7/84

Nowhere to Run

Nowhere to Run

The Story of Soul Music

Gerri Hirshey

Times
BOOKS

Portions of this material appeared, in different form, in *Rolling Stone* and the New York *Daily News*.

Published by TIMES BOOKS, The New York Times Book Co., Inc. 130 Fifth Avenue, New York, N.Y. 10011

Published simultaneously in Canada by Fitzhenry & Whiteside, Ltd., Toronto

Library of Congress Cataloging in Publication Data

Hirshey, Gerri.
  Nowhere to run.

  1. Soul music—United States—History and criticism.
I. Title.
ML3537.H57   1984   784.5′5′00973   83-45924
ISBN 0-8129-1111-3

Designed by Doris Borowsky

Manufactured in the United States of America

84 85 86 87 88 5 4 3 2 1

For David

Acknowledgments

I'd like to thank all the artists who have lent their voices to this book, men and women of great patience and generosity who opened their homes, their scrapbooks, and their memories. Special thanks to Mr. Joe Brown, father of the Godfather, who ferried me and my pesky questions through the Augusta streets and the Carolina piney woods and gently, but firmly, pointed out the trees. I'm also grateful to my other rock and soul tour guides extraordinaire: Joe Billingslea in Detroit, Mary Wilson and Solomon Burke in L.A., Irma Thomas in New Orleans, and in New York, Screamin' Jay Hawkins.

Jerry Wexler, Ahmet Ertegun, and Bob Rolontz were all most generous with industry wisdom and personal reminiscences; Quincy Jones helped me ease on down the road with a well-timed chat on perspective. For their aid in contacting artists, and with publishing and recording information, thanks also to Simo Doe and Noreen Woods at Atlantic Records, Karen Rooney at Warner Brothers Records, and Terry Barnes at Motown.

My interview material was supplemented by research conducted with the help of the staffs at the E. Azalia Hackley Memorial Collection of Negro Music, Dance and Drama in Detroit, and the Schomburg Center for Research in Black Culture in New York. Most appreciated was access to the Wexler Archives, an ad hoc but exhaustive collection of books, notes, tapes, anecdotes, photos, and flat-out horse sense; my heartfelt thanks to the curator in the Muscle Shoals T-shirt.

Chart positions were taken from Joel Whitburn's *Record Research* series, compiled from *Billboard* charts in pop, country, R & B, and soul; information on Stax and Atlantic session dates and personnel, from *Atlantic Records, A Discography,* by Michael Ruppli. Douglas Moody is a killer Motown expert who actually sat through both tapings of *The T.A.M.I. Show* as a Santa Monica teen. He has put together the most complete and accurate Motown discography—we can only hope he'll take time off from his record collecting to publish it.

For good talk, lent books and records, for arguments and encouragements, I'd like to thank Mark Jacobson, Richard Price, and Fred Schruers, and, for his early support of this project, James Raimes.

Carol Mann has managed to be just the right combination of agent, friend, cheerleader, and finger-wagger all the long way through. Alan Weitz first shaped some of this material as my editor at *Rolling Stone* and gamely undertook to read the manuscript with the same care and perception. For all his contributions—the pep talks, the lent materials, and a close, critical read—I am grateful to that Motor City native son Dave Marsh. David Hinckley of the New York *Daily News* is a great concert buddy and R & B nutcase; his reading of the manuscript, along with his notes and comments, was invaluable. I thank him, too, for sharing interview material. Also at the *Daily News,* Jack Sanders and Susan Toepfer gave me the assignments and deft editing that kept this project going. Arthur Hettich, my editor at *Family Circle* magazine, gave me the freedom and, over the years, the confidence, to go out and do this crazy thing.

Iris Brown is the only transcriber/typist I know who can listen to plane engines, shattering glass, and five-part harmony interviews and still get it right.

Fredrich Cantor, whose portraits appear in this book, is a gifted photographer and painter; since our first joint magazine assignment, I have counted him a dear friend and stalwart sidekick on those rambles far, far past the midnight hour.

Thanks, for the hot meals, shelter, and sympathy, to my Washington, D.C., backup group: Peter Isakoff and Tony and Karril Kornheiser. For somewhere to run, love and gracias to Dr. Feelgood, Harry Jaffe. Also on the soundboard: Paul Gardner, Gil Schwartz, Roger Director, Alan Richman, Jay Lovinger, Nancy Cardozo, and Louise Sanders. My *everlasting* devotion to the girls—the Sweet Inspirations, Part II—Sally Boyd, Cathy Brooks, Rosemary De Tore, Lisa Henricksson, Barbara Kukuc, Jane Leavy, Nancy McKeon, Lawrie Mifflin, Sue Mittenthal, and Susin Shapiro.

Deepest thanks to my editor, Elisabeth Scharlatt, who helped me find my own voice.

I am blessed with a family that never saddled a kid with hotshot expectations. Despite their best efforts not to interfere, they are the ones who make everything possible.

Finally—away back in the sixties, my husband, David, flashed a pair of Sam and Dave tickets and secured our first date. *Here, My Dear. I Thank You. Amen.*

Contents

Part 3   Southern Soul   *263*

Illustrations follow pages 144 and 304.

Introduction

IT WAS A SUNDAY NIGHT, during an especially loathsome stretch of junior high; that old poker face Ed Sullivan, introducing his next act, gave no clue to what he was about to unleash. Accompanied by the Famous Flames, James Brown popcorned through the gray snow on the boxy RCA console, screaming, bopping, my God, *sweating* right there on prime time. Watching him dance inflicted a momentary, ecstatic paralysis; the three-cape, collapse-and-resurrection exit left me white-knuckling the vinyl hassock. Next day I deep-sixed the Beatle magazines and worked out in the basement, longing to *be* a Famous Flame. I grew up, but I can't say I've outgrown the infatuation.

"The man gets *out* of himself. James Brown is magic. He's got a kind of freedom. I *crave* it. Every day." This confession came from Michael Jackson, an excruciatingly shy young man who spent his elementary school years peeking out at James from backstage at the Apollo Theater in Harlem. By the age of six, Michael was fronting the family act with his own mini-bag of JB-inspired dance moves. At twenty-five, he had busted into the *Guinness Book of World Records* as the only pop artist to get six Top Ten singles off just one album, *Thriller*. It sold 20 million copies.

Just before *Thriller* was completed, Michael agreed to a rare interview. Though he is completely relaxed performing, talking about himself causes him genuine pain and discomfort. Seeking a break from one taping session, he took me to the mansion he was reconstructing as a self-contained funhouse and refuge. He seemed to grow calmer as soon as he drove through its gates. As we visited his pet fawns and walked the plank over unfinished hot tubs, the formal Q & A mercifully dissolved into chat. Michael wondered if writers, who are also performers, feel the need to conceal their real selves sometimes—to do a flashy, full-tilt boogie in print, then attempt a clean getaway in street clothes. He had me there, and he knew it. We traded a few more insecurities, and it didn't take us long to agree that it was a special freedom we had both long envied in Mr. James Brown— what seemed a total release from any kind of nagging self-consciousness. Michael was black, and in grade school when the longing hit him; I was a white subteen in a suburban tract ranch. Years later, there we sat, trying to dissect it, when Michael suddenly asked if I could help him locate a videotape of *The T.A.M.I. Show,* a 1965 TV teen special that captured the most mind-bending exhibition of JB dance hoodoo ever recorded. It's the same film clip that Elvis Presley used to watch over and over in the middle of the night, when fame confined him to Graceland.

"Studying it would be very helpful to me," Michael said. "I never dared speak to him, but I consider James Brown my greatest teacher. I was too young to think about it as a kid, I just felt it, like an animal senses things. But I think if I look at it on film now, maybe I can understand what I'm all about. You know, why I still am obsessed with escapism, with getting out of myself."

When soul music was at its peak in the 1960s, an entire generation was trying to get out of its post-Eisenhower self. Soul blew a huge hole in *Leave It to Beaver*-land. It was untrammeled, emotional, *different* music, and it fit the times. Soul played black activist centers and white fraternity bacchanals; soul cassettes went to Saigon in rucksacks; soul singers, particularly James Brown, drew the twenty-two-year-old Mick Jagger to the Apollo night after night. A decade before the Solidarity movement in Poland, soul music—albeit by white imitators calling themselves the Blue and Blacks—caused a repressive police action in Gdansk.

The generation of musicians who made the sound were the first black artists to hurtle the barrier between the rhythm and blues and pop charts in a serious way, to make black music *popular* music, worldwide. For young adults, black and white, soul was the fitting bridge between blues and doowop, hardcore and marshmallow pop. Blues were too black and adult and unremittingly realistic; doowop was okay, but too sublimated for the times. Whang—there was soul, with a funky, danceable beat and a delicious code of double entendre applicable to the politics of sex, race, or the playground. It was and is a fine analgesic for pain, adolescent or otherwise. It could get you out of yourself.

It follows that soul music has had to carry a lot of emotional freight.

It happens to a lot of music beloved enough to be called popular, and so it was with soul for me. But personal nostalgia doesn't go far enough, and it's awfully myopic. I know that a greater, more consuming passion than my own moved the people who actually made the sound. Fifteen years ago I'd stand amid the delirious celebrants at the close of a Temptations concert—watching the last flame-orange, belled and sequined trouser cuff set slowly behind the bandstand—and I'd wonder: Who *were* those guys?

I guess, since that long ago JB transfiguration, I've been curious about the singers behind those songs. Like Michael, I wanted to check it out in grainy black and white. I hit the ground in a full-tilt fact dance, determined not to look back.

It didn't last long. The first interview I lined up was with the Queen herself, Aretha. If seeing James Brown had momentarily stopped the world, listening to Aretha Franklin has surely helped me live in it. I hog-tied the fan in me to the record rack and hauled myself to her hotel door in a hair shirt of sober music tech questions. But Aretha spared me the schizophrenia by talking plainly from the jump.

"It's all *about* feelings," she said. "You can't get away from that fact, no matter what you do." Aretha said that singing had taken her places she couldn't get to any other way—to a zone where she was so much herself that none of us would recognize her. It was impossible to take anyone else to that zone, but, she said, she could talk about where she had lived and listened as a child. Conversation doesn't come easily to Aretha, but through a pack and a half of Kools, she walked us back through her first church solo, then out into the Detroit streets outside the Flame Show Bar, where Aretha, still underage, tried to get inside and wrap herself in Dinah Washington's blues.

"Now there's a plain bare fact," she offered. "Soul came up from gospel and blues. *That* much you can write down."

And like gospel and blues, soul was a restless music that rarely sat down to study on itself. Soul was as mobile as American blacks have had to be. City soul grafted urban sophistications to root forms brought up from the South; southern soul stayed rawboned and simple, but southern recording studios opened their doors to northern producers and expatriate singers, Aretha among them.

For organization's sake, this book is divided into sections on city and southern soul, with a preamble on the blues and gospel roots they hold in common. Of course, it's not that clearcut. Artists keep slipping back and forth over the borders, singing "both sides" and living in both places, breaking up and making up with record labels or group personnel that are doubtless still changing as this goes to press.

Al Green, Little Richard, and Solomon Burke, among others, have shuttled between gospel and secular soul. Looking up Motown artists who grew up in Detroit, I'd often find they'd gone "home" to Georgia or Alabama. Memphis session men had moved to Los Angeles; for that matter, so had Motown Records. And James Brown has gone back to producing his own records in his hometown of Augusta, Georgia. Home, as James once pointed out, can be a tricky concept if you've been told to move along for a century and a half.

As it was, the unprecedented success of soul music took the singers to some strange places in America. Before they were stars, they were domestic and assembly line workers, cotton pickers, waitresses and wonderboy preachers, chauffeurs, orderlies, students, janitors, junior deacons, and juvenile delinquents. By the time soul had peaked at the end of the sixties, they had all moved in and out of a lot of very different neighborhoods.

Tracking the artists down, I found I had to keep moving as well. Interviewing singers, musicians, and producers, I often found myself in those twin confessionals, churches and bars, or in that dreamless limbo known as The Road. Often it was 4:00 or 5:00 A.M., after a show, when fatigue or adrenaline could conjure memories I'd never get in a ten-minute phone interview. The answers to my questions, about the composition of a song, a particular performance, often came from that uncharted zone Aretha spoke of. *I had lost her. I had found Him. I was lonely. I was beyond tired.*

Once all the talking was done, I paged through the reams of transcript, waiting for the big picture to lay hold of me. What leaped off the pages were the *voices*. The people who had sung the music so well are its most eloquent historians. Their voices are as distinctive on paper as they are on vinyl. James Brown speaks the way he dances; Mary Wells uses the same frank girl talk you hear on her records.

The sound—the story—of soul music is contained in those voices and the infinite change-ups they worked on twelve notes and an equally basic set of human emotions. Sam Cooke's yodel, James Brown's shrieks, Wilson Pickett's dangerous screams, the Temptations' gorgeous harmony were all as distinct and unique as their fingerprints. Style may have linked clusters of artists; studio locations and production teams created specific sounds on labels like Stax, Atlantic, and Motown. But direct, standout *vocal* expression is the touchstone. And so it seemed clear enough: A book on soul music had to be a book of voices.

It was no accident that the appeal of strong black voices reached its height at a time when Americans, black and white, were raising some pretty basic issues. Nor is it surprising that once the civil rights movement outlived the buoyant optimism of the Martin Luther King, Jr., era, once the Vietnam War was over and a certain numbness or wound licking set in, those soulful voices were all but drowned out by the more arranged and produced forms, such as disco. Much of the new music required less involvement of the singer and the listener. Regional sounds dissolved as record corporations grew. Voices lost out to production technique; rhythm went from being an exhorter to a tyrant.

Nearly every soul singer I spoke to had his or her version of the Disco Diatribe, but of course it was more than disco that nudged soul off the charts. Black American music just won't stay put. And the same restlessness that made the teenaged Wilson Pickett give up on the Ravens sent seventies and eighties kids bopping off to Kool and the Gang, the Commodores, and Michael Jackson.

To go back to the singers, to the voices, ten or fifteen or twenty years after their greatest successes wasn't unlike talking to athletes about a championship season past. There is talk of titles and awards won, and royalties missed out on. Some have continued amassing the hits and the stats, but the majority are working on a more modest level. They are not old—many have just reached forty. They can still sing and play, and beautifully. Having given themselves wholly to a sound, they've had to try to make sense of what became of it.

Sometimes, as Martha Reeves explained to me, that can leave you feeling like you've got nowhere to run. She sang the song by that title with the Vandellas in 1965, and she says she feels a bit like that every day now. Fell in love with the music; can't tame it, can't quit it. Whether you're talking about love or life on the record charts, it all has to do with promise and expectations.

And that is deeply, stubbornly American. Two decades after soul singers vocalized about the Promised Land in terms of God or romantic love or racial equality, a lot of that is, as Solomon Burke sang, "Just out of Reach." Urban rap music made it from the street to the fashion pages but has had a hard time getting airplay on mainstream stations; despite the boom in cable-TV rock video, black artists (with the exceptions of Michael Jackson and Prince) still have been effectively shut out. Reading quotations from black citizens on the twentieth anniversary of the march on Washington was very much like listening to James Brown take off on the subject of restrictive radio format. *Ain't much changed.*

Nonetheless, mainstream American pop cruises along, still trading on the restlessness that moved all those gospel journey songs, that spurred traveling bluesmen and lonesome hillbillies and, later, those car-crazy fifties rockers. After all, riding steerage was the first rock and roll experience for millions of would-be Americans. By the eighties, Bruce Springsteen topped the charts by dipping back into that bag of American journey yarns, stating his belief in "The Promised Land," then lamenting "The Price You Pay."

All of it adds up to a lot of running around, especially for the generation that turned the dreaded thirty around the time America celebrated its two hundredth birthday. The young Americans who made and loved soul music found themselves in a peculiar place indeed. Looking back at the sixties, the years of his son's greatest triumph, Joe Brown, father of James and Soul Granddaddy Number One, summed it up this way: "White folks, some young white folks, run *away* from America," he said. "They ashamed. Black folks, they run all over, up North, everywhere, tryin' to get *into* America."

For a few years, in an era characterized by the word "movement," soul music gave many of us somewhere to run—to get out of ourselves, to *feel* free, if only for two and a half minutes a side.

Twenty-five years after his first hit record, it was James Brown himself who skimmed the romance off a fan's notion of freedom and revealed its price. It was James, with his truck and limo discourses, the 5:00 A.M. phone lectures, James, with his boogaloo Socratics, who showed me how to be adult about sizing up an infatuation. His voice is among the loudest and strongest in this book. It was he who convinced me that in leaving this book to the voices themselves, I could remain a fan and still tell the story.

—Gerri Hirshey
New York City
November 1983

Part 1
Singing
Both
Sides

*Spirituals, blues, it don't matter me pickin'
one or the other. I'm proud to say in my
lifetime I sung both sides. Depends where life
find you. All I can say is you sing what your
voice come to most.*

—JOE BROWN, father of James Brown

1

Sympathy for the Devil

I wish I could be who I was before I was me.

—SCREAMIN' JAY HAWKINS

TWENTY-TWO THOUSAND FANS move between the molded plastic seats in New York City's Madison Square Garden. Most of them entered a vast mail lottery to win the privilege of buying tickets; some have paid scalpers as much as $200 to be here. We are at a Rock Event at the outset of the eighties. Check all bottles at the door; have your tickets ready to show the officers. . . .

"Get yer ya-yas out," bawls a T-shirt vendor at the gate. The escalator is a twitching artery of fifteen- to twenty-year-old haunches vacuum-packed into denim and spandex, all come to shake it with the Rolling Stones, who were singing as a group before many of these kids were born.

Besides solid, reliable, kick-ass rock and roll, some rock theater is anticipated. Enormous plastic bladders hang from the ceiling, bulging with thousands of colored balloons. A squadron of sneakered young men washes the custom-crafted kidney-shaped stage with swirling pastel lights.

3

Stage left, a cherry picker reaches up from below the loge seats like a monster-movie crab claw. Mick Jagger will confer his pouty benedictions from aloft. The question is on many lips: "You think Mick's gonna throw rose petals like he did in Philly?"

There is so much going on no one seems to have noticed the tall black man who has wandered out onstage in a long red cape and gold lamé turban. He checks the miking on a huge concert grand and smiles at a pretty black woman who sits sipping a soft drink just left of the drum set. A four-piece band has begun to fiddle with the clutch of breadbox-size monitors and amps. Before half the crowd even notices that the recorded Top Forty music has stopped blaring from the Stones' mammoth speakers, the band has jumped into a springy blues.

"Ladies and gentlemen," the PA system booms, "will you please welcome blues and rock *legend,* Mr. Screamin' Jay Hawkins."

"Whoooo?" Bewilderment whistles through scores of high-glossed lips.

Screamin' Jay Hawkins, children. Piano sideman turned blues shouter turned rock and roll pioneer. In the mid-fifties he was one of rock's archetypal wild men, a fiendish dandy in polka-dot shoes and zebra coattails, leaping out of coffins and clouds of smoke with the same manic drive that let Jerry Lee Lewis mule-kick a piano stool halfway to the second balcony. Owing to his screaming delivery, his spiritualism (albeit demonic), and his stage antics, Screamin' Jay Hawkins stood, as music critic Arnold Shaw put it, "on the surrealistic borderline between rhythm and blues and soul." After thirty years on the road, he still screams hard but travels light (no coffin). He is selective with his bookings and still proud of his name.

Born Jalacy Hawkins in 1929 in Cleveland, he was renamed Screamin' Jay one whiskey-mist West Virginia night when a lusty club patron shook her size no-end bootie and sent a galaxy of sticky shot glasses into orbit, yelling all the while, "Scream, baby, scream! Go on, Jay, scream it!"

It sounds like a hoarse gargle at first, this scream, snapping heads in the direction of the Garden stage.

"Auwwwwrargaieeeeeee. Ow. Ohhhhhhh. Mmm."

Jay tamps it to a low moan and bears down on the keyboard with a greasy tangle of river-deep blues chords. Screamin' Jay does not so much sing a song as assault it. He will beat, stretch, and hammerlock a lyric and all but suffocate a melody. Though his style and training are rooted in postwar urban blues, his is not the noble detachment of the great midwestern bluesmen. Those guys knew the devil, but they never went so far as to lend him their voices.

Jay's voice, that terrible, changeling voice, is suffused with moans, growls, gurgles, and snuffles, a churning swamp of unchecked emotion that would, in the years following Jay's flaming fifties, be refined, politened, in many cases churchified and pumped out as soul by the next wave of black popular artists.

Singers like Ray Charles would replace the hoodoo spiritualism with a gospel sensibility and, like Hawkins, ignite it with sex. James Brown would raise the soul scream to sacramental heights. The voice of Aretha Franklin would take a holiness shout and wrap it around an audience until it, too, screamed for the sheer wonder of it. By the late sixties, along with other singers like the Soul Screamer himself, Wilson Pickett, they would take the human howl to unprecedented commercial success.

Of course, the soulful scream is as old as the blues, as old as desolation itself, and, in that sense, just as fundamental to gospel. Gospel sufferers can ask, "Why, O Lord?" and seek relief in the balm of faith. The bluesman must listen for his answer in a piney woods wind, a train whistle, a dog howl.

Either way, it's no surprise that America, a nation that began with Pilgrim martyrs and enslaved tribes, that a people so bound up with persecution would come up with a music so ripe with rebellion and a headlong run at deliverance: rock. At its most dangerous, rock *is* a scream. The fads and styles of the marketplace control the volume and the pitch.

What Jay Hawkins and other rock pioneers did was to let the scream loose in a way that both scared and delighted the kids. Crooners were too tame for the postwar baby-boom kids. And classic bluesmen were simply too strong. To white kids, horror was a zit, not a lynch mob. Black kids were familiar with the blues but distanced in their own way.

"As a kid in the fifties I was taught to be *ashamed* of the blues," Isaac Hayes told me. "We thought of it as plantation darkie stuff. And that was miles from where *we* wanted to be."

As a teenager in Detroit Smokey Robinson ignored his mother's blues records. "The blues is torment or some degrading type of thing," he says. "Kids weren't ready for that. I liked Frankie Lymon, Sam Cooke, or Jackie Wilson—the plush, pop kind of singers whose music wasn't hardcore blues."

All in all, fifties kids' tastes were just 3.2 beer compared to Muddy Waters's 90-proof barrel of blues. Screamin' Jay kept the chords and rhythms and learned to burlesque some of the pain. He could conjure fright but make it fun. In doing so, Jay Hawkins became one of the original bards of rock theater, a funky Iago whose favorite prop is still a human skull on a stick.

He is at it now, rushing from behind the piano to center stage, toting the skull and a rubber rattlesnake, big hips rumbling like a haywire Maytag.

"Is he for real?" asks a blow-dried subteen.

"Fuckin' weird," says a boy in a Black Sabbath T-shirt. "Like he's rippin' off the Sabbath."

Black Sabbath's former lead singer Ozzy Osbourne does real neat stuff like bite the heads off live doves. Oz has performed some of his most outrageous stunts at record company conventions to demonstrate his commercial appeal. Such genteel corporate arenas were not available to rock's prehistoric wild men.

Most of the artists Oz went to school on are dead or convalescing now. Elvis, the King, is dead. The Killer, Jerry Lee Lewis, was recently resurrected from yet another near-fatal bout with bleeding ulcers, pills, and booze. Chuck Berry has been quieted by a jail sentence and financial woes. Once again Little Richard has gone back to screaming for the Lord. Jackie Wilson, after collapsing on stage with a heart attack in 1975 and remaining semi-comatose in a nursing home, died in January of 1984. For a while punk tried to butt its matted head into the pantheon of True Lunacy, but with little lasting impact. Sex Pistol Sid Vicious was just perfecting his projectile vomiting when heroin spaded him under.

"Nah, you got it wrong," says Sabbath T-shirt's friend. "This guy Hawkins is rippin' off *Kiss*."

Playing to squealing teen angels, Kiss spit fake blood and wore horror-flick makeup. Kiss sing dem surburban Clearasil blues. Kiss was in diapers when Screamin' Jay Hawkins pumped the full clip of a military automatic rifle into a wild boar on the rim of a Hawaiian volcano to extract the tusk that now thumps against his chest on a big gold chain.

Sweat has begun to bead up above the penciled mustache Hawkins has drawn on his upper lip; rivulets seep from beneath the turban, which is listing to the right with all the exertion. He has roared and shaken through half a dozen songs, gutbucket stuff like "She Put the Wammee on Me," "Lawdy Miss Clawdy," and "Alligator Wine." Now he has retreated back behind the piano, fishing for a wandering mike with his right hand, reaching down past Hades for some sulfurous chords with his left. Remarkably, a good portion of the audience seems to have passed beyond curiosity and into listening.

"I hear," says Sabbath T-shirt, "this guy's an old favorite of Keith and Mick or somethin'."

It is a long-standing habit of the Rolling Stones to pay tribute to the font of their music by touring and jamming with black musicians. The alumni include Howlin' Wolf, Tina Turner, Billy Preston, and Stevie Wonder, among others. Were it not for a last-minute contractual snag, James Brown would have opened this very show at the Garden. One of the first things Mick Jagger did on the Stones' first U.S. tours in the sixties was to make a beeline for Brown's dressing room at the Apollo. It was an infatuation that began in *his* youth.

In the late fifties and early sixties, aspiring rockers like Jagger, Keith Richards, Eric Clapton, and John Lennon would queue up outside the doors of London "palais" like the Flamingo and the Marquis, stubbing out cigarette butts with pointy black boots while they waited in the skanky urban rain to dig the American madmen.

"To English and French kids," Eric Burdon of the Animals has said, "names like Chuck Berry, Etta James, and Screamin' Jay Hawkins and countless others are *gods.*"

The Stones' audience is hardly worshipful tonight, but after thirty minutes they are still with Screamin' Jay. He is gearing up for his finale now, marking the beat with his skull like some satanic drum major, leaning into the mike to howl out the title line of his 1956 hit, "I Put a Spell on You."

Sabbath T-shirt is impressed. "That's a Creedence song," he tells his friends, who nod sagely. He is referring to a 1968 version of the song by a white rock group, Creedence Clearwater Revival.

Screamin' Jay vamps and shakes through the number, waving the skull at bewildered teenies in the front row. About to wrap it up, he signals to the woman who has been sitting beside the drums. She puts down her soda and ambles toward center stage, where she sets a small black box in front of the singer. He has ground the song down to spasmodic growls and yelps.

"Yo' miiiiiiine, mine, mi-i-i-i-ine . . ."

Unrolling an attached wire, the woman walks back to the drums, and at the agreed-upon cue, she throws a switch. The black box releases a flash and a wheezy puff of smoke.

"Aaaeeeeeeyowwwwwww."

The last of the scream whangs off the Garden scoreboard as the artist and his rubber totems exit through the smoke, stage right.

"Far out," says Sabbath T-shirt, rolling his eyes. "We got time till the

Stones," he says to his girl friend. "You wanna buy a T-shirt or some-thin'?"

Afterward the opening act passes on the backstage banquet, the wine and Perrier, the celebrity corner. As Mick Jagger bounds onstage in yellow football pants and kneepads, Screamin' Jay tucks his skull under his arm, collects his snake and his woman, and heads uptown to his West Side apartment.

"Naw, I didn't stay for the rest of the show," he says. "There was some good wrestling on TV. Got home just in time."

In front of the TV is where I find Jay one blustery winter afternoon, seated in a swivel chair, watching the soaps. Cassie, the woman who set off his smoke box onstage, places a steaming mug of tea on the folding snack table beside him, along with two of the government-issue pill vials he gets from the Veterans Hospital down on Twenty-fourth Street.

"Blood pressure pills," he says, thumping his chest hard enough to make the plastic-entombed preserved scorpion dance on its neck chain. The penciled mustache is gone; the lamé turban has been replaced by a wool cap. The thick black-rimmed glasses render him almost unrecog-nizable from the wild publicity shots framed on a desk. At fifty-five, Jay is a tall, robust man, with square shoulders and a long, tensile reach that helped him snare the Golden Gloves middleweight crown in 1947. After turning off the TV sound, he lopes across the living room to perform sur-gery on the door buzzer, deftly inserting a cotton ball over the clapper now that his visitor has been admitted.

Screamin' Jay likes his peace and quiet. Despite war injuries incurred when a grenade blew him clean out of his South Pacific foxhole, even allowing for the sanctioned mutilations of the boxing ring and the daily rigors of Manhattan street life, it is the cankerous human flotsam of the entertainment world that Jay most fears and avoids. He gives his phone number to no one and conducts most of his business through sympathetic intermediaries at music-licensing organizations like Broadcast Music, Inc. (BMI) and the musicians' union.

"I caught more hell on the road than I did in the war," he says, un-plugging the phone and settling back into the swivel chair. Jay's speaking voice is a clear, well-modulated, and enunciated baritone that belies three decades of sustained abuse.

"Really," he confesses, "I wanted to be Paul Robeson." He laughs. Then, in mock-sinister tone: "Now aren't you *terrified* to be in the wild cannibal's den?"

Some guests, he explains, have left suddenly upon noticing the library of voodoo and incantation books. One or two got queasy at being offered a drink from the blood transfusion bottle that hangs from the ceiling over a corner bar. So as not to upset folks, Jay keeps his stage props out of sight in the bedroom. Besides the smoke box, built by a long-deceased electrician at the Apollo Theater, there is a mechanical severed hand and a semiretired set of chattering, self-propelled teeth. Henry, the skull on a stick, rests with them.

Naturally, it's all in fun. Jalacy Hawkins insists he's as peaceable as the plastic coffee-table Buddha that smiles amid dishes of Mary Janes and lemon drops. He has been a reasonable man since 1974, when he made Screamin' Jay quit drinking. *That* Jay was a lodestone for trouble. Everywhere he went, it seemed his body attracted small pieces of metal: penknives, switchblades, razors, slugs.

He proffers a photo of that Screamin' Jay, exiting from a hearse in cape and "Mau Mau" makeup. It is from the 1978 movie *American Hot Wax,* which purported to be a history of the beginnings of rock and roll. The film dealt largely with the flamboyant career of deejay Alan Freed, the man who claimed to have invented the term "rock 'n' roll." Like "sepia" or "ebony," "race music," and "rhythm and blues," "rock 'n' roll" was just another euphemism for black music at the time. Freed was one of the first mainstream jockeys to play black popular music to white teenagers, first at radio station WJW in Cleveland, then at WINS in New York.

Contrary to legend, Freed didn't act alone. Dewey Phillips's *Red Hot and Blue* show broadcast black music to black and white teenagers in Memphis. Isaac Hayes remembers growing up with records spun by Rufus "Do the Funky Chicken" Thomas on WDIA in Memphis, known as Mother Station of the Negroes with its 50,000 watts and all black announcers. By 1951, when Freed began playing black music on a white station in Cleveland, most southern cities already had black stations. And white kids had begun to tune in. The trend did not go long unnoticed in the record industry.

THE LATEST TREND: R & B DISKS ARE GOING POP, bannered *Billboard* magazine in 1954, once that trend had taken hold. The phenomenon was explained in an accompanying article by Jerry Wexler and Ahmet Ertegun, whose label, Atlantic, was to become the greatest soul powerhouse a decade later. They wrote:

Here's what happened. . . . As far as we can determine, the first area where the blues stepped out in the current renascence was the South. Distributors there about two years ago began to report that white high school and college kids were picking up on the rhythm and blues records—primarily to dance to. From all accounts, the movement was initiated by youthful hillbilly fans rather than the pop bobbysoxers—and the latter group followed right along. A few alert pop disk jockeys observed the current, switched to rhythm and blues formats, and soon were deluged with greater audiences, both white and negro, and more and more sponsors.

Of those deejays, Freed was able to take this aural miscegenation to its most outrageous heights.

It had begun with his visit to a local record shack where a Cleveland distributor pointed out the fact that white and black teenagers were buying discs by black artists like LaVern Baker, Della Reese, and Ivory Joe Hunter. Impressed, Freed abandoned his classic format in the middle of 1951 and began playing rhythm and blues. The jive was infectious; Freed began *talking* black on his late-night show, howling like the "Moondog" he called himself, numbing his throat with a pint of cheap whiskey. It made quite a noise in the largely segregated city.

"This cat was stone wild," Jay Hawkins remembers. He first heard Freed's show when he returned to his native Cleveland on leave from his third military stint.

"I went to the station," he says. "I went to find out who we had in Cleveland that would *dare*. I mean, how could a black cat get away with such shit? So I go there, and I say, 'I want to talk to this Alan Freed.' "

He gaped at the short, stocky white man who came at the receptionist's call.

"I says, 'Oh, no, *you're* playing black music on a white station?' and he says, 'That's me.' So I shook his hand, and I said, 'Well, thank you, you're doing us very good.' "

While Jay was away beginning his career as piano player for various bands, Cleveland and Freed made national headlines. Freed was as amazed as anyone when he arrived at the Cleveland Arena on March 21, 1952, and saw the response to his on-air invitation to a Moondog Dance featuring all-black entertainers. The hall could handle 10,000, but 25,000 black and white teenagers stormed the ticket booth. Twenty-six years before the infamous Cincinnati gate crush at a Who concert that killed eleven, the American heartland, and the world, recoiled at the spectacle of the first rock and roll riot.

Once Jay's career got going, Freed played his records, too, sandwiched between the latest from Chuck Willis, Fats Domino, the Coasters, the Dominoes, and the Drifters.

"We *all* had to thank that man."

Jay allows that Freed was no saint. He drank hard, had a hell of a temper and a keen appetite for cash. But you had to hand it to him. . . . "Alan Freed could sell tickets to the end of the world," says Jay. "To the first *and* second shows."

In 1960 Freed went down in flames, charged by a New York grand jury in a payola scandal that shook the music industry. In 1962 he was tried and convicted, having pleaded guilty to two counts of commercial bribery. Two years later a second grand jury indicted him on charges of income tax evasion. Broke and in disgrace, he died of uremia in 1965, obedient to the rock credo of living hard and dying young. He was forty-three.

"History done Alan Freed wrong," Jay contends. "And while I'm at it, so did Hollywood." Though Jay enjoyed playing himself in *American Hot Wax,* he says that what showed on screen wasn't really what went down. He could have told them some things, but nobody asked. Such arrogance galls him as much as recent arguments he's had with Madison Square Garden promoters who refused to include him on a rock and roll revival bill.

"I was *there!* From the mid-forties, before, during, and after the whole mess started. One of the reasons I did the Rolling Stones show was to play the Garden, to all those thousands of people, on a ROCK AND ROLL BILL . . . and SHOW those suckers!"

Jay is riled, living up to his name now, briskly stroking a dainty Siamese cat who has settled on his knee, obviously used to the noise.

"You got a mess of tapes with you?"

He leaps up suddenly and begins pulling open desk drawers, extracting datebooks, check stubs, royalty statements—thirty years' worth of documentation. As he builds the pile, he tosses half sentences over his shoulder.

"Can't get to soul without rhythm and blues. And gospel. And what they call rock and roll, which ain't nothin' but R and B. Labels are bullshit. You wanna get to the sixties . . ."

Three huge scrapbooks thud onto the floor.

". . . you gotta start with the forties and the beginning of rhythm and blues. Late forties, early fifties. Somewhere along the mid-fifties, people started doing gospel and blues, too. You can't make a clean separation anywhere.''

He sweeps a hand toward the phonograph, which has been playing an LP anthology of Motown hits beneath the conversation.

"Now I never sung that stuff, but I like it, what they call soul. That stuff got heaven *and* hell in it." He laughs. "Me? I guess you have to say I spent most of my time on the *dark* end of the street.''

The data are still mounting on the sofa and coffee table: notebooks dating back to the fifties and sixties, detailing time, locale, and earnings for each gig in meticulous script. From another drawer come newspaper clippings from around the world, photographs, Library of Congress copyright certificates.

"Audiovisual aids," he says. "For Jay Hawkins's rock and roll, prehistory of soul home movie.''

During this long, darkening afternoon, he will rail, sing, document, and reminisce. No, he is not surprised that his recollections correspond to facts in rock histories and newspaper morgues.

"I ain't no encyclopedia," he says. "I lived it, is all." He leans over and starts the tape recorder. "Get comfortable. Close your eyes, but don't you *dare* fall out. Now imagine . . .''

Dawn, in a New York City Parking Lot, January 1953

The windows of the battered station wagon have lacy frost curtains. Jay Hawkins's long, lean form is bent double on the back seat like the tenor sax that rests alongside him. The boss, jazz guitarist and bandleader Tiny Grimes, is in a heated hotel room somewhere. Resentment rises in Jay's gullet along with last night's bourbon.

He is unhappy. The pay, when he gets it, is lousy. And playing jazz piano just doesn't feel natural. Jay prefers a new blues that he has been hearing since he came home from the war. These blues sound almost happy, and they *move*. Boogie rhythms have been pepping up the countrified delta blues that came North via the Illinois Central Railroad to Chicago and other midwestern cities. The blues came up like a house afire when industrial jobs lured blacks North for work. The first wave had begun in the twenties. By the time twelve-year-old Jay Hawkins fired the piano teacher his mother had hired for him in 1941, his precocious fingers could rap out blues figures that were the legacy of thirties stars like Bill Broonzy, Tampa Red, and Big Joe Turner. As the forties drew to a close, Jay found himself drawn to an even newer sound. Better, and stronger still to his ears, were the driving, more aggressive combo blues by younger men like B. B. King, Muddy Waters, and Howlin' Wolf.

Jay noticed that these guys were turning up in the Cleveland clubs looking for a bar tab and an AC outlet. Electric guitars were raising their blues above the club din. And Jay was hearing more of a bottom to the bands that carried electric basses. The bass could work a steady, throbbing beat that defied folks to stay in their seats.

But those all were the casual observations of a star-struck kid. An ambitious twenty-four, Jay reads the trades now. *Billboard* magazine has been calling that happy, danceable blues rhythm and blues since the late forties. He thinks it fits and has set to studying it. The vocals, especially, have become warmer, looser, and more emotional. From the time he first dogged the clubs in Cleveland, Jay was drawn to favorites like Bullmoose Jackson, Louis Jordan, Peppermint Harris, Eddie "Cleanhead" Vinson, and Lowell Fulson, a Texan who played blues guitar and carried with him a blind Floridian named Ray Charles on piano and vocals. All the best R & B singers had strong, fearless voices set in front of a muscular band. They didn't hold back like crooners; they wallowed in a song. To Jay's mind, nobody got as down and dirty as his friend Wynonie Harris, a big, strapping shouter who let his horns bray like jackasses and his vocals wander free as his wicked mind.

This is precisely the style Jay has in mind for himself as he leaves his cramped mobile home and heads for a recording session Tiny Grimes has this day for a company called Atlantic Records.

Jay knows that recently Atlantic has scored for black artists like Ruth Brown and Big Joe Turner, and that Ray Charles has left Lowell Fulson and taken himself to Atlantic, recording his own compositions.

Jay has written some songs for himself; he has the band down pat. If the Atlantic people agree, Tiny says that Jay can cut a few songs solo. His optimism pales, however, this day in 1953 when he arrives at the dumpy office on West Fifty-sixth Street that doubles as Atlantic's studio. He is introduced to a young but prematurely balding man named Ahmet Ertegun.

Tiny says he is a Turkish guy, father's a big-shot diplomat in Washington. This Ahmet was a friend of Ellington's, it was said. Had some sort of jones for black music. Twenty years down the road, Ertegun's indulging those infatuations would let him sell Atlantic to Warner Communications for more than $20 million.

But this day he is just a beginning producer, and a nervous one at that.

Jay watches him closely. The man is everywhere, twirling dials, adjusting recording levels, nodding happily as Tiny jogs through his session. It's been decided that once Tiny has finished, Jay can record two sides. He starts with "Screamin' Blues," an original composition that, after too many takes, has Ertegun blinking in frustration.

"No, no. I don't like that. *Again.*"

Four times Jay starts out, bawling over an athletic piano, and four times Ertegun is left frowning. The stuff is too, um, raw. Couldn't Jay pretty it up? The band sits back, shaking saliva out of their horns, watching the confrontation.

Ertegun brightens. "I want it to sound more, um—something like Fats Domino."

"What the fuck you have *me* here for? Why don't you go and get Fats Domino? I wrote the song. I'm just now breakin' into the business. And *this* is the kind of act I want to have. I want to be known as the *Screamer!*"

"Bring it down some. Relax," Ertegun says soothingly.

"You go to hell!" And here Jay commits one of the great mistakes of his career. He tries to belt Ahmet Ertegun.

It is no surprise to anyone that "Screamin' Blues," on Atlantic master disc No. 986, is shut forever in the can. Haunting Fifty-second Street jazz clubs with Tiny, Jay feels he is at a dead end, sleeping in Tiny's car, walking Tiny's dog. Finally Jay and Tiny split in Philadelphia, and as a stopgap Jay signs on with the Lynn Hope Band, a Black Muslim group that bounces Jay for eating a plate of unclean chitlins. Jay does not fail to note the irony as he auditions for his next job. Fats Domino is in town, and he needs a piano player to do opening sets for his show.

With his rolling New Orleans piano style and his jouncy, broad vocals, Fats has nudged himself a wide space on the R & B charts. Along with other club singers, like Nat "King" Cole, Dinah Washington, and Billy Eckstine, Fats knew the market value of infusing pop-style music with jazz and blues. These club singers were cooler, more polite than R & B's great shouters. If Big Joe Turner was shots and beers, the Fat Man was a maraschinoed cocktail—relaxed, affable, and smooth.

The bookings got classier, and Fats's diamonds have grown larger with his rise on the charts. Now he is given to sending Jay up to the theater balconies for reports on how his flashing rings irradiate the cheap seats. Disgusted, Jay places a call to Wynonie Harris, who gets him his first solo gig at Small's Paradise in Harlem. Jay works on his yowling delivery until, finally, Screamin' Jay takes wing.

Summer, 1954, Herman's Bar in Atlantic City, New Jersey

Backed by the house band, Jay is onstage singing when the woman walks into the hot, smoky room and pushes her way through the crowd to the front of the stage. She is staring fixedly at the singer, rummaging in her purse. At the glint of metal a few patrons back off. The lady lobs a shiny object toward the stage, and it lands between Jay's feet. He recognizes his apartment keys.

He looks up to see the woman blowing him a kiss before she disappears back into the crowd. There are still two songs left in the set, and Jay wails through them before he replaces the mike in the stand.

"And how about a nice hand for the band that's been shakin' up this land . . .?"

While the band takes its bows, Jay makes his way to the bar and Mom, Herman's barmaid, a woman so wise Jay calls her Solomon.

"You done lost the best thing you ever had." Mom shakes her head over a tray of beer glasses. "That girl is either out of Atlantic City right now or in the process of gettin' out. Those were your keys, right? Well, she's done locked up your pad. You can get in, but you won't find no girl. The girl *left* you, Jay."

Jay walks next door to his apartment and finds it locked. When he gets in, there is no woman. Her clothes are gone. The mirror has been stripped of photographs.

"Good-bye my love" was all she wrote, in scarlet lipstick, on the glass.

And there is loosed upon the waterfront a terrible scream. Jay will remember it as the most painful of his life. "Only one," he tells Mom later, "that found its way out of my big mouth *directly* through my heart and guts."

The soulful moment.

Jay sits down on the bed and commences to write. Already he knows the key and tempo. The song would be dedicated to *her.* He would just conjure her face and scream out the words.

"I put a spell on you because you're MINE. I love you, I LOVE YOU. I love *you,* baby. And anyhow, I don't care if you don't want me, I'm yours," he finds himself half singing, half yelling at the man from Grand Records in Philadelphia, where he will first record the song. "That's what I mean to tell the girl, man. Now I want this heard around the world. Let the woman know, okay, I was wrong, baby, I love you, I want you back."

On the Grand label, "I Put a Spell on You" is heard by virtually no one, sinking like the seven previous singles Jay has made. But when Jay recuts it for Okeh Records, it is a hit. Soon after its release in 1956, radio stations deem two bars' worth of moans and groans "cannibalistic," and the record is banned. A retouched version without the offending sounds hits even bigger, helped along by record company hype promising to compensate any deejay fired for playing it. And amid all the tumult, Jay gets his woman back.

"Oh, it wasn't 'Spell' that done it," she tells him. "I fell in love with the flip side."

Jay called that one "Little Demon."

December 28, 1957, a Top-Floor Dressing Room at Manhattan's Paramount Theater

"They callin' you a cannibal out in the streets, them parents."

A scout has returned from the tumult in Times Square caused by Alan Freed's holiday rock 'n' roll revue. Jay Hawkins is a virtual prisoner, along with the other artists. The Paramount is under siege.

This is the place where a skinny, jug-eared Sinatra induced bobby-soxed hysteria more than a decade ago. Once again the armies of this night are adolescent. They began arriving at 4:00 A.M., queued five abreast, nearly every one of them in cuffed denims. When Jay got to the theater a few hours later, the line snaked three blocks past the Paramount and into Times Square. Despite the cold, more than 20,000 would plunk down $2.50, roughly the price of three 45's, for tickets to one of the day's six shows.

"They called the po-lice," someone yells into Jay's dressing room. "Some on horses."

Everyone passing through the narrow corridor has some tale of destruction. Almost 200 cops are scooping up fainting girls and chasing punks.

"And the parents. Hooooeee. They preaching Armageddon."

There are small knots of them, along with clergymen, denouncing rock music in stentorian tones.

"Rock and roll is a *disease;* it's the bubonic plague."

Jay heard that one on his way in.

" 'For their rock is not our Rock, even our enemies themselves being judges.' "

Sweet Lord, they are quoting Deuteronomy.

"O Wickedness, thy name is Alan Freed."

The infidel himself sits calmly on a folding cot in a dressing room near Jay's inside the theater. Wearing his trademark screaming-plaid jacket,

Freed sips, a trifle ostentatiously, from a glass of milk and answers a question for *The New York Times*.

"Rock 'n' roll is really swing with a modern name," he says. "It began on the levees and plantations, took in folk songs, and features blues and rhythm. It's the rhythm that gets the kids. They are starved for music they can dance to after all those years of crooners."

As he speaks, Frank Sinatra's box-office record at the Paramount is being broken. And Dean Martin's. Outside, glass shatters: a restaurant door. Earlier in the day it was the glass in the Paramount ticket booth.

Mr. Freed, thirty-five years old, continues his interview.

"I see those scrubbed faces looking up at me from the orchestra and I know they are like my own kids. If they want to jump and clap hands, that's all right. If the theater gets a few broken seats, that's their problem."

"Oh, Lord." The loitering musicians snigger. "The man can *bullshit*."

All of them, his merry band, know him for a marauder, hauling buses full of creased and conked blacks in florid suits along with bands of Vaseline-slick white Romeos, all of them with lust in their hearts and lightning in their thighs when they hit a stage. Tonight is a representative sample: Fats Domino, Chuck Berry, Jerry Lee Lewis, the Everly Brothers, Screamin' Jay.

In addition, there are the groups: the Cadillacs, the Moonglows, Frankie Lymon and the Teenagers. Freed is packing more and more vocal groups into his radio playlists and stage revues. Some of them, older singers like Billy Ward and the Dominoes, have been around since the early fifties. They're what Jay calls more hard-core R & B, with leering hits like "Sixty Minute Man," a song that uses the words "rock and roll" the way black slang intended. That rock and roll was what teenagers spoke of as "the thing." Sex. The Act. This is the rock and roll Jay Hawkins knows, but he has noticed that the younger groups aren't quite so blunt about it. Lots of hearts and flowers, moons and Junes. And Adolescent America is digging it. The Paramount teens have been going crazy when Frankie Lymon shrills "Why Do Fools Fall in Love?" in his nasal kid's falsetto.

Doowop they would call it later, this mannered, closely harmonized group sound. Some of the harmonies are straight from the black church. And some are strictly barbershop. Anyhow, it's polite, and a perfect counterweight to the vocal outrages perpetrated by the screamers and shouters.

Having dispatched the reporter from *The Times,* Freed is darting between dressing rooms, then to the wings, staring at the twitching, mewling chaos he has helped foster. Before the seven-thirty show the New York City Fire Department cleared the house for inspection and hauled a few hundred kids out of the second balcony, fearing collapse.

"Hawkins," Freed is yelling. "Where is Screamin' Jay?"

In his dressing-room eyrie Jay flaps and cackles, well pleased with himself. He has had a dozen suits ripped off his body by female hands at this point, and he likes the way it feels. In his portable playboy lair he has a record player, with all the latest hits, and a three-wall bar: beer on one, scotch on a second, wine along the third.

"Gotta talk to you, Jay." Freed stands in the dressing-room door. He has that look, the one that means another show will be added or the money will be late. Freed pours himself a drink from Jay's back wall and begins to talk.

"You got a hit record. Great. You got a good act, all that screamin' wild man stuff. I got one more thing you need."

Jay is mildly curious. "What's that?"

"A coffin."

He laughs, until Freed explains he wants him to get *in* one.

"Now you don't show this nigger no coffin," he tells Freed. "'Cause he knows he gets in that only once. And when he does, he's *dead!*"

"Jay, I want you to do this for me, I already got the coffin downstairs."

This crazy fool has taken Jay's measurements on the sly. Picked out the style and model of coffin, hipped the stage manager, figured out how they could mike it and wheel it out, have Jay spring out. . . .

"Make them wet their pants." Freed is grinning.

"No, man, forget it."

Jay sees the lid closing, imagines lying helpless in the inky dark, with his arms pinioned in that tailor-fit space.

Freed has reached into his pocket for a wad of bills the size of a turkey club and begins peeling off hundreds.

"Jay, will this change your mind?"

"No!"

"Six? Eight?"

"Cancel me off the show, go ahead, I won't do it."

"A grand?"

"I'm working for a living. I got a record that's still hot, man."

"You got an act to go with it now. You get in the coffin, we'll just open up the curtains slowly to a drum roll, like a firing squad, and the blue lights will be blinking. . . ."

Freed fans the bills and holds them out.

"Fifteen hundred."

"Keep it."

"Two grand."

Jay lunges forward and snatches the bills. "You're not gettin' this back now."

"I would have gone another thousand. I've got cameras down there ready to photograph you tonight in that coffin. I want this to be the weirdest show I've ever done, and on top of that, Jay, I can tell you it will be the last one 'cause they're gonna stop us from doing the shows here. They're claiming we're creating too many riots."

"Well, in that case, then I'll really give them something."

Jay runs down to a Broadway liquor store for the proper elixir, a quart of Italian Swiss Colony pink muscatel. It has all the properties for the job: tastes sweet, gets you drunk fast, and doesn't ferment breath odors that could be lethal in a small enclosed area. Pulling on the bottle, Jay lurches toward the dreaded object to size up the technological problems. Weeks later he would consult morticians to inquire about the oxygen left (three minutes' worth) should the airtight lid accidentally have clamped shut. But tonight he is too drunk and too scared to put too fine a point on things.

Two locks open from the outside of the box; no need to have them operate from within. When the coffin, with its trembling, pickled cargo, is wheeled into place behind the curtain, one finger, its nail blue from the weight of the lid, keeps the box open a life-giving crack. Jay hears the drum roll and the screech of the curtain pulleys.

The sound from the crowd is like a giant steam leak. Now Jay hears shrieks and rapid footfalls. Freed is hugging himself in the wings. He's done it: They're terrified, running gaga up the aisles.

"*Aaaiiieeeeerroooogah.*"

Screamin' Jay has leaped up and out, his black satin bat-wing cape flying from its moorings. The house is hysterical, and Freed is nearly weeping with joy.

Backstage, having returned to his senses, Jay is waxing thoughtful.

You don't know it all, he tells himself. That box is gonna help you when the record ain't hot no more.

"That kept me eating for quite a few years," Jay says. His custom-made zebra-striped coffin is moldering now in a relative's basement in Philadelphia. But no matter where he plays, people still ask about it.

"People to this day look at me as though I'm some sort of madman." Jay is stroking the Siamese again, looking a trifle exhausted by the afternoon's narrative. "People are wondering why good people like Sam Cooke died. And Clyde McPhatter. And Jackie Wilson out of it, and Screamin' Jay Hawkins is still here. Maybe I'm a freak. We are *survivors*. If we lose the talent or the going fad leaves us out in the cold, we shall prevail. By living by our wits."

To be more precise, he says he lives by his wits, occasional gigs, and carefully monitored royalties on the songs he has written.

"Look at all of them," he says, riffling the pages of a fifteen-foot-long Library of Congress computer printout listing his copyrighted works. "People think I'm a one-song artist, but I wrote all of those."

Included in the voluminous list are numbers like "Feast of the Mau Maus," "Alligator Wine," and a number that sold inexplicably well in decorous Japan, "Constipation Blues."

Besides royalties from young rockers re-recording old blues, there are some projects cooking. Jay is headed for a gig in Rome. Eric Burdon's manager has inquired about the possibility of their working together in the States. English rocker and veteran bluesman is a combination Jay has found agreeable enough. He enjoyed going back into New York's Blue Rock Studio in 1979 with Rolling Stone Keith Richards, who lent his guitar to a bit of nonsense called "Armpit #6" as well as a new version of "Spell," a single released in England.

In addition, there has been some television work, most recently a live segment for a special on early rockers. This experience he found much less arduous than the lip-sync segments of the fifties and early sixties, when an artist merely mouthed the words as his record was played. For somebody like Screamin' Jay, this could produce tense moments.

"How in hell," he asks, "are you gonna lip-sync a scream, a moan, and a gargle?"

He has noticed that they still lip-sync on *Soul Train,* the weekly black music and dance show that has chugged across American airwaves for the last decade.

"Now I was on the original *Soul Train*," he says, producing yet another clipping, a TV listing for *The Toast of the Town,* Ed Sullivan's mid-fifties show, featuring R & B stars like Jay, LaVern Baker, and Bo Diddley, among others.

Ed Sullivan?

"The cat was hip. Nobody else had tried a black show. Sullivan had the same instincts as Alan Freed. Black or white or purple didn't matter. All these guys cared about was: *Will it draw?*"

To make sure that his revue was culled from the top R & B acts, Sullivan hired black deejay Tommy "Dr. Jive" Smalls, of WWRL in New York. Dr. Jive also promoted very successful package shows at the Apollo. He was one of the first to recognize the commercial possibilities of that kind of bill. Long before the legendary Motown and Stax/Volt revues, deejays, who knew the market better than anyone, were experimenting with the form. There was Freed, in the Midwest. And in Memphis, Rufus Thomas and Nat Williams organized twice-yearly charity shows: the Star-Lite Review in the summer and the Goodwill Review in the fall.

Once packages gave promoters a way to boost profits with six or seven shows a day, theaters like the Apollo in New York, the Regal in Chicago, the Howard in D.C., and the Uptown in Philadelphia were packed with black teenagers surrendering their allowances and after-school salaries. Mixed crowds jammed shows at New York's Paramount, the Brooklyn Paramount, and the Brooklyn Fox. Considering their numbers, the take was staggering.

"Not that *we* saw much of it," says Jay. "And most times I deserved combat pay."

A few close calls stand out, like the night Ben E. King and the rest of the Drifters shut the coffin lid all the way as a joke.

"The band was playing my introduction, so nobody could hear me screaming. Somehow, just as the air was running out, I managed to rock enough so the thing fell off the cart and busted open."

Often Jay was murder on himself. He confirms a story told by Solomon "King of Rock 'n' Soul" Burke, about one grisly performance at Chicago's Regal. As Burke and Lloyd Price stood watching in the wings, Jay accidentally impaled himself on an iron gate at the foot of the stage during one of his flying leaps. He staggered back onstage and performed for forty-five minutes more. Burke and Price were impressed with Jay's latest gruesome effect. It was soaking his suit bright scarlet.

"Dude has a bag of ketchup in his shirt," Price insisted. "It's fake blood, like they got in Hollywood."

"You should have seen their faces when they carried me off to the hospital," Jay says. "*Fake* blood, my ass."

Hastily stitched up, in a fresh suit, he made it back for the next show an hour later.

Having promised to play the banned version of "I Put a Spell on You," Jay slips it on the turntable, interrupting Smokey Robinson mid-heartache. The offending two bars prove to be merely grunts and growls and absurdly tame compared to the orgasmic pant-rock that has since gained airplay.

As the record ends, Jay switches on a lamp. It has grown dark, and the talk winds down to idle observations about the Rolling Stones' show at the Garden. I cannot resist telling Jay about Sabbath T-shirt, crediting "Spell" to Creedence Clearwater.

The resulting screech sends the Siamese under the sofa.

"FOR YOU, DUMB KID," Jay is bellowing, standing over the tape recorder. "FOR ANYBODY WHO DOES NOT OR WILL NOT REMEMBER. SO ANYBODY READING THIS WILL KNOW THAT THE STATUE OF JUSTICE IN WASHINGTON, D.C., IS NOT ONLY BLIND, SHE IS RETARDED."

He reaches over and extracts a small white envelope from one of his notebooks. The return address says, simply, "Creedence." It is written in labored ball-point by one Tom Fogerty, a white California boy who formed Creedence Clearwater Revival with his brother John and two others. From 1969 to 1970 it was the most popular band in America.

"Read it," Jay insists. "Read it right into that machine."

It reads like this:

> *Dear Screamin' Jay:*
>
> In the long history of rock, some records are standout classics. My brother John and I had our minds blown the first time we heard "I Put a Spell on You." "Spell" is a classic, like "Strawberry Fields Forever" or "Fever." I hope your new album is a monster. Best of luck to you. And keep on screamin'.

Jay unsheathes a hunting knife to cut a blood pressure pill in half. "I ain't right today," he murmurs. "Sometimes life just gets on my nerves."

2
Sweet
Inspiration

I don't think there's much question that "rhythm and blues" is a term that I coined when I was working at Billboard. If I understood then what I know now, I would have called it rhythm and gospel.

—JERRY WEXLER

"NOW MAYBE THERE ARE some folks inclined to see the late fifties as a war of the worlds or something, with rock and all. With the new colliding head-on with the old, the traditional stuff—which, for lots of us, was gospel. But, honey, I am here to tell you it wasn't some freak thing that gospel banged into and got mixed up with what you might call popular music. No, it was *natural*. Mixing the two was *not* blasphemy to my mind. Although, I can tell you, there are some people upstairs here that might give you an argument."

Her voice hoarse from a cold and a recent string of club dates, Cissy Houston stands in the pastor's office in the basement of the New Hope Baptist Church in Newark, New Jersey. Every Sunday morning at eight Cissy directs the New Hope choir on its weekly radio broadcast. She got her own training in this church, as did her nieces Dee Dee and Dionne Warwick. Noon services have just begun in the wide, balconied hall. As

23

we struggle to conduct a conversation, a rolling thunder builds overhead. The sermon is pushing up a rugged slope of scripture and doxology. The wooden floor creaks beneath the tread of the faithful.

Cissy says that she is tired. Besides the choir practice and broadcast, she does club dates, mainly in New York City and New Jersey. Last night it was Washington, D.C. In a couple of weeks she will leave for Los Angeles and backup vocal work on the newest album of her longtime friend Aretha Franklin. It is Cissy you hear behind most of Aretha's greatest efforts, whooping, scolding, or flat-out harmonizing, fitting around Aretha's tasty filling with the snug but airy lightness of a blue-ribbon piecrust. Often it was a group effort by Cissy and the "girls"—Myrna Smith, Sylvia Shemwell, and Estelle Brown—the most heavenly backup group so representative of the best in sixties soul. Producer Jerry Wexler named them the Sweet Inspirations one long night when they had neatly, sweetly stitched up the holes in yet another Atlantic recording session.

Wexler says he learned the inspirational value of a fine, fiery backup group working with Ray Charles and his churchy, supercharged Raelettes. Like tireless sparring partners, they could push a singer's voice, cheer and challenge him to go higher and wilder, trading off a note, a moan, or a well-timed "ow!" until all parties, including the audience, were dropped, rubber-legged, to the canvas.

"A lot of girls got into doing that kind of session work," Cissy says. "But once we got it together in the Inspirations, well . . . nobody could touch us. Except maybe the Blossoms. And they were on the West Coast."

Before she joined the Inspirations in the early sixties, Cissy did session work on her own. Cissy is one of the strong female voices behind the early hits of Solomon Burke, behind Wilson Pickett "and just about anybody else you can name." In fact, she sang backup on both records when Burke and Pickett went toe to toe with simultaneous versions of "If You Need Me." When Elvis Presley decided to make his postcinematic Vegas comeback in 1968, he insisted upon having Cissy and the Inspirations behind him, feeling a need for gospel bedrock in that mirrored oasis. Some nights, between shows, he would knock on their dressing-room door, so they could sit around and talk gospel.

"Elvis did love gospel. He was raised on it. And he really did know what he was talking about. He was singing gospel all the time. Almost anything he did had that flavor anyhow. At least I heard it. You know, you can't get away from what your roots are."

Like Elvis, Cissy came up singing gospel as a child. But she says her

own path to secular work was rockier than his. Like a lot of southern
white boys, the King had access to stalwart white churches and tumble-
down black porches, could bawl blues out one side of the Lip and, out
the other, tear the top off harmonies he learned in the Assemblies of God
Pentecostal Church. Elvis was a born mongrel. And Gladys Presley must
have sensed the futility of threatening her baby boy with eternal damnation
over a mouthful of blues.

"Growing up, mine was a pretty narrow road," Cissy says. "Now I
had been brought up strict, to think that all of it, rock and all, was the
devil's music. But if God gives you a gift, if he gives you a *voice,* well,
I don't think He's gonna discriminate on how you best put it to use. But
I didn't always feel this way. Not at all . . ."

"Forsake me not!"

The hypnotic cadence upstairs is cracked by a deacon's cry. Cissy
smiles, hanging on to her thought. But more than once the tide upstairs
pulls us under.

"Savior, please! Savior, pull-eze! Cleanse the world, Oh CLEANSE
the world!"

"What was I saying, honey? Oh, yeah. The devil. Well now, I remember,
I was reared with that. With that belief that there wasn't but one righteous
way to raise the voice God gave you. And I suffered great trauma when
I went over [to pop]. But I had three children to raise. And I felt compelled
to get . . . I wanted the best for them. So I looked inside. And I realized
that if you had it here"—she thumps her heart through a tailored tweed
jacket—"if your heart was right, well, it was all about love anyhow. Just
with different words. I love my God, and I love my husband. And you
can't tell me it's a sin to open my mouth about either. And sing it *out.*"

The door flies open, and a woman in a starched nurse's uniform and
cap puts her head around the corner, then darts off. A second woman in
a flowered hat walks into the office and asks, "Sister, can I pick up my
envelopes?"

Cissy's tone is firm. "Did you pledge?"

Collection envelopes, boxed in sets of fifty-two, are stacked and waiting
for those who have pledged weekly donations.

"Two dollars a week," says the envelope seeker. "Till my situation
improves."

Cissy locates the woman's envelopes and crosses her off a master list.
Seated behind the pastor's desk, she stops to take a phone call. Yes, the
supper is on. A pot of greens surely won't go wanting.

"I am *trying*," she says after hanging up, "to remember when I noticed. I mean, some groups, like Billy Ward's Dominoes, were using gospel technique for R and B in the early fifties. But I would have been too young to notice. No, it would have been the mid-fifties, with Ray Charles and the like."

This, she points out, was also the *most* amazing time in gospel. A true flowering.

"What you have to understand is that it was no accident. You started to hear gospel in black popular music in the mid-fifties because that's what was going on in black *life*. Everybody was getting crazy that R and B was making it big, crossing over for whites and all. But gospel stations were just as exciting to listen to. Gospel was making folks jump in a big, big way."

Gospel's boom years were roughly the forties through the sixties. It began shortly after Sister Rosetta Tharpe took her big, bold voice and her blues-tinged guitar out of church and into clubs and theaters. In 1938 Sister Rosetta took it to the Cotton Club in Harlem and a feature spot in Cab Calloway's revue. Born in Cotton Plant, Arkansas, she went North to Chicago with her mother at age six and debuted singing gospel to a congregation of more than 1,000. By the time she recorded "Pickin' the Cabbage" with Calloway in 1940, she had a sizable following in both fields. Nobody seemed to mind that she could sing both sides, recording "I Want a Tall, Skinny Papa" and "Jesus Is Here Today." Before anyone had ever heard of Ray Charles or James Brown, Sister Rosetta cut a version of "Jonah" that jumps like a netful of live minnows. Her album *Gospel Train*, an LP assembled from recordings made in 1944 and 1949, is an unmatchable stew of jazz, gospel, and blues. By the time she switched back to gospel exclusively, Sister Rosetta was still commanding crowds of up to 25,000.

Strong soloists like Marion Williams, Sallie Martin, and Willie Mae Ford Smith developed significant followings, but no one did more to spread gospel's appeal than the queen, Mahalia Jackson. Her voice could derail a freight train. And when Mahalia got happy, she would lift her skirt, run down a church aisle, or snake-hip through a chorus. She was born in New Orleans's Storyville red-light district, settled in Chicago, and traveled all over the world, recording prodigiously. She was one of the first black artists to land on the network couches of Johnny Carson and Joey Bishop. Only the majestic Mahalia could induce Chicago's Mayor Richard Daley to help her bring the Reverend Martin Luther King, Jr., into that city.

Only the mischievous Mahalia could challenge Colonel Sanders on the *Tonight Show* with plans for her own chicken franchise. Her word was revered, her wit was wicked, and her combination of talent and personality opened the door further to showbiz gospel, until, by the late sixties, Clara Ward and her hopping, high-wigged singers had bounced from the TV show *Hootenanny* to raising the spirits of high rollers on the Vegas Strip.

The commercial potential of recorded gospel was evident as far back as 1939, when Sister Rosetta nailed herself a certified pop hit with "Rock Me," a song composed by Thomas Dorsey, one of the gifted writers crucial to the gospel boom. Dorsey explained, in a 1961 interview with *Ebony* magazine, that the return to the gospel tradition was due to something he called "the transitions of time," changes largely governed by American economics.

"We tried the gospel songs in the Twenties," he said, "but the time was not ripe for it. In the Depression, the time was ripe. People wanted to turn to something. The time is right for what these young fellows are trying to do. It's the age, the Atomic Age. People are scared. They want something to turn to. They're ready for it."

Professor Dorsey became the deacon of American gospel, but he, too, was familiar with both sides, having started out as an accompanist to blues great Ma Rainey and as "Georgia Tom," partner to Tampa Red. In the twenties Dorsey made a decent living as sideman, writer, and performer. Before he penned gospel classics like "Precious Lord," he wrote double-entendre blues titled "It's Tight Like That." In the beginning of his gospel career, his bluesy leanings sometimes got him thrown out of some churches. But to Dorsey, it was all of a piece. And later, when the back-to-the-roots movement in jazz and gospelized R & B began using the term "soul," Dorsey wasn't entirely approving. These kids, he contended, were not doing anything particularly innovative: "It was first in the Negro church. When I was a little boy, the churches couldn't afford an organ and the sisters sat in the amen corner and kept rhythm by clapping their hands. There is no need for some fellow born yesterday to come up and tell me now that soul is something new. At church, they do more foot tapping and hand clapping than they ever did. Some people go to church for the rhythm. And white people like the same kind of rhythm."

This fact was borne out as more gospel tunes "crossed over" to the white pop charts and as gospel queens were besieged with offers to sing at folk fests and in symphony halls. In black neighborhoods their appearances were less an event than a way of life. Road shows and revivals had never done so well. Nationwide, storefronts, churches, school gyms, and tents opened to receive a new surge of gospel artists. These included popular male groups, like the Sensational Nightingales, the Golden Gate Quartet, the Swan Silvertones, the Soul Stirrers, and the Dixie Hummingbirds. Soloists like Sallie Martin, Willie Mae Ford Smith, and Mahalia Jackson toured to huge followings, as did the Reverend James Cleveland, the "king" of gospel who became mentor to Aretha Franklin. A handful of record companies—notably Chess and Vee Jay in Chicago, Apollo in New York, Savoy in Newark, New Jersey, Peacock in Houston, and Specialty in Los Angeles—pressed and sold gospel singles with the same frenzy generated for producing and promoting R & B discs. Thus the Five Blind Boys' "Our Father" could cross over to the R & B charts in 1950, right alongside Wynonie Harris's "I Like My Baby's Pudding."

On the radio, blues, jazz, rock, and gospel were neatly separated by programming hours. On the road, it was different. Gospel, like the blues, had come North via rail and highway. The Soul Stirrers, the Pilgrim Travelers, the Highway QC's, the Gospel Paraders, the Caravans all were *travelin'* bands, literally and lyrically:

Goin' home . . . goin' over, bound for Canaan.

Even the titles moved: "Rock Me," "Nearer to Thee," "Standing Out on the Highway," "The Last Mile of the Way."

The train was bound for glory, but it wasn't express. As fellow travelers, gospel passed the blues in bus depots and train yards. Sanctified sat down with sinner across the sticky oilcloth of storefront rib joints. It was only natural that they talk.

From this kind of vibrant dialogue, black American music has grown, a call and response between the plain truths of clean, rural forms and the complex sophistications of new lives, new sounds in the city. Blues, jazz, gospel, and their progeny, R & B and soul, all have origins in the South. They're what they are *because* they traveled. By the late fifties the blue note chatter bounced between the fertile crescent of the southern cities and the northern industrial cities strung from the shores of the Great Lakes to the Atlantic. Migrations brought variations. The blues began in the Mississippi delta and got electrified in Chicago and Kansas City. Rock and R & B hatched their root forms notably in Memphis and New Orleans and went national with the heavy urban wattage of well-placed deejay oracles.

"When you are talking about a living thing—and I do believe music to be a living, breathing thing—you have to understand that it will push and change itself, just to survive. And if it's something you do every day, it's going to change right along with what's going down in your life," says Cissy.

She has closed the door against the growing din in the basement as church members prepare for the congregation meal. Pots clang and women laugh. From the wall vent comes the spicy smell of hot sweet potato pie.

"Now gospel will go a long way to help you survive," she says. "But in the late fifties when I started hearing churchy things in pop music, in Ray Charles, in Sam Cooke, when I listened to *my* voice and realized what I *could* do . . . well, I felt I was wronging my children, holding back like that."

There is no holding back when Cissy tilts her face into the bluish spot of some Manhattan club and rattles ice cubes with an out-and-out love song. I saw her do this just a few nights before our talk. That night, when Cissy stepped aside to let her teenage daughter Whitney take a solo turn, R & B swallow Maxine Brown was moved to stand up in the audience and clap and holler, "Sing it, girl. Carry it *on.*"

Whitney is a fine-boned, pretty young woman with a set of lungs that could turn back a tidal wave. Her mother says she has taught her not to hold back.

"Within the love of God, all things are possible," Cissy says. "Playing some club and singing in the New Hope choir, in Newark, New Jersey. I never have trouble with it now, owing to my faith. I received Jesus into my heart when I was fourteen. I can't describe it. I have been pretty peaceful ever since. Listen, I can't expect you to understand. It's a special relationship, between me and my God."

Metal folding chairs bang and scrape as the congregation files in to the meal. Cissy says she is too tired to eat. There is a lot to do before she flies West to work with Aretha.

"My good friend Miss Ree says she has some fine things ready to go, and I have no doubt it's true. You can tell when she is ready. She'll sit down at the piano and line it out for you—Reverend Cleveland taught Aretha to play a *fine* keyboard—and she'll have all the parts ready, all your harmonies. You know you understand gospel when you get a feel for the *wholeness* of the sound."

Though she couldn't have known it at the time, *Jump to It,* the album Cissy was about to work on, would be hailed as a comeback of sorts for

Aretha, more than a decade past her best work on Atlantic in the late sixties. Critics welcomed back a roundness, a full use of the voice that first loosed itself in a gospel shout.

"All I know," Cissy was saying, "is that I'm going to go out there and feel right at home. Always do. There have been a lot of trips since what people called the soul years, or whatever. Took a lot of people places they never dreamed of. And there will be more trips, I can tell you that. I really don't worry about where I'm going." She laughs, stepping out of the office into a current of rushing organdy and Sunday serge. She waves a ringed finger over her heart. "This girl's baggage has passed inspection."

3

Uptown, Saturday Night

It was a quartet. . . . That sound, that driving sound, always makes me see a black cat, face brilliant and sweating in the sunlight, which pours down on his face, pacing, prancing, up a long, high hill. . . . He is surrounded by people urging him up the hill, they are all around him and behind him, but you do not see them. You know, simply, as he does, that they are present.

—JAMES BALDWIN, in *Just Above My Head*

GOSPEL IS SIMPLY *the* original group sound in America. And once gospel was secularized, popularized in some fifties group sounds, with Ray Charles's solo efforts, and at its utmost in sixties soul, it was the community aspect that stood out. Soul would go so far as to *preach,* to become message music for the black community with songs like James Brown's "Say It Loud, I'm Black and I'm Proud" and the Impressions' "Movin' On Up."

But long before soul music reached those late-sixties anthem stages, booming out of black culture centers and university strike headquarters, the fifties group sound drew voices together in the streets for the sheer fun of it. Uptown, in Harlem, one of those voices was that of a teenage Ben E. King.

"Got to watch the pipes."

Ben E. King removes his overcoat but keeps the soft tweed scarf around his neck. His recording contract has just run out, here at Atlantic Records, where we have borrowed an office. Though he is ambivalent about shopping around for a new one, he is still mindful to protect his throat.

Long past the golden years with the Drifters, nearly two decades beyond his solo hits like "Spanish Harlem," "Don't Play That Song," and "Stand By Me," Benny is still working. He is only forty-six.

"I do some rock clubs," he says. "A few oldies gigs. Hotels. And, when I can handle it, supper clubs."

Mainly these are suburban pleasure domes where the prime rib gets top billing and brandy Alexanders close the show, any show, glasses and spirits raised just high enough to make the entertainer feel like a side order of succotash.

From 1962 to 1964, when he headlined at the Apollo, Ben E. King was the main course, dishing up hits like "Don't Play That Song," a tune written for him by Ahmet Ertegun.

"Sure, for a while I was one of Atlantic's big deals," he says. "With the Drifters, then by myself. How would I market a Ben E. King today? Oh, *Lord.*" He laughs and throws up his hands. "People still come up to me and say, 'Hey, aren't you *B. B.* King?' Maybe I'm just a victim of being around too long."

Still smiling, he is not a man given to bitterness or soppy regret. His is a temperament so adjustable, so pacific that his friend Solomon Burke, another Atlantic alumnus, calls him the black Andy Williams. Benny says he can't complain; he's still making a nice living. He only wishes to point out that his current hotel and dinner theater bookings have required a few adjustments.

"I find them [the audience] very, very hard to reach. Even as many times as I've done it, I still stand in the wings sometimes, and I look out at the audience for a while. They're like forty and fifty and sixty, and the drummer can't get but so loud. And the bass can't get funky. If I say 'funky' to them, I have to explain to them *why* I'm saying this."

Dinner theaters and high-rise hotel ballrooms are far, very far from Harlem, where this whole thing started. For Ben E. King, born Benjamin Earl Nelson in Henderson, North Carolina, Harlem was the strange cemented-over place his grandmother sent him to join his parents at age nine, a place where amateur vocal groups collected under corner streetlamps like sharkskinned moths. Sundays, he recalls, most of the boys sang in church, in storefronts and the solid brick-front Baptist churches that sat along Lenox, Seventh, and Eighth avenues like stern and watchful matrons. But until dawn delivered those sweet harmonies unto the feet of the Lord, Saturday night bore a wave of voices tuned to the frequencies of earthly love.

If a neighborhood vocal group wanted to check out the action farther uptown, say, near the St. Nicholas housing projects on 131st, they might let a few trains pass and rehearse on the subway platform.

"On-leeee yoooooooo."

"Higher, man, and hold it two more beats. Benny, hey—you *late* on the harmony."

Sweet pomade battled the subway brimstone of smoke and burned metal. Echoes bounced off tiled walls and vaulted cement ceilings, better than in a bathroom or hallway. Benny remembers that you could hear the sound—your sound—coming right back at you, the way it might on a recording.

Small, independent record companies in and around New York were already hauling kids off the corners to capitalize on this abundance of cheap, eager talent. A good record company scout knew the group turfs. Fat black coupes idled alongside the tinted and fringed chariots of alpacaed pimps as record men worked their own hustles. But most often the recruiting budget was a handful of subway tokens.

"Yeah, they found you where you lived," Benny says. "And they didn't have a whole lot of selling to do. That was taken care of by the guys who had already made it, got a contract and all that garbage. News traveled fast. And those guys were instant heroes."

As soon as his father released him from his chores at one of the three uptown restaurants the family ran, Benny would take the apartment house steps two at a time, discarding the clothes infused with the smells of frying chicken, burgers, simmering onions, and beans.

"I'd hook up with three or four of my buddies. I used to live on a Hundred Sixteenth and Eighth Avenue, and we hung out there."

In 1957, when he was nineteen, Benny would make it to amateur night at the Apollo with his little local group and would come in second. But just getting onstage was a struggle. It seemed there were hundreds of groups and a thousand street-corner versions of "Earth Angel" and "Sincerely." Even after smooth-talking managers, talent show credentials, or outright begging got you the shot on amateur night, there was a lot of work to be done.

Often the next priority was to pool money from after-school jobs to put something down on a sharp set of matching suits, so slim at the ankle that a nylon sock made it tough to slide a foot through. More cash could get choreography lessons from master black dance coaches. Foremost was Cholly Atkins. As a tap duo Atkins and Charles "Honi" Coles had been peerless. They stopped dancing together in 1960, when Coles left to manage the Apollo. But as a free-lance coach in the mid-fifties Atkins was available to help a group of gangly adolescents nail a pirouette, a slide, or a freeze-frame group pose—with or without the glow-in-the-dark white gloves. This could kill when flashed during the silent bridge of a song. Looking in mirrors, groups worked up supercool Polaroids: chins on hands, eyes to heaven, shoulders and pants creases sharp enough to cut paper. When Benny was coming up, Atkins's special prodigies were the Cadillacs.

"Oh, they were so sharp it hurt," says Benny. "The Cadillacs had the best clothes, the best steps. They had a real tight harmony hit, a nice plush ballad, 'Gloria.' You could watch those guys and turn kelly green."

No matter how sharp you were, how big, how successful, no one seemed immune to the fear. It could paralyze, Benny remembers, tap-dance on your diaphragm as you stood, shaking, in the wings of that old vaudeville house on 125th Street. It had caused one big-name bandleader to wet his pants. Ella Fitzgerald said it always made her sweat to play the Apollo. Even the suave Nat "King" Cole could not control his shakes there.

"That audience could love you so you thought you'd died and gone to glory," Benny says. "But some nights, no matter what, they were out for blood."

Most vocal was the cheap-seat crowd high in the second balcony, which was aptly dubbed the Buzzards' Roost. Especially on amateur night, they could descend on a limping bunny of an act, squawking for a kill, relentless, until the carcass was hauled from the stage.

This was a crowd so tough that the projectionist locked himself in his balcony booth, so stubborn that when it was time to clear the house for the next show, only a thirty-minute movie short called *The River* could do the job. It featured a half hour of flowing water. Few sets of kidneys were immune to its subliminal message. Within minutes the seats emptied.

Dismissal of amateur contestants was not quite as subtle. "They really had a hook, to haul guys off if they were bombing," Benny says. "Sometimes, let me tell you, it was for their own protection."

Often a few shots from a starter's pistol proved far more effective. All in all, it helped, in this arena, if you had already earned your stripes trading doowops in the streets.

"Not that we were into street fights," Benny says. "We were pretty cool in my area. We had our fighting crowd—they were the Sultans, mean, ugly, bald-headed dudes—and we had our singing crowd. I never really got into fighting. It drove me crazy to have to run like hell for five or six blocks when I could just as easily smile, and doowop, and duck around a corner."

Vocal groups sacked and pillaged, but in a mannerly way.

"My buddies and I would walk from a Hundred Sixteenth to maybe a Hundred Twenty-ninth. And on those blocks alone you'd find anywhere from three to five groups. We'd stop and listen, and if we felt that we were better, we would challenge them. It was territorial, you know, and you'd have to go out looking for the competition," Benny says. "You'd stand around and check it out; they'd have a crowd anyhow. And their girls, of course."

To the victors went their phone numbers. Friday and Saturday nights were the most popular for such musical marauding parties. And no challenge was issued without great preparation.

"We'd learn from the records, like everybody did. The group to get you over the best would be somebody like the Moonglows. If you could sing Moonglows, you could *kill* the neighborhood. They had great harmonies, the Moonglows. Or the Satins or the Clovers. We tried to pattern ourselves after the tight-harmonied groups."

The lineage of such groups can be traced back to the thirties and forties, with the close-harmonied gospel quartets, with secular black vocal groups like the Ink Spots and the Mills Brothers. Black harmony had long been a sweet and inexpensive form of recreation. Black kids, especially in the cities, had begun to pay keener attention to the group sound when it became apparent that they could become commercially successful with it. The human voice is a cheap and versatile instrument; there was no reason you couldn't teach it new slides and fillips to make it current, exciting, and salable. Even in the slums of Kingston, Jamaica, future reggae star Bob Marley drew his early inspiration from the Moonglows. There was something about this sound, especially the Moonglows' tight, chesty "blow" harmony, that had tremendous appeal in the post–big band era.

"Doowop" is, of course, an *ex post facto* label, and it can be argued that it's inadequate. Especially in the case of early fifties adult groups like the Moonglows, the Orioles, the Clovers, and the Ravens, the harmony was complex and sophisticated and just as "serious" as a heartfelt offering from the gospel Soul Stirrers. "Doowop" effervesced with the advent of pop production teams seeking to make the sound more accessible to kids. In this soft angora niche were groups like the Cadillacs, Frankie Lymon and the Teenagers, the Five Satins, the Platters, Little Anthony and the Imperials, and the Charms. They sang stuff like "To the Aisle," "Church Bells Will Ring," "Twilight Time," and "Tears on My Pillow."

"We knew it wasn't just in New York," says Ben E. King, "that kids were buying these records, white and black kids. And you knew that Alan Freed and Wolfman Jack and those guys were playing it. R and B was on the air nationally, and all that. But remember, for us it all got started as a *neighborhood* thing. And if you came up, like so many of us did, from the South, singing could help you get it all together. Turn you into a city boy, you know? I was in two groups most of the time. I sang with an R and B one, but I stayed with the gospel. I mean, for us it was no blasphemy, that kind of garbage. For me the feeling I got was the same. If it was an old church song, one of those old-timey Dr. Watts hymns, or a new hit you'd been learning off the records, you took a song and made it your own. And your buddies, the guys who did it with you, they were your *heart*. You could get so in tune it seemed you all had but one heart between you. Man, you knew when all the other guys were gonna *breathe*."

Benny catches himself for a moment and laughs, a little self-consciously. He wonders aloud if he isn't getting carried away by memories.

"No, no way," he decides. "I really mean it. I would say that those street years, in the groups, were the best of my life. Not the big successes, the gold records, looking at where you are this week in the charts, all that garbage. I mean, that was great. I loved it, and it's fed my family. But listen, it's just real hard to describe now the feeling a quartet gave you. You never felt alone, is all."

Being in love with the music itself was a group thing, too. Infatuations are catching, especially among teenagers.

"You could dance to the stuff," Benny says, "kiss your girl to it. And, my God, more than a lot of this electronic stuff you have going on now, you could *feel* it. It was a human voice you picked up on. I guess I'd say you could get involved on a real emotional level.

"You got involved with the singer, too. You worshiped these guys, stood at the edge of the stage checking out their clothes, every move, every fancy vocal trick with your little old heart banging at your sweater like crazy.''

Few singers quickened pulse rates with the ease and majesty of Clyde McPhatter, who began with the Dominoes, founded the Drifters, then recorded as a solo. As a latter-day Drifter, from 1959 to 1960, Benny was the fourth lead singer to try to fill McPhatter's high-sheen patent boots. The list of artists who credit McPhatter as an early influence includes singers as diverse as Screamin' Jay, Jackie Wilson, and Smokey Robinson. The elements that would later characterize many soul acts—the emotional delivery, the gospel-oriented call-and-response patterns, even the flashy, drop-to-your-knees theatrics—all were part of McPhatter's appeal.

"It all came together in Clyde," Benny says. "He could sing the blues, but he had that gospel sound since he came up in church. What Clyde did was to bring gospel into pop music in a big way as a lead singer. I guess you could say he made a wide-open space by mixing it up like that. A space a lot of guys were grateful for. Billy Ward knew what he was doing when he happened on Clyde."

Ward was a well-known figure in Harlem, a gospel coach. Affiliated with various Sanctified or Baptist churches or working solo out of home "studios"—usually a front room in someone's apartment—quartet coaches schooled a group in harmonies and phrasings, groomed them, and, once invitations to visit other churches were received, traveled with the quartet, acting as road manager, banker, tour guide, and surrogate parent.

Billy Ward was, by all accounts, a stern master, recruiting and training his students with uncompromising discipline. Ward had pushed himself to learn all aspects of quartet singing. In addition to coaching singers, he played piano and organ, arranged and composed songs, saw to every detail, including personal grooming. In the late forties he was intuitive enough to anticipate the winds of change in pop music. With an eye on the growing commercial success of black vocal groups, he handpicked the best gospel students and formed an R & B group known as the Dominoes. To assume the demanding burden of lead singer, he looked to Clyde McPhatter, who was barely seventeen and fresh out of high school.

The son of a Baptist minister, McPhatter was born in 1933, in Durham, North Carolina. Singing with his brothers and sisters in church, he soloed as a boy soprano at age ten. When he moved North to New Jersey and joined the Mount Lebanon Singers, his voice broke into a fragile tenor. By the time Ward put him in the Dominoes, he had developed a house-wrecking style that set off traditional major-chord group harmonies with the unpredictable minor-note pyrotechnics of the gospel shout.

The Dominoes were successful with McPhatter almost instantly. In 1951 and 1952 they had three hits, including the classic "Sixty Minute Man." Arching his long, supple frame into a backbend, then crumpling to his knees, McPhatter was a box-office dream. But Billy Ward pressed his troops just a bit too hard and lost the best lead singer he could ever have had. It couldn't have sat well when Ward insisted that the Dominoes actually stand for inspection before performances. Fines were levied for lateness, for wrinkles, for unshined shoes. On tour, under the lash of Ward's regime, McPhatter developed attitude problems that got him drummed out of the group in 1953. Waiting in the wings was a young man who had followed the group on tour with undisguised devotion. Jackie Wilson became the Dominoes' new lead, confessing years later that he had been hopelessly in love with McPhatter's voice.

"I was mad for Clyde's voice, too," Ahmet Ertegun told me. "Had to have it at Atlantic." Noting McPhatter's absence from the lineup when the Dominoes played Birdland in Manhattan one night, Ertegun embarked on one of his legendary talent hunts. Tracking down blind blues singers or backwoods piano genius, Ertegun was often party to wild road rallies in taxi and limo, through Harlem or Louisiana bayous, into pricey clubs and cheap hotels. As a mogul in the making Ertegun was tireless—and now and again perhaps downright foolhardy—about pursuing his musical infatuations. He has, as a *New Yorker* profile put it, "taken Louis Vuitton luggage where Louis Vuitton luggage had rarely been before."

The search for Clyde McPhatter led to a furnished room in Harlem. There the deal was cut. As lead McPhatter could form his own group to record for Atlantic. This he did, shuffling personnel until the mix was right. Searching for just the right churchy background for his hooch-and-hallelujah leads, McPhatter chose bassman Bill Pinckney, a pair of gospel-trained brothers named Andrew "Bubba" and Gerhart Thrasher (baritone and tenor), and, on different sessions, Willie Ferbie or Jimmy Oliver.

Calling themselves the Drifters, they hit immediately but only on the R & B charts. "Money Honey" in 1953 was followed in 1954 by a novelty version of der Bingle's chestnut "White Christmas." Its flip side was a doowoppy version of another pious tune, "The Bells of St. Mary's." The same year the Drifters released one of McPhatter's finest efforts, "Whatcha Gonna Do?," written by Ahmet Ertegun.

The draft yanked McPhatter out of the Drifters and off the charts, and after he returned from the service in 1955, he began to record as a solo. His biggest hit was "A Lover's Question," in 1958. Just over a year later he left Atlantic for Mercury Records. There were a few more hits, like "Lover Please" and "Little Bitty Pretty One," in the early sixties, but soon McPhatter slipped into soupy pop orchestrations that all but drowned his gospel fire.

Many fans and rock historians have tried to make sense of his decline. Some point to the British invasion of the early sixties that seemed to over-shadow a good many R & B originals. Others claim that though he was, with Sam Cooke and Ray Charles, one of the standout fathers of sixties soul, McPhatter was simply and fatally ahead of his time. He was found dead, of heart, kidney, and liver "complications," in a Houston dressing room in 1972. He was only thirty-nine, but often, before his death, he had told Ben E. King he felt he had missed his chance and had just given up.

Without McPhatter, the Drifters moved through a few incarnations. David Baughan, Johnny Moore, and Bobby Hendricks took turns at lead. A long history of contractual disputes and personnel changes got the entire group bounced from the Atlantic roster in the late fifties. George Treadwell, who owned the name, felt there could be an entirely new set of Drifters, and in 1959 a Manhattan group called the Five Crowns got the nod. Among them was Ben E. King, who had joined the Crowns a year earlier.

"I was singing baritone and bass," Benny says. "I wasn't doing any lead. So I didn't figure I had much of a future. My parents were saying, 'You should be working here at the store with your dad; you'll never make a living from show business.' I guess I thought they were right until I started doing lead. And I didn't start doing that until we started recording, really."

The new Drifters' 1959 smash "There Goes My Baby" was produced by Jerry Leiber and Mike Stoller, the Wright brothers of American pop. At first listen, Jerry Wexler pronounced the record "a fucking mess"— a wild mélange of kettle drums, strings, vocal *bom-bom-boms,* and Ben E. King's heartsick gospel wail on lead.

Benny liked the record. He liked being out front, lining out the story, cracking a pained *whoa-oh-oh-oh* across the neat, harmonic tattle of the other singers' cant of "there she goes."

The song hit number two on the pop charts, and Benny hung up his skillet and apron and left his father's luncheonette; within a year, when this set of Drifters was headlining at the Apollo, they were also regulars on the pop charts, having finally achieved that crossover dream that McPhatter cherished. More hits followed, with Benny on lead: "This Magic Moment" and "Save the Last Dance for Me," which stayed at number one for three weeks in 1960. Benny's parents, who had reluctantly signed the Atlantic contracts since he was underage, now turned up at the Apollo, along with customers from their restaurants.

By 1961 Benny had a solo hit with "Spanish Harlem," a song written by teen genius Phil Spector, along with Jerry Leiber. His biggest solo seller ever came that same year, with "Stand By Me," a secular version of an old gospel song by the same title. It is a big, emotional record that sets a pair of lovers against a stark, gloomy landscape. Faith and love fend off the darkness, can endure when stars fall, mountains crumble.

"Oh, yeah," Benny says, "that record is straight out of church. And a few parts Harlem. Sweetened up with some plush Broadway strings."

It was, in hindsight, a classy antecedent to the best of Atlantic soul, part of a body of hits that would move the company from a dumpy West Fifty-sixth Street office above Patsy's restaurant to the Warner Communications monolith that now shades West Fifty-first Street.

The young, smartly dressed Atlantic staff is just returning from lunch as Benny and I end our conversation. The walls of the borrowed office have begun to vibrate with the rumbling bass of speakers in adjoining cubicles. Some of the music is new Atlantic "product," some the cassette demos of hopefuls. All seem to pulse with the dominant, almost tyrannical rhythm tracks that have been pervasive since the disco craze of the mid-seventies. Benny closes the door on it, still smiling.

The human voice is such a satisfying instrument, he says, the feeling so physical and terrific that in a way, he is sorry for the children who will never know it.

"They're taken away from all those fun things," he says. "They're being given big radios. And they've got them on their shoulders, and it's driving them crazy."

Benny and his wife have raised their three children in the New Jersey suburbs to keep them safe from the streets he roamed as a kid. He still goes back to those streets. "My training ground" he calls them. But he always goes alone, driving in over the George Washington Bridge, down the West Side to 116th and Eighth Avenue, where the Sultans whopped and the Five Crowns doowopped. And where now, the dominant rhythm is the junkie's nod.

"I park my car and I walk. I see myself there if I don't be cool. And I've seen myself there quite a few times if I didn't be cool to the point where I could say, 'Hey, nothing spectacular about you, babe. You just have a voice. Just that one thing.' "

4
High-Octane Dreams

You harmonize; then you customize.

—WILSON PICKETT

THE NEW YORK GROUP SCENE was hardly an isolated phenomenon. In the late fifties and early sixties street-corner hybrids grew like crabgrass in the sidewalk cracks, especially in the industrial North, where cities had large, still-growing black populations. In Detroit, Cincinnati, Chicago, Cleveland, Philadelphia, and Gary, kids sprouted their own, new sounds from blues and gospel cuttings carried there from the South and tended casually but faithfully on front stoops, in schoolyards, churches, talent shows, and clubs.

Some of the singers were born to the cities. But the overwhelming majority had been born in the South. Just how much baggage they hauled along and kept was a very personal matter, they will tell you. One such traveler remembers working almost obsessively to knock the red Alabama clay off his shoes, out of his talk, out of his very memory—of swearing to wear fine calfskin, instead of watering and tending it. Having walked countless country miles, he wanted to drive, even if it was three blocks to the candy store. He says he is a God-fearing man, but when he left, he swore—and swore viciously—that the next time he saw a ball of cotton, it would be in some fancy glass jar in a downtown Detroit drugstore.

"Baby, I am a *mean* motherfucker. Don't you be *writing* nothin' nice 'cause you'd be jivin' people. I AM THE WICKED. Dig? I AM *NAMED* THE WICKED, I GOT TO *BE* THE WICKED."

Sterno flames have cast a satanic cobalt mask over Wilson Pickett's face. He glares over the tray of Chinese appetizers, sinking lower in a Leatherette restaurant booth, scowling, until the bluster dissolves into a fit of giggles. He downs a fried oyster and brandishes its tiny chrome pitchfork.

"Now," he says. "Ain't I *bad?*"

"Owwww," yelps his friend, songwriter Don Covay. "So very, very bad my eyes can't *stand* to look. Wicked Pickett, my mean friend—how is it I love you?"

Love each other they do, despite some rocky times.

Covay, who recorded and performed solo and with a group called the Goodtimers, still does the occasional gig in New York clubs, and often his friend Pickett will fly out of the wings to help him shut down the late show. He is perhaps best known for the hits he's written that were sung by other singers—among them Aretha Franklin's "Chain of Fools" and "See Saw."

A decade has passed since Wilson Pickett seriously assaulted the charts, but at age forty-three, he has surrendered only one belt notch to middle age and, it appears, a tidy fortune to his tailor. The pinstripe suit is impeccable, tossed over a pearly white shirt.

He still wears silk better than Rita Hayworth, still looks the part of the mean, libidinous Pickett, soul's mythical "Man and a Half," the Pickett with the heart-stopping soul scream, the Stutz, the Rolls, the badass record company moniker ("The Wicked"), and a string of greasy, classic sixties soul wallows like "Funky Broadway," "Mustang Sally," "Soul Dance Number Three ," and, of course, "In the Midnight Hour."

Midnight hugger . . . all night lover. He sang it; he says he lived it. Pickett, the Midnight Mover, who weakened legions of fishnet stocking'd knees with courtly little love poems such as "Lay Me Like You Hate Me." *Midnight teaser . . . real soul pleaser*. Lean, handsome Pickett, who used to blow into the Atlantic Records office in Manhattan like an arctic squall of cool in white rabbit overcoats, wrists and knuckles glacial with diamonds. These days the Wicked keeps his rocks in a bank vault. He says he's afraid of being mugged. He guesses he was just too green and naïve to be scared when he started out in Detroit.

Wilson recalls the fifties and early sixties as jumpy, mobile years. There were high-octane possibilities for country boys who headed North to those cities of the industrial crescent strung like greasy ball bearings along the southern shores of the Great Lakes.

"Me and a million other dudes said 'Later' to pickin' cotton and that shit," Pickett says. The rural South held no promise for him. Of his ten brothers and sisters, he figures he had the hardest head and the most problematic childhood in tiny Prattville, Alabama.

"The baddest woman in my book, *hoooooeee*. My mother. I get scared of her now. She used to hit me with anything, skillets, stove wood. Not too long ago, I said to her, 'You know, there's one thing I never forgave you for.' And she said, 'What's that, baby?'—she calls me baby—and I said, 'Remember when I did all the chores?' There was eleven of us. I done worked my ass off. And I'd go and lay down in front of the wood-burning fireplace. She come in to tell me to go get Granny some dippin' snuff, got to go all the way to the company store to get the snuff, which is five miles. I said, 'Mama, I'm so tired, why don't you ask one of the others?' *Whoooa,* she almost killed me."

Terrified of another whupping, Wilson hightailed it to the store for the two-cent snuff. Then he decided to run away.

"I cried for a week," he remembers. "Stayed in the woods, me and my little dog."

He caught fish and picked and ate raw corn until his small belly cramped and swelled. But it was the nights that drove him home, to another session with the switch.

"I got scared out there. Too many hoot owls."

Things were tolerable until his grandfather caught him singing what the old man called modern profanity. Really, it was just a tame popular song by Louis Jordan: "Ain't nobody here but us chickens, ain't nobody here at home . . ."

Wilson is standing in the booth, flapping his elbows over the egg rolls, singing in a little-kid voice: "So gobble, gobble, gobble . . ."

The lyrics were hardly racy, but Wilson's elders had no truck with *any* secular music. WHAP. He jerks his head, impacted from an imaginary blow.

"My grandfather, he was a preacher, right? He hit me across the head with—you know the Bible weigh a *lot*—the King *James* Bible, mind—WHAP—right across the head. Yellin', 'Don't you hear me readin' the Bible, boy?' WHAP. ' "Ain't nobody home but us chickens," huh?' WHAP."

All the adults agreed the boy was trouble. He had no respect for the old ways and no patience, no tolerance for the quiet acceptance his elders seemed to have for the economic and social gospel according to Whitey. Out in the cotton field, Wilson invented a dangerous game. Pick a bag of cotton; haul it over to the truck; hand it to the white foreman to weigh. Then Wilson would toss it to his partner on the truck, who would then toss it back out the other side, unseen. Wilson messed around in the field long enough to make it look good. Then hauled the same bag back . . . got it weighed . . .

It worked. But his mother worried when irritation over "little" things caused her teenage son to sass the Man. White people had always walked into black homes without knocking, anytime night or day.

"One day," says Wilson, "I asked this white cat, 'Don't you know how to knock on a door?' "

Shortly after, his mother decided he would benefit from the discipline and protection of his father, who had moved North. So, in his early teens, Wilson lit out for good, this time for Detroit and night sounds far, far from the call of Alabama hoot owls.

He says that those mid-fifties city sounds suited him just fine. Nolan Strong and the Diablos, a Detroit group, had begun to record. Jackie Wilson, the Detroit teenager who had replaced Clyde McPhatter in the Dominoes, began a solo career. And another local boy, who had been discovered in a talent show by King Records, Little Willie John, hit with the classic "Fever" and "All Around the World." On the charts, Willie John's dreamy, almost melancholy cool was offset by the frenzy and twitch of Little Richard's "Tutti Frutti" and Chuck Berry's fast-lane road trip "Maybellene." Smooth groups like the Platters, the Charms, the Hearts, and the Clovers continued to score with mellow, close harmony sounds.

Another group sound, less polite, was catching Pickett's impressionable ears. It was less polished, more sexy, and very danceable. It was that sound that the Dominoes and the Drifters, with McPhatter, had begun. Technically it built on the classic quartet harmonies. Lyrically it often required just a few word changes to slip from exalting the Almighty to celebrating an almighty fine woman. Like doowop, "rhythm and gospel" was a street mongrel. There were plenty of church-trained kids in the streets of Detroit who were just as conversant with the backseat sacraments exalted in the Hit Parade. In fact, the same talent show that had spotlighted a subteen Willie John yielded Hank Ballard and the Midnighters, whose silly, salacious "Annie" records (among them "Work with Me, Annie" and "Annie Had a Baby") could drop a deacon.

"Listen," says Wilson. "Just what kind of sound you got into back there, it all had to do with style, you know? And where you were livin', in the body and the spirit."

The Wicked maintains that gospel was all he thought he *could* sing— until a Detroit neighbor named Willie Schofield convinced him that R & B wasn't but a sigh and scream away. Schofield had a group called the Falcons, which also included Mack Rice, who would later pen Pickett's "Mustang Sally," Joe Stubbs (whose brother Levi would become lead singer for Motown's Four Tops), and Eddie Floyd, who would later have hits as a singer and songwriter on Stax Records out of Memphis.

Schofield heard Pickett noodling on the porch with a secondhand guitar and some untrammeled gospel. He invited him to be in the Falcons, "to do the group thing," says Pickett, "and be cool."

Marcelled, processed hair was cool, he recalls. And wide lapels, trimmed in contrasting colors. Pointed shoes were cool. And cars with "porthole" windows. Being in a group—a good one—says Pickett, "could make you so cool you *smoked.*" Thousands of kids teamed in aggregates of four or five to hammer out a sound that worked and was stylish as well. To hear Pickett tell it, the process was not unlike auto shop in any urban high school.

"You harmonize; then you customize. Now what kid don't want to own the *latest* model? And tell me now, what black kid in some city project can afford it? When I hit Detroit, I was eatin' nothin' but beans and rice, rice and beans. Maybe once a month I come up with a chicken liver to throw in it. And pancakes. Aunt Jemima done saved *my* starvin' ass. Anyhow, you got no cash for music lessons, arrangers, uniforms, backup bands, guitars. No nothin'. So you look around for a good, solid used chassis. This be your twelve-bar blues. R and B ain't nothin' if it ain't the twelve-bar blues. Then you look around for what else you got. And if you come up like most of us, that would be gospel."

Both elements went into the first hit tune Schofield and Pickett composed together. Released on Lu Pine in late 1961 and an R & B hit in

1962, "I Found a Love" was the hit that got the Falcons an opening act gig at the Apollo, with Pickett as lead. But he says it took "a lot of messin' around and singin' in Detroit alleys" before it all came together.

"Sure, you mixed it up," he says. "*Customize,* like I say. You see what's in style. You know, we listened to the Moonglows and all that. And the Dominoes, where you could really hear the gospel. But then you had your church favorites—cats who burn it *down,* wreck a church, we call it."

It's not surprising, given his own trademark screams and flaming delivery, that Pickett was particularly drawn to the voice of the Reverend Julius Cheeks, lead singer for the Sensational Nightingales, who was said to have one of the most terrifying voices in gospel. Until his death in 1981, Reverend Cheeks would go down to the basement of Wilson's house in New Jersey to fool around and sing along as they played records from the Wicked's massive gospel collection.

"Anyone cried to the Lord so's He could *hear,* I got down there," he says. Included are seminal recordings by the Soul Stirrers, a gospel group that had its origins in the 1930s in rural Texas. Early on, the group enjoyed the guidance of lead singer R. H. Harris, who, from his travels in and around Houston, also developed an ear for hillbilly music and solid Texas blues. The Soul Stirrers were a traveling quartet, and they came through Detroit often when Wilson Pickett lived there. Actually, he saw a second incarnation of the Soul Stirrers. Once Harris had retired from the road in 1950, nineteen-year-old Sam Cooke was called up from a sort of junior gospel farm team, the Highway QC's. After a few false starts that attempted to imitate Harris, Cooke's clear, bracing tenor found its own combustion point, bursting into cries that melted and flowed into long, molten yodels. His voice transfigured the sound of quartet gospel and, as early as 1950, in his gospel work, heralded the sound of soul. To say that the Soul Stirrers could wreck a church is, according to those who saw them then, a most sinful understatement.

"Them sisters fell like dominoes when Sam took the lead," Pickett says. "Bang. Flat-out. Piled three deep in the aisles."

Among the faithful was the teenage Aretha Franklin, who often heard the Soul Stirrers when they sang at the Detroit congregation of her father, that master of brimstone with a beat, the Reverend C. L. Franklin. She recalls a strange seating shift in the New Bethel Baptist Church whenever Sam Cooke showed up. Suddenly the young people, who always left the first rows for the elders, began crowding up front. Some of them even started Sam Cooke fan clubs. It didn't hurt that his face was nearly as beautiful as his voice. He was tall and slim and profoundly, almost unconsciously sexy at first. Lost in a melody, he had a way of slapping his thigh to bring himself back to the beat.

"Ooh, I loved that man," Aretha told me. "And when I saw he went pop, you know, outside church, that's what made me say, 'I want to sing that stuff, too.' "

It was R. H. Harris, gospel connoisseurs insist, who masterminded the innovations in quartet singing that shaped Sam Cooke and the sound of soul to come. In his history *The Gospel Sound,* Tony Heilbut explains that Harris took the revolutionary step of bringing the lead singer out in front of the quartet and adding a second lead to make it a quintet. Having doubtless come up listening to gospel, R & B groups like the Ravens were alternating leads by the mid-forties; this is a format Motown later used to great pop advantage, notably with the alternating leads of Temptations Eddie Kendricks and David Ruffin.

Harris also insists he was the first male to sing falsetto in a quartet, having done so as a child of ten in Texas, at a time when "even women didn't sing falsetto in church." Falsetto was later taken to secular heights by the likes of Smokey Robinson, Eddie Kendricks, and Curtis Mayfield. Ultimately it fueled the nasal excesses of white pop groups like the Bee Gees. Like so many other aspects of black American music, falsetto singing has been traced from current pop incarnations back to West Africa, where falsetto singing is considered the highest and purest form of male expression. There even the highest-pitched percussion instruments are considered male in nature.

Just how falsetto resurfaced on a country lane in twentieth-century Texas is a story obscured by countless migrations on this side of the Atlantic. It's easy to see why Harris, like other men of a singular genius, can subscribe to his own theory of spontaneous generation. After all, he was just a child at the time. And the voice and the spirit ran naturally high within him.

"If Harris is right," Heilbut wryly concludes, "the falsetto sound that traveled from gospel to soul to the Beatles began as a Texas birdsong mimicked by a latter-day Mozart."

Regardless, once Harris had carried his sound east and north to the cities, once Sam Cooke had seized upon those Harris-inspired fundamentals to forge a style of his own, the bridge from gospel to secular soul, from farmboy quartet to street-corner vocal groups was cemented. The

Soul Stirrers weren't the only gospel quartet to set down the foundations. But few will dispute that they were the most innovative and widely known. Traveling between the brick churches and storefronts in the big industrial cities, they split the urban hustle and honk with a sound that was pure country and as clean as dew-washed clover. Ben E. King and his New York friends called it a "close harmony thing." Pickett knew it as down-home country quartet. But whatever its routes and its subtle regional differences, the sound went national, and across color lines, when Sam Cooke stepped from the pulpit to the pop charts. It was no small blessing that a niche for his smooth, almost courtly pop offerings had been blasted by a cannonball of a record cut by the most fiery prophet of soul, Ray Charles.

As a traveling jazz and blues musician Ray Charles had a rapacious ear. His mind collected and stored it all—blues, jazz, country, and gospel. Segregation tossed traveling bluesmen and gospel artists into the same bed-and-basin roadhouses. Charles remembers passing the time with gospel troupes, trading road tales and harmonies. The music was hardly unfamiliar to him, as he explained in a *Rolling Stone* interview with Robert Palmer. He had grown up with it as a child in Florida: "Greenville was a small town, or a village, really, and in the south, in those years, you went to church *every* Sunday. Whenever there was a revival meeting during the week, you went to that. So naturally I was around church music. The preacher would say a couple of lines and then the church would sing what he said. It was very ad-lib."

And so it was when Charles began writing his own songs, for Atlantic Records, ad-libbing secular words to old gospel tunes, tossing in jazz and blues as well. When he went into the studio with producers Ahmet Ertegun and Jerry Wexler, it was, Wexler recalls, "the most rudimentary, yet sophisticated gospel education anyone could hope for. We'd had a modest gospel line at Atlantic, but I learned far more from Ray Charles. When I came to Atlantic in 1953, Ray was already there. So for me he was the source. Everything—the gospel harmonies, structure, the bar length, the patterns, the idioms—was all there in the studio with Ray. It wasn't until we worked with him that any of us ever listened to gospel in an educated way."

It was business as usual in November 1954, when Charles called Wexler and Ertegun and asked them to meet him in Atlanta to record something he had been working on. Often they met him on the road while he was touring. Ertegun was delighted to have an artist who wrote for himself, relieving him of some of his songwriting chores. Wexler remembers a certain sense of expectation before the Atlanta session. Ray's music had been getting freer, more emotional, and less mannerly ever since he began working with bluesman Guitar Slim, an uninhibited shouter whose real name was Eddie Jones. In between his work with Slim and the Atlanta date, in December 1953, was a New Orleans session Wexler calls landmark Ray Charles. He wrote the material, arranged it, and sang and played it with his own band.

"Having witnessed an act of creation like that, in the New Orleans sessions, you could only have good feelings about what was going to happen next with this guy," says Wexler. "Ray was so full of changes, such a protean type, you could never truly anticipate his next move."

The entry for November 19, 1954, in the Atlantic Records docket of master recordings shows that Ray Charles's "I Got a Woman" was cut in a borrowed radio station studio in Atlanta. Once it hit the air, there was no chart category that seemed able to contain it—not blues, not jazz, not even rhythm and blues. What could you call a fusion of deep-chorded, churchy piano, a strong band, and a vocal that bounced between the bedroom and the blessed? There were low moans and falsetto shrieks. Most important, especially for what would become known as soul, there was no holding back. At Atlantic, this blues/gospel alchemy was being hailed as the genius of Ray Charles. Elsewhere it was condemned as blasphemy.

"I got a lot of criticism from the churches," Charles told Palmer, "and from musicians, too. They said I must be crazy and all that, and then, when they saw it was working, everybody started doing it. It's just like when a manager makes a business decision. If it works, he's a genius; if it doesn't, he's a dog. Well, it worked, so I was a genius."

Charles's amen ad-libbing was its most complete with "What'd I Say?" a song that he improvised at a dance outside Pittsburgh in 1959, trading off groans and phrases with his three-woman backup group, the Raelettes. As the give-and-go heated up, the crowd began to respond as well. Like some of the best of soul, like Screamin' Jay's pain-crazed "Spell" or Percy Sledge's ad-libbed "When a Man Loves a Woman," it was a song born of a perfect, resonating moment.

Ray Charles liked what he felt in that fine Pittsburgh moment. He tried the song out a few more times, live, and the reaction was the same. It moved people, so he decided to record it in New York.

"And so," Palmer concludes, " 'What'd I Say?' was created the way spirituals were created: forged communally out of the interplay between exhorter and congregation.''

What Ray Charles was able to do, which even a great gospel voice like Sam Cooke never quite achieved in his rather tame pop work, was to transfer the gospel fire to the Top Ten with its heat undiminished. And unlike polished acts like the Mills Brothers or Nat "King" Cole, Ray Charles sold music that was undeniably black.

"Ray had the guts and the genius, yes, it *was* genius, to sing and play exactly what he *felt,*" says Jerry Wexler. "It's as simple and basic as that. But in 1954, coming from a black man, that was a *revolution*. Later they called it soul.''

"Several years ago a fella dropped in on me by the name of Ringo. He said, 'Pickett?' And I didn't say nothin'.''

Having wandered through his years in Detroit, Pickett has begun to fast-forward his narrative over a plate of steaming shrimp.

"So then he said, 'Wicked Pickett?' and I said, 'Yeah.' He said, 'You been singin' all around the world about a thing called soul. Can you please . . . can you pullleeeeeze tell me what it's all about?' And I said, 'Ringo. Ringo Starr,' I said; then I screamed, 'SOUUULLLLLLL! Soul ain't nothin' but a feelin'.' He said, 'How you know when you get it?' An' I said, 'Good God.' ''

"For a singer," Covay puts in, "soul is total vocal freedom."

"And *that,*" says Pickett, "brings you right back to gospel. Now you take Sam Cooke. He learned *all* he knew, all he brought to gospel, then pop, from a genius gospel brain, which was R. H. Harris, who had the brains and the spiritual sense, understand, to let that lead singer go free. Let his voice be as soulful as the Lord intended. To loose a sound. Like AAAAAAAAAAHHHHHOOOOOO. Sounds that put ten, maybe twenty notes to one word, like Sam Cooke done, and Jackie Wilson and all them.''

More formal analysts define this as melisma, the vocal art of stretching a word or a syllable up, down, and sideways along the scale. This is what lets Aretha Franklin make one word, like "good," into an entire song. These are the vocal aeronautics that let Smokey Robinson's falsetto soar as easily as a hawk on a mountain air draft. Jackie Wilson used it so well he could get nearly two dozen notes out of a single word.

"Okay, okay, mel-isma. Call it plain or fancy. So, to be comin' back to what I was tryin' to explain, about style and customizin' and all that.

We're out of church now, okay? We're back with Pickett in Detroit. With the Falcons and all. Okay. You got your quartet harmonies. And you got your man out front who is gonna work on ups and downs and other fancy stuff. Maybe he feels like he wants to cry a note, fall up and back on it a certain way. Maybe when the other guys in the group are down singing tight together, almost a hum, you whip a scream across the top. EEEEEOOOOWWW. It just come *out*. You can feel it comin', but you don't let go until the moment is *exactly* right.''

Here the Wicked allows himself a lusty chuckle.

''That timing is somethin' you have inside you. You just *know,* okay? That's how I got to be known as a screamer. And once you get known for something special, well, now, *that* would be your hood ornament.''

Style, for soul music, would become paramount. In a music distinguished by the power and peculiarities of individual voices, the weight would rest on the singer, more than the song, much as it does in gospel. Style would define soul music, and for all its strength and distinction, style would also limit its life-span on the charts. Aggregates of styles—the rawboned southern Memphis sound, the spun-sugar-and-chiffon Motown sound, the rolling Caribbean-infused New Orleans R & B—were molded by time and place. Their popularity nationwide depended on the rhythms of American migrations. And infatuations.

Pop music is, after all, born of infatuations, wave after wave of them, each so true to its era that a two-minute thirty-second song can be a perfectly wrought miniature of a place, a climate, and a time. Some people swear they can smell hot dogs when they hear the Drifters' ''Under the Boardwalk.''

''You play me her record 'My Guy,' and I swear I can see Mary Wells as a young girl,'' Pickett offers. ''There she is, leaning against the brick wall in Detroit, those big eyes, a short, tight mohair skirt. Oooh, she had a *walk.''*

He is leaning back against the red Leatherette, eyes closed, smiling. Abruptly he remembers that he has left his Stutz Bearcat in a lot that's about to close.

''City don't give you no rest,'' he says, patting his jacket for a wad of bills. ''Which is okay, if you a shark.''

Sensing puzzlement, he explains. ''Now I am a fisherman. Sport fishin'. Fish a lot, especially deep-sea. And out there you learn about those suckers. Now you know why a shark is such a tough, mean motherfucker? He don't sleep. Never. Not at all. Somethin' about the way the gills are built. Anyhow, he got to keep that water movin' through him, he don't *ever* stop swimmin', movin' around the ocean, he stop movin'—bang.''

He slaps the table, sending the Sterno flame higher.

''He's dead.''

Laughing, the Midnight Mover drops a $50 bill on the table and heads for the door.

▌5

"We Sang Like Angels"

▌*I'd like to go back to gospel. Really, I never left. Or it never left* me. *The public may not know it, but the Sex Machine first did it to death for the Lord.*

—JAMES BROWN

FOR ALL THE Picketts, McPhatters, Willie Johns, and Ben E. Kings, there were country loyalists who would forge their own brand of southern soul, artists who came up listening to country-western and hillbilly music as well as gospel and blues, who dreamed not of vertical skylines but of wide green vistas. Otis Redding, with the first proceeds of his success, bought up the land near Macon that his ancestors had been slaves on. Percy Sledge, Isaac Hayes, Rufus and Carla Thomas, Clarence Carter, Joe Tex, Allen Toussaint, the Neville Brothers, Irma Thomas, all were homegrown soul artists who chose to stay below the Mason-Dixon Line. Some, like James Brown, tried city life and gave it up. Memory, family pulled him back, he'll tell you. Sure, he says, the South didn't give him a happy childhood. But you don't blame the land for the sins of the men who walk on it.

"I want to, I *can* testify: Quartet singing, gospel singing saved my life. That is the honest truth. Except that I didn't get to sing it in church that much. Or in the streets. I sung it away out in the country, in a place Georgia law sent you to *bury* you. I sung it in prison."

This from Soul Brother Number One, the Hardest-Working Man in Show Business, Mr. Please, Please, Please, James "Butane" Brown.

At the time Ben E. King was first testing his lungs in the subways, when Wilson Pickett was still sassing his mama in Prattville, JB found himself harmonizing in a jail cell. Brown's little Augusta, Georgia, combo played dances and talent shows until James was sentenced to eight to sixteen years for breaking into cars in 1949. Also convicted was his running partner, Johnny Terry, who later became one of the original Famous Flames, James's backup vocal group.

More than thirty years after they did their time together, the two men sit reminiscing amid a rather spirited Sunday dinner in Manhattan. Wide-eyed, the maître d' in the starched dining room of this midtown hotel had to dispatch a crew of waiters to create seating for Mr. Brown's entourage. It is a jolly group of more than a dozen and a half, including one Brooklyn reverend (aka the Rev), a radio announcer, a bodyguard, a hairdresser, a fashion model impresario, dancer Lola Love (aka the Sex Machine), and Ms. Malia Franklin, a lively young woman draped in grimacing mink heads and lace. Currently Ms. Franklin is recording as a Bride of Funkenstein.

"Mr. Terry," James says over the din, "didn't gospel music save us?"

"Oh, yeah."

"Weren't the Famous Flames a bunch of real fine quartet singers? And wasn't it *country* under those fancy suits we went and bought?"

"None other."

Long before his flaming successes of the sixties, James says, he sang for his very life in prison, never would have got out those gates, he insists, if he hadn't formed that little gospel group in prison. Music Box, the other inmates called him.

"We played on pocket combs. Made a bass out of a washtub. We sang like angels. People *cried* when we sang. We sang at other prisons, we were just kids, and these big, tough cats—even the guards sometimes—they would cry. *We* cried when we sang, it was so pretty."

After three and a half years James was released, largely because of his angelic vocalizing. He figures the clincher was the night a bureaucratic snafu left him and his group unsupervised at another prison, where they had been sent to perform. The road before them was wide open. When the slipup was discovered, armed guards rushed to the scene.

"Now they didn't expect to see us *no*how, did they, Mr. Terry?"

"Figured you was clear to Toccoa."

"You can imagine what them guards thought when they walked in and we were still there? Still singing."

"Had them sinners *cryin'* to the Lord."

Mr. Terry is convulsed at the memory. Mr. Brown is tilted back in his chair, roaring. The maître d' looks as if he has just seen a roach boogaloo across the pastry cart.

"Have mercy," Malia wails above the laughter.

"Well now," says James, "they done just that. I sent a letter to the warden on a Thursday, explaining our work for the Lord and our good, good behavior. And by Monday I was on my way home."

As he does fairly often, James muses about recording some serious gospel one of these days. But he isn't sure that gospel purists would cop to a rendition of "Nearer My God to Thee" from a guy who composed soul chestnuts like "Get Up, I Feel Like Being a Sex Machine" and "Hot Pants (She Got to Use What She Got to Get What She Wants)."

Down at the other end of the table, the Reverend Al Sharpton, himself a former Wonder Boy Preacher who toured with Mahalia Jackson at age nine, would like to know James's gospel favorites.

"The Trumpeteers, the Dixie Hummingbirds, the Five Royales—"

"You sure did love that jubilee sound, too," Johnny Terry says, referring to the tight-harmonied, upbeat gospel genre that enjoyed a vogue in the forties with groups like the Charioteers and the Deep River Boys. Left to themselves, the two men talk about gospel quartets the same way they talk about prizefighters, with the passion of fans and the knowledge of connoisseurs.

JB says that gospel has remained a comforting touchstone throughout his twenty-five-year career.

"Gospel can take you home, from anyplace you're at, right Mr. Terry?"

"Amen."

As he speaks, James is frowning, struggling to reseason a plate of Frenchified cuisine with half a bottle of Tabasco sauce. Veal marengo was the closest thing to chicken fried steak the perplexed captain could come up with. He had personally removed the offending mushrooms.

"I don't eat toadstools," James explains, saying that this kind of road food, however high-class, still leaves him hungry for a taste of home. He spends a good deal of time on his ranch outside Augusta now. When he was averaging 350 shows a year, he says, he never stopped missing Georgia.

"Georgiaaaaa, Georgiaaa," he sings, "the wholllle day through . . ."

Deep down he always knew he would give up that funky castle in Queens, New York—the one with the white carpeting and the black lawn Santas—and buy up some land back home.

"I am country. I stayed country. Couldn't do nothin' about it, if you want to know the truth. And entertainers like me, from the South, who truly love it . . . well, you meet up on the road, and you could tell if a guy was missin' somethin'. Lookin' for somethin'. I used to talk about being homesick with Otis Redding. I spent a lot of time in Macon, where he come up. You know, Little Richard, he's from there, too."

Once he resettled down South, James set to collecting cars and real estate. He says he dockets success in mounting acreage and marks the passage of time with the mutations of car chassis. They are complementing elements, the cars and the land. Trading wheels, as JB does incessantly, satisfies a restless impulse; the land offers timeless sanctuary.

"I get chased all over the world," James says. "Get my clothes ripped up, people screamin'. But in my home, in Augusta, everything is cool. I wouldn't have it no other way, couldn't live if I couldn't walk the streets I grew up on. Now Elvis, he got so far away from it he couldn't do that. We were friends for a long time, for twenty years. And he told me, he'd ride around Memphis, around the streets he come up in, all alone at night. Ride around on his motorcycle when he was sure the rest of the world was asleep, just kind of hauntin' them places he hung around in as a kid. He was a country boy. But the way they had him livin', they never turned off the air condition'. Took away all that good air. You get sick from that."

James says he noticed a positive change in his own energy level—though it has always been naturally high—once he moved back South to his ranch off Route 287 in North Carolina. It is just across the river from Augusta and less than a mile from the long-ago collapsed shack where he was born.

"I come off the road," he says, "and home is a long drink of water."

He signals for another Coke to offset the Tabasco, and laughs. "And you may not believe this, but my daddy *makes* me go to church. To a little church, out in the country. I ain't a regular, but it don't mean I don't believe."

He says he tries to be a good shepherd. In fact, just last night, Saturday night, when the midnight show melted into dawn at the Town, Too, a small black club in Brooklyn, the Godfather of Soul closed his set with the Lord's Prayer.

"It was Sunday. And I didn't want to be keepin' those people away from God."

Lola Love, who says she counted no fewer than twenty-four splits before James shook the boogie out and dropped to his knees in prayer, says it was an easy conversion.

"That bar turned into the amen corner," she says.

It was, the Rev notes, a "just folks" show anyhow. No big money, no advertising, no big deal. Just a thank-you to a joint that booked James Brown long before the yawning cow palace gigs.

"Like I told you, I don't want to forget. Don't want to get too far away. Because if it's a time when a record company don't want me or a bunch of radio station playlists don't want me, *they* want me. You know, it's the little things that keep you goin' over the long haul. Ain't it right, Mr. Terry?"

"That's so, Mr. Brown."

James recalls the night, in an L.A. hotel room, when both he and his friend Elvis were starved for something homey and familiar.

"We threw a bunch of people out of the hotel suite," he says. "It was late, real late at night. Elvis had thrown this big party, all kinds of big stars, the Rollin' Stones, all of them. But you could tell he wanted to be somewhere else. And I was tired, and so did I. So me and Elvis sat together in that room and sung jubilee. Yeah, we sung gospel, and Elvis, he could sing it pretty. 'Old Blind Barnabas,' I remember, we sang. He knew the harmony. Me and Elvis never talked too much about bein' superstars or nothin'. Never did discuss it. But when you sing together, real close, jubilee now, like I told you . . . well now, *that* is communication, yes, ma'am. What else you think gospel harmony is?"

If you spend a reasonable amount of time with James Brown, if you pepper him with questions that force him to look back, you hear a lot about Elvis Presley. They were friends, he says, because they had a lot in common. After all, James will remind you, Elvis's "Hound Dog" and his own "Please, Please, Please" both hit the airwaves in 1956. That year both men hammered out sounds that changed the beat of American music. And both had the questionable fortune to outlive their revolutions. Hillbilly rock and niggertown funk, once outlaw southern forms, have long since been sanitized for middle-of-the-road consumption. But the dangerous times, those renegade days in the late fifties, had seemed wide open to a handful of wild young men.

"Oh, I loved it *so,"* James says. "I just loved those times to death. Take a look at the charts back then, and maybe you can understand."

"Then," says Johnny Terry, "it was *tasty."*

Just a couple of years, specifically 1954 to 1956, were banquet years for formative rock and soul. The appetite was there. American kids were proving to be voracious consumers. They seemed born to seize and follow trends. At that time there was ample choice: gritty R & B, and gentle doowop, Elvis's crossover white-boy blues, and Ray Charles's hallelujah hell raising. There was so much going on, in so many places—Detroit, New York, Memphis, New Orleans—that a precise chronology just isn't practical.

"How," one record executive suggested, "are you going to map an atomic chain reaction? Once it begins, it's damned impossible to figure out the *exact* order things banged into one another."

What you can do is chart a course on the luminous standouts. Individual genius can ignite an atmosphere charged and waiting for something to happen. And so it was that just months after Ray Charles melded gospel and blues in "I Got a Woman," the man with one of the most beautiful voices ever raised to the Lord took time off from his gospel chores with the Soul Stirrers and cut his first pop tune. "Lovable," recorded under the pseudonym Dale Cook, was hardly Sam Cooke's most memorable effort, but the move to pop was paramount.

"Please, do *not* forget the man I was opening for in 1956, '57," says James Brown. "Do not pass over one of the most important soulful voices. Little Willie John was a soul singer before anyone thought to call it that. I recorded a tribute album to him after he died. Man died young, died in prison. But the man left his mark. On my music, on lots of singers who understand how to sing with *feelin'.* 'Fever' was a monster record."

It was, and is, an aching counterpoint of raging desire and finger-snapping cool, a record that wrapped longing in velvet and made love to the notion of desire itself.

"Now *that,"* says JB, "will beat what any dictionary tell you about soul."

Unless, of course, you caught the interpretation of the born-funky James Brown.

"In which case," adds the Reverend, "you could say it *all* with one little word."

The word was "please," but the tone was hardly polite.

"Please," fractured, sobbed, squealed, stretched, panted, and wailed a few dozen times on a two-minute forty-two-second side ("Please, Please, Please"), would set ex-inmate Brown on his path to becoming Soul Brother Number One.

"Now nobody had heard anything quite like it on the radio," says JB. "I never heard nothin' like it. But somehow it just hit me that the time was right. I had just been hearin' this certain sound myself for a long time." He laughs. "What you got to figure out is, is the rest of the world ready for it?"

By 1956 the answer was a howling yes. And for soul music, as the Godfather points out, the years from 1954 to 1956 were crucial. The gospel shout that had been cropping up sporadically for two decades in popular music—from Sister Rosetta Tharpe on up through Clyde McPhatter—fused with blues and went public in a bigger way with Ray Charles's "I Got a Woman" in 1954. A gospel prince, Sam Cooke, began getting national airplay as a pop crooner. Urban northern R & B met its rawboned southern cousin when James Brown began touring and opening for Little Willie John behind "Please." Willie John was ultracool; JB sweated through his shoe soles. Soul, as it would come to be known, would be able to accommodate extremes.

By this time white kids were sanctioned to listen. The musical miscegenation that deejays like Alan Freed had begun to perpetrate was cast in durable vinyl by Elvis Presley, whose first record, a remake of Arthur "Big Boy" Crudup's "That's All Right" (1954), led to the phenomenon of "Hound Dog," a remake of Big Mama Thornton's 1953 original.

"Elvis always *had* soul, or he couldn't have done those records," James says. "But don't ask me when they started calling my music soul 'cause I don't remember. It was always that to me. Now I will tell you, I think it is a respectful way to call it. Look how we went from 'nigger' to 'colored.' And then to 'Negro.' And now 'black.' "

James figures that the route from "race music" to "ebony" and "sepia," from "rhythm and blues" to "soul" is some measure of the same kind of growing dignity and respect.

"It's been a long, long trip," he says. "And the music industry ain't there *yet,* no, ma'am. Not as long as white stations still use formats with no room for black music. It has hurt me plenty. But I still believe in the American dream. I got to. How else a shoeshine boy gonna get to be a superstar? HOW ELSE?

"My story is a Horatio Alger story. It's an American story, it's the kind that America can be proud of, but yet if you tell it in detail, if you tell all the things I fought to make it, it's like the Satchel Paige story."

None of it, he says, would have happened without the men who helped him learn the business: white men. Now some of them *gave* you the business. There are enough horror stories to jam up the docket books on Judgment Day. Still, in the fifties Jim Crow resolutely barred the door to corporate America. To get around it, there evolved a biracial coalition of black artists and white businessmen, uneasy at times, but necessary.

It had begun as early as the 1920s, when scouts and field engineers were being sent out by white companies to find and record black singers down South. Profit, not posterity, was most often the motive. Since the records were sold to black audiences, the product was not altered artistically. A producer's aesthetic vision was often limited to technical considerations. Asked, for instance, why his company, Chess, had made so many 78's of black blues singers, Leonard Chess said, "Because the black folks down South like the big records."

Once R & B had proved popular with whites, the connection became paramount. Many black artists were willing to make some musical changes suggested by white record executives, hoping for the bigger crossover paychecks. Business, distribution, and production chores fell to men like Syd Nathan and Ralph Bass at King (Cincinnati), Sam Phillips at Sun Records (Memphis), Art Rupe of Specialty (Los Angeles), Ahmet Ertegun and Jerry Wexler at Atlantic (New York), Leonard and Marshall Chess at Chess and Checker (Chicago), Herman Lubinsky at Savoy (Newark, New Jersey), the Bihari brothers at Modern (Los Angeles), and Joe Banashek of Minit (New Orleans).

Black product triumphed, despite humble beginnings in storefront studios with pawnshop equipment. By the mid-sixties this minority music, marketed by and to a white majority, as well as to blacks, would become the dominant force in pop music worldwide. By 1967 a black-owned company, Motown, would sell more single 45's than any other company in the world, white or black.

"I would be *foolin'* myself, I would be tellin' a lie if I said James Brown would be a *world* star—thank God—without the help of men like Mr. Nathan. And Henry Stone, who produced for him back then. And my manager, Ben Bart, who's passed. White men. Businessmen. Not enough black artists know the business, even today, and I am not afraid to say that. But back then you could get shot for even tryin' to learn. How much business you think I was *ready* to do then? I knew how to pick up change when people threw it at my feet. But I danced for pennies and nickels. I knew what to charge for a shoeshine, sure. But what do you ask for a song? What's a one-nighter worth?''

Eventually a James Brown booking could be worth nearly a quarter million dollars. In 1955 he was lucky to hit double figures for a night's work.

''Mr. Nathan was the first one willing to take a chance on me. I told you I never forget a favor. And that's the truth. Oh, we had differences, you can believe that. Mr. Nathan never did believe I could play keyboards. Had it in my contract I couldn't play and sing on the same record. And he was dead wrong on that one.''

He is grinning broadly, oblivious to the waiter perched like a dour raven behind his shoulder.

''Mr. Terry,'' he yells over the meal's-end clatter, ''didn't Mr. Nathan make one other little tiny mistake?''

Johnny Terry just grins and lifts his glass.

''Let us give thanks,'' says the Rev, ''that he had the vision to correct it.''

The little mistake was firing King Records' artists and repertory (A & R) man, Ralph Bass, for bringing in a demo of ''Please, Please, Please,'' a piece of utter trash according to his boss. Nathan found the record rotten, wild, unsalable.

''Ralph Bass got his job back when the record was sellin' like crazy,'' James says. He directs a stagy look at the floor and then at the ceiling. ''Mr. Nathan, wherever you are, I love you. This one's for you.''

He drains his Coke and announces he must go upstairs to rest. He is beginning negotiations with a new record company the next morning, and he wants to be sharp about it.

''On second thought . . . Rev, call up that limo service. Let's take a ride.''

The Rev looks worried. ''Where to?''

''Times Square.''

''Aw, Mr. Brown, no. Not that, please. Last time we went there, I had to call the police on nine-one-one to get us out. They were swarming all over you in seconds. Messed up your suit and near loved you to smithereens.''

''*Love* it, Rev.''

"How about the East Side drive? Look at the skyline and all? Central Park?"

"Funky *Broadway,* Rev. Time to mix it up."

It is impeccable logic, using Times Square as a sparring partner. All the better to hone the reflexes for the morrow's corporate palookas.

"No record company can tell James Brown how to be James Brown, no, sir. Yo, Rev. Get a skylight on that car. I need some air."

Part 2
City Soul

Me and a million other dudes said "later" to pickin' cotton. Moved North. Learned how to live in the city. Detroit, my Lord, what a place. Singin' in the streets, doggin' them clubs. You want some romance, some sweetness, you scrape together some change for a quart of chow mein. And a pint of Thunderbird or maybe somethin' weird like cactus wine. You and the lady finish it all up. Got to be chow mein or the magic don't work. Lean the lady up on one of them big Pontiacs—we in the fifties now—be sweet, and she slide right down the tailfin and into your arms. Lord bless and keep them automotive engineers. Gave a country boy a reason to sing in that dirty old city.

—WILSON PICKETT

6
Pressing Hits, Spo-Dee-O-Dee

The men in the business knew these things about Ahmet: that he was the son of a Turkish Ambassador to the United States; that he was married to a woman of fashion; that he wore, as a matter of strict custom, blue blazers, dark suits and vividly polished shoes; that in 1947—already known at the Ritz-Carlton, already known at the Howard Theatre (already, for that matter, bald)—he had founded Atlantic Records with a partner named Herb Abramson (later eclipsed) and with the financial help of a friend who was a Turkish dentist; that in the nineteen-fifties, he had taken on two new partners, one of them an expansive man from Washington Heights named Gerald Wexler, and the other his own older brother, Neshui Ertegun; that during the nineteen-fifties, he and Jerry Wexler had made records (with Joe Turner, Ruth Brown, LaVern Baker, Chuck Willis, Ray Charles, Clyde McPhatter, the Clovers, Ivory Joe Hunter, and other Negro singers) that constituted an important sub-genre of the music that came to be called rhythm and blues; that he had been present when rhythm and blues music collided with an unexpected white audience, and thus was as much responsible as any man for the hegemony of rock and roll. . . .

—G. W. S. Trow, in "Eclectic, Reminiscent, Amused, Fickle, Perverse," *The New Yorker*, May 29, 1973

SEATED AT THE large white desk in his office at Atlantic Records, Ahmet Ertegun is inquiring, with lively interest, about the circumstances of some former Atlantic acts I have encountered recently. Yes, he had heard that Ruth Brown was singing downtown. How'd she sound? Looking well? The crowd—did they know what they were hearing? Ah, Clarence Carter. He is one of Ertegun's favorites. Clarence had soul hits on Atlantic in the sixties with "Too Weak to Fight" and "Patches." But beyond that stuff, says Ertegun, the man plays a damned fine blues guitar.

"You know something?" Ertegun stops for a moment, looking almost wistful behind the thick glasses. His manicured fingers have been absently shuffling a deck of cards featuring portraits and bios of blues greats, a boxed set put out by Arhoolie Records. Lightin' Hopkins is on top, and as it happens, he has just died at age 70 in 1982. He was working right to the end.

"You know, there are a lot of things I would like to do, especially with some of the older musicians who are not going to be around much longer. It's just a matter of . . . that."

He points to a sheaf of correspondence. Beside it is a stack of demo tapes and a travel itinerary that reads like a nightmare bargain tour—all one-nighters in the capitals of Europe. Before we began talking, he had been dictating telegrams to the Rolling Stones, specifically to his good friend Mick Jagger, congratulating all on winning the *Rolling Stone* magazine readers' poll for best band for an unprecedented third time. Record men must take such things fairly seriously. When an artist or a group is hot, they pour all their energies into keeping it that way. That's how the business works. But, says Ertegun a trifle mournfully, "it can keep you from having fun. Unfortunately we're running a big business here now, and it sort of . . . well, it drives you away from the kind of music you like, which you know is not gonna sell very much but should be recorded just for the musical value of it. We have our hands full with the important artists who are selling four million albums, and you can't let them down."

Ertegun says he doesn't talk about such things too often anymore. In fact, he doesn't even like to think about it, to remind himself what talent is out there, unmined. He says it makes him feel like a geezer. And after all, beating out geezers was his own delicious triumph when he started all this. He describes his hands-on education in his friend Waxie Maxie Silverman's Washington, D.C., record store.

"When I went into the business, I was immediately successful at age twenty-three because the people who were in their fifties had no idea what was going on in the street. Before I started Atlantic Records, I did an apprenticeship of a year and a half just hanging around a friend's record shop, seeing what people bought, spending seven, eight hours a day watching people come in. See, we used to play records then for them. You watch their reaction and see at what point it gets them. So you find out. So when I started, the old geezers, like I am today, had no idea. They wouldn't make the kind of record that people wanted 'cause they thought that was terrible music.''

Wading amid the marketgoers, watching teens snap gum in the listening booths to the latest from the Dominoes and LaVern Baker, had revealed the golden mean to other music industry seers. Visiting a record store had convinced Alan Freed to scrap his classical format for R & B. For Motown founder Berry Gordy as well, teen chatter was the Rosetta stone that let him understand the language and the flow of the market. Gordy plugged into pop and R & B only after musical snobbery had forced him to close his own Detroit record store in 1955. He was twenty-six then, hardly a geezer, but he had been pushing only jazz, stocking Miles Davis when the kids wanted Fats Domino, the Clovers, and the Moonglows.

"I didn't know what R & B was," Gordy confessed years later, when Motown had become the first black company profiled by *Fortune* and *The New York Times*. "I didn't know until after I started in the record shop. Then I finally started to stock it. It was too late because we were doomed; we were on our way to bankruptcy. But I thought about it, and when I started writing tunes, I found out that's what I really felt. My feeling was really what I'd heard in church and the beats. Whenever I found myself playing, I really had the funky beat. . . .''

Like a lot of other young blacks at the time, Gordy had to overcome his own prejudice against the older, more basic forms of gospel and blues, something that had begun forcing veteran bluesmen to seek out white college audiences or overseas audiences clamoring for something authentic and American.

"I always sort of looked down on R & B," Gordy confessed, "because I always figured I was sort of ultrahip as a kid, you know.''

Ahmet Ertegun was precociously hip. But he was white. And rather than being appalled or embarrassed by the most basic black music, he was enthralled by it. He says he was crazy about its most sophisticated contours as well. As a teenager he was befriended by none other than Duke Ellington, who noticed him hanging around the Washington clubs. Ertegun says he was completely hooked. There was something about this music—a restlessness, an easy changeability. It was often spontaneous, but enviably suave.

"Black taste is sophisticated," Ertegun says. "It's more soulful, but it's soulful like a Cadillac is soulful, as opposed to being soulful like an MG. You know, it's lush. With a really good singer and an eight-piece band. Music is natural to the black, to sing, to listen to, to dance to. It's not a *strange* event. It's all part of a continuum. Black audiences aren't fickle, but they're not nostalgic either. What they liked last year, they don't like so much this year, because they like what's going to happen tomorrow. They not only make the records but make the music. They buy it; they dance to it. Black music evolves. It's a living thing. And it's not intellectually self-examining. They don't analyze it."

Analysis would be left to the corporate types who sought to market the stuff. Still, they could do this only by divining the populist tide and trying to float with it. There have been times, Ertegun notes, when what black tastes ran to musically became a craze for the larger population as well. He points to the worldwide disco rage of recent years, which began with a stylized black dance boogie. So it was, he notes, when R & B group sounds and soloists started the fad that became rock and roll. By the mid-fifties, with the geezers still working on Perry Como retreads, the road was wide open. The only speed limit was how fast you could cut and press it.

Art Rupe, of L.A.'s Specialty Records, which was home to rock daddies such as Little Richard and Lloyd Price, liked to call it FOFing. This was his shorthand for Fill Orders Fast. They FOFed like madmen in the fifties, when there was still enough oil to produce mountains of real, pure vinyl chips for records, and a fast wildcatter could tap a whopping gusher of teenage allowances.

But what kids clamored for one day they might drop-kick beneath their chenille bedspreads the next. With the group sound especially, styles evolved with the high-speed excesses of the wild auto tailfins Detroit was punching out at the time. There were trends, and trends within trends.

The late forties and early fifties saw the ascendancy of the "bird" groups—the Ravens, the Orioles, the Penguins, the Robins (who became the Coasters), the Flamingoes, and the Falcons. Then, especially in uptown Manhattan, the "car groups" named themselves after popular models: the Cadillacs, the Lincolns, the El Dorados, the Impalas, even the Edsels. Romance had its day with the Moonglows, the Hearts, the Charms, the Heartbeats, the Dream Lovers. Royalty enjoyed a brief vogue with groups like the Kingsmen, the Monarchs, and Ben E. King's first professional group, the Five Crowns.

A female group called the Teen Queens was at the vanguard of a trend that would not hit big until the sixties. With the notable exception of the Chantels, whose 1958 hit "Maybe" remains an R & B torch classic, girl groups were rare in the fifties. Quartet singing, both gospel and barbershop, was, after all, a male tradition. It wasn't until the late fifties and early sixties, when girl groups did begin to form in significant numbers, that record companies and producers gave them serious attention.

It took far more than a stylish name to turn a street-corner group, male or female, into a salable recording act. It took good songs and shrewd production. In those early days company executives were not above rolling up their sleeves and diving in. They had no choice. A. Nugetre, a producer and songwriter of that era, says he was driven to his craft by sheer desperation. Spelled backward, "Nugetre" is Ertegun.

"When I first started out," he says, "I *had* to produce. There were no such things as producers then. Whoever ran the record company co-produced the records. And I had a great deal of difficulty finding songs. We had a couple of house writers, a guy named Rudy Toombs, and an arranger named Jesse Stone, who was really like a coproducer of most of the records. He was really an important molder of the music and taste in R and B music. I wrote songs, Jesse wrote songs, some of the arrangers used to write songs, but very few of our artists wrote songs."

And so it was that white record execs penned hits for the likes of that majestic blues shouter Big Joe Turner, for R & B queen Ruth Brown, for the Drifters, and for Ben E. King.

"My songs were not great songs," Ertegun says. "They were songs that were trying to have built-in hooks that would appeal to the record buyer of that year."

Ertegun learned hands on, working in Atlantic's makeshift office-studio long past the hour when the busboys slammed the chairs atop the tables in Patsy's restaurant downstairs. He learned to dangle a hook, jiggle it through a two-minute song, loop it artfully to a lyric with the precise concentration of a fly fisherman tying a lure. It was a strictly manual operation, dependent on instinct and feel. And despite the determined craftsmanship, there were always surprises.

"I should," says Ertegun, "'fess up to the truth behind Atlantic's first big hit."

That 1948 single, a lighthearted dally by bluesman Stick McGhee, was called "Drinking Wine, Spo-Dee-O-Dee." It is still the anthem for devotees of "beach music," an R & B–based genre that grew out of student romps at the Carolina beach resorts. To others, "Drinking Wine" is simply a minor, light blues. To Ertegun and his partners it was the long-sought miracle, selling enough copies to help their fledgling operation stay aloft.

"I'll tell you how we happened to make 'Drinking Wine,' " Ertegun says, laughing. "We had a two-man record company. And every two or three days I would call the distributors to get them to order our records. I called our distributor in New Orleans. Even when we had hits in Harlem here, our records were not selling well in New Orleans because it's always had different taste than the rest of the territories. It's a very musical city, and it doesn't follow the rest of the country. Never has. Anyhow . . .

"Our distributor there was a man named William B. Allen, an older man, very nice, but crotchety. I'd call him up, and he'd say, 'Well, I'll take three of this and five of that.' Now these are singles, you know, twenty-five to a box. Well, I was taking his order, and he said, 'There's a record here on a label that's extinct. It's called "Drinking Wine, Spo-Dee-O-Dee." We just ran out. Can you see if there's any wholesalers who have some? I'd like to have five thousand.' I said, 'Send me the record, and I'll make it for you exactly.' So he sends me the record, and it's a very amateurish bad pressing of this guy singing with a guitar and bass, Stick McGhee. So I said, 'Where am I going to find somebody that sounds as country as this, like country blues, in New York?' Now the only person I knew who had any contact in New York with blues musicians was Brownie McGhee. He had a little rehearsal studio in Harlem and knew all the blues players. Played the guitar and sang the blues himself. So I called up Brownie. He said, 'I could do it; but my brother Stick is the one who did it, and he's right here.' So that night I recorded him at the Apex Studio on Fifty-seventh Street. We made the record, shipped five thousand. The guy was delighted. The thing became a huge hit. We sold unheard-of amounts, four hundred thousand or something, and we were heavily counterfeited on it as well. Stick was pretty happy, too. He made some royalties off our record. He didn't get any off the first version."

Atlantic's first smash, then, was a fluke. Ertegun doesn't know what, if anything, might have happened if McGhee hadn't been passing through New York at the very time he was searching for him.

"You know, when we started Atlantic, my aim was to record really good, strong black blues music," Ertegun says. "But we really couldn't find any. We didn't have the funds to travel all over the country looking for artists, so we had to work with the people we found in New York or Washington or nearby. And the artists that we found in the eastern seaboard area were urban artists who were very sophisticated and were making records that were not especially tailored to the taste of the southern black audience of that time, who really liked soulful blues music. So we had to try to give the artists songs that would force them into a blues feeling. But what came out was something other than the kind of real blues records Chess was making [in Chicago]. Chicago had a vast reservoir of blues musicians who had migrated from the South. Somehow they didn't come to New York. As a result, the kind of music that we were trying to make with these sophisticated urban singers turned out to be something that was much more popular than the real blues music. This is because it appealed to an emerging young white audience. Records by Ruth Brown, LaVern Baker, the Clovers appealed not only to the black urban population but to that new southern white population which was listening to black radio stations down there. Now they [the whites] didn't have that much feeling about a record by bluesmen like Big Bill Broonzy or B. B. King. But they did get something from this precursor of rock and roll. And that was our kind of urban black music with some blues feeling in it.

"Records by people like Clyde McPhatter and the Drifters and Ray Charles, Chuck Berry and so on—those kinds of records were really picked up. They were the models that the Beatles and the Rolling Stones used to form their own music. What we produced back then became the model for these people. Of course, people like Eric Clapton and Mick Jagger go much further back. They're also conversant with blues music of the twenties and thirties. But the kind of music we were making in the fifties became the model for rock and roll of the sixties."

Success—the Atlantic rock and soul dynasty that would eventually include everyone from Aretha Franklin to Led Zeppelin—was largely due to a careful monitoring of that dialogue between rural and urban sounds and the hybrids they spun off. Some of Atlantic's best soul records in the sixties were the result of return journeys, when Jerry Wexler took urban artists like Aretha Franklin and Wilson Pickett back down South—to recording studios in Memphis, Miami, and Muscle Shoals, Alabama—to work with a mix of black and white blues-, country-, and gospel-trained session musicians.

It also helped, Ertegun notes, to get a song down fast, in the first bloom of inspiration. He says that he and Jerry Wexler tried to be flexible enough to record whenever and wherever the muse hit. When Ray Charles called

New York from somewhere on the road, they packed their bags without hesitation.

"It was terrific. Ray would be ready to record, and we'd go wherever he was. Sometimes we'd be in New Orleans, sometimes Miami, whatever. We'd go there, and he'd have his band and he'd have four or six songs, and we'd cut them. And we'd always come away with two or three hits. The other singers we had, like Joe Turner and the groups, we really had to write songs for. Or we'd find other people to write songs. That's how people like Leiber and Stoller developed."

Jerry Leiber and Mike Stoller were easily the most successful team of that era, working with black groups like the Coasters and later the Drifters to lure a Top Ten mixed audience. They were the best and most prolific of a new breed of songwriting and production teams. In the high-speed pop market, they were the pit crews, leaping out to change a bass line, a horn pattern, a lyric, to clap hands and sing backup, if need be, to complete a session and drop a tune into the groove of the moment.

Leiber and Stoller became one of countless partnerships that turned out Brill Building customizing kits. Many of them shuttled in and out of cramped offices in that Broadway office tower. What Seventh Avenue was to the fashion industry, the Brill Building was to the record world, vertically stacked. Teams like Doc Pomus and Mort Shuman (they wrote the Drifter hits "This Magic Moment" and "Save the Last Dance for Me"), Carole King and Gerry Goffin ("Up on the Roof" for the Drifters and "Will You Still Love Me Tomorrow?"), all were considered "Brill Building school," in the sense that they churned out custom-tailored songs and, in some cases, entire sounds for certain types of acts. Among their clientele: male R & B groups like the Coasters and the Drifters and the newly emerging girl groups like the Crystals, the Ronettes, the Dixie Cups.

The system developed its assets and its flaws. Artists capable of writing their own material often came to chafe under it. But for vocally gifted artists who could not write, record companies began to hire teams to seek out and shape appropriate material. At some points—and this happened in the sixties with Phil Spector's famous "wall of sound" production technique and at Motown with teams like Holland-Dozier-Holland—the producers could become more crucial than the artist. Their sound became so distinctive they could try a song on any of a dozen artists and be assured of a hit.

The ideal balance, for soul music, would be reached by a few classic teams. Jerry Wexler and Ahmet Ertegun, with the wizard engineering of

Tom Dowd, were a magic combination for Atlantic, along with Arif Mardin and, early on, Bert Berns. Kenneth Gamble, Leon Huff, and Thom Bell produced for a variety of companies and artists out of Philadelphia. In Memphis, Isaac Hayes and David Porter wrote and produced in almost mystical tandem. Working with a host of Stax and Atlantic acts out of his own studio in Muscle Shoals, Alabama, a white country boy named Rick Hall produced a solid stack of masterly soul sessions. Nearly all of these producers got their initial experience cutting R & B in the fifties. The best of them, Ertegun maintains, did well to study the shrewd flexibility of a team like Leiber and Stoller.

Their music could be raw and mocking, like "Hound Dog," a song Jerry Leiber scrawled on his brown lunch bag for blues singer Big Mama Thornton. Leiber and Stoller could also turn out delightful nonsense, like the Coasters' "Yakety Yak" and "Charlie Brown." But often their songs had bite. The Coasters' "Shoppin' for Clothes," with the lead spoken in canny ghetto jive, outfits a black dandy in pure, pure camel hair, gold buttons, and "herrin'bone," then strips him when his credit is refused. Man can't understand it. Has a fine, *fine* job, sweepin' up. . . .

Black teenagers tuned in loud and clear. And for white kids, there was the surefire seduction of rebellion, if only represented by a firm twist to the radio dial. Long before Sly Stone produced his incendiary Vietnam era album *There's a Riot Goin' On* (1971), Leiber and Stoller had the Coasters singing exactly those words in "Riot in Cell Block No. 9" in 1955. The lead voice was a hairy growl; the singer was clearly a black man in prison, doing time for armed robbery. It was peppered with B-movie sirens and tommy-gun effects. It was theater—albeit a theater of cruelty—and it sold like crazy.

Sensing a good thing, Atlantic persuaded Leiber and Stoller to produce for its subsidiary Atco. The formula and the Coasters' success continued. Leiber and Stoller worked well with the individual singers' voices, letting them speak/sing in musical playlets that often had hilarious pantomime routines for those all-important stage shows at the Apollo. Just as easily, they could switch from black "in jokes" to story lines that were as basic as Romeo and Juliet. What fifteen-year-old could not understand the glandular obsession and insomnia of the poor chump who had nearly swooned watching "Young Blood" pass by on the street, yellow ribbon in her hair? In 1957 love at first sight was a universal teen construct. Better still, it was a passion play you could dance to.

"The music we've always made has danceability as an important part,"

Ertegun says. "The danceability is caused by the motion, the swing of a song. If it doesn't have that inner buoyancy, it's very hard for a record to become popular. Now what was danceable in 1932 was not danceable in 1940. Rhythm patterns change, and you have to find new and more exciting ones to replace what was in fashion three years ago."

It is the changing rhythms, he says, evolving things, with lives of their own, that confound the efforts to label them neatly. Sometimes it is the dance step of the time that names a music—a cha-cha, a lindy, a jitterbug, a waltz. But just as often it is the rhythm itself.

"Bebop, swing, rhythm and blues," Ertegun says. "I think of the dominant *rhythms* behind those words."

Soul, as a form of musical classification, first came to his attention because he was a jazz buff. It was a term adopted by black jazz musicians, mainly in New York, in the late fifties and early sixties. The soul movement in jazz arose as a sort of backlash against the snobbery some musicians felt had invaded and stultified the music and, in effect, made it less black.

Ertegun recalls that in the forties, even as far back as the thirties, black jazz musicians would twist themselves in knots to avoid using blues changes in their work. Or if they did use them, they would try to disguise them by dropping camouflage half notes here and there.

"They were," he says, "extremely cautious to avoid what might be considered retrogression."

Extremists on the subject turned so far away from blues roots that they seemed closer to European conservatories.

"This music, cool jazz, as opposed to hot jazz, sounded very abstract to a lot of people. Factions developed around the issue of avoiding or embracing the blues."

The dispute is drawn in more detail by writer Lerone Bennett, Jr., who sought to interpret it for the black readers of *Ebony*:

> Outraged by the growth of classical-oriented jazz and inspired by the success of artists like Mahalia Jackson and Ray Charles, the young New York musicians began in the late Fifties to reassess the Negro folk idiom—the cries, chants, shouts, work songs and pulsating rhythmic vitality of gospel singers and shouting choirs. Then, in one of the most astounding about-faces in jazz history, the fundamentalists (most of them are conservatory-trained liberals) abandoned Bartok, Schönberg, and "all that jazz" and immersed themselves in the music of Thomas A. Dorsey, Roberta

Martin (gospel artists) and Howlin' Wolf. Jazz, which had been rolling along on a fugue kick, turned from the academy and faced the store front church.

The self-conscious shame, the reluctance to embrace bedrock black music, had begun to erode. As Bennett reported, "Young musicians who had shunned the so-called emotionalism of the Negro church began to discourse learnedly on the polyrhythms of the [African] ring shout. It became chic to dig Blind Lemon Jefferson. . . ."

In such an atmosphere, "funky"—a concept that tied up all things earthy, emotional, and spiritual in black life—became an acceptable, even respectable word for all things soulful. "Once," as Wilson Pickett explained, "funky was something you do in the dark with very *basic* equipment." Suddenly journalists and musicologists were using the word. In the record industry the adjectives "soulful" and "funky" were becoming synonymous with profits.

"Beginning in the late Fifties and continuing in the Sixties," Bennett explained, "the Soul Movement caught the eyes and ears of the pacesetting record buyers in the big urban centers (especially Chicago, Detroit, Philadelphia, and Los Angeles). . . . Record makers, hot on the scent of a marketable commodity, turned out stacks of vinyl: *Soul Brothers, Soul Junction, Sin and Soul. . . .*"

Atlantic Records, typically, was at the front of the pack. A scan of its master recording list for the fifties turns up titles like "A Bit of Soul" (1955) and "Hornful of Soul" (1956), both by Ray Charles, followed by Milt Jackson's "Plenty, Plenty Soul" in 1957.

Jackson was a vibraphonist with the Modern Jazz Quartet; in jazz circles he was known as Brother Soul. When journalists and fans pressed him for a precise definition, he tried to accommodate them. Soul, he told them, "is what comes from within; it's what happens when the inner part of you comes out. It's the part of playing you can't get out of the books and studies. In my case, I believe that what I heard and felt in the music of my church . . . was the most powerful influence on my musical career. Everyone wants to know where I got that funky style. Well, it came from the church. The music I heard was open, relaxed, impromptu—soul music."

Jackson didn't have to bother explaining all this to one of his favorite collaborators. Ray Charles had never had much patience or need for categorical nit-picking. Nor was he skittish about incorporating wilder, less sophisticated blues and church-based forms into his jazz. In 1957 the two men did some Atlantic sessions together. The resulting album came to be called *Soul Brothers*.

"It was people like Milt and Ray Charles who did a lot to allow black musicians to embrace the blues again," says Ertegun, remembering the sessions. "Because Ray was, after all, an accomplished jazz musician. He had the skill and the credentials, and he had the wisdom to embrace the whole musical heritage—the suffering, which was the blues, and the celebration, which could come out in gospel."

Strangely, Ertegun's memories of how the Jackson/Charles album was named have little to do with musical issues: "We called it *Soul Brothers*, but I wasn't thinking so much of the notion it conjures today. 'Soul brother' wasn't part of the language then. But in Turkey we have this concept. People who become very good friends declare one another brothers or sisters in the hereafter. They call themselves soul brothers or soul sisters. It's a Turkish Muslim phrase. And I thought that it would be a groovy thing, since they dug one another so much, to call the album *Soul Brothers*. But it's accidental."

Serendipity of any sort is rare now, he concedes. "Spo-Dee-O-Dee" probably couldn't happen today. And there are no more wild talent chases through Louisiana bayous or Harlem rooming houses. For a while, he says, there were a lot of dull visits to suburban American garages. It seemed the sixties rock and soul explosions planted a garage band next to every Country Squire station wagon in several thousand tract developments. He found that most of them were more noise than voices, and it was depressing as hell.

"I find myself longing for melody and artful arrangements," Ertegun says, "which is not there in a lot of this crashing, atonal amateur music."

Letting go of the production end was his own choice, of course. Still, he misses the excitement. Falling in love with a sound, a voice, then courting it, grooming it, squiring it into the marketplace, into the populist salon, had to be exhilarating. And like so many affairs, these musical flings were destined to cool into friendship or memory. As Ertegun's interviewer G. W. S. Trow observed keenly: "Ahmet was himself always infatuated and always disappointed, and . . . at the heart of his achievement there was no answer stated or question posed but, rather, only this: the rhythms of infatuation, smartly expressed."

It has been a long time, Ertegun confesses, since he fell deeply in love with a voice. And it's been a while since he hung out in a record store, trying to crack teen codes. He had to call a halt, too, to letting managers and A & R men drag him into those nightmarish garages.

"Sometimes it's hard," he says. "I mean, some of these punk rock groups really stretch your imagination as to how *anyone* can like this particular thing."

He smiles and lays a hand, lightly, on the receiver of a buzzing, insistent, blinking phone. "I try," he says. "I really do. I'm trying to fight off becoming an old geezer myself."

7
Broadway Fricassee

> *Ahmet would come in to a session and ask you if you
> wanted a pastrami sandwich. He'd order it from the
> Jewish deli, then start yakking in French on another
> phone. Some wheezy cat from Bogalusa's on tenor sax,
> working at a carton of takeout Cantonese. A pleasant
> Jewish man name of Wexler is cussing out a late
> drummer with some mighty greasy Lenox Avenue jive.
> Me, the black preacher, the apprentice mortician from
> Philadelphia, standing at the mike. Singing country
> and western. Now what would I call those years at
> Atlantic? Broadway fricassee.*
>
> —SOLOMON BURKE

"AHMET HATES TO dwell on the past. He hates to talk about the old glories. He likes to talk about what's coming."

Jerry Wexler is sitting in the office of his Park Avenue apartment, his silver hair still a bit wet from a shower. He wears a paisley dressing gown over a Muscle Shoals T-shirt. It's midday, and in between calls to his office at Warner Brothers Records, where he is a senior vice-president, he is recalling, with archival detail, a few old glories and assorted mysteries. Unlike his former partner, Jerry is an inveterate curator. His has been a fascinating life, and he has held on to its artifacts: artists' handwritten session notes, work tapes, correspondence from southern writers and beat poets, clippings, photographs. Gold records—souvenirs of his collaboration with Ray Charles, Aretha Franklin, Willie Nelson, and Bob Dylan, among others—line the walls. Above the gold records, custom-built shelving holds rows of LPs—jazz, blues, gospel, classical, western swing.

Though he worked side by side with Ahmet Ertegun producing artists like the Drifters, Ray Charles, Clyde McPhatter, and others, Jerry is best known to soul fans for his sides with Aretha Franklin. Anchored largely on her stupendous talent, sixties soul was crucial for Atlantic Records and nothing short of a triumph for Jerry Wexler, who coaxed some stunning performances from a wave of young black singers. White rock groups like the Rascals, the Bee Gees, Cream, and Led Zeppelin would cement Atlantic's success in the late sixties. But soul was a vital turning point. The modest margin of profits from Atlantic's early R & B days jumped well into the black thanks to the most distinguished roster of soul artists anywhere: Aretha Franklin, Wilson Pickett, Solomon Burke, the Sweet Inspirations, King Curtis, Clarence Carter, Percy Sledge, and Joe Tex. By virtue of a distribution agreement with Stax/Volt in Memphis, Jerry added a southern firmament, which included Sam and Dave, Otis Redding, the Mar-Keys, Rufus and Carla Thomas, Booker T. and the MGs, the Bar-Kays, and Eddie Floyd. If the fifties bore the stamp of Ahmet Ertegun, the next decade owed much to Jerry Wexler. He is very proud of his work. But he is not fool or egotist enough to call himself a seer.

"Who knew?" he says. "Ahmet and I flew along. When you're living it, you don't consider something an era. It is only with the comparatively cheap wisdom of hindsight that you figure out what the hell you were doing. I mean, the whole setup was so damned *unlikely.*"

On the wall, just over a sofa, is a cartoonist's rendering of that unlikely trio, brothers Ahmet and Neshui Ertegun and Jerry Wexler, bouncing along on a camel. The Erteguns are dressed in robes and Arab headgear; Jerry wears the frock coat and prayer curls of a Hassidic Jew. They became partners in 1953, when Jerry was thirty-six, and worked together for the next twenty-two years.

Jerry was born in New York, in 1917, the son of a German-Czech immigrant and a talmudic scholar with Polish and Austrian roots. Harry Wexler, the scholar, turned window washer in this country. Sometimes Jerry worked with him, rubbing and rinsing, hauling buckets full of dilute Manhattan soot. Evenings Jerry serviced a grateful clientele as a liquor store delivery boy. He says he divided his time between books—he graduated from high school at fifteen—and the bookie joints, pool halls, bars, and clubs where writers like Damon Runyon, Ring Lardner, and Langston Hughes drew their best thumbnail sketches of barflies and hustlers. Jerry wanted to write, too, and enrolled in Kansas State's journalism program. After an Army hitch he turned out some prose for *Story* magazine and took a job churning out hard-boiled industry reportage for *Billboard*. In Manhattan and Kansas City he had always haunted jazz and blues clubs. As a writer, he says, he liked giving voice to those infatuations. Even after he had left the fourth estate to produce records, there was a conscious literacy that persists in his conversation. He can talk bebop with a horn player and quote Faulkner on the backbeat.

"Listen," he is saying, "I can't always recall all the minutiae. I tend to take the Tolstoyan point of view of the infinite number of small events that make up a historical trend or movement. Who knows what they are at the time? What makes a thing pass? One day you're making hit records, and the next week you can't get out of your own way."

He doesn't claim to have foreseen the sixties soul boom, but once it got going, he felt it might end as quickly as it began. "I'll say I had a hunch it was going to happen. Purely intuition. I told Ahmet that, and he laughed at me. Said, 'What in hell are you talking about?' But I maintained—and I was right—that this big part of our business, which was then called soul, could go just like that."

When soul gave way to hard rock and disco in the seventies, he did not waste time mourning its slippage from the charts. He says he just kept working—with Dr. John (New Orleans piano man Mac Rebennack), Allen Toussaint, Dire Straits, Willie Nelson, and Bob Dylan. He left Atlantic in 1975. By then his former partner had already left the studio for the boardroom at Atlantic.

"What a great record producer Ahmet was," he says. "Most people don't remember. He and I took different roads. I stayed with the music, making records. And he stopped making records. He does administration, having to travel and attend meetings and all. He likes to go home and play B. B. King records to cleanse himself after a Led Zeppelin concert. I still don't know that much about what goes on inside him. But he got out of the studio. It's as simple as that."

From the outset Jerry and Ahmet worked in close tandem, but in different keys. Bob Rolontz, who was then head of publicity for Atlantic, recalls that the dynamics between their different natures kept the office humming nearly twenty-four hours a day.

"Wexler was probably the spark plug during the day," Rolontz says.

"Wexler was morning and afternoon, and Ahmet was an afternoon and evening man. There would never be anything formal. Maybe that's why it worked so well."

Jerry agrees that while the intent was never casual—they both set out to make hit records—their success had a lot to do with letting things hang loose.

"We weren't into what you call creative tension. None of that bullshit managerial rubric. We simply appreciated our differences and made them work for us. The only thing homogenous about the whole operation was what I'd call Atlantic's bel canto policy. We aimed, above all, to find and produce beautiful, exceptional *singers*. Atlantic was distinguished by its *voices*. But to achieve that end, we had some pretty wild combinations. Turks, Jews, blacks, red-necks—the human forest primeval in a cruddy midtown office."

Jerry has read and reread Faulkner. And he shares that writer's fascination with the notion of juxtaposition and odd couplings. Nothing so drastic as a giant slue-foot bear set against an immutable Mississippi forest. Or African/Chickasaw hunters . . .

"But basic," Jerry says. "Musical comminglings. Some damned basic confrontation and symbiosis. We tried a lot of weird shit in the studio."

He was intuitive enough—perhaps initially perverse enough—to take the self-proclaimed citified soul man Wilson Pickett and drop him into the midst of black and white country boys in the Stax Studio in Memphis. And once that got old, he pushed Pickett even deeper South, to the Fame Studios in Muscle Shoals, Alabama, and producer Rick Hall.

"I looked down out the plane window," Pickett remembers of his first trip to Muscle Shoals. "And I see black folks pickin' cotton, and I say, 'Shit, turn this motherfuckin' plane *around*, ain't no *way* I'm goin' back there.' "

When he saw the big southern white man waiting for him at the airport, he was beside himself.

"Look just like the law. Look mean. How did I know Jerry Wexler gonna send me to some big white southern cat? Woulda never got on that plane. And I woulda made the biggest mistake of my life. Rick Hall made things grow down there. What happened was beautiful. I love Rick Hall. But I never would have believed any of it before it happened."

He says he was completely floored by the Stax and Muscle Shoals musicians as well. At least half of them were white, and they turned out the deepest, funkiest sound Pickett could stretch a scream across.

"Those guys play so damned well," Jerry says. "White country boys from the mid-South that take that left turn away from country music and go toward the blues. It's the best. There is something about the southern approach to life—you find it in the writers and musicians down there. They don't have the narcissism."

This is not far from what Ahmet Ertegun says about the refusal of black music to become self-conscious and overly self-examining. It is grounded in immediacy, but it never loses its heritage. Southern history is like that as well. In the South, history is never ignored. It is taught and learned as a living thing. More mythic than textbook formal, southern history can be as precise as a quilting stitch and as mysterious as a piney woods blues.

What they called soul, says Jerry Wexler, is of the same fabric: music created at a precise moment but sung by voices that house a vast collective memory of blues, gospel, and hillbilly plaints. You can't define it in words as well as you can recognize it in a note or a phrase. It's like a family resemblance that can creep into a smile.

"You could cut a record in one or two takes, with just a head arrangement," he says. "But it might have a resonance that took in generations."

Racial memory may have been the chief wellspring for soul. But Jerry learned to trade on an equally basic relationship to the land.

"Hillbilly music and the blues and gospel all are soulful in a way that is fundamentally southern. Of a *place*," he says. "Now Pickett wasn't crazy about returning South to record, but doing so loosed something he couldn't quite let go of in Detroit or New York. He could work with white studio musicians because they were southern boys. And by the way, that truth holds when black singers get ahold of white material. There's a type of southern black R and B singer who sings basically in a country format: Joe Simon, Arthur Alexander, Joe Tex, Percy Sledge. Percy sings the *hell* out of country songs."

Black artists singing country songs were nothing new by the time Atlantic began experimenting. Syd Nathan had done it on King Records, cutting a cover of Hank Penny's "Bloodshot Eyes" on Wynonie Harris. Also on King, Bullmoose Jackson did Wayne Raney's "Why Don't You Haul Off and Love Me?"

But none of these records achieved the success enjoyed by Atlantic when, on a hunch, Wexler paired a newly signed black vocalist with a country tune in a New York studio. It was, in the minds of both Wexler and Ertegun, a key moment for the beginning of the soul era. This was in 1961, when Jerry Wexler signed a former boy preacher from Philadelphia named Solomon Burke. Burke was a strong, emotional singer—an exhorter. He recorded in Manhattan, but his appeal bypassed local tastes and went straight to the Dixie heartland.

"He could connect with a white southerner and a black," Jerry says. "The link was Baptist. Regardless of color, they all talked in tongues. What they were saying might go over the head of a white middle-class kid up North. But it hit dead center in Atlanta and Birmingham."

Solomon Burke had recorded for Apollo, rather unsuccessfully, before he found his way to Atlantic.

"We were aware of him," Ahmet Ertegun remembers. "He was one of the important young black singers of the time. He had a kind of gospel feeling to his singing, and he was also a little bit country. We all thought he could become what we considered an Atlantic star."

One day someone told Wexler that Solomon Burke was in the Atlantic office, visiting a friend. "I went out, shook his hand, and I said, 'Solomon, come on in, you're on Atlantic Records,' " Jerry says. "And we worked out the contract right there. And on the first session we did that country tune."

"Just out of Reach" was Solomon's first hit in late 1961, and it made inroads in the R & B, pop, and country charts. Ray Charles, who had already left Atlantic for ABC by then, recorded a country song in 1962. His version of "I Can't Stop Loving You" (done in 1958 by both Kitty Wells and Don Gibson) was a hit, and subsequently ABC released two Ray Charles country albums.

"Actually," Jerry says, "Ray Charles had done country songs on Atlantic before he did them at ABC. He did 'I'm Movin' On' by Hank Snow. I've got work tapes that Ray did in, oh, 1953, doing 'That Sweet Kentucky Moon,' I think, in a very hillbilly style. Ray used to work with hillbilly bands in Florida. In live gigs he did many a country song. But technically it's true that Solomon Burke did precede Ray by actually getting a country hit."

Solomon Burke had worked with urban church choirs, not hillbilly bands. The key element was the emotional quality in his big, lush voice. Heartbreak or hellfire, it telegraphed well. In 1962, almost a year to the day after cutting "Just out of Reach," Solomon Burke and Jerry went back into the New York studio and cut one of his best records, "Cry to Me," written and coproduced by Bert Berns.

Again, the record was especially well received down South. Solomon's delivery has an Elvis-like stutter, with a few churchy "oh yeahs" grafted on. His hybrid style and his status as a soul pioneer were crystallized at his next session, on March 15, 1963, when Jerry took him into the studio to cut a song he had picked off a demo tape that had come to him from Detroit. The singer on the demo record was destined to become one of Solomon Burke's best friends and an Atlantic costar. But at the time Wilson Pickett was not pleased that Jerry had paid for publishing rights to "If You Need Me" and released Solomon Burke's version while his own was struggling for airplay. Jerry admits that Pickett's version might have had a bit more spin to it. But with the undeniable edge of a heads-up promotion, the Atlantic version proved the bigger hit.

By the mid-sixties, soul was becoming very bankable, but, perhaps still remembering his scuffling days in Philadelphia, Solomon was forever hedging his bets. By the time his recording career hit its peak in 1965, his record company had to compete for his energies with sidelines in food concessions, a church ministry, a pharmacy, and funeral homes.

"I guess I should have expected it from his behavior at that first session," Jerry says. "There was this tremendous blizzard. Somehow we all made it in and did the session, and we started to run the playbacks. It was his first record, you know, and Solomon started to leave without hearing it. I was amazed. I said, 'Don't you want to listen?' and he said, 'No, man, I've got to go back to Philadelphia. I'm running a dump truck to pick up the snow. Pays four dollars an hour.' "

Solomon was the headliner at the Apollo when Ertegun got a call from Bobby Schiffman, whose father owned the theater. It seemed the star of the show was insisting on selling Solomon Burke's Magic Popcorn in the aisles between appearances. The Apollo already had a food concession, and the proprietor was fuming.

"I went to Solomon and told him he couldn't sell his popcorn," Ertegun says. "I explained that they had a deal for popcorn, potato chips, soda, all that."

"Does that include pork chop sandwiches?" Solomon wanted to know.

When it was determined that nothing in the concession agreement covered said delicacy, Solomon set up a grill on the sidewalk, and between shows he stood there in a cloud of greasy pork smoke, cooking and selling his wares. He was no less resourceful on the road when he traveled with the large rock and roll package shows.

"He knew what happened to people after they were on the bus for an hour or two," Ertegun says. "So he'd order ten fried chicken dinners at the motel where they were staying, and he'd make these sandwiches and wrap them up. Then he'd get ten gallons of cold orange juice or Kool-Aid. Well, after the show everyone would get drunk and so on. They all piled into the cars and buses and passed out, and three hours later everyone was waking up, hungry and thirsty. Paul Anka told me about this. He was just a kid, dying for something. He told me Solomon would sell these sandwiches for, like, ten dollars apiece.''

Soul as a formal category got a boost when Solomon sought to repackage himself so that he didn't look like just another pork chop sandwich. Deploring the limitations of being labeled an R & B artist, he cast about for a term that could gain him a toehold in at least two sets of record charts. He decided on the "King of Rock and Soul" and commissioned a Baltimore deejay to make it official.

"Well, it's like somebody has to anoint Charlemagne," Jerry says, laughing. "You have to have an anointer. So Rockin' Robin, this deejay, was it. I think this was Solomon's attempt to achieve peer footing with James Brown, who was what then? The Godfather? Or the King of Soul?"

Title agreed upon, Solomon added the trappings: a crown, a scepter, a cape, robes, dancing girls, and colored lights. On his considerable back, and with the three-cape, collapse-onto-a-hospital-bed operatics of James Brown, with the Temptations' dandified road suits, with Rufus Thomas's wild hot pants and Funky Penguin outfits, soul would combine a healthy sense of play with the broad theatrics of black vaudeville and the church. Solomon Burke's delivery was so preacheresque, black audiences often stood when he made his entrance. The effect was made more dazzling in coats of many Vegas colors. One time, as Jerry Wexler remembers it, such trappings nearly cost Solomon Burke his young life.

"He was on a long string of one-nighters in the South. He was playing a place like a tobacco barn. I think people came on mule back to this gig, somewhere in the Carolinas. They announce Solomon Burke, and he comes on with this flourish, and some farmer in the front row pulls out a gun. And he says, 'I paid my money for Solomon Burke. If you're Solomon Burke, where's your gold suit?' He had this gold suit, and he told me he had probably done sixty days in it. Thing was crumpled into a ball, filthy and reeking, ready for the cleaners. But the guy had the gun on him, so Solomon had to go back to the parking lot, where he changed into the gold suit behind a station wagon. The whole audience—especially the guy with the gun—followed him out. He comes back to the stage; the guy looks at him and says, 'Okay, sing your music. *You're* Solomon Burke.' ''

Solomon's big laugh booms through the phone as he confirms the story from his Hollywood home.

"True, true, every word, my Lord, yes. Certainly. Did you know I also had a midget? Strange little guy, three-foot somethin', but he could sing just like Sam Cooke. Little Sammy we called him. Had all my show girls after him. Oh, yes, I had show girls. I had an exact replica of the crown jewels of London, for onstage coronations—King of Rock and Soul, oh, my, yes. I hired Sammy for the cape at first. It was trimmed in real ermine, beautiful thing. This really killed them. I'd walk onstage, this big old cape draggin' fifteen feet behind me. I'd toss it off, and then the cape would exit, stage left, by itself. Or so it seemed. Little Sammy could haul ass under all that velvet and fur, yes, sir. Sammy carried the jewels, too. They stopped me, at the London airport once, when I tried to bring them in, even though I told them they were paste. Said, 'Mr. Burke, what is this *soul* business?' And for a brief time they detained me, on suspicion of promulgating a new religion in the queen's domain. Can you imagine? Ah, but there are so many stories. You're here in L.A.? Fine, fine, very good. I am rippin' and roarin' today. Doing a little business, tending the fields of the Lord. We will give you the rock and soul tour. Do dress comfortably, please, low shoes, ready to rip and roar. I'll have my costume designer pick you up. Gorgeous black lady in a pink jump suit. I trust you know what you're in for. . . ."

Hanging around with Solomon is never boring. Not when we're put on earth, as he says, to have one boogaloo good time. Solomon can bless a child with one hand and pinch a fanny with the other.

"It would be a sin," he notes, "to pass up the pleasures the Lord made just for us."

Fittingly, Solomon has gone Hollywood. He owns two houses there, and several businesses. The big silver sedan that picks me up is one of a modest fleet he owns, including limos kept in other cities. To signify their deductible sanctity, they bear the special license plate "We need a miracle."

Reine, Solomon's costume designer, is accompanied by Dr. Kenneth Breaux—"my twin Rev" Solomon calls him, as they look remarkably alike. We set off for International Silk and Woolens, a huge fabric emporium on Beverly Boulevard catering to the stars. Reine says that Dr. Burke will be needing twenty-two ensembles—tunics, pants, and capes—for upcoming club appearances and church dates. "In concert and revival" is his term for the upcoming campaign. Reine has been dressing him since

1969. She says that today's mission is not nearly as trying as the days when she was called upon to dress as many as eleven of his twenty-one children identically, every day.

The store is a riot of flashy, in-your-face yard goods. We walk beneath an archway decorated with eight-by-ten glossies of happy clients like Tina Turner and Donny and Marie Osmond. Reine's business is conducted upstairs in the designer room, where beaded and sequined fabrics start at $90 per yard.

There is a stirring in the stairwell, and up comes Solomon in monumental pinstripes, with a diminutive salesman who has attached himself like a limpet to this very good client.

"You would like maybe a nice flocked velvet? I gotta shantung knock your socks off."

"Meshugenah," says the good Dr. Burke, and introduces his wife, Sunday, a small, pretty Oriental woman with dark hair that reaches to the waistband of her jeans.

"Bee-ooti-ful silks we got . . . you want lamés? Lamés we got, too."

"Have mercy," Solomon says. "I must consider a wide range of needs."

There is so much to do, he says. He will be appearing with the likes of the Wicked Pickett and gospel queen Shirley Caesar. Different events, of course. Negotiating with Ted Turner's cable network for a gospel show, working, too, on a new sold-on-TV album to be finished up, new floral concessions, a string of mortuaries.

"I am, I trust you know, a practitioner of mortuary science."

Certainly. Joe Tex had told me, "Solomon Burke knock you dead from the bandstand; then he gift-wrap you for the trip home."

It is a trade he learned back in Philadelphia. He joined his aunt's funeral-home operation when he started out, he says, "because it was murder trying to buy that first Cadillac hearse. So she took me in, and we did some great promotions. Worked a deal with a car-painting service. Give you any color coffin and a limo to match. You really want style, we color coordinate the pallbearers."

He admits he has always had a weakness for the grand gesture. As he talks, he runs his fingers over his selections: a black flocked velvet, a gold brocade, a rainbow velveteen, a blue velvet paisley embossed on navy silk. The average price is $100 a yard, and by his own estimate, draping a man of his girth is a mighty pricey business. But imperative.

"We will be in gospel caravan," he explains. This generally means a motorcade of sorts through black sections of whatever city, limousine or two, followed by buses, sound trucks, mopeds. Solomon likes to fly through city streets, in a flutter of banners, with the crack and bawl of bullhorns, calling the whole shebang to unannounced halts at fast-food parking lots and street corners, to "meet the people."

"Somebody gonna see Solomon Burke at the Chicken Shack, they're gonna go home knowing they've seen Solomon Burke," he explains. The Lord may work in mysterious ways, but his servant Solomon is candid about his own approach. It is very showbiz. People like it. And they remember the gold suits.

He is just as meticulous about his secular appearances. He will descend from the upstairs dressing room of modest blues clubs like Tramps, in New York City, a great, undulating vision of sea-green satin and rhinestones, and, without need of microphone, fill the room with his big, energetic voice and sheer force of will. The magnetism is such that often women will attach themselves to him in twos and threes. Sometimes he gently shakes them off; other times he is most gracious about permitting the sisters access to his special radiance.

"I have discovered," he will announce, "that there are one thousand and one ways to make love, oh, yesss. But you know there is only *one* way to say it."

It is shocking what women say to a man of the cloth in response.

"My dear ladies," he breathes, "it seems you are asking Solomon Burke to give you one boogaloo good time."

"Oh, yesss."

"You know, a minister in bed is just a *man.*"

"Amèn."

"You will be shouting that, darlin'. And you will be praising a few other things when I'm through."

We all praise his timing, for the man knows just when to turn off the talk and slide into a song.

"If you neeeeed me . . . call me. . . ."

Solomon slides through "The Price" and "Down in the Valley," then flies into the sermonette beginning of "Everybody Needs Somebody to Love."

"And I am so glad, so very glad to be here in your beautiful city tonight . . . and you know I need . . . I say I NEED . . . you don't know how much I NEED a witness here tonight."

He is swamped with volunteers. By the time he rips the top off "Cry to Me," perspiration is spreading through the felt above his hatband.

Smiling, wet-faced, Solomon leans down to offer comfort to the orange jump suit at a front table.

"Don't cry, darlin'. And please don't you tell *no*body that Solomon Burke left his audience wet and drippin'."

He says this with a smile so big it seems to linger once he has disappeared through the crowd and up the stairs. For a large man, he can move quickly. Before the faithful can touch the hem of his tunic, he is buttoned into a limousine and off into the night.

"I am always in a hurry," he is saying as Reine frantically scribbles yardage figures on a sales slip. "The Lord has given me much to do. Dr. Breaux, shall we jump to it?"

Leaving Reine and Sunday juggling bolts of fabric, we head out to the parking lot on our way to the next stop. Over the hum of the car air conditioner, Solomon talks.

"I thought that one day I would write a book. About how to be a legend. Without really trying."

Lesson number one is the Chicken Shack Principle.

"*Do* stop at the Chicken Shack, and be real with people. Remember that it's the little people that make you. The big ones do not buy your records. They get them free. It's the person on the street, the maid, the guy who works in the gas station. It's important to get out and say hello, leave a free record."

And as ye sow, ye shall reap.

"My grandmother told me I was chosen to spread the word of God. I am now the spiritual leader of one hundred sixty-one churches across the nation, and soon we may be blessed with satellite capability if Ted Turner exercises his cable option. There, on your left, is just one of our churches."

Mother Taylor is waiting on the back steps of the Greater Grace Memorial Church of God in Christ, an aging but sturdy building on Compton Avenue in West L.A. The church was founded and built by her husband. Gospel king James Cleveland has rattled windows here; other distinguished alumni include Sister Rosetta Tharpe, Billy Preston, and the peripatetic Richard Penniman, better known as Little Richard.

Mother Taylor tightens the crocheted shawl around an ankle-length paisley dress. Rhinestones sparkle from her glasses. Mother Taylor is radiant. There are kisses, "God blesses," and handclasps all around.

"Life, life, *life*," she murmurs. This church has always been brimming with it, but today it is especially frenetic. Tomorrow is Martin Luther

King's birthday, and there will be a dinner, fifty cents for those who can afford it and free for those who cannot. This is a poor neighborhood of blacks, Hispanics, Samoans, Vietnamese, Filipinos.

"Some deal," Solomon is saying. "Half a buck gets you chicken, rice, gravy, potatoes."

One hundred and twenty pounds of frozen fried chicken, extra-crispy, have just been delivered. Solomon begins to inventory the cartons before lugging them to the kitchen. Floorboards creak as Dr. Breaux conducts a tour of the church itself. Up in the balcony, the wood floor is gullied with the tread of the faithful. Below, near the front entrance, there is a coffin-size plaster of paris grotto sculpted to look like stone, where caskets bearing the congregation's dead are brought to receive a final blessing beneath plastic ferns and flowers. Behind the altar a Plexiglas baptismal tank stands, drained.

Back from counting the boxes of chicken, Solomon leads the way to a small meeting room where a lean black man stands, paint-spattered and beaming. He has painted rainbows on the walls and clouds on the ceiling.

"My ghetto Sistine," he says.

Amid canvas-covered pews, he has ranged a jumble of sculptures and mobiles fashioned from bedsprings, bottle tops, and odd bits of costume jewelry. A painted obelisk bears the message *"SOUL"* beneath a collage of black faces. The man moves between his sculptures, pinging a tin can dove with one finger, setting off a wire waterfall with the next. He says he is building a prayer garden out of items scavenged from the inner-city neighborhood.

"The Lord can reveal his word in the castoffs of men."

"Ain't it the truth?" says Solomon, squeezing past a pile of coat hangers to the door.

The next stop is at an abandoned-looking building on Santa Monica Boulevard. We rap on two doors and a boarded-up window until Ellen Shannon, a tiny woman in boots and snug black pants, opens a side door to let us in. This is Alco Records, a functioning record plant where bags of specially ordered red vinyl chips have just been delivered for Solomon's latest sold-on-TV album, a collection of his greatest hits recorded live at a Washington, D.C., club.

"Seventeen hits in forty-six minutes," he says, sinking into an ancient bamboo chair. On the wall over Ellen's desk framed copies of 45's hang at odd angles: "Sleepwalk," by Santo and Johnny, Little Richard's "Long Tall Sally" on the yellow and white Specialty label, the Teddy Bears'

"To Know Him Is to Love Him" on Dove, and the Crystals' "He's a Rebel."

"Phil Spector and Lester Sill did that. Cut it, pressed it here on the Philles label," Ellen says. She and her husband, George, have run Alco for years, pressing the efforts of rock and soul daddies, girl groups, gospel singers—anyone who can deliver a clean master and enough cash for vinyl, covers, labels, and manpower. As Solomon settles in to make some phone calls, Ellen offers a tour of the plant.

It is a grimy late-fifties throwback, but everything works. The five-man night shift has just come on. Two men have taken their places before a pair of ancient Presa record presses. From large sacks of pure vinyl chips, they extract wads the size of hockey pucks and place them in the center of the presses. Without benefit of gauge or automatic timer, they cook them deftly, lifting the big steel tops to reveal shimmering discs, heady with the smell of hot petroleum.

"They use polystyrene in most places now," Ellen says. "It's cheaper and easier to come by. But these records will stand up better."

In garage-size plants like this most of the R & B classics were pressed in the fifties and early sixties, when small independent record companies flourished. Often the artists themselves would back wheezing station wagons to the loading area to pick up enough 45's to make the rounds of deejays and promo men.

"It's a dinosaur," Ellen says. "But I guess I love it."

We arrive back in the office to find Solomon on the phone negotiating with the artist designing his *Golden Classics* album cover. Within fifteen minutes all the details—pressing, labels, jackets, shipping—are attended to. Solomon is pleased with the package. He says that he has been most successful at gift-wrapping himself since the early days, when he reclassified himself in the charts.

"Understand, there was nothing bad about being called an R and B artist. But if you had that classification, you had to work your way all the way to the top of the R and B charts before you could make the national pop charts, *white* charts. That was just as plain as day, okay? I just refused to work myself up from the bottom of those R and B charts all the way to the top, then start the struggle again. I just refused to accept that. So I went to Ahmet with this rock and soul thing. I think it was sixty-two or sixty-three."

Solomon insists that despite use of it as a marketing concept, the notion of "soul music" was a valid one.

"I said 'rock and soul' because soul singing to me is just basically singing from your soul. Whatever you do can be soulful. And that especially went for the country stuff. That got me a lot of bookings in the Deep South, in some places no other black artists could get into. That kind of country soul bridged a lot of waters. Of course, once or twice it darn near killed me. . . ."

Occasionally a white southern audience would not know that Solomon Burke was a black man until the curtain parted. Even more frightening was a gig in Alabama when the artist was unable to see the faces of his audience.

"It was to be one of those big outdoor deals," he says. "We got down there early, about four in the afternoon. And the sheriff came up and said, 'Now don't you boys worry 'bout nothin'. We have a whole setup over here for you.' "

On a ridge, in the middle of a large field, there was a huge tent. "There were beds and radios, and oh, Lord, all the beautiful black girls were out there with their mothers, cooking chicken and potato salad, slicing watermelons."

The white sheriff let it be known that he had spared no effort in orchestrating his idea of a black man's paradise. "He said, 'Now you boys remember this is sponsored by the county sheriff, so you don't have nothin' to worry about. Eat here, sleep here. Got an outhouse, four outhouses just for y'all. The ones with the green crosses is *your* outhouses."

As the sheriff walked off, Solomon counted the money, $7,500 in cash. The band rested in the cool early evening, ate the food provided by the women, and met with a sheriff's emissary for final instructions.

"The guy says, 'We want your band to hit just as dusk starts falling and let them play until it gets dark. *Dark*. And when it gets dark, I want you to come on with 'Down in the Valley.' Then if you could make the next number 'Cry to Me.' And I said, 'We'll do it, we sure will, by God.' "

The man smiled and made to leave. "You boys is all right," he said.

The band went on at dusk, as requested, and played until dark. The emissary reappeared and told Solomon it was time for him to go on. Though he could see no people beyond the stage, he walked out and began "Down in the Valley."

"All of a sudden I could see lights. Lights coming all around us, from all directions. You know, glowing over all the ridges. Thousands and thousands of lights it seemed. They were coming closer. And then I could see beyond the lights. It was the KKK, in robes, with torches. All KKK—

husbands, wives, children in bitty little sheets. Walkin' in out of the field towards us. I want to tell you, that's when I knew that the Lord had called me to ministry. 'Cause I said, 'Jesus, if you walked with me ever in my life, *run* with me now. And if you can, show me which way to go, Lord. Like straight up.' "

The band was in a 4/4 coma of fear, keeping the beat with ice-cold fingers and pounding hearts. The drummer was able to croak to his boss, "Man, you said this was the greatest gig we ever had. You didn't say nothin' 'bout it bein' the last."

The crowd had begun to yell at Solomon. To his relief, they were screaming the titles of his hits.

"We did the show, and when we got to 'Travel On,' well, I think we did 'Travel On' for thirty minutes. I'm singing and wishing, you know, 'Feel like I got to travel on . . .' and some guy in a sheet yells, 'One more time.' Okay, no problem, buddy. Thirty more times if you say so. I tell you, it was one of the greatest performances my band ever came up with."

When at last the torches burned down and the robed hosts departed, the sheriff presented Solomon with a sticker for his car that would ensure him safe-conduct in all Klan territories.

"You boys is all right," he said again, and drove off across the field.

Dark has fallen when we finally leave the office at Alco and head out into the smoggy night. Alas, it is too late for a tour of his mortuaries. Most likely the embalmers have gone home to dinner. Solomon directs Dr. Breaux toward the center of town and a large restaurant atop a sky-scraper where you can see for miles way up into the Hollywood Hills. Solomon's is a rich, happy life, and he likes to sit up there and think about it. His two marriages have blessed him with twenty-one children.

"Man sent out for Cantonese one night," Wilson Pickett had told me. "Just for the family, you know. We go down to fetch it, and it takes half an hour to get it all in the car. Bill comes to three hundred and sixty dollars. You believe that?"

"That was just a snack." Solomon laughs and says that he and Wilson are very good friends. It's clear when you see them together. In fact, at one Manhattan press conference, when the Wicked was shaking down the thunder around the cringing media, when he was stalking around in his bad leather pants, threatening to hang a promoter, to bash a reporter, to kill and *maim* all the dumb motherfuckers who refuse to give R & B its due, it was Solomon Burke who walked in and laid a big hand on

Wilson's yellow silk shoulder to calm him down. As he sat decompressing, Wilson hugged all he could of his substantial friend and said that really, being friends with a preacher could try a man's soul. He got mad, but he got over it, the time Solomon overloaded their car with Bibles he was selling and blew out all four tires. In fact, the only time Wilson got downright testy was the night the good Dr. Burke made his mama cry. She and his sister boohooed until he thought he'd lose his mind.

"Oh, that was on Wilson's birthday," Solomon says as the maître d' recedes. A crisp bill has gotten us a booth overlooking the city. Over an arc of blue-brown haze, a few stars have ventured forth. Solomon is staring into a candle flame, smiling at the memory of that crazy southern night.

"Wilson is not wicked. His is a gentle soul. He's had a lot of hurt. He has a big family, and he has taken care of them. That night, at the house he bought for his mother in Kentucky, they were giving him the greatest birthday party I'd ever seen. All his family there, everyone ready to party down. And I say, 'Let us pray.' Wilson's mother grabs my hand. And pretty soon the whole circle is interlocked, and there are all these beautiful dark faces. So quiet you can hear June bugs hitting the screens. The mother held to it all so tight. So tight. Eleven grown babies, and their babies, too. And she started to cry for joy. For *joy*. Because she had never let herself dream it could turn out well for them. And her big baby, Wilson, her protector, looked like he would *die* from it all. She brought him up hard because she had to. Sent him away from her when he got too dangerous, too bold to stay down South, and it broke her heart. But she would have driven him off with a shotgun. And if she had to hurt him, it was so other people could not come along and hurt him worse. Wilson is a great, great singer. And I am sorry to say this, but it comes from a long acquaintance with pain."

For a moment the good-natured blarney has vanished, and Solomon is not smiling.

"God. And sex. And rock and roll. And children. Making love and making music. Without restraint. It is a pleasurable life. I *am* blessed. But there was a lot of hurt, a lot of pain, a lot of suffering. You asked before why a man of God, a mortician, is afraid to fly the way I am? Why I am so terrified by the thought of a plane crash? I have faith, but I am no fool about how much it can *hurt* to die. I've witnessed the attitudes, the agonies of death. So I go full tilt boogaloo at life. I have done a lot of funerals, and some of them get way out. And what the people don't understand is that once you're dead, it's finished. There's no 'Let's do it again next week.' I buried countless strangers and far too many friends. Otis Redding, Sam Cooke. They were babies. *Babies*. Otis was twenty-six. Otis loved planes too much. A woman killed Sam Cooke. She claimed self-defense; she said she was afraid. It is hard to believe you could look at that man and be afraid.''

I wonder aloud if maybe it wasn't Sam Cooke's exceptional beauty—musical and physical—that made some people uneasy.

"You mean, if he found it to be a curse sometimes? I'd say yes. I'd say yes because I was there and I saw it. It happened in Shreveport.''

Solomon was with Sam Cooke in that sticky Louisiana town, was witness to the reason Sam wished aloud the rich black earth would heave up and swallow the damned place and wipe it from memory.

What Shreveport did was this: It singled Sam Cooke out for his talent and his beauty and humiliated him beyond his imagination.

As Solomon begins the story, he notes that Sam Cooke was shot to death in a motel not far from here. But he says that something got killed—at least gravely wounded—earlier on, in Shreveport.

"Sam was a very proud man,'' he says. "He was a star. But for a minute he forgot what he was in the South.''

It began in a small flyspecked restaurant, next door to the motel where Sam, Solomon, and others had put up for the night before their next date in New Orleans.

"B. B. King's backup orchestra was with us, too. And I think Jerry Butler. Maybe Bobby Blue Bland. I'm not sure of the show lineup, but the rest I'll never forget. We were in these little row houses, like motel cottages, and the restaurant was next door. We went in there, and they wouldn't serve us. But another waitress recognized Sam. You know, he was so good-looking.

"Anyhow, she was a white girl, and she came over to the motel and said to him, 'I'll get you what you want to eat. Send your road manager or somebody to the side door, and I'll give it to them.' So she took all our orders. We gave her the money, and we were waiting on her to call us back on the phone at the desk so we could get the food. The next thing we know, police are coming into the room from everywhere. The police took Sam and I out of there.

"They took us to the fire station and made us take off our clothes. They said, 'Now get your microphones, boys, and start singing.' They had us do the whole show.''

He is smiling at the visual memory now, of the tall, slim Sam Cooke and himself, both sweating like Niagara, dancing naked for the red-faced firemen and cops, trying to sing with fear-parched throats.

"You should have seen me singing 'Cry to Me.' Shreveport, Louisiana. Okay. My Lord. We did all our records. I did the background for Sam's pop stuff, the *ooh-doo-doos,* and Sam did my background. And when we had finished, the guy told us, 'Get in them stolen limousines, boys, and don't ever bring your band to Shreveport again.' We were happy to oblige."

"Just another day," as Sam had sung with the Soul Stirrers. *"Just another day my Lord has kept me."*

"He never did get over it."

8

"Lady, You Shot Me"

> *Paul did not know if Arthur knew why he was singing.*
> *It was something Arthur had come to all alone, and at*
> *the age of thirteen. He had not claimed to be saved.*
> *He had not been baptized. And yet, he sang—indeed,*
> *he sang, and there was something frightening about so*
> *deep and unreadable a passion in one so young.*
> *Arthur's phrasing was the key—unanswerable; his*
> *delivery of the song made you realize that he knew*
> *what the song was about.*
>
> *Your reaction to this passion can destroy the singer.*
>
> —JAMES BALDWIN, in *Just Above My Head*

GIVEN THE YOUNG but long-winded history of rock journalism, it was a pleasure to come across the most succinct and perceptive record review I'd ever read. It was penned by the late Lester Bangs, about a reissue of Otis Rush's *Groaning the Blues* LP. Old Lester got right to it.

"It's better than killing yourself" was all he wrote.

I can't think of a better way to describe the effects of listening to Sam Cooke singing "Wonderful" with the Soul Stirrers. If ever there was a reason to live, you ought to be able to find it in that scant two-minute song, whether you are a believer or not. Sam Cooke died in December 1964, more than a decade after he had cut "Wonderful," but in all his work, gospel or pop, there hardly exists a better example of Cooke's bottomless, wellspring soul. The word "wonderful" becomes a song in itself.

There is a great gentleness to it, yet the sure, deft phrasing reveals a singer of exceptional confidence and strength. Wonder-*ful,* God is so *wonderful.* The notes are clean as spring water and teeming with life.

Soul, as defined by Sam Cooke's singing, depended less on formal technique than on drawing out the emotional, almost subconscious qualities of the human voice. It didn't so much matter if you could reach a high C; it's where you could take the listener on your way there. In just the first word—Jesus— of "Jesus, Wash Away My Troubles," Sam Cooke shoots the rapids all over the scale and straight to that point just beyond the ear that answers back, "Yes. Of course."

"Sam could take you to the water," says Solomon Burke, "before you even knew you were thirsty."

Having cut their best records in the fifties and early sixties, Sam Cooke and his bluesy counterpart Little Willie John were peerless soul men. Their voices have an emotional fidelity no amplifier, no studio sweetening could improve upon. Between them, they could reach every feeling—passion, pain, euphoria, melancholy. Both were precocious talents. Their lives were short, and their ends tragic. Both cut some unregenerate schmaltz, but they are best remembered for their definitive soul.

Listen to Sam Cooke sing "Touch the Hem of His Garment" or "Jesus, Wash Away My Troubles" or "Pilgrim of Sorrow," or Willie John singing "Fever" or "Need Your Love So Bad." It's all there—loneliness and redemption, agony and ecstatic release. Soul would enjoy its greatest vogue after their best work was completed, but never, except perhaps in the work of James Brown and Aretha Franklin, would it find better vessels. What made it all the more enthralling was the control both men exercised over their instruments. They knew their power, and even very young, they wielded it with conscious authority.

To be both cool *and* soulful was possible for them because their art drew heavily on the tension of opposites. The beauty of performance was not possible without a working knowledge of the hideous aspects of life. In their music, and in their lives, Sam Cooke and Willie John struck a resonance with rock's archetypal soul man Robert Johnson. Johnson died young, in 1938, under mysterious circumstances—it is said a jealous woman poisoned his whiskey. He recorded only twenty-nine blues in 1936 and 1937, but many of them stand unequaled—magnificent ruins of a tormented soul. Those ruins have been worshiped ever since by generations of bluesmen and more recently by white rockers like the Rolling Stones and Eric Clapton. Robert Johnson was too black, too soon for popular music to canonize him like a Hendrix or a Presley. But in a convincing, historic way, Greil Marcus showed him to be a pioneer rock martyr. It's all very American, as he argues in *Mystery Train:*

> The most acute Americans, in the steps of the old Puritans, have been suspicious, probing people, looking for signs of evil and grace, of salvation and damnation, behind every natural fact. Robert Johnson lived with this kind of intensity. . . .
>
> This is a state of mind that gives no rest at all. Even if you have sold your soul to the devil, you cannot rest with him; you have to keep looking, because there is never any end to the price you have to pay, nor any certainty as to the form that price will take. Every event thus becomes charged with meaning, but the meaning is never complete. The moments of perfect pleasure in Johnson's songs, and the beauty of those songs, remind one that it is not the simple presence of evil that is unbearable; what is unbearable is the impossibility of reconciling the facts of evil with the beauty of the world.

Sam Cooke met that unbearable truth in Shreveport, among other stops, and succumbed to it in an L.A. motel. Little Willie John killed a man and died for his sins in a Washington State prison.

Perhaps under the burden of his sin, and his lesser success in entering the pop market, Willie John would never earn substantial credit for his contributions. It is, as James Brown argued late one night, an injustice that he is keenly aware of.

"I loved that man's voice to death," James said. "I used to open for him in the beginning, you know. Willie John was a singer that could take you places, and when I recorded my tribute album *[Thinking of Little Willie John and Other Nice Things]*, it was partly because I did not want this fact to be lost to man: And that is that Willie John was a *connection*. Now I loved the Five Blind Boys and I loved that early R and B, and I heard *everything* I loved in Willie John. He was a small man, you know. He wore these sharp, sharp little hats, smoked a pipe, and looked like a kid playin' grown-up sometimes. But I don't care how old he was when he started. I think twelve or thirteen, right? He open his mouth, step up there, lay his hand on the mike, just eyeball the crowd. Look kind of dreamy-headed sometime. Tilt his head a little and go, 'Talk to me, talk to me.' When he found his trouble in life, I heard the quiet come down. I missed that voice.''

Asked what that voice had said most plainly to him, James thought for a few moments and asked me if I was familiar with his own "Lost Someone." Sure, I said. It's a sad, lonely ballad. James nodded and said that was true. But the song wasn't just about loneliness. To his mind, it had to do with the special, excruciating loneliness that follows togetherness.

"Now look here," he said. "You can only miss somethin' if you had it. If you been hungry, and I have, and your tongue is rememberin' food, good food, somethin' you love, your mind and your mouth be *screamin'* just a half a second before somebody set a full plate down in front of it. And if you been missin' love, if you had it . . . or you thought you did, if it's nearby, but not close enough . . . well.''

James is an able poet of need himself. He has crawled across the stage on his belly, singing "Please, Please, Please," and sobbed unashamedly during "Try Me," that flaming testament to want. Onstage and on record, he'd likely follow such a confessional with some macho denial. For every "Lost Someone," there is a preening "Sex Machine" or a "Superbull, Superbad." Needing and getting. It's the old push and pull. And at bottom it's nothing short of the longing to make the world whole.

What James Brown would later paint in such broad strokes, though, Little Willie John could do in a whisper. "Fever" is about the same kind of missing James describes. So is "Need Your Love So Bad"—a whole catalogue of need in which the singer longs for soft lips, soft voice, someone's arms. Willie John's recording of that song and Irma Thomas's later version of it are His and Her bookends on the heaviest volumes of love and loss.

"Missin', like I said," James concluded. "Willie John's songs were about knowin', *then* missin'. Kind of missin' makes me scream. Willie John did not scream it. No. But you could hear it. To me it was very loud. And like I say, I missed it when he passed. I don't understand why people miss Sam Cooke so, and *not* Little Willie John. I don't. I don't deny Sam was great. No, ma'am. I guess Willie John never did make it to the Copa. People forget where you been. And get it stuck in their minds where you *ain't* been.''

Rock and roll never forgets, as Bob Seger sings. But it's never been big on credits, and it makes a lot of noise about living for the moment.

Given this jumpy state of mind, it follows that kids don't have to know that Eric Clapton idolized Robert Johnson to appreciate his latest album. Nor did they have to know about Little Willie John to dig James Brown. It's enough that the artists listened. It must be through them, as well as Willie John's scant recording catalogue, that this short, tough life is granted its legacy. The facts themselves are few.

William Edward John was born in 1937, in Camden, Arkansas, the youngest of seven children. His father, Mertis, moved the family north to Detroit, where he took a job at Dodge Main. Willie started singing in a gospel quintet. He was just a teenager in 1951 when bandleader Johnny Otis saw him in a talent show at the Paradise Theater and included him in his scouting report to Syd Nathan of King Records. He was barely five feet tall, but the high, elastic tenor could stretch across a precocious range of blues, love ballads, even goofy novelty songs. Nathan passed on the pint-size solo act and signed another of the night's top talent winners, the Royals (later to become Hank Ballard and the Midnighters).

Willie John was seventeen when Nathan changed his mind and signed him to King in 1955. Producer Henry Glover hunted up a blues for his first release, a bawdy bit of nonsense first recorded by Titus Turner, called "All Around the World." The singer is pledging his love, but the effect is hardly courtly. Listening to Willie John's easy, cocksure swagger on that cut, I was reminded of a remark overheard late one night in a Seagram's-scented ladies' room: "Ain't nothing more dangerous than a man that KNOWS you love him." Willie John knows on that record, and he's intent on enjoying the dividends.

While "All Around the World" was still on the charts, Willie John came back with "Need Your Love So Bad," hiking up his macho armor enough to reveal vulnerability and the soul man's nightmare, dependence. "Fever" took it further still, and need became delirium. Though his obituary in *Billboard* listed him only as "co-writer of 'Fever' popularized by Peggy Lee," Willie John's performance of it was his biggest hit, outselling Peggy Lee's by far and holding on for six months in the R & B charts of 1956. A few more minor hits closed out his lightning half decade. They included "Talk to Me" and "Sleep." The big quiet that James Brown spoke of descended in 1961, when he was arrested after stabbing a man to death in a Seattle café brawl. He was convicted of manslaughter and sent to Washington State Penitentiary, where he died, of pneumonia, on May 26, 1968, six months shy of his thirty-second birthday.

The same night that Johnny Otis scouted the Detroit talent show that turned up Willie John, another solo act upset the crowd impressively. A few years older than Willie John, Jackie Wilson was a native Detroiter who came up singing in church and turned himself out onstage as an enthusiastic cheerleader for S-E-X. Like Sam Cooke and Willie John, Wilson was fated to be an early soul comet, effectively burned out by the time singers like James Brown, Wilson Pickett, and Aretha Franklin were hitting their stride. Wilson's beauty—he was exceptionally handsome—and his passionate, almost suicidal delivery nearly undid him.

He knew early on the ecstasy and power of a seduction performed live, onstage. He has said that he fell hopelessly in love with Clyde McPhatter's early fifties flamboyance and with his voice. Clyde bore the wild man's stigma, the mark that would also touch Jackie Wilson and James Brown: None of them could get through more than two or three songs in a performance before twin patches of stage grime marked the knees of their snappy slacks. But before he bore the mark himself, Jackie Wilson studied Clyde McPhatter's moves. So complete, so obsessive was his absorption that by 1953 he had incorporated the twists, shimmies, and knee-drops, the moans, even the high-pitched choke into his own presentation. That year, when Billy Ward was looking for a replacement for Clyde on the Dominoes, Jackie Wilson was the logical choice. He sang lead for them for three years, until a Detroit club owner named Al Green agreed to book him as a solo act in the new Flame Show Bar. A young man Wilson later described as a hustler, Berry Gordy, also dogged the Flame. He was a beginning songwriter, and once he had persuaded Wilson to try some of his compositions, he cracked the charts on Brunswick Records, beginning in 1957 with "Reet Petite" and in 1958 with "To Be Loved" and "Lonely Teardrops."

It was the live act, more than the records, however, that made Jackie Wilson a dyed-in-the-mohair soul man. An ex-prizefighter with the heart of a lion or a fool, he would willingly leap into a sea of female arms that tore the clothes from him and raked at his flesh. In New Orleans in 1961, diving into the frenzy he had caused got him arrested when he shoved a cop who was roughing up swooning women. In black clubs he had the icy effrontery to come at them with "Danny Boy" and wail away at it until they banged the tables and screamed. Jackie Wilson was well aware of his dangerous potency. And still, he pushed it.

"Your love keeps liftin' me, higher and higher. . . ."

Between Jackie Wilson's sets, stagehands sopped up pools of sweat like the towel boys who daub at the hardwood during NBA time-outs. He threw himself around without regard for his safety or his wardrobe. Besides having dirty knees, the fancy stage clothes were soaked in funky brine. Many suits he could wear only once. Taking the stage at the outset, he was icy-cool devastation in a boxy silk suit and spectator shoes. Leaving it, he looked like a man who had walked ten miles in a driving rainstorm.

It followed that female hysteria popped and crackled dangerously around him, wherever he went. One night, in a New York hotel room, a woman brought to the edge pumped bullets into the cause of her madness, and Jackie Wilson nearly died. It happened in 1961, the best year of his career, in which he had six best-sellers. After a long convalescence he hit again, in 1963, with "Baby Workout" and "Shake! Shake! Shake!"

On record Jackie Wilson's performances were far less consistent than his stage shows. In the studio he could lapse into creamed corn; like Clyde McPhatter at the end of his career, he would allow the magnificent voice to be obscured beneath mushy string arrangements. Still, all was forgiven when he took the stage.

He was out there in October 1975, eight years after his last solid hit ("Your Love Keeps Lifting Me [Higher and Higher]"), pouring it on for the crowd at the Latin Casino in Cherry Hill, New Jersey, with Dick Clark's Good Ol' Rock 'n' Roll Revue, a golden oldie just in his mid-forties, when his heart gave out. He survived, but the destruction was so complete he spent the remaining eight years of his life semi-comatose in a nursing home. A local court had inexplicably conferred guardianship on his much estranged ex-wife. When Jackie Wilson finally died, on January 21, 1984, his family refused to allow the hospital to disclose his cause of death.

Sam Cooke made it to thirty-three. The day they buried him, the temperature was near zero in Chicago, but more than 25,000 people tried to attend the rites at the Tabernacle Baptist Church. Fifty policemen contended with the hysterical mourners. When gospel singer Bessie Griffin was too overcome to sing, Ray Charles stepped in to replace her. Young Muhammad Ali was granted a private viewing of his friend's body once it had been flown back from Los Angeles.

On December 11, 1964, the L.A. police had retrieved Sam Cooke's body from a $3-a-night motel, dead of gunshot wounds and marked with contusions suffered by his having been beaten with a blunt object. He was wearing a sportcoat and one shoe. Bertha Franklin, the motel clerk,

claimed she shot him, then clubbed him in self-defense when he charged
her office at the Hacienda Motel, shouting and in a state of extreme agitation. Mrs. Franklin was able to report the deceased's last words: "Lady,
you shot me."

Police found Sam's tomato-colored Ferrari, valued at $14,000, in the
motel lot, with a copy of *Muhammad Speaks* in the back seat. In a phone
booth nearby, they found Elisa Boyer, a twenty-two-year-old Eurasian
woman who claimed that after offering to drive her home from a party,
Cooke had forced her into a motel room. She said she had escaped when
he went into the bathroom. She had taken some of his clothes with her
for her safety, she insisted, and not for his wallet. He was looking for her
at the registration desk, where Mrs. Franklin testified he attacked her.
She stopped him with three bullets from a .22-caliber pistol, and a large
stick.

There were and still are rumors that the scenario was orchestrated, that
it was, in fact, a mob hit—a white reprisal for Sam Cooke's growing popularity. His gospel contemporaries also insisted that such an immoral end
was impossible, that it had to be a setup. Sam Cooke's widow, the former
Barbara Campbell, sued her husband's killer for $3 million, a counter to
Bertha Franklin's suit charging slander and damage to her reputation by
the widow's statements to the press. Neither matter reached trial, and
three months after the killing Barbara Campbell Cooke married her husband's former guitar player, Bobby Womack.

Whatever the truth, to his fans Sam Cooke died a martyr's death. He
was a hero, whether he was struck down by a murderous plot or just a
fatal evening's dalliance. He died young and handsome and at the peak
of his career, had crossed over but never sold out, had worked for and
with white men, but always on his own terms.

Few people who were close to Sam Cooke, including his family, will
speak about him. His former manager, J. W. Alexander, told me he'd
signed an agreement to withold interviews pending the making of a film
on Sam's life. I was able to track down the men who produced his records
for RCA, a pair of Italian cousins named Luigi Creaturo and Hugo Peretti.
They were journeymen producers with a background that was more
Broadway/big band than R & B. Both are retired now, Luigi in Florida,
Hugo in New Jersey, where he oversees various business concerns. When
we met at his hardware store, Hugo admitted that Sam was unlike anyone
the cousins had ever dealt with. He says they were shocked at the moment
they heard the news of his death but, all in all, not surprised. They say

that the ugliness was not in keeping with his character—he was a gentle and honorable man—but the drama was consistent.

"Sam was a very excitable guy," Hugo says. "Very colorful. Sam *did* things to people. When you have the power to excite like that, there's always the possibility of weird stuff."

RCA released a Sam Cooke single just days after his death. It was a slow, slightly ominous song Sam wrote called "A Change Is Gonna Come," and in hindsight, the record had all the portent of Martin Luther King, Jr.'s final "Free at Last" speech and Otis Redding's mournful and posthumous "Dock of the Bay." "Change" would be recorded, respectably, by the likes of Aretha Franklin and Otis Redding, but when you listen to Sam Cooke's version, it's clear he wrote it for and of himself. Those who knew him characterized him as restless, as a habitual searcher. And there was no disputing the fact that Sam Cooke had been through a lot of changes since he started singing gospel as a pretty-voiced child.

He was born in 1931 in Clarksdale, Mississippi, one of eight sons of the Reverend Charles Cooke. The family moved to Chicago, and like so many black teenagers in northern cities, Sam divided his time between singing with a junior gospel group, the Highway QC's, and harmonizing on the street corners and at poolrooms around Thirty-sixth and Ellis. He was capable, but intimidated, when the QC's coach, R. B. Robinson (the Soul Stirrers' baritone), suggested Sam step into the huge void created by lead singer R. H. Harris's departure from the Soul Stirrers to retire from the road.

At first Sam foundered beneath the weight of the mantle passed to him. By all accounts, his first outings as a Soul Stirrer were tentative, uneasy affairs as he sought to mimic Harris's sound. But it did not take long for him to put his own twists on falsetto singing and develop a mind-bending yodel that would wilt the cloth gardenias on any Sunday hat.

"Nobody has put more people on stretchers than Sam Cooke, nobody," says Jerry Wexler. "He's got to be the best singer that ever lived, bar none. I mean *nobody* can touch Sam Cooke. When I listen to Sam everything goes away. Modulation, shading, dynamics, progression, emotion, every essential quality—he had it all. I speak of his gospel work. The pop stuff never came close to making the fullest use of his talents. Most people don't realize how bad those records are. That he overrode a lot of the sterility in them is a tribute to his genius. Listen, I was as excited as anyone when I heard whisperings that Sam was going to try some secular stuff.

"There is a story about how Sam got away from Specialty with his master records of the pop stuff. You know, Sam had done one pop record for Specialty, under the name Dale Cook ["Lovable"]. Well, as soon as you heard it on the radio, you knew it was Sam. Anyhow, Specialty and its owner, Art Rupe, owed Sam fifteen thousand dollars. Now Sam had cut these pop records, with Bumps Blackwell producing. Art didn't think they were gonna sell because they were the devil's music and all, and Sam Cooke was entrenched in gospel to his fans. Anyhow, Art gave them the release on the pop stuff free and clear. They walked out with the masters, and that was it. Art saved himself fifteen thousand dollars. And they ended up on this tiny label called Keen. Bob Keene was an airplane manufacturer or aeronautics engineer or something. Sam had a couple of records out on Keen. I think 'You Send Me' sold over a million and a half. That was in 1957. But I guess they didn't have such a tight contract, and RCA jumped in."

Dozens of independents would have mortgaged their entire catalogues to sign Sam Cooke. But two years after he had joined the Keen label, Sam opted for the mainstream. RCA had only one other black pop singer, Harry Belafonte, who was already considered a crossover act. Signing with a major label held similar promise for Sam Cooke. His manager, J. W. Alexander, declared it was a route he'd mapped for his client long before.

"Well now, we went over to RCA, and we started bringing people in," Luigi remembers. "We were scouting, developing new kids. Sam Cooke had had one hit at the time. Then he went cold. He had nothing going, and he was loose, and we heard about it. Sam stopped by one night on his way to a gig in Brooklyn; but he had a cold, and he couldn't use up his voice to sing for us. He told us he was writing. He sat down at the piano and showed us a few things."

Hugo and Luigi were encouraged. It was always a boon to have a singer who could write for himself.

"He wrote like crazy. He'd come in with twenty or thirty songs," says Hugo Peretti. "We didn't mess with Sam. He knew his mind. He'd play a few bars of twenty or so songs he'd worked up, and we'd weed them out together."

Sam's first release on RCA in 1960 was a treacly thing called "Teenage Sonata." It did decent business, but the next record shot him into the Top Ten. Luigi says it was cut almost as an afterthought.

"We were working, and Sam says, 'There's another song I haven't finished.' And he started to play around with it, all these *oooh-ahs*. Said it was supposed to be men working on a chain gang. I said, 'Finish it, we're recording on Tuesday.' ''

"Chain Gang" was not what you'd call gritty realism. Like the Coasters' "Riot in Cell Block No. 9," the record has sound effects, of hammers hitting spikes, of chains clinking, and a studio "work gang" doing the grunty *oooh-ahs* that punctuate Sam's vocal. The kids loved it and made it a huge hit in the summer of 1960.

"Sam was on his way," says Luigi. "After that he was in the Top Forty, even the Top Ten like clockwork." He and Hugo nicknamed their artist the Consistent One. On their album liner notes they described him as "tall and slender, with looks that remind you at once of Belafonte and Poitier." RCA did its best to turn the former gospel shouter into a smooth, all-around entertainer. He was photographed in starched white shirts and cardigans and fitted with a repertoire suited for both record hops and supper clubs. Whatever was thrown at him, from teen anthems like "Only Sixteen" and "Tammy" to pop standards like "Summertime" and "The Wayward Wind," Sam obliged.

It was a function of the times that he did not resist doing the schlock rock that had crept into the Top Ten once the fifties wild men had cooled down. Presented with "Everybody Likes to Cha-Cha-Cha," he did not recoil. After all, America was, as his hit claimed, "Twistin' the Night Away" in 1962. Just as Motown was beginning to hit with songs billed as "The Sound of Young America," Sam Cooke's "Having a Party" sketched a scenario straight out of Ozzie and Harriet's rumpus room— Cokes in the icebox, popcorn on the table. And above it all, that American teen mantra "Please, Mr. Deejay, keep those records playin'."

Since 1960 the twist had had millions gyrating hard and fast enough to prompt plans for America's first discotheque, the Whiskey à Go Go, which opened in L.A. a year later. Mushy valentines, like Shelley Fabares's "Johnny Angel" in 1962, were also hitting number one. White city kids were coming into their own as a bunch of adenoidal Italians, the Four Seasons, hit with "Sherry." There was still room for flat-out silliness as well, with records like "The Monster Mash" and the hit debut, in 1962, of the TV series *The Beverly Hillbillies.* John Kennedy's Camelot was still playing at the White House. It took one discreet phone call from Kennedy to get Dr. Martin Luther King, Jr., released from an Atlanta jail following a sit-in arrest. And in the public mind, the civil rights movement was still as nebulous as the concept of soul.

In both the teen and adult markets, black artists found themselves in that frustrating limbo between pop and R & B charts. It was no less confusing with live engagements. Coming off an era of Comos and Damones, the supper-club success of Nat "King" Cole was still a shimmering grail to black entertainers who had come up on the chitlin circuit. Rock package tours could push a record and plump a bank account, but the rigors and the rip-offs made even the biggest stars look toward Vegas or the Copa.

Given this marketplace schizophrenia, versatility was the key to survival for soul men who came along before *Soul Train* and Afro-Sheen. Sometimes it took comic proportions—Sam Cooke worked a Purim date with Myron Cohen at the Copa in 1958. And RCA was not reluctant to play up the artist's crossover idiosyncrasies and parlay them into a sort of outré charm. One press release burbled that Sam had once "amazed a deli owner" by ordering hot pastrami topped with blueberries and sour cream.

It seems Sam was also resistant to the dyspepsia that so many of his fans suffered when confronted with his more showbiz recordings.

"Sam was game," as Luigi puts it. "And Sam was always a fine, fine vocalist. He was a perfectionist. And he wouldn't release a record if his voice didn't sound good to *him*."

On all those RCA cuts his voice is never less than pleasant and impeccably controlled. But sometimes even that formidable instrument loses out to overblown or ill-timed arrangements. Having Sam Cooke sing "I Cover the Waterfront" was a wonderful idea, but the framing is incredibly, inappropriately up-tempo—complete with finger snaps. The mismatch— and the lost possibilities—are all the more apparent next to Billie Holiday's version, which pulls lazily like the tide itself. It was only when the arrangements were minimal—like the light French horn and flute on "The Great Pretender" or the muted backgrounds on "Unchained Melody"— that the voice is given its just display.

There was, in all his ballads and old standards, one vocal distinction that resisted the camouflage of any arrangement.

"Oh, we all heard it," Solomon Burke says. "In a lot of that pop stuff he'd give you the high sign. Pull a Sam in the middle of a note, let you know it's him. New pop audiences heard that yodel, that *woah-ah-oh,* like it was a shiny new thing. But if you knew Sam from gospel, it was him saying, 'Hey, it's me.' "

The songs that Sam Cooke wrote for himself were his biggest hits and, naturally, those with the built-in opportunities for his vocal loop-the-loops.

"Sad Mood," released in 1960, is simple, blue, and to the point ("My baby done left me"). "Bring It On Home to Me," one of his most beautiful records, also calls out to a departing lover, and in its sorrow and loneliness, the song is very close to the weary solitude of the gospel pilgrim. The jilted lover is distraught, penitent, pleading, and resigned all at once. He offers money, jewels, unconditional forgiveness; the voice is strong, almost hoarse with pain at times, and amplified by the gospel harmony of Lou Rawls, who was a session singer at the time. The English is black, the sexual circumstances are frank, and it all ends in a crescendo of churchy call-and-response "yeahs"—in short, a soul masterwork.

Occasionally, while Sam was recording a pop song, there would be a brief, tense moment in the studio when he could not lose a black inflection.

"Once, when we were working on one of those love songs and Sam got to the height of it," Luigi says, "he sings, 'And if you ax me, I will,' and I said, 'Hold it. It's "asked." ' Sam says, 'What'd I say?' 'Ax,' I tell him. So we did another take and got to the same spot, and 'ax' appeared again. We did it a third time, and I guess I was getting a little annoyed. And Sam looked at me and laughed and said, 'Hey, man, you're taking my heritage.' "

The fourth time Sam said "ask." It was one of the few times his producers had to lean on him for anything. His voice was so consistent yet surprising that Hugo and Luigi often huddled behind the soundboard, sure of the sheet music but having no idea when their artist would detonate one of his quick, melismatic flares.

"You know, the things he did, the yodel, the *oh-wo-woah,* you know. You'd be listening intently, and on a certain note, he might come in on a place you initially thought was wrong. You'd look up through the glass and realize that it was only his beginning. And he was gonna run, coming up to the note you're looking for on your chart. He'd reverse things, work changes you could never expect. But they always worked."

Luigi says that despite these surprises, sessions were always smooth. Sam Cooke's tapes were the cleanest he can remember. "He just sang. We had to pay attention to the background, if the balance was right and all. But the trouble was never with Sam. If we did another take, it was because the guitar goofed, not him."

Luigi feels that Sam liked to write and record his own songs for the feeling of control it gave him. When the time came to do his second session with Hugo and Luigi, he told them he wanted to have more input on the material.

"He said he'd been writing some more stuff," Luigi remembers. "He said, 'I don't want to be Perry Como or Tony Bennett. I want to be me.' "

Once he was on his way, Sam Cooke was generous and encouraging with other performers. He persuaded his guitar player, Bobby Womack, to record his first hit, "It's All Over Now," which was later covered by the Rolling Stones. Sam formed his own recording company, Sar/Derby Records, with the intent of recording the Soul Stirrers and the young man who had replaced him as the group's lead, Johnnie Taylor. He began planning a pop career for Taylor and started his own music publishing company and management firm.

"Control was very important to Sam," Hugo says. "He saw what had happened to a lot of other black artists, and he didn't want to get ten percented to death. He was always looking for investments. He even bought a beer company—Cooke's Beer. I think it went right down the drain, but he bought it. He had some problems. People screwed him. And legitimately—that is, legally. They just took advantage of him. Like anybody else, he was better off sticking to what he knew, which was music. His record company was in the black from the start."

Sar/Derby went pop shortly after its incorporation in 1960, and with the help of his manager, J. W. Alexander, Sam began to map pop careers for some of the gospel singers in his stable. Besides Bobby Womack and his brothers, who performed as the Valentinos, and a duo called the Simms Twins, Sam signed and encouraged keyboard virtuoso Billy Preston and set Johnnie Taylor on a soulful road that would eventually lead him to Stax in Memphis.

Sam intended to produce many of the acts himself. When he wasn't recording, he would sit in on Hugo and Luigi's sessions, asking technical questions, watching and listening. Once, when they were recording in California, Sam was also working with a young singer whose records he was hoping to produce.

"We did Sam, say, from eight to eleven, and when we finished, he said, 'You know, I'm producing at midnight. Why don't you come back?' So I came back about two in the morning. Same studio, same engineer, same musicians, same arranger. Sweat was coming out of Sam's forehead. He looked *awful*. And he says, 'It's not coming right. I got all the same things here. How do you do it?' And I said, 'Schmuck. *I* used Sam Cooke.' "

Occasionally after a session Sam socialized with his producers. But more often he disappeared in the small sports cars he favored. Outside the studio, his was a restless way of life. He lived mainly in California but preferred hotels to houses or apartments. He settled down enough to marry his childhood sweetheart, Barbara Campbell, but was most often on the road, as he had been with the Soul Stirrers. The birth of a son drew him happily home, but eighteen-month-old Vincent Luncy Cooke drowned accidentally in a swimming pool in 1963. Hugo remembers that Sam plunged deeper into his work. And though he was well established nationally as a top-venue entertainer, he never lost the wariness that prompted phone calls from some motel road stop to his producers in New York. There were questions—about royalties, investments, gate percentages.

It was at Sam's request that Hugo and Luigi secured the services of a solid show business conglomerate. It was arranged that he be represented by the prestigious William Morris Agency. Every few weeks Hugo would get calls from the agency, in search of its client.

"Sam would disappear," Hugo says. "No one knew where he was. I'd play dumb to William Morris for a while, but then Sam would call. What he'd do is this: He'd go on the road. He had a little truck and a sports car. And he and a band and a few guys would just go down South and hit a little town, say, Wheeling, West Virginia. And he'd go to the local promoter and say, 'Tomorrow night we're gonna give a concert and dance.' They'd put up banners and all that, and Sam would do the gig. He made all cash, put the money in his pocket, and left. Then he'd hit another town. You could never pin him down. He moved so fast there was no way to prove he was doing it. Maybe taking those secret trips helped settle him down. You know, he felt that he was always giving so much to agents. He'd say, 'I want to make some money for myself.' A few days out there, and he'd put a roll in his pocket all right. It may not have been what he'd earn in a night at the Copa, but I guess it was worth more in peace of mind."

It doesn't seem inconsistent that Sam Cooke, the entertainer, would harbor a need to get away from the abstract success of royalty statements and hit the road, in secret, to see how he was playing out of town—to control it entirely, with a road map and his own will. Perhaps he was, in the manner of Robert Johnson, that restless, intense, and wary soul man.

Few black artists were in a position to advise Sam at his level of success, and he called Hugo and Luigi often for advice on how to deal with the corporate higher-ups. Likewise, RCA executives weren't quite sure how to treat their first black pop star.

"When we were recording him, he dealt with nobody but us," Hugo says. "There was hardly any relationship with the company. Then one day the president of RCA called us down. He says, 'Do you realize Sam Cooke sells next to Elvis Presley for us?' At the time Sam was making a guarantee of thirty thousand dollars a year. Now that wasn't too much, but when we signed him, he was cold."

The RCA honchos looked again at their figures and decided that their artist might appreciate a gesture of some sort. They suggested luncheons, press junkets, dinners. Hugo and Luigi told them to let it alone; Sam didn't go in for that kind of stuff.

"Well, they gave him a luncheon," Hugo says, laughing. "Then they took him through the building. And on the way they said, 'Look at your new album cover. What do you think?' "

Sam did not realize that this, too, was meant as a gesture, so he told them exactly what he thought. He didn't like it. And as long as the gentlemen had opened this dialogue, it seemed appropriate to chat—with Sam's legal counsel—about the contract that needed renewing.

"One thing led to another," Hugo says, "and before you knew it, Sam got a million-dollar contract."

RCA acceded, delighted with his sales. They were less pleased with his insistence on remaining black.

"Some of the people at RCA didn't like that," Hugo says. "They felt that Sam should be doing the Waldorf. 'Cause he was big enough. He used to say [about the Waldorf], 'They're not my people. I don't belong there.' He would rather work . . . well, there was a place here on Eastern Parkway in Brooklyn. He used to *kill* them in that place. When he got through, his shirt was off, his tie was off, he was sopping wet. People would stand on the tables, faint. There were bodies everywhere."

Even when he was long past the need to play small black clubs, he would confound promoters by insisting they be fitted into his bookings. He said he needed it as much as the black club patrons who could afford only an uptown shot-and-beer cover charge.

It was a sorrow to Sam that in courting his secular audience, he plummeted in the esteem of the sanctified and generally older fans who had loved his gospel. They jeered him when he took the stage with the Soul Stirrers at their anniversary concert in Chicago, calling him a blues singer, which was, in church, the meanest way of calling him down. He cried as he left the stage. Once again Sam Cooke was caught in the middle. His record company called him Mr. Soul, but the church folk damned his blaspheming soul. They might have been cruel and unjust to cast him out,

but in terms of what they lost when Sam Cooke stopped singing and recording gospel, they had a right to grieve.

Technically, and in terms of their use of the singer's natural gifts, Sam
Cooke's gospel recordings with the Soul Stirrers on Specialty dwarf anything he did at RCA. The stamp of his gospel soul was audible early,
indelibly, on his first session with the Soul Stirrers in 1951. He was only
twenty when he recorded "Jesus Gave Me Water," and it is nothing short
of chilling. The word "water" becomes liquid. Sung once, it splashes
through seven notes; repeated three times, it cascades over the solid
background voices. Shortly after, Sam followed with a piercing, almost
a cappella performance on "Pilgrim of Sorrow," and it is as desolate, as
haunting as any blues.

Lyrically the singer is "down in this world all alone," with no hope for
tomorrow and no place to roam. The rest of the Soul Stirrers roll a dense,
fluid baritone hum; a slight but responsive guitar echoes the singer's
plaints, softly at first, then ringing louder on his rising tide of misery.

"Sometimes, I'm tortured, Lord, and driven."

The voice breaks under it, loosing itself from the melody to crack into
a hoarse "whooaa, Lord," lining out a cry for the guitar to shadow. For
a very young man, it was an awesome beginning.

It was hardly intentional, but Sam Cooke's last hit record closed the
parentheses on his work with an almost identical gospel feeling. Though
there were five posthumous single releases after "A Change Is Gonna
Come," "Change" is remembered as his last and as the record most wor-
thy of his talent. It had an almost funereal tempo. But there were heavenly
strings, and the lyrics are straight from the church: *"It's been too hard
livin', and I'm afraid to die."*

Just like the singer in "Pilgrim of Sorrow," the man in "Change" is a
searcher: born by a river and been running ever since. Like the pilgrim,
he turns to ask for help—to brother, to mother—and again he is left running, alone. Yet there is nowhere to run. He says he doesn't know what's
up there, behind the clouds.

It is that terrible loneliness, the kind that sentences the soul man to his
incessant searching. He may rest in a momentary carnal romp, may move
thousands to communal hysteria when he gives the unspeakable willies a
voice, as Willie John did in "Fever," when he wrestles with it, literally,
as Jackie Wilson did onstage. But like the traveler in all those terror-shot
Robert Johnson blues, he finds himself marking highway miles alone.

"Hellhound on My Trail" was Johnson's mean animism for that re-

lentless solitude. Sam Cooke's gospel leanings let him sing of hope that he might be changed from the tortured pilgrim. But the voice on "Change" is not entirely convinced.

The year after his longtime friend Sam Cooke had died, Otis Redding recut the song on his album *Otis Blue*. Redding's is a broader, less subtle version, snagged on a few oversouled asides, but it is beautiful and full of ache. By 1965, at Stax, in Memphis, with "soul" a full-blown chart category, there was no longer great concern about masking a black man's language. Sam Cooke would surely have smiled when he heard Otis launch the verse about seeking comfort: *". . . and then I axed my little mother . . ."*

In an interview not long before his death, Otis Redding said that it was his intention to carry on the great tradition begun by Sam Cooke. And in that spirit Otis would soar—and wallow—in what came to be called deep soul, pumped undiluted out of Memphis, Tennessee.

Back North, in the city where Little Willie John and Jackie Wilson upset the first waves of urban soul children, where Sam Cooke made his fateful leap from the New Bethel Baptist Church to the Flame Show Bar— in Detroit—another kind of city soul had taken root. It dared confront and capitalize on the market schizophrenia that had plagued pioneers like Sam Cooke by deliberately aiming black-made music at a white audience. The year Sam Cooke died, 1964, the Motown sound was battling, successfully, with a quartet of white Anglo-Saxons from Liverpool for Top Ten dominance. Motown would accomplish the ultimate crossover. Unlike gutbucket soul, sprung from a moment, Motown was built, layer by layer, with a conscious aural blueprint. Like the small frame building it was housed in, it borrowed from many styles and expanded itself with whatever was on hand. It could have come only out of a city. Motown might have cribbed from the gospel and blues of a South left behind. But the children who sang there were committed to a slick new city life and sound. The Temptations gave it words: *"Just keep on walkin', don't look back."*

▮9
Motown Redux

*Going to Detroit, Michigan, girl you got to stay at
home
Going to Detroit, Michigan, Mama you've got to stay
behind
Gonna get myself a job on the Cadillac car assembly
line*

*Tired of whooping and hollering, looking down that
Mississippi Delta road,
Tired of whooping and hollering, picking that nasty
cotton
Gonna catch a bus away up north, I won't have to be
saying "Yessir, boss."*

—"CADILLAC ASSEMBLY LINE"*

ON JULY 24, 1967, General Motors chairman of the board James Roche took the elevator to the roof of GM headquarters in Detroit. From that vantage point, not far from the studios of Motown Records, he watched the plumes of smoke and flame that fueled the worst riots in that city's history. At the time, 36 percent of Detroit's population was black; so was over a quarter of the auto industry work force.

John Lee Hooker would make a blues for the Big D shortly after, about

---

*"Cadillac Assembly Line," Lyrics and music by Mack Rice, Copyright © 1975 EAST/ MEMPHIS MUSIC CORP. Copyright assigned to IRVING MUSIC INC. (BMI) 1982. All Rights Reserved. International Copyright Secured. Used by Permission.

117

how it was consuming itself. Hooker grieved for his hometown, burning down to the ground "worser than Viet Nam." All anyone could do was watch. *Wasn't a thing old Johnny could do.*

Triggered by a routine raid on a premises at Twelfth and Clairmont, the violence left 43 dead. Seven thousand people were arrested; more than 1,200 homes and businesses were destroyed. The ruined black neighborhoods, sociologists opined, perhaps weren't "communities" to begin with. In Detroit the ghetto is spread out, horizontally, in small dwellings, rather than the vertical tenements in other American cities.

"Something go bad, it spread fast and far as a crack in lake ice," a Detroit counterman told me over the pop of his griddle. "To my mind, this town ain't come to much but the miseries of fire and ice."

Everything burned easily in July 1967. Since the volatile mix of poor whites and blacks began filling the projects and factories in the twenties, Detroit has been a hospitable locale for spontaneous combustion. The rioters, city fathers were heard to observe, were largely the "hard-core unemployed," inner-city blacks who still lived and tried to work in Detroit proper.

Looking out over the devastation, auto industry executives realized, in hindsight, their grave mistake. They had still been recruiting assembly-line workers from Appalachia and the Deep South, rather than from the neighborhoods that sprawled beneath their corporate headquarters. Many of these "hard-core" Detroiters were the children and grandchildren of the first wave of workers who had come North on the strength of Mr. Ford's $5-a-day promise in 1914. By the sixties the auto industry had begun "dialogues" with the black community, but only too late did they realize the conversations were misguided.

"It turned out that we were talking to the wrong Negroes," Henry Ford II confessed to *The Saturday Evening Post* in the riot's wake. "The middle class black is as far removed from what's happening in the ghetto as we are."

One of those upwardly mobile blacks was Berry Gordy, Jr., a former chrome trimmer for Ford who had built Motown Records into a $30 million corporation by that hot summer day in 1967. Some of his artists were onstage when the trouble began. Motown Records did not burn, but the studio and offices reeked with the smoke of the fire storm a few blocks away.

Something like this had happened in Detroit when Gordy was a small child. The riot that tore the city in 1943 was a racial clash very similar to that of 1967. Since the twenties, millions of poor whites and blacks from the mountains and deltas of the South had migrated to what was being dubbed the American Ruhr, a wide coal- and iron-fed industrial belt that included cities like Chicago, Cleveland, Saginaw, Gary, Buffalo, Cincinnati, Toledo, and South Bend. Detroit, with its easy access to Great Lakes transportation, was a prized industrial stronghold.

In just the decade between 1910 and 1920 the black population had increased by more than 600 percent from before Emancipation. By 1926 Detroit's largest employers, paying an average wage of fifty-five cents an hour, were Ford, Dodge, Studebaker, Packard, and Cadillac. From the beginning, labor recruitment was concentrated almost exclusively in the Deep South. By June 1943 nearly 200,000 blacks had come to live in the Motor City, also known as Dynamic Detroit.

The blues came, too, and they adapted to their new surroundings. There was hope at first. Blind Blake sang of a faith that work in Mr. Ford's place would "stop them eatless days." Work was hard, but payday offered release in the boogie-woogie piano stylings of Cow Cow Davenport and scores of other local or itinerant bluesmen. People screamed for Big Maceo Merriweather to play his "Detroit Jump," a local favorite that helped crown him king of piano men in the night life of the roiling, smoky Black Bottom section of town. Big Maceo enjoyed the friendship and musical company of guitar great Tampa Red. From the twenties through the forties, Black Bottom twitched and jumped to the offerings of John Lee Hooker, Sippie Wallace, Little Eddie Kirkland, and Washboard Willie. Much of it went down on Hastings Street. Hastings was to Detroit what Beale Street had long been to Memphis after hours.

From nine to five, discord began to cause misfiring in the factory rhythms. Poor whites and blacks, competing for the same jobs and low-cost housing, were coming into direct conflict. Animosity deepened on both sides as blacks were forced to go beyond black neighborhoods to find housing. With the wartime industrial boom, the situation became desperate. The first sign of serious trouble was at a Packard plant turning out bomber engines for the war effort. In June 1943, when 3 black workers were upgraded, 25,000 white workers struck in protest. One white striker explained their action this way: "I'd rather see Hitler and Hirohito win than work beside a nigger on the assembly line."

In such an atmosphere it took just a small incident, a dispute between blacks and whites on the crowded Belle Island bridge one hot Sunday night, to detonate citywide violence. The riots began on the night of June

20, 1943, and left thirty-five people dead, twenty-nine of them black. A report to U.S. Supreme Court Justice Frank Murphy confirmed that nearly all the dead blacks had been killed by a police force made up of many southern whites. The report also found that some of the dead had been shot in the back and concluded that "anti-Negro motivations of the Detroit Police Department" appeared responsible for a good deal of the carnage.

From that point on, Detroit was known as Distress City. It responded briefly to the boom euphoria of the Eisenhower years, building portholed and finned gas guzzlers for a car-crazy nation. Progress of this sort muted the blues; Hastings Street and its clubs were bulldozed in the fifties to make way for the Chrysler Freeway. Bluesmen scattered to clubs and bars on Mack Avenue and Twelfth Street. By the mid-sixties that musical community was as divided and weakened as the rest of the inner city. Like many of its midwestern industrial neighbors, Detroit had begun to feel its age and regret the excesses of its youth. It was too set in its ways to kick the dependency on a single industry, which itself depended on fossil fuels. Its economic vulnerability became the butt of a popular saying: "When the rest of the nation gets a cold, Detroit gets pneumonia."

"Now I'll tell you the joke of the day," says Joe Billingslea, a forty-six-year-old Detroiter who has been, with varying degrees of satisfaction, a Motown singing star (with the Contours), an auto worker (for Chrysler), and, currently, a Detroit policeman. Rocking his big, aged Chevy into an icebound parking spot, he is telling the joke to dispel any tension about the pearl-handled revolver strapped to his right hip.

"Crime is the only thing that *don't* freeze in a Detroit winter. But anyhow, the joke goes like this. When you land at the Detroit airport nowadays, they frisk you for a weapon. And baby, if you don't have one, they *issue* you one before they let you in."

Which is why, he says, no fool is going to walk into a place like Jimmy D's Celebrity House restaurant out here on Livernois without some form of metal-alloy life insurance. Besides a lot of ice, there is a good deal of broken glass outside on the sidewalk. Dispositions are a touch brittle, too.

"Been one of them weekends," Joe mutters as we pick our way to the door.

Super Bowl XVI, held two days before in nearby Pontiac, did little to lift the deep freeze of economic gloom. Nor was it especially soothing to Jimmy D's clientele when Mr. Reagan smiled benignly over the TV and, right at the outset of his first State of the Union address, intoned: ". . . and for you auto workers in Detroit . . ."

Seems the man was going on about some new economic plan he had, something called enterprise zones.

"Detroit cops are payin' for their own gas to patrol," Joe says. "Now I guess that's what you call enterprise."

Joe is off duty tonight and has called a group meeting of the retooled Contours. He and Council Gay, better known as Count, are the only original members. Joe recruited the others—Bean, Breeze, and Arthur—"from around." They all worked on some harmonies and steps and listened to the old records. They have gotten a few decent gigs around town, and tonight the group, whose average age is about forty-five, will be negotiating with a local promoter for a weekend club engagement.

"Beanie, Beanie. Where you been?"

We had stopped by Bean's small brick house minutes before and found it dark. Now Joe finds him at the bar, staring disconsolately into a glass of orange juice.

"Couldn't stay in that house. No. Not tonight."

His wife has gone with their daughter to the hospital where a fourth grandchild is being delivered. His house is scheduled for foreclosure within the month.

"There's the man," he says to Joe, eyeballing a slick type in a knee-length leather coat who has swept in and commanded a large table. "Let's get us that gig," Bean says. "You know I need it."

"Watch it, Bean. Man got some buzzard in him. Don't let him know your troubles."

Within minutes the others arrive, drinks are ordered, and the moneyman lets it be known that he's hip to the shape of things as far as the Contours go. He knows that Count and Arthur got laid off the factories, that Breeze is still hanging on at GM, but barely. Somehow he even knows about Bean's foreclosure. Nobody has money; that is why his offer for the two nights' work is so insultingly low. In trios and in pairs the Contours repair to the gents' to discuss it, while Mr. Compassion works on whoever's left.

"You wanna keep your house, right, Beanie?"

And to Arthur, the handsome lead singer who is wearing a suit and a tweed cap: "You pretty, that's true." He snatches the cap off Arthur's head before he can stop him. "But you goin' *bald*, man."

After an hour only Bean has weakened. Joe is staring into his beer, mute with rage.

"Keep it," he says finally. The meeting breaks up, and the moneyman is left alone at the table, counting off empty glasses to match them to the check.

"How it is ain't how it was," Joe says as we head back into town on Livernois. Might be nice to stop in at the Motown office and take a look around.

The following afternoon the Motown sound is sharp and unnerving. Tires spin and whinny on greasy, road-blackened ice. Joe lets the Chevy shudder its engine down in front of 2648 West Grand Avenue, the address known worldwide in the sixties as Hitsville, U.S.A. The sign on the peeling blue-trimmed white frame house still says that, though the building is now kept more for sentiment than for function. Beginning in 1960, it was the home of Motown Records and its subsidiary labels, Gordy, Tamla, and Soul. Motown was, in its PR slogans and on the airwaves, "The Sound of Young America." But since 1973 Motown's main offices have been relocated in a steely gray skyscraper on L.A.'s Sunset Boulevard. Those offices house the Motown Record Company and a clutch of film, publishing, and management subsidiaries. All of them were built on a shoestring operation that began with a $700 investment in 1960 in Detroit.

It was the calculated gamble of Berry Gordy, Jr., the restless son of a plastering contractor. The seed money was borrowed from the family credit union. At the time it was hardly a safe bet. Gordy had tried professional boxing and given it up. A stint as an $86.40-a-week assembly-line worker was even less promising. Retailing was a bust as well; Gordy's 3-D Record Mart had gone bankrupt in 1955.

In 1960 Detroit had the fourth largest black population in America, more than half a million. Blacks liked and made and bought music, but there were no substantial record companies there to press and sell the abundance of local black talent. Artists like Della Reese, Hank Ballard, and Little Willie John had all been recruited by companies based in other cities, notably Cincinnati's King Records. Brunswick, a revived black subsidiary of Decca, survived on the strength of Detroit's Jackie Wilson, who could credit his early solo successes in part to the songwriting help of Berry Gordy. The two had met in a Detroit boxing gym. Wilson's "Reet Petite," "To Be Loved," and "Lonely Teardrops" were cowritten by Gordy, his sister Gwendolyn, and Tyran Carlo. Encouraged by this success, Gwen

Gordy founded her own record label, called Anna. Her husband, Harvey Fuqua, himself once a singer with the Moonglows, also started Tri Phi Records. Later, both labels would merge with the new company Berry Gordy founded and named after his hometown.

Joe Billingslea announces us through the intercom to the Motown receptionist, who buzzes us inside. It was twenty years ago that Joe and his four friends auditioned right here, in the minuscule reception area. They called themselves the Contours, shortened from the Rhythm Contours.

"Yeah, the Con-*tours.*" Joe pronounces it with the accent on the second syllable. "Don't mean nothin'. I just liked the way it sounds. Con-*tours.* Me, Billy Gordon, on lead, Billy Hoggs, Sylvester Potts, Hubert Johnson— we all come in, right on this spot, and gave it all we had."

Berry Gordy, leaning back on the receptionist's desk, seemed unimpressed with the group.

"Uh-huh. Thanks, guys. Come back in, oh, maybe six months."

But they were back in fewer than two hours, following the intercession of Jackie Wilson, who was Hubert Johnson's cousin.

"We sang the same song the same way," Joe remembers, "and got our contracts half an hour later."

The receptionist, an old friend, informs Joe that he missed Diana Ross by twenty minutes. Diane, as everyone knew her then, had stopped by in her limo to visit with Berry Gordy's sister Esther Gordy Edwards, who runs the Detroit office.

"Diane looked *bad,*" the receptionist is saying. "Fur coat. Maybe silver fox, I don't know. *So* beautiful, I swear. Better-looking than ever."

"I know," Joe says. "I saw her on the news."

Except for a few partitions and the persistent grind of a swiveling TV security monitor, he notes that little has changed since he swept the floors back in the early sixties. Until a group got on its musical feet, odd jobs were parceled out to singers like Joe, who already had four children to feed on his $50-a-week salary. As the operation grew, there was always something that needed doing.

"I *built* that studio on West Grand," Temptation David Ruffin had told me. "Me and Pops. Did it all by hand."

Pops was Berry Gordy, Sr., a cotton farmer from Georgia who had moved North in the twenties, with hopes of bettering his lot. He was a model of ambition to his eight children, expanding beyond his plastering business to a grocery store and print shop while his wife, Bertha, looked after real estate and insurance interests. Sweat equity was a family bylaw. And so, when Berry, Jr., set up shop in the house on West Grand, the small but growing Motown "family" undertook the renovation. Pops and his teenage work crew nailed up the acoustic wall tiles, painted, and partitioned the tiny cubicles that would accommodate songwriters/producers like Holland-Dozier-Holland and Smokey Robinson.

"You know," Joe is saying, "it looks so much the same I'm feelin' a little weird."

Atop battered file cabinets, there is a yellowing cardboard promo for a 1971 Diana Ross TV special. Just past the reception area, the narrow passage to Studio A is blocked by a glossy life-size cardboard figure of current Motown luminary Rick James. James is a former staff songwriter, now a glitter/funk act given to S & M album art, onstage dope smoking, and X-rated lyrics that would have caused sixties Young America to swallow its retainer plate. In 1981 he was easily selling out 80,000-seat stadiums. The cardboard James's costume is *Marat/Sade* meets *Star Wars,* body parts cantilevered by strips of leather and vinyl.

Joe is peering at the braided and beaded hair construction, which, it has been reported, takes twelve hours to complete. Gently lifting the smirking Mr. James, Joe carefully moves the thing aside. "Up against the wall, my man."

There is a perceptible drop in temperature as we step through the door into the control room. It is largely unused and, so, unheated. Breath fogs the plate-glass window as Joe peers down into the studio itself. The tableau is ghostly, like a crime scene photo that freezes on a family's unfinished dinner.

The space itself is no larger than a suburban rumpus room. Sheet music lies open to a "Supremes Medley." The stool is pushed back from a huge black concert grand. A set of drumsticks is propped against the acoustic wall tiles. These yellowing squares bear the hieroglyphics of some boisterous past civilization, punctured by producers' ball-points, gouged by swinging guitar necks, sliced in demure patterns by the sharp, lacquered fingernails of nervous young girls. Toward the back lies a clumsy, battered brown speaker, its rubber diaphragm exposed and slightly cracked from the cold.

"It all came out of that sucker," Joe says. "To this minute I remember what it sounded like. The groups worked right there in front of it. The tracks came out of that thing and hit you square in the chest. Made you jump, you know. Made *everything* move."

Backup singers went one on one with the single yard-long speaker. Lead singers were sometimes cosseted in a phone booth-size cubicle raised to the right of the gray metal control board. Marvin Gaye was incarcerated in that booth for hours, Joe remembers, while producers whipped up on his voice until it was raw enough for his 1963 hit "Hitch Hike."

The Contours' sound, he says, was naturally rough, more R & B. There was nothing polite about "Whole Lotta Woman." Their biggest hit ever, "Do You Love Me?," was the subhysteric rant of a frustrated lover. Unlike the majority of the other Motown acts in 1962, the Contours had a high voltage stage show to support the record.

"We were the best dancers, that's the truth," Joe says. "We did splits, jumped through each other's legs, dove headfirst, did spins, slides, all that stuff. People would *scream*. Kim Weston used to hate it. She had to follow us a lot, and it was hard because some of those people would still be screamin'."

By the fall of 1962 Berry Gordy had bullied and cajoled a string of bookings for his package show, citing sales of national hits like the Marvelettes' "Please Mr. Postman" and "Beechwood 45789," Mary Wells's "The One Who Really Loves You" and "You Beat Me to the Punch," and the Miracles' "Shop Around." Once he had the dates lined up and the logistics figured, he assembled his troupes to lay out a plan for conquering Young America. A bus and five cars waited outside for the forty-five nervous and excited passengers, among them the Contours, the Marvelettes, the Supremes, Mary Wells, Marvin Gaye, and the tiny Steveland Morris, a precocious blind twelve-year-old Motown had renamed Little Stevie Wonder.

"It was right down there, against that back wall," Joe says, pointing to the far end of the studio. "Berry lined us up. The bus was already started up. And he gave us this little speech, you know, that we were representing Motown, that we should be men and women and all."

Turning his collar up against the cold, he leads the way out of the frigid studio and upstairs to the warren of rooms that function as a museum of sorts. Keeper of the guest book is company executive Esther Gordy Edwards. Seated behind the desk in her second-floor office, she is a startling contrast with the slapdash surroundings, a serious, businesslike woman in designer Ultrasuede with matching burnt orange accessories.

Suggesting a tour, Mrs. Edwards points to a small room that has a glass case in one corner. A set of suits from the Temptations' last tour (before the departure of David Ruffin and Eddie Kendricks) hangs limply from hangers above three pairs of matching ankle-high boots. The boot tops are flopped over, limp from the exertions of the Tempts' ball-bearing ankle joints. Sequined flames lick up the arms and trouser cuffs of one suit. The scalloped lapels are curling on a shiny white tux.

"Hey, look here."

In a room around the corner Joe has found the first publicity still of the Contours. "Just look at us," he says. "Like kids at Christmas. Like the party never gonna end."

End it did, in the late sixties. The Contours would never eclipse the success of "Do You Love Me?" although "First, I Look at the Purse" and "A Little Misunderstanding" did creditable business on the R & B charts. The group knew something was up when Berry Gordy called them off a tour, all the way back from New York, to work a low-rent Detroit record hop. In the dispute that followed, three of them quit. They turned over the keys and registration to the group's car, got their royalties, and walked out with their pride and their name—something many other Motown acts were unable to do. Motown still owns, in total or in part, the names the Temptations, the Vandellas, the Marvelettes, the Supremes. Even the Jackson Five were forced to become the Jacksons when they switched labels.

"Well, then I went to work in the factory," Joe says, still looking at the photo. "Worked for Chrysler. Worked for a year as a crane operator and got in union politics and ran for chief steward. I was CS for about four years. Then, all of a sudden, I was in the union room, listening to the radio."

"Do you luhhhhhv me?"

Joe looked up from the container of vending machine coffee and heard Billy Gordon's hoarse, frayed-libido lead: *"Well, do you love me?"*

"Somebody said, 'Whatever happened to the Contours?' And I said, 'Hey, I'm not supposed to be in here.' So I quit, right then. But then I joined the police department. 'Cause when I thought about it, I didn't want to sing anymore. I'd been through that circus. Then I started going to clubs again, watching. And I'd realize we were better than lots of these guys they got now. So I hooked up with some of the guys, and we said, 'Aw, man, let's try it.' Then we found Billy Gordon, our lead singer, he had come out of the penitentiary . . . aw, but enough of this shit."

He moves down the wall, chuckling at a photo of Little Stevie Wonder, perched stiffly like a ventriloquist's dummy on Muhammad Ali's knee.

On a wall by itself is a framed copy of the Motown company song, a treacly all-for-one and one-for-all pep chant penned by none other than Smokey Robinson. Employees are neat and clean, it burbles. The company is swinging. Unity conquers all at Hitsville, U.S.A.

"Hey," says Joe, "check this out. It's exactly the thing I was telling you about."

He is pointing to a ten- by twelve-inch glossy snapped moments before that first Motortown Revue hit the road, in the fall of 1962.

"We were just kids," Joe says. "And at that moment we thought we were the luckiest alive."

The group in the photo does look like the pep squad for an inner-city high school. There are long-legged Miracles; grinning Contours; Diana, Mary, and Florence, the Supremes, clutching tightly to Leatherette purses. There is a full complement of shiny, pointed boots, mohair sweaters, boxy cameras slung around necks. Two stout, stern-faced women chaperones stand among them. Like most of the photos that line the walls here, the graduating class is beaming its best "most-likely-to" smiles.

"Aw, look at us all," Joe says. "We had no idea in the world where we were *really* off to."

Officially the first stop was the Howard Theater in Washington, D.C. The tour wound through the Midwest and as far South as Miami. By December, after about twenty-five one-night stands, it had reached the Apollo in New York. During that ten-day engagement Berry Gordy contracted to have his road show recorded live.

Poorly recorded and mixed, *Recorded Live at the Apollo, Vol. I* is as telling an aural portrait as the photo on the wall. Some of the voices are still woefully untrained. Fear and the obvious strain of the tour snag notes and phrasings.

Doing "Whole Lotta Woman," the Contours' lead, Billy Gordon, sounds more like Wynonie Harris, more hard-core R & B than the sound Motown came up with for later acts. The "new" act at the time, the Supremes, gets only tepid applause for a nasal rendition of "Let Me Go the Right Way." Mary Wells worries aloud about making "boo-boos." Stevie Wonder borders on the hilarious as he kiddie-vamps the adult stylings of singers with quadruple his testosterone level. As Marvin Gaye struggles through "What Kind of Fool Am I?" trumpets fart in all the wrong places.

Throughout that show, the band chickabooms along with wedding hall mediocrity, and this early, live Motown sound is almost unrecognizable from the slick productions the company would come to trade on so heavily.

Only one act that night came close to approximating its sound on record, a group the emcee describes as one of the "early pioneers" in rock and roll "as far as girl groups are concerned—the Marvelettes!"

Berry Gordy reinvented the name when staffer Robert Bateman brought the Marvels to his attention. Bateman had heard five teenage girls from Inkster, a Detroit suburb. They auditioned with the Chantels' "Maybe," a record that was to girl groups what "Earth Angel" was to male quartets. By the time the Marvelettes' "Please Mr. Postman" hit big enough to spin off "Twistin' Postman" in 1962, the group had been whittled to three: lead singer Gladys Horton, Wanda Young, and Katherine Anderson. Onstage and on record the Marvelettes were polite, but to the point:

You better watch out, girls, for that playboy.

Back off, and don't mess with Bill. Like what you see? An' the number is Beechwood fo'fiveseveneightnine.

Whispering confidences, snapping out warnings, Gladys Horton could conjure the aura of a high school girls' lav, cigarette smoke curling from the stalls, the wastebaskets heaped with lipstick-kissed Kleenex.

"Them girls," Joe Billingslea is saying. "They were always whisperin'. You know, wonderin' did Berry think they were cute, gossiping about Marvin and how handsome he was, all that kind of stuff. Sometimes they would do a little office work, you know, filin' session notes and whatnot, all these little chicks just chatterin' away. Berry or Smokey [Robinson] walk by, they clam up, just like the principal's cruisin' the halls."

They wanted to be model pupils above all else, Joe says, "and get a hit offa Smokey."

In those heady, got-to-have-another-hit days, Gordy passed out Smokey Robinson songs like nickel candy to the best and brightest. William "Smokey" Robinson wrote hits for nearly everyone as well as for himself and the Miracles. Joe points out the spot where Gordy erected a four- by six-foot cubicle to accommodate his master composer.

"Smokey is a Motown vice-president now," Joe says. "Did you know that? Got a big suite, secretaries, the whole bit. And he should. I mean, just as much as Berry, that cat *is* Motown."

10
Still Smokin'

I will always bless Smokey Robinson for those slow dance records. I was about sixteen, and back then, on a Saturday night, you know they're gonna play Smokey's "Ooo Baby Baby," you'd think how you gonna dress. You go to that party in dark *pants. Yeah, that was a black slack record for sure.*

—DEXTER, a fan

BERRY GORDY HAS CALLED HIM Motown's Honorable Undergrounder and a bread-and-butter artist. Nearly thirty years into his career, William "Smokey" Robinson has only to release a record and several hundred thousand people will buy it not because it is a hit or is getting airplay but because it is Smokey. His fans are as faithful as the lovers in the thousands of songs he has written.

On stage, and on his last few album covers, there is a hazy, airbrushed look about him. It may be due to a decade of California living, or the technology of Lurex and stage lighting, but to true believers it is an aura: foxfire on the dusky perimeter of erotic memory; first love, first kiss, first base, home run. If you came of age in sixties America, chances are Smokey was there with you, soothing, encouraging. Amid the awkward fumbling, the back seat wrestling, Smokey held out the promise of endless, ideal love. And when the tension got unbearable, he could make you dance. *Going to a Go-Go,* with Venus last stop.

Smokey—steadfast keeper of the eternal flame of pop romance. He carried it through the sixties with the Miracles and a fusillade of hits like "Ooo Baby Baby," "You've Really Got a Hold on Me," and "The Love I Saw in You Was Just a Mirage." He tended it quietly in the studio when disco froze out soul and substance in the seventies. And now, at forty-four, Smokey is still carrying torches, blazing into the eighties with gold singles and albums and titles like "Being with You" and "I've Made Love to You a Thousand Times." The adolescent sentiments have settled into a comfortable maturity; the voice can still pull a note like taffy and keep it sweet.

As a songwriter he remains an undaunted humanist. Smokey Robinson's lyrics are peopled with perfect lovers, men who don't just like, they *love,* and forever, not just till payday. You can hurt them badly, and they'll still love you madly, will tell you unflinchingly that you really got a *hold* on them, that you're forever. You're his now, and his then. Smokey—here was a Galahad in a glinting sharkskin suit of mail, riding on a water-smooth melody, that gallant voice leaping into reeking school gyms, into dim paneled basements, cutting through playground jive on a three- by five-inch eight-buck turquoise Japanese transistor, pleading, sweetly, "Baby, baby, don't cry." This was no Wicked Pickett, no tomcattin', predatory man-and-a-half Teddy Pendergrass type who might snack on a woman's heart and throw the rest to his Doberman. Smokey would serve his own heart up on a platter, with a side of endearments.

"Honey," Smokey says, squeezing a plastic bottle of Sue Bee pure honey. "I eat a lot of it. Don't smoke, don't drink, don't eat meat."

"He just *don't,* period," says road manager Randy Duncan. "Cat only eats oatmeal and raisins."

Fried egg is the *air du temps* in this Manhattan hotel suite, cooked by Smokey's secretary on the hot plate he insists on toting along into the most la-di-da tower suites. He says he himself is a fair hand with a skillet.

"Let me show you something," he says, and disappears into the bedroom. Amid much clanging he reemerges juggling a matched set of olive green saucepans and skillets.

"I started cooking on the road because of segregation," he says. "Now I can get anything I want from room service. And I can pay for it well enough. But I'll be damned if I'll pay seventeen-fifty for frozen orange juice and a pair of vulcanized eggs that are gonna terrorize my insides. On the road I prefer to be sufficient unto myself.''

In a maroon Lacoste shirt, jeans, and soft slippers, he looks more like a suburban squire than a road-toughened soul man. The eyes are light, nearly green, and the modest Afro of the late Miracle years has relaxed into tiny ringlets. The mustache is wispy and nearly always fringing a smile. Suspended on a gold necklace is the message "Try God." He says he believes deeply in God, though he never found a church liberal enough for his let-it-be world view. He is, in fact, one of those rare post-Eisenhower wonders, a truly happy man. He is a prospering vice-president of Motown Records, a millionaire, and is still, after so many years, a million seller. He is a devoted husband to his childhood sweetheart, Claudette, and doting father of two subteens. The girl, Tamla, is named for one of Gordy's record labels; the boy, after Berry himself. Smokey is a company man, he says, since the company was founded largely on his music. And if there have been occasional blue notes, the more dominant harmonies have washed them away.

He moves the set of saucepans from a coffee table and stretches his legs. He says he has finally learned to make being on the road bearable for himself. It has taken nearly two decades to work out the delicate balance among lover, husband, daddy, and heartthrob. He says he finally got it together in the early seventies, after a bit of enforced meditation.

"I was burned-out. Fried, you understand? I was sick to death of the road. By 1972, when I decided to split with the Miracles, my son was four, and my daughter had just been born. Claudette [a former Miracle and his wife of twenty-six years] had had a number of miscarriages. So we really *wanted* those babies, and once we had them, I didn't want to be a celebrity to them. I said, 'This is it for me; I'll never go onstage or record again. I'll write, I'll produce, and that will be it.' "

It was, for a time. He says he played a lot of golf and discharged the official duties of his company vice-presidency, signing payroll checks, scouting new talent, and reading memos.

"I guess it took about a year to come on me. I found myself in the audience of every act that came to L.A., spooking around the back row, listening, aching somehow. I was happy but unhappy. Just kind of doldrumming away."

Watching him around the house, Claudette and the kids suffered the restless fallout of an energetic thirty-two-year-old retiree. "You're going stone crazy," she told him. "And if you don't do something, you'll take us all with you. Get into that studio and record something on yourself. I don't care if you never release it. Just *sing*."

He sang, and he released it, and still the hits came, first "Baby Come Close," next "Cruisin'," then "Being with You." Singles and albums went gold again, as did his disposition. The woman always had sense, he says. He has loved Claudette since they were teenagers, madly, faithfully, just like in his songs. But in that first audition, back in Detroit, a talent scout warned him that the girl in the group, this Claudette chick, would be nothing but trouble.

"Understand, it was real typical, our start. We had our little groups. So we sang, all of us, in the recreation centers with about a thousand other groups, had battles of the groups, the whole bit.

"If boys and girls were really tight, the brother/sister group was a big thing. You know, the boys had a group, and the girls were the Whateverettes. We had a little group first called the Matadores. Same personnel as the Miracles—myself, Pete Moore, Bobby Rogers, and Ron White. And early on Bobby's brother Sonny. And we had us some bad little Matadorettes."

One of them was his future bride.

"We used to practice at the Rogers', and Claudette was their sister. Sonny decided to go into the service. We had this audition coming up. It was the summer I graduated from high school. And suddenly we were one voice short for the five-part harmony we did. Just two days before the audition we decided to put Claudette in the group."

Smokey sinks back on the sofa, twisting the long body into a position that will ease a pinched nerve in his neck. He says he can't stand wearing the foam surgical collar the doctor gave him. Worse, it's just a little embarrassing to tell people he got the injury playing in a celebrity golf tournament in California. If anyone had told him, after that first audition, that he would someday purr across velvety Beverly Hills putting greens in a canopied golf cart, well. . . .

"We *failed* that audition. And miserably. Guy told us it was because we should have used Claudette like the girl in Mickey and Sylvia. They were real popular then, and their sound was more duet-type stuff.

"We were slinking out of there like dogs when this guy stopped us. He introduced himself as Berry Gordy, and he wanted to know where we got this little song we did, 'My Mamma Done Told Me.' I told him I wrote it and showed him my notebook. I had about a hundred songs in it, and out of the hundred, he really liked that one."

Since he bought his first Big Chief writing tablet with earnings from his Detroit *Free Press* paper route at age eleven, Smokey had been doodling at songs. He says that most of the compositions he showed Gordy were in the moon-June, teen angel mode, "all mush, with no commercial edge." With Gordy's help, he worked to smooth the edges in the songwriting and the singing. Ever hopeful, the Matadores became the Miracles.

"When we first started to record, there was no Motown Records," Smokey says. "But Berry got us on End [out of New York], which was a real big deal for us. Little Anthony and the Imperials, all our heroes were on End."

The Miracles' first End release, "Got a Job," came out on February 19, 1958, Smokey Robinson's eighteenth birthday.

"[Miracle] Bobby Rogers and I were actually born on the same day in the same hospital," he says. "But we didn't meet knowingly until we were fourteen. So yeah, we got the record for our birthday. And I guess you could say, technically, we sure did—got a job. We were working recording artists. But contractually things didn't work out. There was this little problem of money."

He says that Berry Gordy still has the $3.19 royalty check they received after "Got a Job" hit number one on the R & B charts nationwide. The fee was actually for four songs; "My Mamma Done Told Me" was the flip side to the hit, and the Miracles recorded another 45. Its titles were "I Cried" and "I Need Some Money." Berry Gordy had the check framed and hung it on his wall, Smokey says, for inspiration.

"Berry had been screwed enough. He decided to start Motown. We had maybe four people, and Berry had an apartment. We were working with Marv Johnson, who had the first ever Motown disc ["Come to Me," in 1959]. Berry and I drove up to the pressing plant, up north in Owosso, Michigan. We went to pick up Marv's records, about two hundred and fifty of them, and took the records out to the radio stations ourselves. And suddenly the record was breaking so big locally we couldn't handle it. So Berry arranged a distribution deal with United Artists."

If the financing and the distribution weren't yet in place, the dream was. And it was carefully constructed from the very beginning.

"Berry wanted to make crossover music," Smokey says. "Crossover at that time meant that white people would buy your records. Berry's concept in starting Motown was to make music with a funky beat and great stories that would be crossover, that would *not* be blues. And that's what we did."

The blue note was leavened by pop hooks that grabbed across color lines. The blues, Smokey says, meant torment to him. Things kids weren't ready for. Kids saw torment in their parents, but they themselves weren't about to succumb. Dance fast enough, and you can cross a hot tin roof barefoot. "I Got to Dance to Keep from Crying" was the title of one of Smokey's early compositions. Like many of the songs he wrote in the early sixties, it had a youthful, urban jumpiness.

"I guess you could say there was an air of mobility to them," he says. "Me, Berry, everybody. Wasn't any of us about to stay put."

At the time America was still buying that eight-cylinder promise. Gaudy, voracious cars grew to look more like flying ships. Over the centuries the notion of freedom may have mutated from fifty acres of bottomland to a full tank and an open four-lane. But that American obsession with promise has never disappeared. There is a kind of stubbornness to it all.

"Well now, despite all the wrecks on the highway, you still keep getting in your car and driving, don't you?" Smokey says. "Call it stupid or call it an act of faith. It's a lot like love. Even if you've been hurt, I mean almost terminally, you keep looking for it. I am an optimist, a romantic in that way, and I always have been. In the stuff I was writing, early on, and still, there was pain, but there was hope, which the blues didn't have. And that's the kind of music I enjoyed. We took it a step further to try and make melody and words memorable and a dance beat very, very audible. Berry was just a business genius in that regard."

There were, as anywhere, misses as well as hits. Gordy recorded a number of groups and individuals that sank like lead lug nuts. Some of the masters he released himself. Others he leased to more solvent companies like Chess that could chance floating a few so-so singles. Smokey recalls names like Lee and the Leopards, the Valadiers, the Satintones, Mike and the Modifiers, Bunny Paul, Henry Lumpkin, Singin' Sammi Ward, the Gospel Harmonettes, and a funky bunch calling themselves Popcorn and the Mohawks. Gordy also recorded white sixties TV stars, among them Soupy Sales, Irene Ryan (Granny on *The Beverly Hillbillies),* and Paul Petersen of *The Donna Reed Show.*

"Lamont Dozier, Eddie Holland, everybody fooled around and recorded themselves, too," Smokey says. "They knew a lot about music, and some had very nice voices. Most of that was for fun, though. We got very serious with the acts that hit."

The Miracles hit again in 1958 with "Bad Girl." Again it broke too big for the four-man, three-room, one-car operation, and the record was released through Chess. Again no cash flow.

"We cut 'Way over There' next, and Berry and I decided to go national with that record. We had moved the whole mess to a two-family house; we had a downstairs flat."

"Way over There" was a hit, but still, distributors didn't have enough confidence in a black label run "out of a Roach Motel," as Smokey says.

"We just decided we'd have to keep at it and not let up, so we came right back with 'Shop Around.' Now I'd written that song for Barrett Strong. I was playing it on the piano, and Berry loved it. 'We're gonna cut this on you,' he told me. I had the flu, I felt like a dog. He called us into the studio at three A.M. He said he heard another beat in there somewhere, and he wanted to change the feeling. Well, we did it. And 'Shop Around' became like the Motown national anthem. It finally caused the distributors to have faith. 'Shop Around' put Motown on the map."

The phone in the suite has begun to trill with inquiries about the evening's concert. Sound check will begin soon; has the band been informed? Guitarist Marv Tarplin, whose melodies have long interlocked with and helped invent Smokey's lyrics, would like to noodle out some song ideas. Can they? When should the limo come by? Anything he would like in the limo refrigerator?

When the Miracles first hit the road, gas was about seventeen cents a gallon, and buying half a tank ate up the entire travel budget.

"Our first professional date was in Ypsilanti," he remembers. "With B. B. King. It wasn't a nice place, but it wasn't too bad, and B.B. made sure we were as comfortable as we could be. B.B. knew the road. Was wrestling with that old witch long before we gave it a thought."

Ann Arbor, Flint, and Ypsilanti offered a rugged apprenticeship to a bunch of kids too young to order a beer. "We played everywhere, even the back of hay trucks, places where you had to stand on the bar and sing, in a room the size of this one. In fact, if you'll stand up, I'll show you what it was like."

He leaps from the sofa and pins me against a wall, so close I can count his eyelashes.

"See where I am? In your face, right? Can't breathe? Can't see over my shoulder? Now imagine. I'm skinny, don't weigh much more than you at that point, and everyone in the room is a head bigger. So I'm singing into some big dude's chest. And the guy behind him is screaming, 'Wait, I can't hear that little motherfucker sing his little motherfuckin' *song.* ' "

Young America wasn't supposed to sound like *that*.

"Ten minutes later I'm ducking wine bottles and high-heeled shoes that could pierce your heart. Most of those gigs turned out one big riotous fight. We got out by the skin of our teeth. Money? Honey, nobody stuck around for that. Berry had this big old car and he'd have the thing started up outside the door with the windows rolled down. We'd fly in the windows, doors, any which way, and jet off.''

He is laughing, having released his captive, and offers to continue the narrative at the sound check for the evening's concert at Radio City Music Hall.

Hours later, after a nap, Smokey stands on the huge Music Hall stage, peering out at the darkened house.

"*Whooaa.* Flashback. I'll be right back, I want to see something.''

He jumps from the stage and sprints up the center aisle. When he reaches the back of the theater, he stands in the dark for a few moments until an usherette spots him and her squeal rouses him from a reverie.

"I was remembering,'' he says when he returns. "I was a kid. It was 1958, I guess. And somehow the Miracles got a weeklong gig at the Apollo. Really, by rights we should have been on for amateur night. It was the most frightening thing that had ever happened to me. It was daytime, but the theater was pitch-black, so dark. We walked in, and our knees were knockin' ''

When their eyes adjusted, the Miracles saw the Apollo house band dead-eyeing them from the stage.

"Let's have 'em.'' The rehearsal director held out a beefy hand.

"Excuse me?''

"The arrangements. Ain't you got no arrangements, boy? Chord sheets at least?''

"Well, no, we just worked with some guys in the studio, guys from around Detroit you know, and—''

"Then get lost. Beat it. You can't be in no show without arrangements. Not at the Apollo.''

Smokey's bony shoulders slumped beneath the humiliation when suddenly a hoarse voice boomed from the darkness at the back of the theater: "WHY YOU GUYS DOIN' THESE BOYS LIKE THAT?''

It was Brother Ray Charles, heaven-sent via 125th Street. Smokey remembers that Ray stalked up to the stage without bumping a seat and stopped just a few inches from the awestruck group.

"Oh, God sent him, I *swear* it. Ray said, 'Who's the leader?' and I squeaked out, 'I am.' He called me over to the piano, sat down, and once I cued him, he started to sing 'Bad Girl.' It was like he already knew it.''

Sung in his soulful, roughed-up way, it had a musky wallop that was far from Smokey's fluty piping, but Ray knew how to frame the melody with the right touches from the Apollo band.

"He said, 'Okay, you horn players do this here; you in the rhythm section, hit it when I nod.' By the time he was finished we had an arrangement. It went beautifully. I was frightened to death, every show, for that entire week. But we killed. Oh, yes, I will *always* love Brother Ray."

For Smokey, the next truly memorable date at the Apollo would be that first Motortown Revue. As elder statesman and as "Shop Around" hit maker he was both the headliner and, he says, "the chief worrier." Foremost on his mind was the material he had worked up for and recorded on the pretty nineteen-year-old Mary Wells, a favorite of Berry Gordy's and, in that year, 1962, responsible for three of the ten Motown records that reached the Top Ten. She was Smokey's first major success as a producer.

What could be finer than the Poet of Eros coaching the ripe but vulnerable Miss Heartbreak? A man who wrote so often, so convincingly about love could peer out from the glass control booth, lock eyes with the pliant, eager-to-please young woman behind the mike and tell her, "Mary, sing it like you are really *hurt*."

"Mary wrote that first record of hers, 'Bye Bye Baby,' " Smokey says. "But after that, it was up to us. I kept doing those things Berry told me—you know, put a little story in the song to keep people's interest. That's exactly what I tried to do in 'Two Lovers' for Mary."

The lyrics had a crafty reverse spin in the finest tradition of a *Twilight Zone* script of that era. The singer has two lovers, and she ain't ashamed. She goes on about loving them both in a light, almost vampy way until the end, when we learn that both mysterious lovers are different sides of the same man. A split personal-a-tee.

It is a twist that would become a Robinson trademark, part of the irresistible buoyancy that would induce even the dour Bob Dylan to pronounce him one of America's finest poets. Besides all the Motown artists, singers as diverse as Linda Ronstadt, Johnny Rivers, and the Rolling Stones have found success with Smokey Robinson covers.

By his reckoning, Smokey has written more than 4,000 songs and published about 1,500 of them. He says they just come. Sometimes it is a phrase; sometimes, a few bars of a melody. Very often it is that quirky desire to turn language on itself. "Sort of like holding words to a mirror," he says, "and checking out reverse images."

And so it is that Smokey has written about choosy beggars, miragelike loves. The hunter gets captured by the game in the Marvelettes' hit by that title; the lonely glad-hand, in "Tears of a Clown." For his old neighborhood friend Aretha Franklin, Smokey wrote "Daydreaming at Night," which she recorded on her *Jump to It* album. Once, when he was Christmas shopping in a Detroit department store, he took a friend's conversational slip of the tongue and made it into a hit song, "I Second That Emotion," in 1967.

He says that songwriting, rather than performing, is his first love and what he hopes to be known best for. Still, he is the foremost interpreter of his compositions. The high, seductive tenor can make the schmaltziest lyrics seem soulful. Only Smokey would dare, as late as 1982, to rhyme "possum" with "lotus blossom" in a song.

He says he was amused but not dismayed when his 1979 hit "Cruisin' " brought critical raves and clerical cries to ban it from the airwaves. "It is in the ear of the listener," he says. "Now you can hear it as—well, pardon me—what some people have called a fuck song, that it's about the act of making love. Some people think it's about gays cruisin' each other, that sort of thing. Or you can take it just as an idealistic, old-fashioned love song. You know, baby, I just love *bein'* with you, cruisin' around."

It's a sexual ambiguity that clearly delights him. Just as his idealized, silhouettes-on-the-shade romance sold in the early sixties, the dreamy ambiguity of "Cruisin' " was boffo in the bi- , tri- , multisexual eighties. It put him back on the charts in a big way for the first time since his self-imposed layoff. And no one was more surprised by its success than he was.

Motown had decided to push another single off that *Where There's Smoke* album, a discofied remake of the Temptations' 1966 hit "Get Ready." Disco was never Smokey's thing, but in the wake of the world epidemic loosed by *Saturday Night Fever,* Donna Summer, and the Bee Gees, the Motown elders pressed for the product of the moment. They planned to release "Get Ready" as a standard 45 and as a twelve-inch disco dance cut.

"Daddy, *this* is your single," Smokey's eleven-year-old son, Berry, argued when he heard "Cruisin'." He is, according to his father, "an up front little dude," already playing a bass guitar and collecting fifties doowop. "Such a nostalgic little cat," Smokey says, "I feel like he's been here before."

The kid had it all figured out. "For the album cover, you have to get a big sports car convertible, Daddy. And you've got to drive it down the highway with a scarf flying on your neck and you got to call the *album* 'Cruisin',' too."

At such a tender age the child had more soul than his namesake. "Get Ready" was the single release, and it did creditable business; but it was, in the artist's words, "nothin' to jump around about." Then, one day, a deejay from WVON in Chicago called him to double-check the details of a benefit Smokey would be doing there.

" 'Smokey,' the guy told me, *'later* on this "Get Ready" shit. When you come here, leave it *home*. We've been playin' a better cut. Chicago is *cruisin'*. And that's what people want to hear.' "

Released as a single shortly after, "Cruisin' " jetted to the top of the charts.

"Can you believe I was elated when 'Cruisin' ' just buried 'Get Ready'? It took off when disco was hot, and it's not at all disco. It let me know you don't have to prostrate yourself for a hit."

The sound check is under way, and guitarist Marv Tarplin has begun to shade the onstage clatter with a few practice riffs from the bridge of "Cruisin'."

Trading hand signals with a soundboard technician stationed in the center of the theater, Smokey picks up a mike to get down to business. He breathes a gorgeous, three-note *oooooh-ooh-ooooh* into the spongy rubber bulb. The man at the board jumps and begins adjusting dials frantically as the sound falls from the ceiling arches like some warm vibrato rain shower.

"Guitar now," the sound man says, and Tarplin shoots off a dense, plangent riff that snaps Smokey's head around.

"That what you got in mind to fool with?"

Tarplin nods and grins.

"Later, in my room," Smokey says, "let's knock it around some."

11

The Girls, Part One

This business takes your life and puts it on hold. Gives you a lull you don't know what to do with. And I just can't settle down.

—MARTHA REEVES

DOZENS OF PLIANT, eager-to-please young women passed through Berry Gordy's charm school from 1960 on. Since then many of them—Kim Weston, Brenda Holloway, the majority of the Marvelettes, Vandellas, and Supremes—have left the company. At least half a dozen of them have tried to sue him in disputes over royalties, group name ownership, and contract terms agreed to when they were minors. But none of them will deny that he changed their lives dramatically, even saved them.

"Until Motown, in Detroit, there were three big careers for a black girl," says Mary Wells. "Babies, the factories, or daywork. Period."

Mary was Motown's first big female star, yet she has just crossed the crowded dance floor of this new wave beer hall without turning a head. It is her they've paid to see, this crowd of punks, preppies, teen queens, and slumming fortyish stockbrokers. A dozen of them are clutching old,

140

musty-smelling album jackets bearing the likeness of the twenty-one-year-old Mary Wells.

The *My Guy* album cover is soul's Mona Lisa, circa 1964. Mary is smiling faintly beneath a carefully teased bouffant, almond eyes drawn into a near-Egyptian slant by twin strokes of eyeliner. Mary was mohair and sequins, vulnerable and tough. Nothing could tear her away from "My Guy," but she walked away, head high, from the low-life lover in "You Beat Me to the Punch." Sometimes toughness was forced on her in the recording studio, where the producers demanded twenty or thirty takes until sheer hoarseness got the pain across. Like acting coaches, they would ask her to imagine the heartbreak in those 2½-minute love comics. They gave her the songs, the sound, and the Look. Mary says it was so stylized, so "sixties sharp girl" that she's not surprised no one recognizes her on the dance floor tonight.

No one has ever seen Mary Wells perform in pants, for one thing. The purple wool slacks are tucked into low white boots. Her hair is tied back simply, no curls, no Dynel House of Beauty wig. She wears only a bare trace of eye makeup. A heart-shaped pendant rests on her collarbone in the V of a cashmere sweater. She says she travels light, often with her manager/companion Curtis Womack, brother of her ex-husband, Cecil. Though she has a recording contract with Epic now, she is still reliant upon union pickup bands at live dates. She says she takes enough gigs to keep her family fed, but not so many as to make her three kids think of her as anything but Mama.

"Girl," she says, "I am a *working* woman. I wear pants all the time, and it doesn't make me feel less a woman. My mother was one of the first liberated women in Detroit to really get into pants. You know why? She scrubbed floors, did domestic work. Daywork they call it. And it was *damn* cold on hallway linoleum. Misery is Detroit linoleum in January—with a half-froze bucket of Spic and Span. It was just me and her. My brothers were grown and gone. I started helping my mother with the work when I was around twelve. When you get that old, and if it's just the two of you, a kid can see somethin' goin' out of her mama's face, you know. Like a dress you can wash but so many times and it ain't gonna size up so smart on the hanger. We were just two women alone, helpin' each other out. Now church helped. She always stood better when she come out of there on Sunday. And I was singing there since I was a baby. Like I say, two women alone; but we were always clean and neat, and we had *something.* My mother taught me independence, and I tell you, I need it more than I need a man or a career. I couldn't let go of that, oh, no. Girl, I'd be too scared. See, because you always know what *you* think, but you never know what the other person—the man—is thinking. Or how he might change. But you know *you'll* always love you. You know you can depend on *you.*''

Two marriages and that fickle lover ''the business'' have made her hang on to that independence in a fierce way, she says. But musically it's tough. In the beginning she did not realize the depth of her dependence on the Motown team productions that shaped an artist's style and sound. Looking back, she says she loved working that ''family'' way and mistakenly assumed it was the same everywhere. When she left Motown in 1964, saying that a twenty-one-year-old woman did not have to renew the contract she'd had at seventeen, she was unable to find another producer and writer who could give her the same concentrated attentions of a Smokey Robinson. She signed with the Atlantic subsidiary Atco in 1966, after an unsuccessful stint at 20th Century Records, and left voluntarily when she was told she'd have to wait a year, until after the initial promotional push for Aretha Franklin, before Atlantic producers could get to Mary Wells.

Romantically the realities were just as ungentle. ''Well, it's like the business,'' she says. ''In a marriage the killer thing, the death bullet, girl, is a loss of respect. And with a woman like me, an entertainer, respect gets mixed up with what people—or should I say men?—expect.

''I think the majority of entertainers should never get married anyway,'' she says. ''People expect too much. They're expecting you to wake up like a movie star in the morning, to have a hit record out every day. You are a symbol, a dream, a myth, you know. So when you choose that profession, you have to think about living up to it. The love from thousands of people out there . . .''

They are outside the dressing-room door, in fact, a random mix of fans: one black car salesman, one white dentist from Staten Island, two orange-haired punkettes, and a pony-tailed sixties holdout named Stan, who has been nervously smoothing the yellowed cellophane on his stack of old Mary Wells albums. When we'd talked earlier, Stan worried aloud that he'd be too nervous to thank Mary for her help. For what? All those nights he closed out the crapola of his parents' fights, the old man's harangues after the Friday supper highballs. Those nights, Stan would lock himself in his room with Mary singing ''The One Who Really Loves You.'' ''My Guy'' on a tinny Nash radio melted one young lady enough to get him a date for the senior trip to Freedomland, an amusement park sunk into the swamplands of the Bronx. Thanks to Mary, he didn't have to close out high school as a total chess club nerd.

"White kids could get their own blues in a two-family dump in Flushing," Stan said. "Mary saved me. I love her."

Being custodian to a generation of such precious memories is dicey. But before the night is over, Mary will listen patiently to a dozen such confessions.

"I used to be very hurt by this oldie goldie thing," she explains. "But really, the term is 'oldie but *goodie,*' right? And we all have a ball. I know now that the labels are just a game anyhow. It can't hurt me. I say, let me just sit back with the kids and relax, just go off and work. Work some tiny club someplace or these big ten-thousand-person gigs outdoors I do in California. Those pull real mixed crowds, oldies types, kids, lots of Spanish and Mexican people; they just go crazy. I don't know what pulls them. I give what I can; then I go my own way, back to my three kids. I know my way now. Twenty years ago I guess I was a lot more tentative in my movements."

Freed of company guidelines and the very real constraints of a sequined sheath skirt, Mary moves around a stage more than she used to. She still has one of the *primo* stage "yeahs," the kind that could raise the neck hairs on the most leaden VO-5ed DA. *Ooooh, hee-yeah.* Mary's soulful shorthand does the work of six paragraphs of proper English.

"When I listen back to that, to those records, I can really hear the difference in my voice all the way. From when I was seventeen or twenty-one. I'm a divorced mother struggling with family and career. I don't have the peace of mind I did on those early tours, you know, bein' on the road and free. But we were all kids on those big tours, just a bunch of kids that cared about each other, just havin' fun. Growin' up together. It's something like what I've heard people describe about their college years, I guess. Those were *our* years of higher education. When you get older, of course, you grow apart."

She says she still keeps in touch with Smokey and Claudette Robinson since they live nearby in California. They don't talk too much about the past. It's mainly strangers who talk her into those trips down a memory two-lane. Like the people outside the dressing-room door. They always seem to be looking for something themselves.

"I truly do love those people, though," she says. "It keeps *me* goin' sometimes. Like this guy who sat next to me on a plane recently. He says, in this beeyootiful accent, 'Are you Mary Wells?' And he told me I should come to Paris to work, that they love me in France.''

This is true, I tell her. In Le Palace, the Parisian equivalent of Studio 54, *tout chic* Paree, in Levi's, pink vinyl, and Saint Laurent was shaking it all night to Motown discs. When "My Guy" hit the turntable, people clapped and hollered. The barkeep handed off another $7 Heineken and bawled along: "Nossing yew culd saaay culd teahhh me awaaaay from mieeeee guieeeee.''

"Whatchu think, Curtis?''

"Paris in the spring?''

"I can dig it.''

Mary has done her share of intercontinental touring, mainly in the early sixties, when she was one of the few Motown acts hot enough to run neck and neck with the Beatles in the Top Ten.

"They never did mind it,'' she says. "Those boys were real sweet.''

At nearly every stateside news conference the Beatles confessed they were just gone on Mary Wells. They invited her to tour with them, and when she accepted, she found them to be perfect gentlemen.

"They were very friendly. They'd stop by my dressing-room door on the way in, say, 'Mary, you all right?' or, 'You want us to get you something for dinner?' John Lennon was funny but always gentle to me, always respectful. I have a *hard* time with the fact that some fool murdered the man.''

She says she has had her share of warped suitors over the years, but she never lost a lot of sleep trying to puzzle out that fine line between fan and freak. It took her some time to realize that early sixties shows in southern theaters were played to white orchestras and black balconies. She was literally blinded by the lights, and only after her eyes had begun to adjust could she see the crowd divisions.

"When I first caught a glimpse of racism, serious stuff, it caught me off guard. It was in New Orleans, and I wasn't thinking. You know, the Martin Luther King trip was well on the road and all. Anyhow, I was down there, and I just walked into City Hall. It was a hot day, and I started drinking out of this water fountain, and all these people started *lookin'* at me. And me, so much a fool. I say to myself, 'Oh, they know who I am, I'm Mary Wells.' Then I look up and see the sign. Yeah, you got it. WHITE ONLY. Me in my little Motown star bubble. All of a sudden everything kind of crushes.''

She learned to deal with it. Everyone had to. There has been just one

Sam Cooke's gospel soul was far more influential than his pop work on the generation of young singers coming up at the time of his death in 1964. A year later, another gospel-trained singer leered into the pop charts with his soul classic "In the Midnight Hour." Having since survived "that disco bullshit," Wilson Pickett (below) insists, "I changed my clothes, but I didn't change my soul."
Frank Driggs Collection.

The teenage Mary Wells was Motown's first princess — pretty, sweet, and ever loyal to "My Guy." "Mary," her producers had to coax her, "sing it like you are really *hurt.*"
Alan Betrock Collection.

"I'm the one who said, 'Hey, come on. Dance! Boogie! Dammit, *rejoice!*'" says Martha Reeves. Martha (below, right) and her Vandellas were Motown's most soulful trio.
Alan Betrock Collection.

Long before the Supremes had a definite sound, Diana Ross (top, center) had Mary Wilson (top, left) and Florence Ballard working hard on a look. "Style," she insists, "is a real important expression of self." Motown's Artists Development Department provided the veneer, with wigs, gowns, and lessons in etiquette.
Frank Driggs Collection.

Though he started as a pliant session drummer, Marvin Gaye proved to be a stubborn kind of fellow during his stormy twenty-year tenure at Motown. *Don Paulsen.*

The Miracles (below) released their first hit, "Got a Job," on Smokey Robinson's eighteenth birthday. Now, at forty-four, Smokey (seated at far left) is a sellout solo artist and a Motown vice-president. *Frank Driggs Collection.*

Little Stevie Wonder auditioned by playing every instrument in Motown's Studio A at age ten. By the time he was twenty-five, in 1975, he had negotiated the largest, and most autonomous, recording, producing, and publishing deal Motown had ever agreed to. *Alan Betrock Collection.*

Motown's most exciting act drew on alternating leads and pinpoint choreography. Here, the Temptations (below) pose backstage at the Apollo with guitarist Cornelius Grant. *Don Paulsen.*

Motown could call itself "Hitsville U.S.A." largely due to the talents of songwriting/production team Brian Holland, Lamont Dozier, and Eddie Holland. *Alan Betrock Collection.*

Atlantic Records successfully teamed black and white, country and city musicians. Working on a session in Muscle Shoals, Alabama: (left to right) Richard Tee, Jerry Wexler, Bernard "Pretty" Purdie, Aretha Franklin, Gordon Edwards. Kneeling: Hugh McCracken, Cornell Dupree.
David Gahr.

Otis Redding was at the heart of the Stax/Atlantic collaboration. Partying with the Atlantic side of that sixties soul clan: (left to right) Don Covay, Ahmet Ertegun, Jerry's daughter Anita Wexler, Otis Redding, an unknown deejay, and Percy Sledge. *Courtesy Jerry Wexler.*

Just out of church, and a rookie at Columbia Records, the young Aretha Franklin gets some coaching from master choreographer Cholly Atkins. Aretha says she was inspired to go pop when Sam Cooke made the change from gospel. She knew him from his appearances in her father's church. "I truly loved that man," she says. "He would come to the house, so polite and gentle. And so handsome. Wow! As much as anybody, Sam made me want to sing. He would just say, 'Sing, girl.' And believe me, that was enough."
Frank Driggs Collection.

set of demands she has never been able to put out of her mind. These demands, now aged nine, fourteen, and fifteen, kept her off the road for a good while, but she does not regret it. Now that her children are getting older, she actually finds herself worrying about their going off and leaving *her* alone.

"When I'm traveling, mostly what I feel is guilt. It seems like I should spend all my time with them. But they *are* growing up. Even the baby, he's nine, and he don't want to be kissed anymore."

That Mommy is *the* Mary Wells is something her children are still coming to understand. Curtis has taken them to her concerts when she plays near home, and watching them watch her cracks him up every time.

"They have no idea, you know. And they see their mama getting people wild and happy. And before I know it, one of them will be saying to me, '*Whoa,* look at Mama *get down.*' You know, these kids are into Michael Jackson and whatnot these days. They see their mother up on a stage, and they just look so surprised."

Out in the sweaty, converted beer hall, the opening act—a new wave band given to gauze bandages and torn Banlon—has cranked into a finale that sounds like dueling Dumpsters.

"Ten minutes, Mary," someone yells through the door.

Mary stubs out her cigarette and reaches for a mascara wand.

"Some women just can't be at home. I can do both. I like to come home, take care of the kids, wash the clothes, clean the house myself, enjoy my kids, help them with their homework. And *then* go back out there and work. I just cannot be idle. It makes me feel like I want to climb the fuckin' *wall.* I think a lot of people feel like that, don't you? That's why you be runnin' *all* the time. . . ."

Mary Wells was already history at Motown in the mid-sixties when female acts like the Supremes and Martha and the Vandellas hit their stride. Within the company, Martha Reeves was thought of as the most outspoken. Martha says that this is true and that she's still given to plain talk. More than a decade after the '67 riots Dinah Shore asked her talk show guest just where she was, where all those Motown stars were when the trouble started.

"Dancing in the street," Martha Reeves told her, and she wasn't being flip. She was singing that song onstage in Detroit when the message came from the wings, and she was obliged to stop the set and tell everyone to go home, that their families were in trouble. She says that the Motown

Revue left Detroit right away and went to New Jersey, but when rioting broke out there, they fled South to Myrtle Beach, South Carolina. They had heard there were no riots down South, and comparatively speaking, this was true. Word was that blacks there were still convinced rioting was suicidal.

"Then Rap Brown was coming through there, we heard," Martha recalls. "So we hurried and just got out of town. We went to L.A. I wasn't in no riot. But right after that, when I went to England on tour, someone sticks a mike in my face and accuses me of being a militant leader. They said that my song 'Dancing in the Street' was a call to riot. My Lord, it was a *party* song."

Now, she says, it's a harmless oldie, and the days of running to keep ahead of the smoke and madness are just memories. The time lapse is all the more apparent on a winter night when Martha stands onstage in a heatless Manhattan theater, trying to teach "Dancing in the Street" to a pickup band that was probably in kindergarten when the song first hit in 1964.

"Uh, sweetheart? You there on keyboards. Can you please give me a C? C. *C.* Yeah, honey, that's the one."

Martha is wearing a fur-trimmed overcoat against the chill. Out beyond the molting curtain, benumbed patrons have begun to stomp and bleat: "Heat, heat, give us some fuckin' heat."

Five minutes to showtime Martha gives up on rehearsal and heads to her dressing room to change. There is no road crew, no wardrobe mistress, and, since their breakup in 1971, no Vandellas.

Minutes later Martha waits in the wings as a promoter tries to get the attention of the testy audience. "Ladies and gents, the one, the only Miss Dancin' in the Streets, Heat Wave, and Nowhere to Run, Miss Jimmy Mack . . . Martha Reeeeeeeves . . ."

Tossing off her manager's sport coat, she shivers and hops over a tangle of cables in silver lamé boots, her white fringed top glittering like fish scales over pearly stretch knickers. And suddenly it is not a ghost show.

Martha charges the footlights, banging a tambourine on the backbeat, urging on the plodding band, planting her feet, swinging her hips, glancing back over her shoulder at the drummer as if to say, "Now, honey, you got yourself a metronome."

He gets it, and things begin to move. Martha vamps into "Heat Wave," her voice and body stabbing at the darkness and the chill beyond the stage perimeter. Twice she must stop the band to search for that elusive C.

"Aw, fellas, can you *try* and get *down?*"

Still, she is undaunted. The audience is on their feet, shaking off the cold, dancing in down jackets and overcoats.

If anything, Martha seems more determined to turn the place out and raise some temperatures. There is no better choice for her encore than "Nowhere to Run," one of the hottest singles Motown ever pressed. Sixteen years after she first stood in Studio A with the Vandellas whooping behind her, Martha has no trouble handling this one solo, balling into that frenzied juggernaut of a song—one of the handful of Holland-Dozier-Holland compositions that went past adolescent pop spooning and talked about sex:

> *It's not love I'm a runnin' from*
> *It's the heartbreak I know will come*
> *'Cause I know you're no good for me*
> *But you've become a part of me. . . .*

Could be a man. But for Martha, at this point, it could be the music itself. Can't tame it; can't quit it. It is so good in the beginning, but it's bound to cut you deep in the end.

> *Nowhere to run to, baby, nowhere to hide*

She is fairly biting at the lyrics now, moaning the Vandellas' chorus alone. The body bends and snaps back, skittering to the left, to the right, leaning out into the darkness as if it were the woman's tenth blind alley and the footsteps were closing fast behind her.

> *Everywhere I go, your face I see*
> *Every step I take, you take with me*
> *NO!*

Her head is shaking back and forth, eyes closed.

> *How can I fight a love that shouldn't be?*
> *When it's so deep, so deep, deep inside of me?*

This love is a brick on the chest, a killer, making her hallucinate.

> *When I look in the mirror to comb my hair*
> *I see your face just a smiling there*
> *NO! Nowhere to run to, baby*

She does a dance of the possessed, palms thrust out at some invisible barrier, pushing at it with her arms, kicking. Martha never had the studied daintiness of the Supremes. Martha always got down, and she is feeling right about it tonight, living the song past the minimal requirements of an oldie recitation, crashing the tambourine against a sharp hipbone, wincing while the crowd bumps happily to a steady, straight-time thud of over- whelming ache. And then, the borrowed gospel cant:

> *My love reaches so high, I can't get over it*
> *It's so wide, I can't get around it*
> *NO!*
> *Nowhere to run, nowhere to hide**

She has made it to the final verse, is teetering back on those fragile high heels to push out the chorus, and the crowd is on its feet. Martha's chest is heaving as she stoops to pick up a plastic rose that has landed near her feet.

As she heads for the dressing room upstairs, clutching the rose, she passes other members of this latter-day one-night-only "Motortown Re- vue." In one tiny dressing room Mary Wells is adjusting a midnight blue sequined dress. In the hallway saxophonist Jr. Walker is sitting calmly, waiting for his band, all second-generation All Stars, to make it in out of the parking lot. He and Martha hug in the stairwell.

"That was *hot,*" he tells her. "Love that 'Nowhere to Run.' "

"Yeah," she says. "I'm glad I recorded that one. Some part of every day I'm like that song. I feel like that every single day."

Whether Martha is running or planting her feet to make a stand depends on just when you catch her. We had talked, a few times, over the space of a year, before and after shows, in borrowed offices, and once on a spring afternoon, watching lunchtime lovers neck on the stone benches around Rockefeller Center. Martha is the first to tell you that the intensity of her performances and her moods varies greatly. Some nights she will gaze over the shoulders of a so-so crowd, almost on automatic pilot, and deliver a set that has all the fire of a K-Tel TV oldies ad. Other times she

---

*"Nowhere to Run," Words and music by BRIAN HOLLAND, LAMONT DOZIER & EDDIE HOLLAND, © 1965 Jobete Music Company, Inc. Used by Permission. International Copyright Secured. All Rights Reserved.

can make Motown seem like grade school with a long, soulful ad lib. One rainy spring night the band looked puzzled when she called for "Dixie Roads," got partway through it, and held her hand up to the drummer for a break.

"Honest, girls . . ."

She walked out to the edge of the stage and looked a clutch of women straight in the eye, then snapped her gaze up toward the ceiling.

"Honest, girls . . . this man up and left on a rainy night just like this one. Um-hum. I mean, the door CLOSED!"

Blam. The drummer made it final.

This was a Martha Reeves no Motown fanatic ever had the chance to know, having added two decades of living and two octaves' worth of range to her voice. Tonight, despite the cold, she says she felt things moving. It felt right. The crowd was kind of sparse, but *they* moved. They cared. "Tonight was good, being with Motown people again," she says, "because you know those people came to see *us.*"

Too often, she says, it's been Martha Reeves plus the Bad Brains or the Cramps or the Catholic Girls or some other punk outfit. She knows that promoters book her since these kids think, wow, you know, old Motown is, like, really hip. These are the same kids who have appropriated their parents' Buddy Holly records and hang around secondhand clothing stores looking for anything "fifties," preferably in pink and black Good 'n' Plenty colors. Attitude brings these kids through the door, the way Martha understands it. But it's something else that makes them quit popping gum and amyl nitrite and get into the music.

"I'm the one who stood there and said, 'Hey, come on. Dance! Boogie! Clap your hands. Dammit, *rejoice!*' "

It was a hip, no-bullshit, let's-party stance, and it made the Vandellas Motown's most adult girl group. Sometimes their exuberance made Martha the chaperone's scourge.

"The girl couldn't help it," she says of herself, smiling. Some people went so far as to call her bullheaded, even tough. The way Martha sees it, she was just determined.

"See, I am one of those people who really did fall in love with a dream. I guess I was three or four. I went to the New Liberty Baptist Church, and Della Reese was the featured soloist. She was singing a song called 'I Hear the Thunder.' Real early on I fell in love with show business. There was church stuff, too. I'm one of eleven children. My brothers sang in a gospel group as teenagers, and they wouldn't let me sing with them.

I'd get angry 'cause I knew I had a voice. I'd stand up on the side anyhow and hit a note higher than a tenor.''

Barred from the male quartet scene, she formed her own girl group in high school, the Delphis. "We actually recorded on Check-Mate, a subsidiary of Chess, before Motown. When I went to Motown to try and get an audition, we were put on a list of maybe about ninety people. There was also a job for A & R secretary, so I took it."

She sat in the basement, jamming session notes on spindles. Newly appointed A & R chief Mickey Stevenson convinced her to stick around and wait for that break.

"I had ten bosses then," Martha says. "I was *the* secretary to Mickey, to Smokey Robinson, Robert Bateman, Holland-Dozier-Holland, all of 'em. I think I made thirty-five dollars a week. That's after I worked there two weeks for nothing, I wanted to be there so much. Then I had to tell them, 'Hey, give me a salary 'cause my dad's tired of giving me carfare to come here.' I made it there every day around nine, and I worked till about ten. Sometimes I did handclaps on sessions, sometimes backup. At that time the Andantes [one of the first Detroit girl groups] were the staff backup singers. But one night they were on another job in Chicago. I called in my girls—Annette Sterling, Rosalind Ashford, and Gloria Williams. I think the first person we worked behind was a blues singer named Hattie Little. They gave us some name like the Bel Jeans or whatever. We worked with Marvin Gaye on 'Stubborn Kind of Fellow' and 'Hitch Hike' and some other things. I think they liked the marriage.''

It was no hardship for the Delphis, who, since they were technically under contract to Chess, changed their name to the Vandellas. The Van was for Van Dyck Street, where Martha's mother still lives. The Della was for the inspirational Miss Reese "and maybe just a remnant of the Delphis.'' They were thrilled to be backing Marvin Gaye, who had begun his singing career with Gordy's brother-in-law Harvey Fuqua in the Moonglows. He also worked as a studio musician.

"Marvin was a session drummer," Martha says. "I kind of followed him around 'cause he was awful cute. But he wore his hat down on his eyes all the time. Nobody could really see what he was up to. To this day Marvin is a very—well, let's say he has a tremendous inner life. He'd come in, he smoked this corncob pipe, and he just did sessions and left. And one day he got discovered. Next thing you know, he was married [to Gordy's sister Anna] and was a big star. That first time with him, once he heard us, he put us on the whole first side of his album, and we toured with him. By then we had our own record, 'Come and Get These Memories.' So we weren't just his backup girls. We were an act on our own."

Once they were a Top Ten act, and the Motown Revues were leaving Detroit like commuter shuttles, it fell to Martha to groom and advise the succession of Vandellas—there were about a dozen over the years.

"I had to give my girls a crash course on what Motown wanted and what they didn't. We did have rules to follow. The poise and beauty stuff was new to me, too, at first. I mean, I didn't know what all to do with a wig when I first got it. But it was part of the *costume*.

"Under the lights those wigs could poach your brains, I swear. Listen, we had recorded, we were professionals, but we had never been in show business. And we had to adjust to it and hurriedly get in the right frame of mind. Like I say, we were chaperoned. They were elderly ladies that basically sat and watched and taught us poise and how to use our knives and forks correctly."

She collapses into giggles. "Now we were doing just fine before all this. I mean, I don't think I ever offended anyone with my *eating* habits."

On the road she did find some Americans with atrocious manners. They wouldn't let her near their dime-store cutlery. And no matter how polite she was, she couldn't lay a bill on certain luncheonette counters and come away with a cheeseburger.

"It's an awful insult when you walk around and you got all kinds of money and you can't eat. We got shot at in the bus down South. They thought we were freedom riders. You ever had a meal of popcorn and sardines? It's good."

Leaning her head on the graffitied wall, Martha demonstrates the stiff-necked sleeping posture that preserved a carefully constructed bouffant.

"We always had to sit up because there wasn't enough room for everybody to stretch out. But we'd have a twelve-piece band, the Temptations, the Supremes, the Marvelettes, the Contours, and the Miracles, Stevie Wonder, Mary Wells. I think all the stories about how tough it was just came from one tour, though, one ninety-four-day tour where we had three nights off. We slept in beds just three nights. It was a promotion that put us all on the map, so I can't say it was a bad move. Motown knew what they were doing. It might have been tough, but we made it. I mean, people died on those tours, just getting worn down, getting in the station wagon after playing onstage, then trying to drive three hundred miles."

She is thinking of an awful wreck on the highway that killed Gerald McFarland, the Marvelettes' driver, and seriously injured Thomas

"Beans" Bowles, who survived to become Smokey Robinson's musical director.

"Fortunately the Marvelettes were put on the bus at the last minute, or they might be dead."

After the crash they all were pretty badly shaken, but they kept going. Wanting things badly enough gives you stamina you never knew you had, Martha says. Besides, they were young and strong, and it beat slinging hash or taking steno.

"We'd do five or six shows a day at the Apollo or the Brooklyn Fox with [deejay] Murray the K. Now let me tell you, they couldn't put on one of those punk rock shows five times a day. I don't think these kids could stand up under that kind of pressure."

She has heard about the way they record, how some rock stars take a year or two to make a single album. The Vandellas' *Heat Wave* album was done in a few hours.

"We flew in from Baltimore after doing five shows. We got in around midnight and went right into the studio. We did 'My Boyfriend's Back,' 'Wait 'Til My Bobby Gets Home,' 'Just One Look,' all those songs. Recorded that whole album, then did three songs, backup, for Marvin Gaye. We returned to Baltimore the next morning. We all had to get shots for our throats because they were suffering from overuse. Understand, I'm not complaining. If I were that age, and the circumstances were the same, I'd gladly do it again. You know how it is. You do stupid, dangerous things when you're really in love. And if you're swept away by it, you don't stop for one minute to think. You say, 'Go get it, girl,' and you don't look back."

She says she did suffer some permanent physical damage. She has had a loss of hearing in one ear and is very sensitive to light, having injured her eyes from staring into so many megawatt spotlights. Once, in the beginning, she tried wearing sunglasses onstage to protect herself.

"The chaperones told me, 'How *dare* you go on and not let your audience see your eyes?' Once I used 'damn' in a song and was heavily chastised."

Sex wasn't dripping from Motown lyrics, but it did show up at the stage door. The chaperones were vigilant, shooing off the packs of young men sniffing around. Martha says she found herself feeling just as protective. Even in the toughest part of town, in the projects, she says, at least you had an idea what might be lurking in the hallway. You take precautions. In show business the muggers wear three-piece suits and send you roses.

"When people say, 'Where are the Vandellas?' I say *men* broke up my group. Sure. Men. I get one cute and all properly trimmed, you know, the modeling school and etiquette and all. And some men come along and say, 'Wow, that's a hot number.' And before I know it, she's gone.

"I've loved each one. And I'm godmommy to their babies. Annette Sterling and her husband live in Detroit; they have two children, and she works for a hospital. Rosalind Ashford was an eight-year member. Now she works for the telephone company. She's got a little boy."

Every time she lost a Vandella Martha says she was sad but stubbornly determined. She never considered giving it up herself. Just kept training new members and stayed out on the road. Her big mistake, she says, was in trying to check on matters outside the recording studio. She asked to look over royalty statements and cash allowance vouchers and was heard wondering, a bit too loudly, about their size and frequency.

"I think I was the first person at Motown to ask where the money was going," she says. "And that made me an enemy. Did I find out? Honey, I found my way out the door."

Martha left Motown in 1972; the Vandellas were disbanded the year before. Also in 1972, Martha gave birth to her son Eric, whose father she could not and would not marry. For a year she tried to support Eric by cashing in annuities, clipping coupons, and watching for sales. And every morning, without fail, she says she "woke" her voice up by running through "The Lord's Prayer" or "The Star-Spangled Banner."

Those songs have what she calls an invigorating range, and she still sings them, the way another forty-three-year-old woman might run through a set of morning calisthenics, glancing for quiet reassurance at the muscles tensing in calves and thighs. Martha feels her voice is in its best shape ever. She can work her way through four octaves without breathing hard.

It was Eric's voice, squalling alongside her own, that compelled her to leave him with her parents and move West. MCA Records and a promised contract were in Los Angeles. So were TV shows and a lot of her old friends and contacts at the relocated Motown headquarters. Martha and her father packed the car with a few suitcases and headed to L.A., and she says she cried nearly all the way.

"That little man-child was not going to lose it before he could walk," she says of Eric. "I could *not* let him become a government statistic. I didn't want to be on welfare, and I wasn't about to seek another career. Singing is what I do best; it's the only thing that God ever let me know I could really do. Now I wouldn't say the last ten years have been real profitable, but every time I think I'm gone, I'm on *Sha Na Na*. Or I'll be shown on a rerun of *Hollywood Squares* or *The Gong Show* or the *$1.98 Beauty Contest.*"

She also gets a fair number of live oldie but goodie gigs, and whenever she can, she arranges them so that she can pass through Detroit to see Eric. It's strange, rearing her son long distance, in her mother's house. But she's sure that things would have ended up a lot worse if she'd never left that neighborhood and taken the bus over to West Grand Avenue. And despite the company disagreements that landed her in this long-distance career/motherhood chasm, she says she respects Berry Gordy and never doubted his marketing genius.

"He's got a great mind," she says. "Back then every female vocalist had a crush on Berry."

The fortunes Gordy reinvests now, in racehorses, in real estate, in film ventures, all are courtesy of that golden decade, between 1962 and 1971. After that his company ceased to dominate the charts. Though Motown's record division is still better than solvent with "new" acts like Lionel Richie, the Commodores, and Rick James, and standbys like Stevie Wonder and Smokey Robinson, Martha believes that the latter two prevailed because they were producer/composers as well, with distinctive sounds of their own. That wasn't true for a lot of the groups so dependent on production teams like Holland-Dozier-Holland, Norman Whitfield, and later Nick Ashford and Valerie Simpson. Just the way starlets needed carefully crafted vehicles during Hollywood's studio years, a company like Motown, with such standardized product, was bound to suffer when styles changed.

"I think Berry got caught in the middle of a tragedy," Martha says. "Because he had everyone working together. Then the networks—radio—and the systems, concert promoters, all of them, started calling for groups that were self-contained. So he started signing a lot of self-contained acts. And the ones that didn't have a band or couldn't produce their own sound just lost ground with him."

Even Diana Ross, who never lost ground in Gordy's ambitions and affections, found the company incompatible with her goals and left for RCA in 1981. The list of the other dearly and clearly departed reads like a long-ago marquee on the Apollo: the Contours, the Miracles, the Supremes, the Isley Brothers, Martha and the Vandellas, the Spinners, Gladys Knight and the Pips. Some groups, like the Temptations, lost vital parts—notably leads David Ruffin and Eddie Kendricks. Some, like the Four Tops and

Jr. Walker, left and only recently returned. Others, by contract, left behind just the dried husks of their names. Occasionally the company fills them with varied sets of live bodies and ships them out on the goldies' circuit.

"Everyone does that," Martha says. "Out on the road now I've seen about three sets of Coasters and God knows how many sets of Drifters. And I've been told, though I haven't seen, that there's another set of Marvelettes."

Nobody gave much thought to legal fail-safes like owning your own name back in the early sixties, Martha says. Things were played so fast and loose you could toss off a lifetime of royalties without knowing it.

"The Marvelettes' name, as I remember, was lost in a gambling party one night. Just lost the name. Berry loved to gamble, a lot of people did, and there were some very heavy card games. That's how easily your life can get tossed from one place to another. I don't own the name the Vandellas. Never did, I guess. So if they wanted, tomorrow they could send another set out on the road.

"I tell you, if I had it to do over again, I'd probably go to college, business college, for a couple of years, then come back with the talent *and* the business sense. I don't think I was ever really rich, so I can't claim any rags to riches story. If I've been rich in anything, it's been love and fans, and my relationships with the girls. Some people you stay tight with; others you don't see. Look, Diana [Ross] and I were very close when she was eighteen and we had a hit record, and they [the Supremes] were coming around the studio and Berry wouldn't record them yet."

Once things started happening for the Supremes and the Vandellas' soulful grit took a back seat to prim valentines like "Baby Love" and "I Hear a Symphony," Martha says all the other "girls" knew what was going down.

"Sup's on!" deejays were shrieking as they cued up "Baby Love."

One night in a Philadelphia club, a love-smitten fan pressed three bottles of bourbon on the Vandellas, and when they read the card, it said, "To the Supremes."

From that point on, it was hard to stay close. But Martha doesn't blame personal relations for it. It was the business—Berry's business—that took Diana on its well-tailored arm and walked off with her.

12
The Girls, Part Two

> *In the beginning, when someone said "the girls," it meant everyone. But past a certain point, when Berry referred to "the girls," he meant only the Supremes.*
>
> —MARY WILSON

"DON'T BE AFRAID TO PERSPIRE, people. I want you to *work* that body. Get up and get down, two, three, four. Yeah, work that body. But please, don't leave your *space,* okay? Stay in your own space."

Ten thousand bumping, flying, cheering Dutchmen obey, parting decorously as Diana Ross wades into a sweaty marsh of waving arms in this Rotterdam sports arena. She blows kisses and touches fingertips, cooing into the cordless mike, "Ooooh, I've been waiting twenty years to love you this *close.*"

Prancing on high, glitter-shot heels, in a succession of Bob Mackie-designed confections, Diana has peeled to a sequined tank suit cut high on the hip and low on the bosom.

"Bump, two, three, four, work it, shake it."

She is well into the spirit of her album cut, "Work That Body," a song engineered to fit the Richard Simmons/Jane Fonda/Olivia Newton-John "let's get physical" groove of the moment. Hopping back onto the center of her custom-built portable stage—one of two she carries with her—Diana is getting physical in ways unthinkable when she was a prim Supreme confined to mohair sheath shirts and hand gestures.

"Get down, girl" was not something they hollered at the lead singer of the Supremes back then. But now, at age forty, Diana is given to licking a finger and applying it to her hip as though testing a steam iron.

"Tssssssss," she hisses. "When I'm good, I'm good. And when I'm bad, I'm better."

It is, at bottom, a PG-rated kind of bad, no more threatening than the monologue of a Sonny and Cher show. Diana Ross is still family entertainment. And this is not so much a concert as a well-paced stage and fashion show. When she disappears for another costume change, the Asbury Jukes, a white New Jersey band chosen as her touring horn section, fly into a manic imitation soul band choreography, all bent elbows and swinging brass, cheerfully distracting the crowd until Diana reappears for her encore.

When the spot finds her, people gasp and clap. Over the tank suit she has donned a neck-to-ankle three-foot-wide creation that appears to be made out of nylon net. From the cheap seats, the lovely head seems trapped in a giant crumpled Kleenex. Moments after she has left the stage and stepped out of it, it takes two wardrobe mistresses to wrestle the thing into submission. From within her dressing room comes a kittenish protest: "Mercy, have mercy. You rat. Not *now.*"

Pleading postconcert "yuckiness," Diana cringes prettily as a video cameraman assigned to shoot highlights of her European tour advances.

"This is a candid," she explains.

The lens begins to pan the skimpy length of her, stretched on a dressing-room sofa. She wears only a black terry-cloth robe and pantyhose. Perspiration still glosses her cheeks and collarbones. The black, shoulder-length hair flies about untrammeled in that sophisticated *sauvage* coif favored by women like Diane von Furstenberg and Cher. Camera lights flare, and Diana's eyes flash to meet them, mouth moist and red in that trademark stretch-limo smile.

"I feel I'm peaking," Diana says when the camera has retreated. "Yes, that's it. You can say I'm in my peak experience."

She is, among other things, the head of a multimillion-dollar corporation, Diana Ross Enterprises, Inc., and her most recent recording successes have afforded her sole ownership of another rock trivia category: only

female vocalist in rock/pop history to have number one records as part
of a trio (the Supremes), a duo ("Endless Love" with Lionel Richie), and
a solo. In 1981 she left Motown Records after nearly twenty years, for a
reported $20 million deal with RCA and EMI. And after leaving her Beverly
Hills mansion and her marriage to producer Robert Silberstein, Diana has
made sure that everything in her adopted home, New York City, is definitely A list.

Her clothes are by Nancy Reagan favorite James Galanos, by Issey
Miyake, and by Bob Mackie, who dusts the likes of Cher and Raquel
Welch with scant constellations of sequins and bugle beads. All her de-
signers, Diana says, "are geniuses who really know my body." Lest they
forget, plastic molds of the star's upper torso have been commissioned
as stand-ins. The body itself is by Ross of Detroit ("we *are* a beautiful
family"). Her *Silk Electric* album cover was a Warhol original; Manhattan
evenings are arranged by fashion icons like Halston and Calvin Klein.
Frequently Diana has been photographed for *Women's Wear Daily* and
The New York Times. In the city Diana installed herself and her three
daughters in a toney midtown hotel. Weekends are spent in WASP country,
Connecticut's Fairfield County, on an estate she bought from tobacco
heiress Nancy Reynolds.

"Can you believe it? I have learned to grow zucchini."

Weeding her expensive truck patch for recreation, Diana has crossed
over into areas where even Berry Gordy does not tread, to a world where
both *Vogue* and the Burpee seed catalogue are required reading. The journey has not been easy, Diana will concede. As far back as 1966 she confessed to the readers of *Seventeen* that even during breaks from the Supremes' hectic tours, she labored to improve herself.

"When we were home," she said, "I went to finishing school for a
week to learn how to do the things that other people have known all their
lives and never think twice about."

As an adult she continued that relentless self-improvement with acting
lessons, Nautilus weight training, and, when she lived in California, an
encounter with est.

"I have been to the mountain, oh, yesss," she booms in mock preach-
erese, referring to the est training retreat she attended on a California
mountaintop.

Giggling, Diana sits back and stirs two spoons of sugar into a steaming
cup of tea.

"So," she says, "what's doing back in New York? What story did you do before me?"

"Dreamgirls," I tell her, and she frowns. That Broadway show, under the direction of Michael (*A Chorus Line*) Bennett, is a certified smash, and for months people have been trying to get Diana to comment since its story line, about three ghetto girls who become pop stars, bears such a startling resemblance to the history of Motown and the Supremes.

In that musical, it is not the glamorous Diana Ross type of Dream who is the focal point; instead, it is the overweight, underappreciated Dream Effie who steals the show. Reviewers have commented on Effie's likeness to the late Supreme Florence Ballard. Like Florence, who was expelled from the group in 1967 by Berry Gordy, Effie gets the heave-ho from a Gordy-like manager, who, as it happens, falls in love with and decides to promote the Diana-like Dream.

Diana Ross's ascendancy became clear when she began appearing at social functions on the arm of Berry Gordy, while Florence and Mary were required to show up separately. According to Mary Wilson, she and Florence were stung when they heard from others that their name was to be changed to "Diana Ross and the Supremes." It was that or lose her to a solo career, Berry Gordy explained when he finally told them of his decision.

Florence was gone soon after, having missed radio and performance dates, pleading unexplained "illness." She was replaced by Cindy Birdsong in 1967; two years later Diana Ross was replaced by Jean Terrell as Gordy offered a future of solo albums, TV specials, Vegas revues, and, ultimately, movies. A "farewell performance" was arranged; they closed the show with their last hit record, "Someday We'll Be Together."

Michael Bennett ended his Broadway show with the Dreams' glitzy public farewell. He had been at the Supremes' last show, he'd told me. And long before *A Chorus Line* made him famous as a choreographer, dancer, and producer, he had shing-a-linged behind the Supremes as a dancer on the sixties TV show *Hullabaloo.*

"I adored them," he said. "And I would do nothing to take away from their accomplishment."

Diana Ross does not agree, although she has steadfastly refused to see the show.

"I didn't want to validate it that way," she explains. "The people that produced it were and are good friends of mine, and I thought at least it could have been passed by me."

She will not permit her daughters to see the show either. Lots of their schoolfriends have seen it, and their speculations have caused some trouble.

"I don't want my children to see *Dreamgirls* and to think that what they see there is how it really was."

Millions of fans, worldwide, are dying to know just how it really was. Despite offers from "two very prestigious hardcover houses," Diana has resisted all the offers to write the ghetto-to-glamour autobiography. After all, she says, she's still living this rather young life. If she did one now, it would have to be the first part of a trilogy. The only things she writes down are for her personal reading and for her daughters.

"There was a girl giving me a massage," she recalls, "and she said, 'Gosh, what a great story your life is going to be.' And I told her, 'This is my *life;* this is not a fucking story.' "

The long, silver-tipped fingers curl into a fist, and the little-girl voice has risen tighter and higher.

"Dammit, this is serious for me. And it hurts me if it's turned into ice cream. There's pain there, and there's wonderful things. It's like in my song 'Mirror, Mirror,' where I say, 'You, you turned my life into a paperback novel.' "

Real tears have begun to bead up on her mascaraed lower lashes.

"Listen, this is real strong stuff for me. I heard my daughter talking to one of her friends on the phone, and she was saying things that she had heard or read. I called her into the room and said, 'Sweetheart, that's not so about me. That's something that someone has written about me.' "

She thinks that her daughters have coped with her celebrity fairly well. When she took the girls to buy sneakers in a Manhattan store, a crowd of 200 gathered outside on the sidewalk as they padded around trying on different styles. They know that major department stores will open at night just for their mother, a rare courtesy extended to the likes of Barbra Streisand and the queen of England. Diana walks through half-lit aisles with only the sound of her footsteps. All this she can explain to her children satisfactorily since it's happening now and they can see it. The past is something else.

"If there's some way I can make sure that they understand from *my* point of view what it's all about," she says. "My relationship with Berry especially."

Diana Ross has only good things to say about the man who molded her career. She says that not a day goes by that she doesn't think of him, and fondly. Over and over she insists her split with Motown was amicable.

"Look," she says, "I had to grow. I'm not one of those little bonsai trees, snip it off at the top and the bottom. You've got to live; you've got to leave home. It's a natural part of life. If I were to stay where I was, I think I would have been giving up some of my livelihood, my *person*. I just had to do it."

In her estimation she has finally become, as an album title proclaimed, the Boss. Sometimes she is surprised at just how pliant she was twenty years ago. Occasionally an old photo or an album cover will trigger flashbacks that remind her just how eager she was. When I mention that I'd visited the Motown "archives," she asks, "Weren't you shocked at how *small* that room is? That studio shocks me when I look back. When I was out there in Detroit, I stood there and said, 'Gee, it was so much bigger then.' "

She says she wandered through the upstairs rooms at Motown, looking at the photographs and album covers, and she got worried. She asked Mrs. Edwards if she could please install a few more smoke detectors in the old wooden building.

"I have none of those things," she explains. "I saved no clippings when I was with the Supremes. I didn't keep a scrapbook. I think we were too busy. We were always ahead of ourselves."

I ask her if she remembers seeing the photo of that first Motortown Revue. She laughs and says that she stood in front of the very same picture for about five minutes.

"It just hit me. There was a time on that first tour that they wouldn't let us off the bus until everybody had their makeup on. It was the day of the beehive, and your hair had to stay teased up like that for days."

She raises her arms above her head to indicate the probable height of such constructions.

"I just saw another photo—in the English papers. There was a shot of me opposite one of the princess. They called it 'the other Lady Di' or something. And it triggered something. I remember the color of the suit I wore to Europe the first time. It was pink, with this nice skirt and a cape top. I was really into fashion, and I thought I was *so* classy." She laughs. "Lord, you look at that picture now, with a Sassoon hairstyle. That picture didn't look like me at all. I mean, I have changed so much. I look at that, and I realize what it was. I was just trying so hard to *please*."

She's sure she tried that hard because she remembers wanting so much, so badly. In high school she had a job as a busgirl in Hudson's department store, and on her way to the kitchen she would daydream about shopping there. Like so many midwestern emporiums, J. L. Hudson's was a gleaming hood ornament on that first industrial boom. It was the last department store left in the blasted center of downtown Detroit when it closed its doors after Christmas of 1982.

When Diana Ross worked there, Hudson's covered a full square block on Woodward Avenue, with four restaurants and fifteen selling floors. On the street level, a brass-buttoned doorman opened limousine doors for the wives of auto barons from Grosse Pointe and Bloomfield Hills. To get to her post, Diana walked along plush-carpeted aisles, down wood-paneled halls. She remembers pulling her coat over the dowdy uniform that, despite the starch, hung on her bony frame like a sack. On her breaks she studied the manikins, and between her job and school she taught herself to sew.

"I'd see all these beautiful things and come home and make them," she says. "There's a picture somewhere of the Supremes' first look-alike outfits. I sewed them myself. They were black and gold, and we had a string of gold fake pearls from the dime store."

In the beginning Diana, Mary, and Florence shopped for fabric and patterns for all the local talent shows and those first days at Motown.

"You remember those balloon dresses? The skirt looked like a balloon? We made some of those in a very bright flowered print. And we had these bright orange shoes with big flowers stuck on the front of them."

Long before the Supremes had a distinct sound, Diana had them working hard on a look. "Personal style," she explains, "is a real important expression of self."

For the Supremes, and for the record company they came to represent, style would all but supplant soul. By the late sixties Berry Gordy's stylistic aspirations would set the Supremes in New York's Copacabana, sporting cutesy straw boaters and rattling nary an ice cube with perky renditions of "The Boy from Ipanema" and "Put on a Happy Face." By then style was the province of the Artists Development Department. But long before the ministrations of wardrobe mistresses, makeup artists, and hairstylists, the teenage Diana worked out an exhausting regimen on her own.

"I didn't feel I was college material," she says. "I didn't know what I wanted to do in school, couldn't select a career or anything. Really, all I wanted to do was sing and wear pretty clothes."

She credits her success in achieving that goal in large part to her mother, Ernestine Ross, who always understood. "She believed in me more than anyone, until I met Berry Gordy. If I said I wanted to do something—be a singer, a model, a fashion designer—she said, 'Go for it. Go ahead.'

"I was doing everything then. I'd go to school in the morning, then come home and work at Hudson's in the evening, so I'd have to change into my uniform. And I went to modeling school on the weekends. And then I was studying cosmetology to do hair, which was time-consuming. You know, you used heat on black hair then."

Her grandfather, who lived with them, clucked at the passing parade of garment bags, fashion magazines, sewing notions, and hair potions. "Daughter," he would say, "where *are* you going?"

Her parents asked the same question when a tall, handsome young man named Paul Williams came calling to ask if their daughter could be in a sister group that would perform with his group, the Primes (later to become the Temptations). Shortly after, the Supremes began their career as the Primettes.

"We were singing all the time anyway," Diana says. "Not exactly on street corners. But out of doors. Everybody had their little record players outside on long cords. Nobody had air conditioners in those days, especially in the projects, and everybody would sit outside all the time. The first batch was Betty [Travis], Mary [Wilson], Florence [Ballard], and myself. Betty left to go steady. Then we got Barbara [Martin], and she got married. At one point Florence's mother took her out of the group because she wasn't doing well in school. We were in high school then. We were just *courting* Motown, you know. Making pests of ourselves. Mary and I started doing duets. We picked songs and did harmony, but we needed our old girl friend. The two of us *begged* and persuaded Florence's mother to let her come back to the group. We promised we would help her with her schoolwork."

It was no secret that Florence Ballard had the most distinctive voice, a clear, high tenor that soared above Mary Wilson's alto and was far more sensual than Diana's adenoidal keening.

"Some of the first stuff we tried was the Drifters' 'There Goes My Baby,' " Diana says. "And one Ray Charles song, 'Night Time Is the Right Time.' Oh, I had a very high voice, and very nasal. I was listening to 'You Can't Hurry Love' the other night. . . .

"Yew can't hurry luvvvv, naw, yew jushavtowait . . ." Pinching her nose with her fingers, she imitates herself and giggles.

"Since I had such a high sound, we'd always pick the singers to imitate, like Frankie Lymon."

The Primettes started getting a little work. They sang backup on some Eddie Floyd sessions, and at record hops they appeared with the Primes. Sometimes they found themselves on the same bill with that raucous gospel shouter Wilson Pickett, who was then fronting the Falcons. It was only through the intercession of Diana's former neighbor Smokey Robinson that they got an audition at Motown. It would be a fair trade-off since Smokey and his Miracles quickly appropriated the Primettes' accompanist, guitar player Marv Tarplin. Whenever possible, the girls dogged the Motown offices. Gordy steadfastly refused to record them until they were through with high school, tossing them only handclapping session chores at $2.50 a shot.

Their first record, "I Want a Guy," flopped in 1961; "Let Me Go the Right Way" reached only number ninety. It wasn't until Gordy teamed the Supremes with the writing/production team of Holland-Dozier-Holland that they hit the formula that would net eleven number one singles.

"It was funny," Diana remembers. "Mrs. Edwards had to practically twist Dick Clark's arm to get him to take us on his tour, Dick Clark's Cavalcade of Stars. Gene Pitney was starring, people like that. We were the 'and others.' I guess that was 1964. We started out opening the show 'cause no one knew us. But 'Where Did Our Love Go?' broke while we were out there, and by the time we got back we were closing the show."

By the end of that tour Clark was glad to renegotiate the Supremes' contract. "Where Did Our Love Go?" was followed by four successive number one hits: "Baby Love," "Come See About Me," "Stop in the Name of Love," and "Back in My Arms Again." As the Beatles continued to crash the American charts, the Supremes box-stepped into the British Hit Parade; by 1966 they had five number one hits there. Gordy saw a world market opening up. And as his product became less black and more processed, there were enticing new possibilities at home as well.

With the Supremes especially, the Motown sound made a sharp right turn, heading, with good speed, to the lucrative circuit of white supper clubs and Vegas casinos. Besides the straight, four-beats-to-a-measure rhythm of their own hits, the Supremes followed Gordy's directives on how to court the mink and monogram crowd with a repertoire of "standards." While chaperones and beauticians fussed with gowns, wigs, and mink eyelashes, Gordy turned to a canny showbiz vet named Maurice King to work out the act itself.

King is an energetic retirement-age gentleman, still Pops to those he has taught. He says he couldn't leave Detroit and his ailing mother when Motown moved West, and since that time he has been special consultant to Gladys Knight and the Pips. When I caught up with him, he had become musical director for the Spinners, working supper-club dates in large hotel chains like the Fairmonts. He says he can't imagine not working. Ask any of his former students—Tops, Tempts, Supremes, Spinners—and they will tell you they can't imagine what the Motown sound might have been without his harmony coaching and his spit-shined staging.

"I have seen a lot of action, darlin'," he admits. In the forties, having worked his way through Tennessee State, King moved to Detroit, where he worked as an arranger for society bands like the Sophisticats. In 1944 he took charge of an all-female orchestra called the International Sweet-hearts of Rhythm. The troupe toured the United States and entertained overseas at the behest of the State Department. In this way Maurice King says he learned "musical diplomacy" early on. The Sweethearts were black, white, American Indian, Chinese, Mexican, and Jewish. They performed songs like "America the Beautiful" in European cities still smoking from bombing raids. They were in the middle of a dance set in West Germany when the emcee broke in and announced that an atomic bomb had been dropped on Hiroshima. Mr. King remembers that people danced like crazy the rest of the night as the Sweethearts played to exhaustion. In 1948 they recorded a bit, songs like "Sweetheart's Jam" and "Ain't the Gravy Good." By 1950 King decided he had had enough of travel and returned to Detroit. A new club called the Flame Show Bar had just opened, and its owner asked King to put a band together. There would be good money, big names. . . .

"Well, I went in April 1950, and I stayed until January 1961," King says. "And like the man said, they *all* came to the Flame: Dinah Washington, Harry Belafonte, Johnny Ray, Brook Benton. I got to direct shows for all of them."

At the time King was also musical director of the Fox Theater (from 1951 to 1958). The audiences there were packed with teenagers like Eddie Floyd, Diana Ross, Wilson Pickett, and the future Temptations. King's move to Motown, however, came through a connection at the Flame.

"Berry's sisters Gwen and Anna owned the concession there. You know, it was an enterprising family. I saw them nightly, and Berry quite often. He heard I had a private studio. He had some cute teenage singers. But he was smart enough to know he needed *acts*."

King's studio wasn't unlike the studios of the gospel quartet coaches who rented out front parlors in Harlem.

"You'd secure a place in homes that had pianos and things. They'd rent you their front suite. At first this is the way the Temptations, Mary Wells, and the Supremes all rehearsed. The Temptations were scheduled at ten in the morning, and the Supremes would be scheduled at noon. And they'd meet going in and out. One day Berry came to me and said, 'Why are you rehearsin' your brains out in somebody's front hall? Why don't you just come on into the company and teach them all?' "

And Motown's fabled Artists Development Department was founded.

"That included a vocal coach, the choreographer Cholly Atkins, and me. I was executive musical director. I had a great assistant named Johnny Allen, and there were a couple of piano accompanists. There was a lady in charge of the girls' wardrobe, makeup and so on, a Mrs. Paul. Harvey Fuqua was director of the whole department. Now say a group had a smash record. Well, they'd have to do a performance. They got to do twelve songs. So while the producers may have taught them the hit record, I have to get them prepared to do the eleven others. We used to say that I was responsible for the in-person how-they-sounded stuff and Cholly Atkins was responsible for how they looked."

Atkins gave the Supremes their sideways head-over-the-shoulder stance, the stylized hand gestures. Maurice King would work up the order of the songs, the pacing of a show, even the between-song patter delivered breathlessly by the doe-eyed Miss Ross. Berry Gordy took a personal, almost obsessive interest in the nightclub productions and would not permit the slightest change without his approval. When the Supremes secured that prized first gig at the Copa in New York, King took them out to four or five other club engagements beforehand.

"By the time the Supremes got to the Copa it was no guesswork, sweetie," King says. "It was all cut-and-dried. Now in the Copa the age-group is maybe twenty to sixty, so they do their records but a lot of show tunes, too. And some real Las Vegas things. And I'd give them a little transition."

"Well, now that you've heard some of our very favorite songs—and we sure hope you enjoyed them—we just wonder if maybe you've heard this one. . . .

"*Ooooohwoooowooooo."*

"They'd fly into the introduction of 'Baby Love' like that, and I want to tell you the audience *screamed.* Because they were hungry and waiting for it. We knew just how long to make them wait." King chuckles. "It's all in the timing, honey."

If an act didn't talk those little transitions well, Maurice King would rewrite them so they could sing them. Gordy would watch rehearsals and shows, and he could be extremely rough if an act wasn't polished to his satisfaction.

"There's one little thing Berry Gordy used to say to a lot of the acts," King says. "And I thought that it was maybe a little cruel at the time. But it was true. He'd say, 'If you can't talk to the people out there, you're gonna have to sing and dance like *hell* to fill up the space.' "

This was particularly painful for some kids from the projects, facing a tuxed white café crowd. They could sing beautifully, but theirs was not the type of English spoken at bridge clubs. Gladys Knight was a good talker, Mr. King recalls. So was Martha Reeves since Martha was never afraid. Diana Ross was very good. She could deliver her lines without stumbling even if Gordy had rewritten them five minutes before curtain. As a vocal coach King never suspected she'd be the one to make it on sheer, raw talent. But Diana Ross always had that theatrical presence. It won her an Oscar nomination for her portrayal of Billie Holiday in *Lady Sings the Blues*.

"The lady *works*," King says. "The lady has always worked very, very hard."

I'm gonna make you love me, as the song says. After all these years, Diana Ross is the first to tell you that she still has to work, even sweat, to win the applause.

"Listen, I'd be lying if I said that any of it came easy," she is saying, withdrawing further into the terry-cloth robe as the body cools down. She drinks more tea, steaming off the last of the lip gloss. She is beautiful but tired now, especially around the eyes. Having it all, and keeping it, do require discipline, she admits. For Diana Ross this means a topflight personal staff to run her business, two households, tours, and recording interests. There are chauffeurs, nannies, traveling beauticians, wardrobe mistresses, secretaries, and maids. And her mother is still her rock. They called her Mama Supreme when she traveled with the group as a chaperone. Now she stays with her granddaughters when their mother is on the road. Sometimes they complain that she is too strict. But discipline worked for Diana, so she tells them to *behave*—they'll thank her later.

"We did have quite a few chaperones, which was really strange," she says. "I mean, for a teenager to grow up traveling so much yet being so sheltered. I didn't date for years. I mean, I'm really happy I met this guy that I married and had my children. It was really very hard. Even now it's hard to date somebody. Anyway, my children keep me balanced. But I think it's difficult. It's a strange life. When I leave all of that. . . ." She waves a hand at the racks of stage costumes, the lavish buffet, the flowers, the cases full of makeup. "I mean, when I go home and go to bed—by myself—it's confusing."

For some performers, that confusion can pose serious adjustment problems. This worries her about her very dear friend Michael Jackson, who missed out not only on normal teen years but on a childhood as well. He has been the featured player since he was old enough to tie his shoes, never knew the inside of a school bus, and watched cartoon shows from the back seats of limousines. He was only ten when as part of the Jackson Five he came to live in Diana's Hollywood home once Motown moved West. By the time he was twenty-four he had written for her and produced her single, "Muscles."

"It was weird," she says, "but I had to force him into being the dominant one when I was singing his song 'Muscles.' One night in the studio he said, 'I just *can't*. I can't tell *you* what to do.' And I said, 'You're the man. You're the boss on this one.' I know him so well. But sometimes even I'm stunned at how he can be so shy. He'll hide, he'll talk like this"— she lowers her voice to a halting whisper—"then you let him onstage and he turns into this sexy, macho *thing*. Offstage I try to get him to step out socially, to get a little more out of himself. He spends a lot of time, too much time by himself."

She asked him to go see *Dreamgirls* for her and give her a report. She tries to coax him to Connecticut for quiet weekends. Once, when she was really concerned, she rented a yacht and took Michael and her daughters sailing in the Caribbean. On the boat he was like one of her children, running across the decks, playing hide-and-seek. Over dinner he was her friend and confidant. When they are photographed together, the physical resemblance is arresting, all angles and eyes. Together they possess all the elements for success. He is a naturally gifted composer, arranger, and performer; she is the sepia Cinderella, spinning style and desire into world superstardom. Offstage they are very different, but in the lights Diana thinks he has created himself in her image.

"There was always an identification between Michael and me," she says. "He kind of idolized me, and he wanted to sing like me."

For fun, producer Quincy Jones had them record some of the sound track to the movie *The Wiz* in the same key. Michael was the scarecrow to Diana's thirty-plus Dorothy. "We did 'Ease On Down the Road,' " she says, referring to the sound track record, "and people couldn't tell which was me and which was Michael. He's matured a lot, but when he was younger, he used to try and move his hands like I did onstage. Everything."

It is growing late, and in the arena below, the yellow forklifts have ceased trundling sound equipment. The road crew has headed back to Amsterdam, and Diana herself must get dressed for the ride back to her hotel there. First we must locate her shoes.

"My old pair was easy to find," she mutters, ducking under a coffee table. She says she had a pair of fuzzy blue slippers, the kind you buy clipped together in Woolworth's. She loved them, but wardrobe deep-sixed them when she wasn't looking. Divas don't prance in matted blue dust mops.

"*There* you are."

From beneath the sofa, she extracts a pair of tiny black kid sandals imprinted with the name of a Manhattan boutique given to charging a few hundred dollars for a few strips of leather. From the racks she chooses a black angora pullover and a pair of buttery leather pants. Fashion is her pleasure, she says, her way of expressing herself. It's one of those nice things women have. It's harder for men to express themselves, she thinks, especially without the degree of fashion and cosmetics acceptable for women.

"I wanted to have a son," she says, "but when I started thinking about it . . . well, I had brothers, and I saw the difficulty of being a male. Right now my brothers cannot get a job."

At the time we spoke, only Diana's older sister, who "went for it" in a serious way, was employed, having worked her way through medical school and become a doctor. The Vietnam War yanked one brother out of school and sent him back, Diana says, "confused and without a useful trade." Two other brothers are looking for spots in show business; a second sister, formerly a flight attendant, is considering opening a boutique for used maternity clothes in Detroit.

Diana pauses for a minute, pulling on a sandal. "She's beautiful, too," she says. "Very beautiful."

Diana's staff except for her driver has departed now. She is always the last to go. That's the way it is for the Boss. She will try to sleep until noon tomorrow, but there is another show to prepare for. She figures that she has spent the better part of her life just *getting ready*.

"I've always spent a lot of time rehearsing. I like to woodshed at home before going to the studio. It's like clothing to me. You spend time putting your outfit together so when you walk out on the streets, you shouldn't think about it anymore. When you go onstage, your clothes need to be *right*. The effort is in *preparing* it. The work itself should be effortless."

All this image stuff is perfectly livable with, Diana says, if you maintain a sense of humor. A lot of yucks have come her way courtesy of that other pop goddess Cher. The two women share a lot: Both are given to lavish stage shows with an average of six to eight costume changes; both use designer Bob Mackie; both are rearing their children alone. Diana and Cher have even been involved romantically with the same man, Gene Simmons, a rock performer conveniently unrecognizable to the public without his Kiss stage makeup. Both women have substantial gay followings, in the *grand dame* tradition of Mae West, Judy Garland, and Dolly Parton. Female caricature, rather than real sex, is the currency.

"I get a lot of gays at my shows, and it's my pleasure," Diana says. "They can dress up like me; they can put on makeup and probably look a lot like Diana Ross. In fact, someone said to me, 'I saw you on Cher's stage show.' Cher has a female impersonator in her show. His name is J.C. This guy has all my moves. He's quicker than I am. I watch *him*, and I see how *I* look."

Perhaps this is not the crossover Berry Gordy had in mind. But Diana thinks he was wise in limiting overt sexiness in the Supremes' presentations. A little went a longer way in white America.

"Someone said, and I agree with him," says Diana, "that the Supremes were such a crossover for young black and white males in our country because there were three black girls and they could openly enjoy them and even lust for them—without thinking what color they were."

She is pacing around the dressing room now, still a bit wired from the show.

"Hey, let's have some beers." She hooks a finger beneath the pop top of a cold can of Heineken. She sips it cautiously, making her way to the steep metal stairway that leads to the loading dock. A low black Jaguar crouches below; the driver holds a door open. Handing off the beer, Diana clings to the railing, placing the spike heels carefully on each step.

"How," she wonders, "will I ever get *down?*"

*   *   *

When Diana and I spoke in 1982, Florence Ballard, the "quiet Supreme," had been dead for six years. Florence liked to say that despite all her years singing with the Supremes, she had never revealed her true voice. She said she started singing at her father's knee. He played guitar, and he played deep blues.

"I'd sing with him," she said. "You know, the public hasn't really heard me."

During the peak years she rarely spoke up in group interviews. In the studio Lamont Dozier, who supervised backup vocals for the Supremes, moved the mike farther away from Florence's arresting tenor lest it outmuscle and outsoul Diana's lead.

"Flo had the pipes," one ex-Motown staffer told me. "But Diana had the poise."

Once she had left the Supremes in 1967, Florence Ballard tried it as a solo, briefly, on ABC Records, with no success. Out of place again, the voice wandered forlornly through soppy show tunes or ill-crafted pop vehicles.

In the interviews she gave at intervals after leaving the group until her death in 1976, the voice was, in hindsight, impossibly blue. At first the quotes were stiffened with anger and wounded pride; progressively the words grew weaker, and the circumstances more ominous.

Eighteen months after she had left the Supremes, *Ebony* magazine visited Miss Ballard in her home on Buena Vista Avenue in Detroit, just across the street from Diana Ross and a few houses away from Mary Wilson. As she answered the reporter's questions, she rolled up the ranch mink sleeves of her at-home gown in order to heat up bottles for her infant twin girls.

"I've told people over and over again," she said, "that we didn't have any 'fight.' We had arguments and things just like sisters have because we grew up just like sisters and we were together all those years. Now as far as the so-called 'jealousy' is concerned, Mary Wilson and I always knew that Diana had the most commercial type voice, so she took most of the leads. We knew that all along . . . so I just wish people wouldn't read more into my leaving than is actually there. All I have to say is that I wish the group all the success in the world. They're doing their thing, and Flo Ballard is going to do hers."

She added that her husband, Thomas Chapman, Berry Gordy's former chauffeur, had great plans for her. The same Mr. Chapman would appear in later newspaper interviews as a vigilant duenna, stopping his wife's more pithy responses with warnings like "Mr. Gordy wouldn't like that." Chapman was undaunted by the fact that Flo's first ABC releases, "It Doesn't Matter How I Say It" and "Love Ain't Love," were flops. He told interviewers of the deals he had arranged and the important people he knew.

"I believe I can make it," Flo insisted. "I wonder if people know how many flops the Supremes had before we made it big?"

On certain subjects, *Ebony* reported, Miss Ballard "maintained secrecy." There are no details of the "illnesses" that caused her to miss shows, no comments on the serious truancies that did her in. After failing to make a date at the Hollywood Bowl and a high-stakes run at the Flamingo Hotel in Las Vegas, Florence was asked to leave by Berry Gordy and was replaced by Cindy Birdsong, who had been singing with Patti LaBelle and the Bluebells.

In place of juicy revelations, *Ebony* was obliged to flesh out the report with a description of Flo's home. The house was large, with a wedgwood blue interior and a "feel" of Oriental splendor. The drapes were velvet; the upholstery was deeply sculpted; the crystal chandeliers were tinted. A "unique" table hung suspended from the ceiling by a chain. All in all, fewer more intimate details were learned except for this: "Her husband is the only person known to have any influence on Flo now. He is completely in charge, except Flo has told him flatly that she'll have nothing to do with trading in their 1968 Eldorado for a 1969 Cadillac limousine."

Chapman had put in heavy mileage from the front seat of Berry Gordy's limousine; for years Florence had ridden in back. Now she was uneasy with the whole idea.

"Suppose I wanted to drive downtown and buy something," she said. "I'd look stupid sitting up there driving a big limousine."

Shortly after, in 1970, *The Michigan Chronicle* found Mrs. Chapman counting out change to buy a head of cabbage and a box of cornmeal mix. At twenty-seven, she was broke, had lost her home, pawned her jewelry. The quiet Supreme complained to the press about mysterious harassing phone calls and threats of "public humiliation."

"Someone was always talking about exposing me," she said, "which is funny now that I think of it. I didn't even have a reputation."

She said that it was often pointed out to her, in heated corporate moments, that after all, she had never finished school (she quit after the eleventh grade). She would not say directly who her tormentors were, but she did not accuse her old girl friends.

"I was in such a bad state for a while, almost to the point of being bedridden," she explained. "For a year I didn't set foot out of the house. I guess I can't really accuse my close acquaintances of being fair-weather friends because I just withdrew into a shell."

In 1971 she emerged to file a lawsuit against Motown for $8.7 million, charging conspiracy in ousting her from the Supremes and failure to report the group's earnings accurately. The suit was dismissed in court as groundless.

Over the next few years she was mugged, robbed, and separated from her husband. By January 1975, to support her three daughters, she was forced to appeal to the Aid to Dependent Families with Children program, a form of welfare. She told a reporter that she was looking for work, perhaps as a receptionist. "It's something around people," she explained.

She was alone, on February 21, 1976, when she called her mother at 3:00 A.M. to ask her to keep the children awhile longer. She complained of shortness of breath. At thirty-two she weighed 198 pounds and was reportedly on medication for high blood pressure.

Some hours later Thomas Chapman called Florence's youngest sister, Linda, to tell her that he had found Florence lying on the floor. She was conscious but had difficulty speaking. She could not move her legs.

Dr. Werner Spitz, medical examiner, later reported that she had been admitted to Mount Carmel Mercy Hospital complaining of a numbness in the extremities. He stated that the patient had ingested an unknown amount of pills and had consumed alcohol. She died at 10:05 A.M. of cardiac arrest. And for the first time in nearly a decade, hysteria marked the public appearance of Florence Ballard.

Weeping fans tore at the flowers and wreaths. One terrified funeral home attendant grabbed the base of a stripped floral arrangement and brandished it as a spear to fend off the crowd. The organ played the Supremes' "fare-well" song, "Someday We'll Be Together." The Four Tops and Marv Johnson were pallbearers. The eulogy, in the New Bethel Baptist Church, was delivered by Aretha Franklin's father, the Reverend C. L. Franklin. Berry Gordy did not attend. There was tension in the church as Diana Ross was escorted from her limousine by a cordon of bodyguards. She was photographed holding one of Florence's daughters.

"I love you, Blondie" was the message on the satin banner of the flowers that Diana had ordered.

*   *   *

The third Supreme, Mary Wilson, lives in Los Angeles now. She has another set of good, good girl friends to see her into her fortieth year. Some are from the business; some, not.

"And this," she says, "is where the ladies lunch."

On this warm, unusually clear afternoon Mary has driven us to a small Japanese restaurant, a quiet place that shares a parking lot with some gas pumps. She and her friends find it very relaxed. They settle into the soothing half dark, knowing just what they want. They take a moment to admire the beauty and precision of the Japanese still lifes on their stoneware plates, then tear into them with good cheer. They drink sweet plum wine and pale green tea. Mary says they sit here for hours, dishing and scolding, boosting and bitching.

"Two plum wines, please."

"Will there be more to your group?"

"Just a duet today," Mary tells the waitress, musing aloud as the wine arrives.

Girl groups were surely a phenomenon in the sixties, a fad if you will. But if you think about it, it doesn't take a record company or some Svengali producer to make one. "Just a few good, good friends sitting around," Mary says. "Everybody has her voice. After a while you fall into parts naturally. And when the harmony's right, girl talk's a real pretty song."

Formal performance music doesn't fill her days the way it once did. As an alto she was best suited to group work. She's done some solo work, mainly in Europe, but just now she's on a sabbatical from supper clubs and TV shows. But she says she does not go long without checking in with that familiar circle of voices.

"The girls. I could not live without them," she says. "You know, you love men in those wild up-and-down ways. But the girls will get you through it *all* every day, if you know what I mean. They are always right *there.*"

She raises her glass.

"To the girls?"

"To the girls."

Mary Wilson smiles often—not the wide beauty-queen smile you saw on album covers and on *Ed Sullivan*. Those smiles could make your cheeks ache, Mary says, and these days she is not into pain of any sort, no, thank you. She is comfortable in just a light sheen of lip gloss. Her hair is long and gently waved beneath a wide straw hat. The jacket and skirt are a well-fitting compromise between sensuality and style. The leather purse has been lived in, and the conversation is easy.

"I'm glad to talk," she says. "The time is right."

For the first time, she says, she is really trying to look back. She has kept a diary since she was a teenager, but only recently has she been going back and reading those loopy ball-point entries. She thinks she herself may do a book and call it "My Life as a Supreme." Interviews like this help her with her own research. So do encounters with old friends.

Not long ago she ran into Marvin Gaye in London and spent an evening in his rented flat, listening to sounds from his old life and his new one. After twenty years he had finally broken free of Motown contractually and had signed with CBS Records. He was working on his new album, and only the rhythm tracks were on the work tape he had. He put on the cassettes for Mary and sang the vocals he intended to record over them. He closed his eyes and tilted his face upward, the way he always had, and it was all so free and nice—so *out* there—that for a moment Mary had no idea where they were in space or time.

Neither of them had any idea that a year later the resulting album, *Midnight Love,* would outsell some of the biggest names in pop, rock, and soul and that one cut, "Sexual Healing," would be Marvin Gaye's first number one song on pop charts since "What's Going On?" in 1971.

"I'm so happy he's gonna give us more of those sounds that are *his,*" she says. "He told me, 'Well, baby, I'm doing it now, I'm really into it.' And I am *so* glad. You know, when we first went to Motown, this guy was sitting there at the piano, and he was so handsome and so soulful, about the most soulful singer that company ever turned up. And we just sat there in a trance. I mean, I fell in love with him, and so did Florence and Diane. He knew we all had crushes on him."

She laughs, remembering how she and Florence used to give each other the high sign when Marvin walked into the Motown building and they tried, so very hard, to act nonchalant.

"You know, if Florence were here, and if she laughed, everybody in this restaurant would laugh. She had that kind of happiness in her soul; it just came out like Santa Claus, that laugh, *ho-ho-ho.* And when she was sad, *everybody* would be sad. You'd *know* it. She just couldn't stand for any injustice to happen. And when she realized that life was what it was— that it just wasn't fair—well, she couldn't handle that."

Mary still misses her girl friend Florence. But so much happened to stomp on the spirit of the buoyant, soulful schoolgirl she came up with, it's almost as if *that* Florence had died before her body did. There have been so many rumors about how and why she died. Mary says that no one has gotten it quite right yet. Someone has to. But for now . . .

"It's always a very touchy thing for me to talk about. I feel sad because there's so much about Flo—so much talent the girl had—that will never be known. She was a *great* singer. But no one will ever really know that. That play *Dreamgirls* was dead on, you know. Florence sings—sang— just like that."

She is referring to Effie, the Dream played by singer Jennifer Holliday, herself a troubled, overweight twenty-two-year-old. Holliday won a Tony Award for playing Effie, the soulful singer who hits the skids after being forced out of the group. Effie has one searing solo, "And I'm Telling You I'm Not Going." It ripped up audiences nightly while Holliday was still in the show. Mary says the sight of that young woman, arms reaching up, that big body racked with hurt and shame and a hundred other things . . .

"Well, it just tore me up," Mary says. "The guy next to me kept giving me hankies. I just felt like I was transported back to 1965, and my heart just went back there, and the tears were coming out. I couldn't stop them. I mean, I had makeup on, I was trying to be cool, to be Mary, the Supreme, and I just boohooed my way through it and made a mess of myself."

Unlike Diana, who took offense without having seen the show, Mary says she was curious and ultimately pleased. "I'm sitting there, just thinking it's going to be a play based on our experience, but not on *us*," she says. "Well, it *was* us. It hit me like a bolt. I was sitting with all these people, and everybody was watching my life."

She was amazed, sitting in her $35 seat, at what lengths Broadway went to to re-create their poverty. It was always a crisis to come up with the twenty-five-cent bus fare to get from the Brewster projects to the studio on West Grand. Michael Bennett spent a then-record $3 million on sets, costumes, and talent. The Motown soundboard had all the sophistication of a ham radio; Bennett told me he used more than eighteen miles of electrical cable to wire his productions.

"I don't think it's amazing that he [Bennett] came up with the right visuals, the picture, you know," Mary says. "My amazement is that he actually went ahead and developed it into a play the *way* he did. Anyone would imagine that if you were doing a play on the Supremes—even though they *say* it was not the Supremes—you would play up the Diana Ross character. So I was surprised that they featured what Florence was going through instead, that they were capable of that insight.

"After I got over the initial shock that it was about my life, I felt very proud. I said, 'Wow, this show that millions of people have been watching is our lives. We've actually made history. Me, and Diane, and Flo, my Lord. We never thought about it. We were just doing what we enjoyed. And fortunately it paid well.''

In hindsight, Mary agrees that the Supremes' is a very American success story. *Dreamgirls* is, after all, a white Broadway production about a black enterprise, a commercial dramatization of young artists' struggles with commercial artifice. Onstage the Dreams peer out through backstage mirrors, and reverse images collide: black art and white business, reality and appearance, greasy soul and Vegas glitz.

"That show was much more about Motown than the Supremes," Mary Wilson says. "It was a marvelous idea they had at Motown. Reminds me of the Hollywood days when they took over a star and completely groomed them.''

It was a disappointment but no surprise to Mary that friendships had to suffer.

"In the beginning, I'd go to fight for Diane in a minute. And she'd go to fight for me. We were inseparable, like sisters. And Flo, the same. I mean, *we* could get angry at each other, but nobody else could. By the time the name changed [to Diana Ross and the Supremes] it had already gotten out of our hands. It was already *Motown*. It was all business, period. And you know, Motown was growing, growing so very fast. It happens in a lot of situations where you have a small business and then it becomes a big business. A lot of things are taken out of your control.''

She found it a bit degrading to be a millionaire in her early twenties and unable to withdraw bank funds to buy herself a car without the written permission of Berry Gordy. In 1977 Mary sued her former employers, contending they had taken financial advantage of her being a minor and charging that those underage agreements still allowed Gordy to authorize withdrawals from her own savings. Special permission had to be sought for large purchases such as real estate or cars. In addition, she charged that funds were withheld over long periods while she received only $200 to $300 per week. As part of her legal struggle, Mary Wilson came away with 50 percent of the rights to usage and interest in the group's name. The whole business was messy and painful, but she says she came through with her sense of humor intact.

"Florence found it all very difficult," she says, "and surely most of the other acts did, too. We could not really grasp how we could be so important. Then, all of a sudden, we become nothing, and the company itself is the star. This really hurt a lot of people. But it was only natural. I'm sure it happens in every big corporation that started as a family-type hole in the wall.''

Money and fame weren't the issues to high school girls in the beginning. Motown was the club everyone wanted to join.

"It was just cool, you know?'' Mary says. "And if you are sixteen, cool is the meaning of life itself.''

After school she and Diana and Florence took turns at the mirror, practicing long, even strokes of eyeliner, blotting the kinds of lipstick that came in flavors, the air heady with the scents of cologne and scorched hair. Diana wielded a rattail comb like a field marshal's baton; she always had the inside track on the latest 'do and considered it her business to work out the battle dress when another girl group picked a clean three-part-harmony fight at a neighborhood rec center.

"Them Fondas think they're so tough. Hah.''

Florence was head cheerleader. She sat there in her clingy Orlon sweater, conjuring pep. "They can't outdo us. You just see who they clap for the loudest tonight. You just see.''

"Awriiiight.''

"But first, girl, fix that hem.''

The girls were at a similar powwow at Mary's apartment when they first heard themselves on the radio.

"All of a sudden, we were screaming,'' Mary says, " 'Mom, Mom, come here, listen to *this!* This is us!' ''

The noise traveled fast around the Brewster projects. Diana, Mary, and Flo had made the club, had earned the right to sport its colors. The new, redesigned Motown label was midnight blue with a map of the Motor City superimposed.

"We became heroes of the project overnight. You were hearing, 'Hey, Mary lives there.' You walk by, and they yell, 'Hey, Mary, right on! Hey, Diane, hey, Flo.' I think it was the best experience I ever had in my life. It was probably more exciting than our first million seller.''

That first gold single, "Where Did Our Love Go?,'' convinced them that they were really going to make it. And at Motown, Mary said, it made them *the girls.* Other groups, like the Marvelettes and the Vandellas, were girls, of course, but already distinctions were being made as it became clear the Supremes best fitted Berry Gordy's optimum requirements for Top Ten crossover success.

"We weren't as—well, masculine is the wrong word. Maybe tough. The Vandellas were a bit more soulful than us, let's put it that way. More R and B than us; they'd move more, with different kinds of gyrations."

Hip sliding was not in the Supremes' repertoire of stage moves. In fact, they hardly moved at all, except for the celebrated hand gestures taught them by Cholly Atkins. Done in perfect, elbow-length-white-glove synchrony, those moves are a bit harder than they looked.

After laying aside a chopstick, Mary demonstrates the famous traffic cop gesture that signaled the chorus of "Stop in the Name of Love." Berry Gordy and Temptations Paul Williams and Melvin Franklin helped them invent it on the spot. The hit was so new that there was no choreography when a sudden live TV show in England came up. All six repaired to a cramped TV studio men's room to work it out.

"STOP. Oh, no, not like that. Bring the arm up close to the body; try not to bend your elbow way out. That's it, palm out. Not in front of your face, girl. They always have to be able to see your face."

A startled waitress observes my lesson discreetly, then wonders if more plum wine wouldn't be nice.

"Cholly gave the Temptations all those great acrobatic steps. But since we were girls, we were restricted, so we worked on the hand motions."

Even offstage the girls were shown new, more proper forms of body language by an etiquette instructor named Mrs. Johnson.

"She'd teach us how to get in and out of a car correctly. You know, you're supposed to put your leg in and scoot your behind in, never bend over, never have your rear showing. But every time we'd get out of her class and she'd go out and get into her car we'd die laughing. Because she did just the opposite of what she taught us."

Fittings for gowns and wigs were a part of the regimen. Songs were not presented to them until all three parts had been tailored to their voices.

"The guy who handled lead vocals was Eddie Holland. He had a way with lyrics and melody that was compatible with the Supremes' sound, and the Four Tops'. Why, I don't know. It's just like going to a tailor. Somebody just happens to fit your things perfectly. It was Eddie on lead vocals and melodies. Brian Holland took care of the tracks and overall composition. Lamont Dozier also did tracks and melodies and handled backgrounds. It worked for the Vandellas and for the Tempts. Most of the success is due to their giving us the right material, knowing what each lead singer could do and pushing them. Eddie pushed Levi [Stubbs of the

Four Tops] and Diane an awful lot because both of them were very stubborn. And Eddie was the kind of guy who said, 'Hey, man, this is the way *I* want you to sing it.' The artist had to sing it his way, and thank God, we did.''

They obeyed their producer, Mary says, because they flat-out adored Berry Gordy.

"We stuck to him so close, all three of us, that if he stopped in his tracks, we'd all pile up behind him. The guy happens to really know what he's doing. People would die to be around him. All the artists would like to be his favorite. And once he started referring to the Supremes as *the* girls, once it was clear where we stood in his eyes, most of the other girls really didn't like us. I mean, Flo and I could hang out together with the other girls and be comfortable. But it was very difficult for the other girl groups to like Diane.''

In terms of glamour Ross was clearly the front-runner with her manikin's figure and devotion to style. But vocally the others had sized her up and found her lacking. To build her leads, she was coached individually, often by Berry Gordy himself. Sometimes she would be given tapes of other Motown artists, like Brenda Holloway, to study. Mary points out that even on the Supremes' last single together, if you listen closely, you can hear Motown staffer Johnny Bristol leading Diana through the vocal on "Someday We'll Be Together," cueing her with phrases like "you tell 'em" and "sing it *pretty.*"

Before the name change, before Flo's departure and all those blue times, the Supremes had a lot of fun on the road. They were still star-struck enough to feel faint when their road manager arranged for them to meet Sam Cooke one night while he was playing the Flame in Detroit. During one long tour, desperate for just an afternoon's freedom, they persuaded Diana's mother, then their chaperone, to let Jackie Wilson "baby-sit" while she went to lunch.

"Oh, sure, I'll watch them little girls like a hawk," he told her.

"Jackie Wilson and the Dells," Mary says. "Some baby-sitters, huh? We all behaved, of course, but it was a pretty funny concept. On those big tours you couldn't fool around. You'd only have time between shows, when those movies were playing. So maybe you could squeeze in lunch or go to someone's dressing room and play cards. You couldn't be hanging around the guys, though that's what we really wanted to do.''

For America's sweethearts it was a PG-rated existence.

"We really became what Berry had imagined," Mary says. "And the message to all those guys was loud and clear. You can look, but don't even think about touching. We were off limits to fans and to other performers."

Rolling a transparent coral fish egg around with a chopstick, Mary giggles. "I should tell you what really happened when the Supremes met the Beatles."

The Supremes were in New York to do an *Ed Sullivan Show*. In town to do their historic Shea Stadium concerts, the Beatles had turned a few blocks near the Warwick Hotel into a riot zone. In the midst of all the volcanic hype, management for both groups thought it would be nice if these seven Top Ten heavyweights got together.

"Of course, the Beatles couldn't get out of their hotel," Mary recalls. "So in between one of the rehearsals for the *Sullivan Show,* we went for a limousine to go over there."

Inside the car the Supremes primped a bit for their presentation.

"Oh, we had our little outfits, you know. I had on my chinchilla, Diane had on her mink, and Florence had her fox and our little gloves. *Ooooweee,* my dear, we were just *so* chic."

They had to struggle to maintain their smiles when the door opened to the Beatles' suite.

"There's all these guys laying around; they looked like slobs. Maybe they were totally out of their heads, I don't know. Just sitting in their jeans, looking raunchy. They took one look at *us,* and they freaked."

The visit lasted only minutes. John Lennon retreated to a corner, wall-eyed with terror.

"He said maybe three words. Paul talked to us for a few minutes. We were whispering to our people, 'Get us out of here,' and they were saying to their people, 'Get them out of here.' Eventually, about five minutes later, we left."

She didn't think much about it until she ran into George Harrison about ten years ago. Yes, he said, the Beatles were mighty freaked. He laughed and explained.

"When you girls came up, we thought the Supremes were gonna be three hip black girls. And you girls come up there in your little fur coats and all prissy and everything. We were *so* paranoid."

It's getting late, and behind the counter the sushi chef is hanging up his array of scabbards. In between the talk and the choreography lessons, a sizable pyramid of tuna and yellowtail has gone untouched. We decide to have it packed up and head out, blinking, into the bright afternoon.

Mary can't find her car keys, digging through a welter of notebooks, mascara, cleaners' tickets, and the like. We are doing a Lucy-and-Ethel with the carton of fish and her purse contents when she leans against the car and laughs.

"You know something? For years, I didn't have to carry around so much as a Kleenex. Or a key or even a purse. There was always someone there, trailing after me. It's pretty funny when you think about it. I am always pulling these little scenes, losing keys and whatnot. After all that's gone down, I guess it's not a terrible side effect, huh? That I can't get used to carrying my little freight?"

In the spring of 1983 the Supremes—Diana Ross, Mary Wilson, and Cindy Birdsong—were reunited, briefly, for the finale of the two-hour TV special celebrating Motown's twenty-fifth anniversary. Those present at the taping saw Diana Ross shove her old friend Mary Wilson and knock the mike out of her hand. Smokey Robinson was dispatched from the wings to airbrush the awkward moment with his considerable charm. When the show was aired, it drew an audience rating double that of any show in the time slot; the dicey moment had been neatly spliced out of the tape. Speaking to *People* magazine shortly after, Mary Wilson politely characterized Diana's behavior as not "a personal thing."

Mary went on to a summer of small revival shows with a reconstituted set of Supremes. Diana Ross held a free concert in Central Park that cost the city of New York $650,000 in damages and police overtime. More than a quarter of a million people stood in the downpour of a predicted rainstorm, yet before she canceled the show until the next night, Diana was moved to ask them, "Do you love me?"

The show went on the following night, and afterward roving youths, working in packs, robbed and beat the exiting crowd and passersby in streets surrounding the park. In the wake of the civic uproar in her adopted home, Diana flew to L.A. to appear on the *Tonight Show*. She showed Johnny footage of how she calmed the crowd; no mention was made of what one radio station was calling "the night New York got mugged."

The majority of the perpetrators were identified as unemployed minority youths—kids who could not have gone unnoticed in previous park concerts by Elton John and Simon and Garfunkel. No one could blame Diana Ross for their crimes, but when Anaid, her production company, and Paramount, which co-produced and televised the concert, announced there were no profits, the press was less than sympathetic.

Despite having sold world film and video rights to the event, the concert backers claimed to have lost money; the city of New York would not get its promised 7.5 percent of the profits, nor would the children of New York get the playground Diana had pledged to build in Central Park. *People* magazine ran a full-page photo of New York's Mayor Koch holding out his empty palm. Days later, Diana and "Hizzoner" kissed and made up at a news conference when she presented a check for $250,000 "out of my own pocket" for a playground to be named in her honor.

"Yes, you put pressure on me," she told the press. But she insisted that she had intended to ante up regardless. Building the playground, she explained, was always very real in her mind. Like so many other wonderful things in her life, it had started as a dream.

13

Are You Ready for a Brand-new Beat?

Now it was the standard joke with blacks, that whites could not, *cannot clap on a backbeat. You know—ain't got the rhythm? What Motown did was very smart. They beat the kids over the head with it. That wasn't soulful to us down at Stax, but baby, it* sold.

—ISAAC HAYES

DURING MOTOWN'S BOOM YEARS, when it dominated the charts from 1962 to 1971, the biggest star was the sound itself, personified by groups like the Supremes. That it was heavier on style than soul assured its crossover success. As the teen record raters used to say on *American Bandstand,* "It has a good beat. You can dance to it."

In record stores nationwide the kids were giving it a 95. In fact, Gordy liked to boast that if a record sold a million, 70 percent would be bought by whites. This being the case, Europe was a logical second frontier. On that continent the entertainment firm of Pathé-Marconi launched a catalogue of European pressings of Tamla/Motown hits in 1965, as the Supremes and the Beatles traded off the number one spot on the charts like a pair of slam-dunk NBA forwards.

The same time Pathé began its catalogue, agreements were made for

Tamla/Motown European tours. The first show at the Olympia in Paris was a sellout, with the Supremes, Martha and the Vandellas, and Stevie Wonder, all backed by the Earl Van Dyke Sextet, a ground-breaking backup band straight from the Motown studio.

Soul was selling worldwide, be it Motown or Memphis. For style-conscious teens, it was one of those prized imports of American cool, the sort that had had Czech subteens and Munich lounge lizards learning the phonetics to Elvis's "Don't Be Cruel" a few years earlier. Like blue jeans, American black music seemed the real thing. European imitators were well intentioned but often hilarious.

One Franciszek Walicki, billing himself as the "Polish Alan Freed," caused riots by playing soul in Gdansk. Polish authorities had no choice but to crack down, they announced, when self-styled "soul exponent" Wojciech Korda ripped things up with his group, the Blue and Blacks. Spain offered Los Pop Tops. It would take a bit longer in reserved Japan for a music so baldly emotional to gain a foothold. But when it did, in the early seventies, Tokyo teens rushed to barbershops demanding Afros, renaming themselves Rocky and Tyrone, getting as funky as possible in clubs like the Afro Rake, the Mr. Soul Disco, and the Big Together Club.

To young black performers with hot records, the fad made sense. To older bluesmen, who were "rediscovered" by the renewed interest in black music, the paychecks were welcome, but the patronage was a trifle nettlesome.

"I had to come to you behind the Rolling Stones and the Beatles," Muddy Waters told an American college audience. "I had to go to England to get here."

NOD FROM BEATLES PUTS DETROIT SOUND ON MAP, the London *Sunday Times* reported, with muted but genuine enthusiasm, on a twenty-four-day British tour by the Supremes, the Vandellas, the Contours, the Temptations, and Stevie Wonder in 1965. The Fab Four had been most complimentary. In fact, they were mad for Motown and had been saying so to reporters wherever they went. Berry Gordy, touring with his troupes, replied in kind: "We are very honored the Beatles should have said what they did. They're creating the same type of music as we are and we're part of the same stream."

That stream was pop, more than R & B, and it was running solid gold. It stood to reason that Motown soul would get a firmer toehold, and faster, than the blacker, less compromising gutbucket soul pumped out of Memphis and points south. After all, one Motown veteran recalls, in 1965 things hadn't gotten too ugly yet, and the mood was still upbeat. Lyndon Johnson was constructing his "Great Society"; Martin Luther King, Jr., had been awarded the Nobel Peace Prize. And Vietnam was still confined to three-inch dispatches between the obits and the tire ads.

"People were still partyin'," says the Four Tops' Levi Stubbs, "before it hit the fan."

The hi-fi set was sixties state of the art, rumbling Mary Wells and the Supremes above the party din as the jumpy host collated his international multicolored guests. Brian Epstein, the Beatles' manager, had arranged and promoted an English tour for the Four Tops, and he had orchestrated it with the same media ballyhoo that had dropped the Fab Four in the colonies—airport fan scenes, banners, press conferences, flashbulbs, and headlines: THE FOUR TOPS ARRIVE!

They stood, a trifle nervously, in Epstein's London flat, celebrating their first Atlantic crossing with the leading edge of the British invasion. The Beatles, the Rolling Stones, the Who, and the Moody Blues mingled with the Tops and Motown staffers. Clusters of feathery, miniskirted English "birds" sang aloud to "My Guy." The rooms were awash in integrated sixties cool. Mod paisleys and vented sharkskins, ashy white lipstick, Old Spice, Yardley cologne, cognac, rum and Coke—all passed beneath the wide porcelain stare of mink-lashed Jean Shrimpton eyes.

Mutual awe began to melt with the ice in the drinks. Someone heard Jagger confess admiration for Smokey Robinson's courtly love poems, flip side to Jagger's secret heart journeys to catch the funkier James Brown live and low-down in the belly of Harlem. Laughter rose with the music, a thudding Motown medley. Suddenly John Lennon raised his voice above the din to shout to the Tops' Larry Payton. "Tell me something, man," he yelled. "When you cats go into the studio, what does the drummer beat on to get that backbeat? You use a bloody *tree* or something?"

The late session drummer Benny Benjamin was an essential element in Motown's secret formula; when drugs and alcohol weakened his mighty reach, it took two drummers to replace him. Bassist James Jamerson, who died in 1983, was finally credited in his obituaries for his innovative genius. But while both men were doing their best work, the sound confounded thousands of Top Ten hopefuls who wore out copies of the Tempts' "My Girl," looking to distill its magic into understandable essences of drumbeats and hook lines. The Motown sound was loosely definable as a mélange of R & B, pop, even Vegas stylings, strung along with gospel harmonies and rhythms. It was crafted on simple 4/4 "straight time," with a thumping backbeat even the clumsiest—or whitest—dance klutz was sure to pick up on.

Long before pop synthesists like Lionel Richie and the Commodores carried Motown's high-tech pop/soul into the eighties, Berry Gordy had made a conscious decision to turn his company toward the most commercial forms of black music. Gospel and blues, despite their migrations, have remained essentially rural and simple. The urban forms are far more arranged and, in response to rapid changes in city styles, a bit jumpy and erratic. This nervous complexity allows for borrowing bits and phrases from nearly anywhere. Motown blended church, cha-cha—whatever it took to craft the crossover hit.

"The Motown sound," Berry Gordy liked to tell interviewers, "is made up of rats, roaches, and love."

The house poet was somewhat more eloquent, but equally vague. "People would listen to it, and they'd say, 'Aha, they use more bass. Or they use more drums.' Bullshit," says Smokey Robinson. "When we were first successful with it, people were coming from Germany, France, Italy, Mobile, Alabama. From New York, Chicago, California. From *everywhere*. Just to record in Detroit. They figured it was in the air, that if they came to Detroit and recorded on the freeway, they'd get the Motown sound. Listen, the Motown sound to me is *not* an audible sound. It's spiritual, and it comes from the people that make it happen. What other people didn't realize is that we just had one studio there, but we recorded in Chicago, Nashville, New York, L.A.—almost every big city. And we still got the sound."

Just like the wave of country music homesteaders who set up storefront record companies on Nashville's Music Row, Detroit did develop its share of Motown imitators. In the mid-sixties an investigator for the Toronto *Star* found that "on nearly every block in some neighborhoods, there seems to be at least one small record firm, sign over door, Cadillac in driveway."

Only one competitive studio, run by a man named Ed Wingate, gave Berry Gordy cause for concern. He bought it and renamed it Motown Studio B.

As he expanded his operation, Berry Gordy borrowed a phrase from heavy industry for a new department overseeing the goods. He called it Quality Control. Standards grew more rigid, tightening the funky parameters of the sound. The raw R & B edges of early groups like the Contours would all but disappear. After 1965 there was less gospel audible in the arrangements and harmonies. As the soundboard was upgraded, Motown made concessions to other market trends, adding synthesizers and wah-wah pedals to the stewpot in order to faintly psychedelicize acts like the Tempts.

"Nothing was left to chance, that's for sure," says Temptation Richard Street. Before he joined the group to replace Paul Williams, he worked at Motown as a "quality control evaluator."

He trained for six years under the tutelage of Motown's fabled engineers, among them Larry Horn. Chief engineer Mike McClean jerry-built the eight-track mix and soundboard himself. They rigged speakers and mikes and developed a reliable, if funky, listening lab to test the product. Yes, Street says, they really did listen to the cuts and mix them by trying them out on speakers you might find in a car radio or a cheap transistor radio.

"We'd have small to medium and large speakers," he says. "You'd put in the small one and turn the dial, and if you couldn't understand the words or it wasn't clear enough, you'd write a little memo back downstairs, like 'Turn up the drums' or 'Too much bass' or 'Can't hear lead vocals loud enough.' "

He says he learned a lot from his good friend Earl Van Dyke, who was in charge of the studio musicians.

Saxophonist Eli Fountain and keyboard player Earl Van Dyke were the founding members of the original Funk Brothers, Motown's studio band, which, with various personnel changes, often went on the road shows as well. Sometimes they were billed as the Earl Van Dyke Sextet. At varying times the studio crew included guitar player Robert White, bassist James Jamerson, guitarist Joe Messina, drummer Benny Benjamin, plus Fountain and Van Dyke.

The Funk Brothers, Van Dyke estimates, were responsible for the instrumentation that shaped and sold the sound on 250 million records. Their biggest strength was adaptability. And though they seldom received publishing credit and the resulting royalties, they composed and improvised along with producers.

Smokey Robinson waxes lyrical about James Jamerson's stunning, distinctive bass lines and says he could not have amassed his huge catalogue of songs without melodic inspiration from Marv Tarplin's guitar. Stevie Wonder credits Benny Benjamin with schooling him in percussion and rhythm. Yet despite their obvious contributions, Motown treated its musicians with the take-it-or-leave-it attitude auto companies exerted on their replaceable human parts. They were usually on call twenty-four hours a day, unable to record as acts on their own, and generally paid flat salaries, no matter how long the hours or how big the hit. No special incentive was offered to Earl Van Dyke when Motown headed West; without raises, he insists, many of the musicians could not afford to relocate to L.A. once Motown moved there.

"Earl is a modest, generous, professional man," Richard Street says. "No matter what incredible thing he came up with in a session, you'd never hear him braggin' on it."

In fact, he could be downright sardonic about how the rest of the world reacted to what he felt was just another day's work. Asked about the Supremes' 1964 smash "Baby Love," Van Dyke told his interviewer: "After it became a hit, somebody wrote about the genius of handclapping on the backbeat. Said it was a new sound, revolutionized pop music. Hell, it wasn't even handclapping. Ain't no way we gonna pay twelve people session fees to clap hands. It was two by fours, man, two by fours hooked together with springs and some guy stompin' on them to make a backbeat. We knocked that song off in two takes."

For echo, they recorded in a bathroom adjoining the studio. Cries of "Don't flush yet" rang out during works in progress. Wood blocks, ball-points, hands, feet, combs, shoes—anything handy could become a per-cussion instrument. That old gospel standby the tambourine was used in ways that Clara Ward might never have imagined. Holland-Dozier-Holland used it on their Top Forty audience the way kindergarten teachers pass out sticks and blocks. Banged incessantly, the tambourine helped even the fumble-footed lock into a beat. But the same instrument is made to sound like a venomous rattler on the introduction to Marvin Gaye's "I Heard It Through the Grapevine."

Systematic fail-safes grew with the company's assembly-line reputation. When others in the industry began accusing Gordy's staff of producing a sound rather than songs, he responded with unabashed candor.

"You probably haven't any voice," he told a Detroit *Free Press* reporter in 1965. "But there are probably three notes you can sing. I can take those three notes and give them an arrangement and some lyrics. That makes a song. And your song will sell."

"Rock and roll shows us the plum," a member of the Artists Development Department told a *New York Times* reporter investigating the nation's most successful black enterprise. "Our job is to bring it in here and can it."

Quality Control could be an exhausting place to work, according to

Richard Street. "On a Monday or a Tuesday I would get about twenty records. First we would judge them from one to ten, and then on Friday we'd take all the records into Mr. Gordy's office. Twelve people would vote on them. If we gave something an eight or a nine, it usually turned out to be a million seller for Motown."

Occasionally, perhaps remembering the failure of his record shop, Gordy would haul a group of local teenagers into his studio, play some records, and solicit their opinions over snacks and Cokes.

The teenage guinea pigs Gordy invited in were nearly always black kids from the neighborhood, and he listened seriously to their feelings about a tune or a beat at his playback parties. But when it came to lyrics, he had a larger constituency to consider. Given its huge white audience, Motown tended to update its sounds faster than its lyrics. Gordy's demographics could countenance no overt militancy, even at a time, in 1967, when Aretha Franklin was scoring with "Respect."

Only after the rubble had been cleared from that incendiary year, only after James Brown had opened his mouth in 1968 and bellowed "Say It Loud, I'm Black and I'm Proud," would the "Sound of Young America" chance a little sass and grit. Late in 1968 the Supremes recorded "Love Child," about an illegitimate daughter, and the tremulous "I'm Livin' in Shame." The Temptations cautioned against materialistic excess in "Don't Let the Joneses Get You Down," followed by "Ball of Confusion" ("that's what the world is today, hey hey"). On their *Psychedelic Shack* album, there was a fairly campy cut called "War," which, without mentioning Vietnam, did go on about war's "causing unrest in the younger generation," all framed with a lot of hup-two-three overdubs. More than 4,000 students wrote in to Motown asking that it be re-recorded and/or released as a single. Producer Norman Whitfield approached Edwin Starr, whose broad, soulful singing was somewhat of an exception at Motown by then. Starr says he agreed to record the song only if he could do it the way he felt it. He did, with a full complement of "huhs" and "good Gods," and within weeks, students were singing through the tear gas, call-and-response style:

WAR.
Huh!
Good God, y'awl.
Whutizzit good for?

"We were in Japan during the Vietnam War," Martha Reeves says. "They sent us over to do a USO thing. Stevie Wonder was with us, and Stevie was really into it. Stevie could always focus on the *big* picture, you know?"

It was Stevie Wonder who would produce some of the first Motown product that had any bite, Stevie, who would come up with that grim ghetto holograph "Living for the City." "Front Line," on his *Musiquariam* album, is a mean-edged, sardonic look at a black war hero who got his leg shot off in Vietnam—and suffered worse wounds when he returned. In 1983 Stevie was still holding benefit concerts and making appearances before legislators in an effort to get Martin Luther King's birthday declared a national holiday; on the eve of the bill's passage in Congress, he celebrated onstage at Radio City Music Hall.

Younger by ten years than most of his studio contemporaries, Stevie Wonder may have been better able to put idealism and activism before the more practical concerns of taking care of a family. Joe Billingslea, who had a houseful of children, says the footing could be perilous for an entertainer who wanted to stay solid with his friends in the old neighborhood, even after working like a dog to move out of it.

"Motown got caught in some funny crossfire," he says. "Here's a bunch of black kids going flat-out after the American dream, you dig? The nice house, the clothes, the car. Just what everybody else has always gone for. But with what was going on, the riots, the Vietnam mess, it was the *down* side of the dream. And so just when some cat gets enough to afford the Continental—bang—it's not *cool* to drive it, disrespectful to the movement or whatever. Just when you're making it in the company, maybe, like Diana Ross, you see your brother pack off to Vietnam, when all them kids you play to in theaters, baby, you know they gonna have college exemptions from the draft. In your own home you *whipsawed*. You get your mama out of the projects first. *Then* you buy the car. Still, somebody got somethin' to say."

In the late sixties, as the civil rights and antiwar movements grew, Berry Gordy and his employees found themselves in the peculiar position of visibly enjoying the good life while the ashes fell around them. There was a Motown Mansion, an opulent stone palace originally built for an auto magnate. Gordy lived and entertained lavishly there. Color Sunday supplements in the Detroit *Free Press* pictured his rooms, with Lalique chandeliers and furniture modeled in the style of half a dozen dead kings and emperors. The house had an oil portrait of Gordy in Napoleonic regalia. His mother, wife, and sisters were prevailed upon to provide descriptions of their evening wear for society reporters. At the same time that Black Panthers in fatigues were breaking white bread canapés with white liberals, golf became the Motown company sport.

"In a way, it just wasn't fair," says Martha Reeves. "It was rough timing. Because you are black and it's 1967, a cute teen song gets viewed as some statement. People make you out to be what they think you should be. Like I said, I never called anyone to riot. I was calling my ten brothers and sisters to the table. All I wanted was a little gravy. For all of us."

■14
Shake Me, Wake Me (When It's Over)

Why stop? If you stop, there's nothing to keep you driving. You just stop and get old. I'd keep driving, all the way. Just like this bus we're on.

—TEMPTATION RICHARD STREET

"WE HAVE ALL ALWAYS wanted this life," says Abdul "Duke" Fakir. "Always."

Eighteen years after their first Motown hit, "Baby, I Need Your Loving," twenty-eight years after their first crazy gigs together as the Four Aims, three of the Tops—Levi Stubbs, Duke Fakir, and Larry Payton—sit in the office of their post-Motown record company, Polygram, enjoying a takeout lunch of Broadway deli. Renaldo "Obie" Benson is back at the hotel, trying to sleep off a cold tugging at his vocal cords. The Tops are touring on the success of their new album, *Tonight,* and its hit single, "When She Was My Girl." Though they have never stopped performing, though their ballad-heavy Mills Brothers style has made them regulars on the supper club and college circuit, they have not had a good, solid hit in more than a decade. They say this new one feels good, but they aren't going to get bent out of shape about it. Nor will they forget the bad old days.

"We were all born on the north end of town; it's called the new center area now," Levi says. "It's by General Motors—a very poor, hardworking part of town. We were neighborhood friends, kind of knew each other from being around."

"We fell into it," Duke says. "Seemed like a perfect mixture. I had the right kind of tenor for the top, Lawrence had the right kind of voice to be a second tenor, Obie had the kind to be a baritone, and Levi was *definitely* the lead."

It is the distinctive, soulful capacity of Levi's leads that has shuttled the Tops easily between teenage and adult audiences. It was his voice that leaped out on "Reach Out, I'll Be There," "Bernadette," and "Ask the Lonely." Lately he has been duetting with his old Detroit friend Aretha Franklin, in concert and in the studio. And new product or not, the Tops, as an act, are offered more live bookings than they care to take.

They feel that the key to their longevity has been their adaptability. Ten years of borscht belting, song and dance revues, clubs, a brief stint with Chess Records, and countless miles in wheezing station wagons preceded their signing with Motown in 1964. They sang in French in Montreal; they did country and western, the Four Freshmen, anything that paid, "anything," says Duke, "from 'My Yiddische Mama' to 'Paper Doll.' " They could do a Dinah Washington blues over an accordion backup. They will still sing in the living room of a long-ago southern frat boy, name of Earthquake, who regularly rounds up some college cronies—and hires the Four Tops to provide the sixties ambiance. Earthquake and his buddies once flew them to Mexico for a poolside serenade, in tropic togs.

One of the first vacation spots the Tops played was Idlewild, a black resort area near Baldwin, Michigan, on the edge of the Manistee National Forest, an obscure spot they feel is greatly connected to Motown's success. The Tops think that Berry Gordy shaped his own Motortown Revues not so much on the rock show packages of the fifties as on the more middle-of-the-road pastiche he enjoyed all those summers in Idlewild.

"Really," says Larry, "I think that's basically where the Motortown Revue came from. Berry and everybody from Detroit used to go there. It was sort of the black Catskills. It was a bunch of cottages and a big hotel. And two clubs. One had big shows, and one had little shows. Before Berry signed us, Arthur Bryce, who owned this club there, would keep us working all summer. He'd put us together with some show girls and two or three acts; maybe Jackie Wilson would be on the show, and a male dance group. He called it the Idlewild Revue. We learned a lot up there. Matter of fact, we came to Broadway, here in New York, based on some work we did there. It was still called the Idlewild Revue when we played here.''

"The Idlewild Revue was seen by a guy who was in the original *Shuffle Along* cast waaaaaay back," Duke says. *Shuffle Along,* produced in 1921, was the first black musical on Broadway, with such distinguished alumni as songwriting partners Noble Sissle and Eubie Blake.

"Anyhow, this guy from *Shuffle Along* knew his business. He got us together in this thing singing and dancing. It was a musical. We played right there on Forty-seventh and Broadway, and we traveled around the country with that show. It was real all-round type entertainment. And I think Berry was hip to that.''

The tradition was black vaudeville, and he thinks it had a great influence on Gordy's idea of showmanship. It crept into a number of Motown acts: in the Supremes' hat-and-cane stylings, the stagy between-song patter Gordy liked to write and arrange, and his penchant for musical "salutes"—to everyone from Ray Charles to Rodgers and Hart.

The Spinners' "Brown Beatle" parody, complete with wigs, was one of Gordy's favorites. According to the Spinners, whose greatest success came only after they had left Motown, Gordy became truly committed to the concept of an Artists Development Department after he watched them burlesque all his acts in a nightclub revue they were doing at the Twenty Grand Club in Detroit. Harvey Fuqua was the Spinners' manager at the time. They were on his label, Tri Phi, but they had no hits. Fuqua came up with the idea of having them do a mock revue, with imitations of the Marvelettes, Stevie Wonder, and Marvin Gaye. They took the show on the road as part of an early "Marvin Gaye Revue," and by the time they got back to the Twenty Grand, where Gordy was in the habit of showcasing his own acts, the moment was ripe for some serious discussion on the concept of corporate image.

Fuqua laid it out simply: The Spinners didn't have a hit, but they had a hell of an *act*. And it sold tickets. Shortly thereafter Tri Phi was folded into Motown, and two of the Spinners drove a station wagon to New York City to pick up choreography teacher Cholly Atkins and his belongings and move them to Detroit. The Spinners note, with some irony, that they unwittingly benefitted from all those classes, since Gordy rarely gave them a record release that would send them on the road. Though they missed out on much of the glory, they got a full course in show biz basics by being kept after school so many times.

"It's okay," Spinner Pervis Jackson insists. "While other acts like the Tempts and the Four Tops were out on the road working, we had nothing to do. So we would be in Artist Development all day, like in school."

Model students, the Spinners were able to cruise comfortably on their well-crafted stage act long after they had left Motown for Atlantic. But not all the acts were willing to accept instruction in all areas. Choreography class had four deliberate truants.

"The Four Tops had been working decently on a stage for ten years before Motown," Duke says. "They attempted to sic choreographers on us, but we just wouldn't show up. It came down to, what do you want to do, sing or dance? We chose to concentrate on singing."

Their natural elements were harmony, melody, and other sorts of vocal tap dancing. Once they started working with the songwriting team of Holland-Dozier-Holland, it was an easy collaboration.

"They'd write around us sometimes. Others they'd work right with us," Larry says. "We'd sing a part, and they'd say, 'Oh, yeah, I like that phrase,' and they'd put the melody in. We bounced off each other quite a bit."

The Tops' own conversation, as it builds, has fallen into a casual harmony. After a bit questions aren't even necessary, so seamless are the memories. They yield to one another instinctively on various subjects and come together for a laugh. Asked about the most spontaneous session they can remember, they nod at one another and begin:

LARRY: We were watching the Temptations at the Twenty Grand. We were all in the audience. And Brian Holland came up and said, "I think I got a hit for you cats. After the show is over, come back to the studio and listen to it."

LEVI: It was like three o'clock in the morning. So we went back to the studio and listened, and Brian called in one of the engineers, and we recorded it ["Baby, I Need Your Loving"] that night.

LARRY: Everybody was used to being hauled in out of bed. There would be an in-house engineer there all night. Guy would be sittin' up in the studio sleepin'. And somebody would bounce in and say, "Let's turn it on."

DUKE: When it was good, being with the entertainers in town and being at the studio, that was our whole life. We only went home to sleep. We'd come in, into Brian and them all's office; we'd just be sitting around talkin', maybe playin' cards. Kibitzin' around. Wrote a whole lot of tunes like that just sittin'. . . .

LARRY: Over at their house, drinkin' beer and wine. And somebody would say something. And somebody else would say, "Hey." And bang—cat would fall down and say, "Wow, what key was that in?" Everyone was so in tune in those days, it was *all* about music.

DUKE: Had some work every day. Berry would just like to see our faces in the place. If we'd miss a day, he'd say, "What happened, where you guys been?"

LARRY: And every day you could look forward to somebody calling you and saying, "Let's go listen to something," or, "Help us out." If the Supremes were recording and needed some male voices, you'd just go in and do it. You might have heard us on almost anything you hear male voices on from that era. Sometimes it would be one of the Temptations and Marvin Gaye and Stevie Wonder. Or two of the Tops.

DUKE: I remember sitting around during the time Marvin and Tammi [Terrell] were recording "Ain't No Mountain High Enough," and Marvin says, "Hey, man, come in here and help me sing the song 'cause I can't make it alone."

LARRY: Couple of times, I filled in for a couple of Temptations. . . .

LEVI: Whatever it took . . .

LARRY: It was a friendly competition. We used to bet. You know, "I bet you two hundred dollars we'll have the next hit," and all. That was the big thing around the company, the producers were betting with each other, you know, who was going to be number one which week. It wasn't really who or if, but *when*.

A secretary steps in to say that Levi is needed for a meeting with some lawyers. The Tops make sure, after all these years, that they stay in touch with the business end of things. Disputes over the accounting had ended Holland-Dozier-Holland's tenure at Motown, and as a result, the Tops'.

From 1963 to 1966 Brian Holland, Eddie Holland, and Lamont Dozier had turned out twenty-eight Top Twenty hits, crafted of so-so lyrics and irresistible hooks. Their structures were simple and direct; sometimes a song barreled to number one on the sheer force of repetitive hooks, like a fast-food jingle that lurks, subliminally, until it connects with real hunger. "Heat Wave," cut by Martha and the Vandellas in 1963, was the first swell; the numbers crested when H-D-H were turned loose on the Supremes and the Four Tops.

"They were really the whole thing for us," Larry says as Levi heads for the door. "I mean, they had us *down*. They would write one song for Levi, and they would say, 'Oh, no, that sounds like Diana [Ross].' And they would do it on her, same key and everything. Levi would sing sort of high and brilliant 'cause he would sing in the same key as Diana."

They alternated hits, the Tops' "Ask the Lonely," then the Supremes' "Stop in the Name of Love." Days after the release of the Tops' "It's the Same Old Song" in August 1965, the Supremes had "Nothing but Heartaches." And so it went, until the music stopped in 1967. Holland-Dozier-Holland demanded an accounting of their royalties. Motown countered with a $4 million suit, alleging that they had "failed to deliver compositions" since the dispute began. MOTOWN ENGINE MISFIRES, read the Detroit *Free Press*.

In describing the suit and the subsequent departure of Motown's million-dollar team, news reports noted a growing incidence of defections and exiles. Shortly after Mary Wells had left in 1964, other artists walked out over artistic and financial issues. Motown's first money-maker, Barrett Strong, departed, as did Brenda Holloway, Kim Weston, the Isley Brothers, the Miracles, the Temptations, Gladys Knight and the Pips, Jimmy Ruffin, Eddie Kendricks, and the Four Tops. The Jackson Five came and went. Gordy was always willing to point out that artists were replaceable. Perhaps more damaging was the loss of support personnel such as Harvey Fuqua, Maurice King, and songwriters Ashford and Simpson. Still, in terms of sales and morale, everyone in the company felt the loss most keenly in the wake of the H-D-H defection.

"When they left, it devastated us," Larry Payton says. "Without them, we couldn't get a hit record. Nobody else could do it for us. Besides, we weren't getting much action anymore as an act. As Motown grew—and I think Berry would even agree with this—they couldn't concentrate on everybody. They got *so* big. And so we just had to leave. There was no real animosity. We're all still friends. It was just a business thing."

An era ended when Motown left the Motor City. In 1971, despite pleas by most of his artists, ignoring the books Smokey Robinson sent him outlining the perils of living along the San Andreas fault, Berry Gordy got himself a Hollywood address. He was intent on piloting his empire into the film world, largely on the glamor of Diana Ross. Along with a number of other acts and musicians like Earl Van Dyke, the Four Tops declined to leave home.

LARRY: When Motown left Detroit, there was a great void. It was something else.

DUKE: It had been our whole thing, being with the entertainers in town, being at the studio. Man, it's hard when all your friends leave town. It was dismal. It took me a while to adjust.

LARRY: And our wives are still trying. They especially miss Claudette [Robinson]. As a matter of fact, they stay in touch more than we do. They talk to each other once a week. It was hard on the women, being taken away from their best girl friends.

DUKE: A little like athletes' wives, holding each other up all those years while the old man's on the road, you know.

LARRY: Baby, if you read this, thank you for being my wife. Baby, I need *your* lovin'.

DUKE: Got to have all your lovin', *oooh ooooh* . . .

They sing, slapping five over the pickle container.

Eventually, the Four Tops would go back to Motown after their appearance on its twenty-fifth anniversary TV special in 1983. Another Motown-promoted event a year earlier reunited the Temptations, but only for the duration of a two-month tour. Lead singers Eddie Kendricks and David Ruffin had been out of the group for eleven and fourteen years respectively. Founding member Paul Williams had died nearly a decade before. Originals Otis Williams and Melvin Franklin had never left; Richard Street, Dennis Edwards, and Glenn Leonard had come in at various times to plug leaks in the harmony and personnel. For three months, all of the surviving members worked on harmony and choreography; some did roadwork, up to eight miles a day. An album was recorded on Motown as part of the reunion package. When the tour reached New York and Radio City Music Hall, it had been sold out for weeks.

In the orchestra seats, Instamatic flashes illuminate black celebrities like Jim Brown and Marlon Jackson who have come to bear witness. Everyone seems a bit apprehensive. The *Reunion* album itself is nothing to weep for joy over, and many of us have seen too many dead-in-the-water revivals. I had seen one late seventies Tempts show where the exiled David Ruffin sat, gazing up from the audience, wearing an expression so desolate you had to look away. Other nights, in the past, road managers had had to restrain him from leaping onto the stage with his old group.

"LADIES AND GENTLEMEN . . . SEVEN OF THEM . . ."

The rubbed mahogany voice of deejay Frankie Crocker cuts through the anxious din: "THE TANTALIZIN' TEMPTATIONS."

Huge risers lift a yellow Checker taxicab up through the stage floor. All the Tempts are perched on it, in black tux, of course. It is one of those perfect freeze-frame moments when it's enough for them just to stand there and *be* the Temptations, so sharp, so sub-zero cool your eyeballs feel a draft.

They are moving now, bouncing down twin ramps, hitting the stage at exactly the same second, lighting into a flurry of dips and spins, easing, elbows bent, into the trademark Temptations' walk. Up front, big Jim Brown is on his feet cheering.

In their prime nobody could work a crowd like the Tempts. No one dressed as well; no set of voices could match their full-court give-and-go. And surely no one could outdance them. Even gravity was just a pissant nuisance to the Tempts. They popped, jerked, and flew their bodies, spun like a quintet of sequined gyroscopes that somehow always stopped at exactly the same second on the same spot. Monogrammed sweat towels flew through the air as the crowd snapped and fought for them. In front of it all, there was always that lamppost in horn-rims. David Ruffin's frame was as angular as the skinny, square glasses he wore, but the body language was fluid. Ruffin had better movement than a Longines, casually tossing a mike, playing cat's cradle with the cord, cracking the long whipcord legs into split after split, then straight into a spin.

He is spinning now, but when he comes out of it, it's clear it's been in the wrong direction. He looks down the row at the other Tempts' backs, catches himself, and laughs. The faithful forgive him this lapse, as they will many more before the night is over.

The show itself is a two-hour time capsule, constructed with typical Motown genius and excess. Still, the high points far outshine the cringers. Ruffin's notes are tenuous on "Ain't Too Proud to Beg," but when he settles into a lower register on "I Wish It Would Rain," the baritone strikes deftly at a crystal of pain and the familiar phrasings gleam. Taking his solo turn, Eddie Kendricks ventures into the audience amid a hail of plastic glow-in-the-dark roses picked fresh from lobby hucksters. "Just My Imagination" comes across like a soothing massage. Before Eddie can clamber back onstage there is much laying on of hands, and security guards have to gently untangle a love knot of arms and legs.

Romance slides briefly into psychedelia as Dennis Edwards takes a muscular lead on "Psychedelic Shack" and "Ball of Confusion." Then the group does a fast rewind as the guitar player sounds the ominous opening chords to "(I Know) I'm Losing You," a song so full of dread and sorrow that heartbreak seems to be chasing Ruffin's voice along like storm clouds coming in off Lake Erie. Though that song was as danceable as any Motown product, it always held a small, larval terror. *Don't want to lose you.*

"I don't wanna lose *you*," a woman screams from the darkness. By the time it is over, two and a half hours later, the audience filing out is testament to the relative success of this revival. Collars are loosened, sport coats over arms. Women's eyes are ringed, raccoonlike, with dark mascara runoff.

"Get ready," a road manager is yelling across Fifty-second Street to his bus driver, " 'cause here they come."

Outside the Berkshire Hotel, liveried bellmen are loading the Temptations' luggage into a custom tour bus that has been idling nearly an hour. There was a party tossed by Frankie Crocker last night, and everyone is moving slowly in the noontime heat. David Ruffin is the last to appear, in shades and a baseball cap. He is moaning softly; in blue jeans, without the camouflage of a tux jacket, he is impossibly skinny. He walks stiffly and slowly, wincing in the sun. He wonders aloud whether eating wouldn't help him feel better and ambles to a sidewalk vendor for two hot dogs, with everything.

"Not doin' so good," he says to no one in particular as he climbs onto the bus. His fourteen-year-old son, David, Jr., is already aboard, tinkering with a new camera that bassman Melvin Franklin bought him. The incessant flashgun sends his father, groaning, to a bunk at the back of the coach. David, Jr., is a tall, muscular boy in gym shorts and a polo shirt. And he is handsome—a dead ringer for the young Marvin Gaye. Having barreled off a roll of film, he switches his attention to a video game on the color TV console.

By some rock standards, this is a modest touring bus: sound system, curtained sleeping area, velour and corduroy upholstered lounge, refrigerator, and sink. A hotel porter struggles in with a tub filled with iced sodas, Perriers, aloe drinks, and fruit juices.

"Yeah," Melvin Franklin answers in his big, round bass. "This bus is different than the first Motown bus. Sure. This one has wheels."

He says the vintage model was a draggedy-ass contraption with a rounded back end, hard upright seats, a minimum of forty passengers.

"I used to sleep in the luggage rack," he says. "Wasn't any of us under six foot one. I can't climb like I did then. Got rheumatoid arthritis. Maybe it's from being a six-foot-one sardine all them years, who knows?"

Throughout the trip to the next concert site in Philadelphia, most of the other Temptations will sack out, comfortably, in curtained bunks. Typically it is Melvin and Otis who do most of the talking. They are the heart and brains of the group, "married," Melvin says, in their desire to make singing together a life's work, as long and as steadily as possible. Otis was reared on a farm in Texarkana until his family moved North in 1950; Melvin came up from Alabama. Both of them plunged into the group scene early into their teens. They began singing together in a group called the Distants, after a less than auspicious first meeting.

Otis, who was recording with the Distants, found himself without a bass singer for one session. He had heard of Melvin and went out looking for him. He found him on the corner of Woodrow Wilson and Seward streets, walking along with a nervous, over-the-shoulder glance that was the result of his getting jumped and stomped on by a gang two days earlier.

"Cat across the street looked like more of the same," Melvin remembers. "Black leather jacket, process 'do, walkin' real fast, starin' hard . . ."

The two did a strange arabesque back and forth across the street. Each time Otis would cross over, Melvin would skitter to the other side.

"Hey, man," Otis finally yelled, "I just want to *talk* to you." Next, Otis talked to Melvin's mother, and once she had consented, Melvin became a Distant for a time; so did his cousin and sidekick Richard Street. The late fifties saw Melvin and Otis and one Eldridge Bryant drifting through groups like the Questions, the Elegants, and Otis Williams and the Distants.

Another young quartet had worked its way up from Birmingham in the hopes of reviving a southern group called the Primes. Paul Williams and Eddie Kendricks left Alabama and headed North on 75, shooting for the southern shores of the Great Lakes.

"We stopped for a few days in Dayton," Eddie Kendricks remembers, "then a little longer in Cleveland. We performed there. There were four of us. Me, Paul, Willie Waller, and Kell Osborne. We called ourselves the Cavaliers. Then we dropped from a quartet to a trio and changed our name to the Primes." In the early sixties, the Distants merged with the Primes to form the Elgins, recording for Motown with no success. It was only after their name change, and the substitution of David Ruffin for Eldridge Bryant, that they became the Temptations.

It was as the Primes that the new arrivals from Alabama courted the would-be Supremes as their sister group, the Primettes. Paul Williams was the emissary who visited Mary Wilson's and Diana Ross's parents. He was polite, handsome, and very earnest. He was so much a part of things from the beginning, Kendricks says, that his death left them all drifting and bewildered.

"Paul and I came to Detroit with plans to do a lot of things together," Kendricks says. "Most of them just didn't work out, for various reasons. So I guess, maybe a little, Paul's problems did relate to my leaving the group [in 1971]. But Paul had too much spirit for that to be the main cause. I really thought he'd pull through those problems, that if he could have worked them out, he'd have been okay."

Poor health, due to a drug problem, caused Williams to miss perform-ances in the late sixties. Some nights, if he was well enough to stand onstage, he was still too weak to sing. Richard Street was hauled out of Motown's Quality Control Department and recalled to performing duty to help carry the act.

"It was rough," Richard says. "Paul was there, but Paul was sick half the time, so he would be just moving his mouth while I would be singing his part from the wings."

As Williams grew weaker and more disoriented, Richard Street was encouraged to pay attention to the stage routines. He says he felt a bit like a buzzard, waiting there backstage. One night, when Williams couldn't even make it to the theater, Richard found himself singing for a missing person.

"We were in Cherry Hill, New Jersey," he says. "Muhammad Ali came

backstage and called us the greatest group in the world. He said, 'Because
I saw four guys and I could have sworn I heard five voices.' "

Shortly after, Street formally replaced Williams. In September 1973,
three years after ill health had forced him from the group, having failed
at running a Celebrity Boutique in a ghetto neighborhood and owing about
$80,000 in taxes, Paul Williams drove his car to a spot a few blocks away
from the Motown offices and shot himself to death.

Nobody had imagined that it would get that bad for Paul Williams, Eddie
Kendricks says. Nor could any of them imagine a reunion without his
presence in some form or another. They chose the songs they did for his
tribute section, "The Impossible Dream" and "For Once in My Life,"
because they felt they had a spiritual context that fitted him well. Even
when the Elgins had been wheezing along, even amid the flops, he was
turning backflips and working out new routines. Suicides can begin life
as the most faithful of men. Most unbearable, Williams's friends surmise,
is to lose that faith and let the blues overtake that gospel stoicism.

"Paul," Kendricks says, "had very strong gospel overtones in his
background. And so did David."

David Ruffin was born in a cabin in Whynot, Mississippi, an eyeblink
hamlet outside Meridian.

"I heard gospel," he says, "before I could think."

His mother died shortly after his birth, and he was reared by his step-
mother, Earlene, who shooed him onstage at the age of six when gospel
shows came through. In grade school he found his skinny self bouncing
on springy plywood stages with the substantial likes of Mahalia Jackson,
the Five Blind Boys, the Soul Stirrers, and Clara Ward. At fourteen he
headed for Memphis, got through high school there, and signed on for a
two-year hitch with the Dixie Nightingales. He drifted to Detroit and got
to Motown as a friend of Gordy's sister Gwen. He worked building the
studio with Pops Gordy until the Temptations needed a replacement for
Eldridge Bryant in 1964.

"David has always been lucky for us," Kendricks says. "He gave us
the right chemistry." His floaty, ebullient lead gave the Tempts their first
hit, in 1964, with "The Way You Do the Things You Do." The quintet
developed an unbeatable combination as Kendricks and Ruffin followed
the two-lead tradition pioneered by the Soul Stirrers and the Ravens.
Kendricks's angel-hair falsetto took care of the ecstatic side of love; Ruffin's sandpaper baritone ripped through heartbreakers like "Since I Lost
My Baby," "(I Know) I'm Losing You," and "I Wish It Would Rain."

When they traded leads, in "You're My Everything," it was grandly theatrical. Before they both left for solo careers, they were coached by Smokey Robinson and Norman Whitfield in the studio and by Maurice King in Artists Development.

"Maurice King was the vocal coach that the average, stand-on-the-corner singer never got the chance to have," Melvin says. "We knew triads and basic sevenths and minors and stuff like that you learn doowopping on the corner. But Mr. King made us sophisticates. Had us doing a lot of doubling. Doubling is when different guys sing the same notes, even if they're an octave apart. I'd love to have Mr. King come periodically, once or twice a year, and just sharpen things up. I can still hear him yelling, 'Get that right, get that *right!*' "

Choreography coach Cholly Atkins was just as demanding. He rehearsed them hard, beginning with forty-five minutes of floor exercises, then putting them through a series of punishing routines that were designed to make a hit record into a heart-thumping live act.

"Paul Williams was actually our first choreographer," Melvin says. "I think he's the best dancer I ever worked with. There's a guy named Peg Leg Bates, an old hoofer. Paul used to hang out with him."

Bates headlined in the forties on black revues with the likes of the Ink Spots, Coke and Poke, and Eddie "Cleanhead" Vinson. "Show me," Paul Williams would plead, and the older man, who actually had one wooden leg, would execute a brush step, a turn, an ankle roll.

"Afterwards, at night, Paul would come over to my house," Melvin says. "We'd go down in the basement, and he showed me how to do stuff. He showed me how to do a 'round-the-world spin and splits and stuff that David did naturally. David was another one. You'd be walking down the street with him, and he'd turn a flip, just like that."

Williams was a great ad-libber with his feet, and should a hit record bloom while the group was on the road, where the ministrations of Cholly Atkins were unavailable, they would work it out themselves.

"When we did *The Dick Clark Show* for the first time, it was with 'Get Ready,' " Melvin says. "It was just released, and Paul had us pull up in the middle of one of those dressing rooms and made up the choreography in less than thirty minutes. And we're still doing the same choreography for 'Get Ready' now."

The Tempts' choreography was like their music, citified and stylized and characteristic of the distinctions between Motown and southern soul. In a northern city Paul Williams could seek instruction and inspiration from a black vaudevillian. In rural Georgia, James Brown says he let his feet do whatever it took to draw a rain of coins when World War II troop trains slowed or stopped at a crossing he knew. "I probably had some years-old African beat in my brain," he says. "But that was pure Georgia clay on my feet."

Ethnomusicologist Alan Lomax traced the roots of black dance back to a circular group dance called the ring shout in this country. It was a stateside variant of circle dances done in West Africa. In the Mississippi delta, ring shouts were done to spiritual songs, but words and melody often disintegrated as rhythm asserted itself. Possession, "getting happy," was less a product of words and music than of a hypnotic, driving beat. And as the spirit began to speak through the body, gospel lyric flattened to grunts, moans, and shrieks.

This is the kind of choreography practiced by James Brown. Sure, he will tell you, he rehearsed and invented moves, practiced in his home until he fell down, panting and sweating on his living-room floor. But possession, the ultimate ad-lib, is the only way to describe his best stage efforts, when he has bludgeoned his own lyrics into screams and cranked up his funkier-than-thou horn and rhythm sections past the limited realm of Anglo understanding.

The Temptations' stylish urban choreography could get people almost as crazy, but it was the exact opposite of JB's seizure boogie. Instead, the thrill was perfect, synchronized athleticism. They ran routines the way a football team could run textbook plays. Precision, not possession, was the name of their game.

"Now you want to know when we really got sharp-sharp?" says Melvin. "Girl, we went on a show at some theater in Ohio in 1961. Shep and the Limelites were on the bill, Gladys and the Pips, and we were the opening act. Those Pips were so beautifully choreographed—Cholly was coaching them—they virtually ran us off the stage. We didn't even exist in those people's minds. So Otis approached Cholly and had him come to the Howard Theater in Washington, D.C., in 1963 and start working with us. It was his relationship with us that brought him to Motown and later brought Gladys and the Pips to Motown as well."

Sharpening the choreography for the reunion tour has been hard work. Melvin has taken to jogging for his muscle tone and for aerobic reconditioning. "I have to work at my concentration. It's strange to me because I never had to before. It's like playing the fifth quarter of a football game or double overtime in basketball."

Otis Williams has reappeared, shaking off a catnap, and out of consideration, Melvin lowers the camera he had pointed at him. He says he has thousands of photos, taken over the last twenty years.

"I don't want to lose any of it. Not a single moment," he says. "My house in California has a whole Temptations wall."

"We gotta sit down with some of those pictures, man." Otis has settled on the seat next to Melvin, and as the bus hisses along the southern end of the Jersey Turnpike, they take care of a little business, as they have done all these years. They talk quietly, heads bobbing in unison with the road vibrations.

"Yeah, the heart and brains," Richard Street says, looking at them. "They keep us going."

The blips and shrieks of a video game are getting more frantic as David, Jr., pushes Sea Battle to its limits. Most of the adults are dozing. They sleep *all* the time, David says. Ten to one, as soon as they hit Philadelphia, his father will be out cold on the bed before the porter can unfold the luggage stand. Coming along on this tour is a sort of summer vacation for him. Sometimes he helps out with equipment and things. He isn't sure if he'd want to be in the music business. "I got time, right?" he says. "I mean, I got a lot to pick from."

"Amen, handsome boy," says Melvin. "Long as you remember what a blessing choice is."

Bored, David, Jr., has abandoned video blackjack for a road race game. He cajoles Richard Street into a duel, and within seconds Street's gaudy magenta racer has crashed into a barrier on the screen, bursting into a million tiny dots.

"Look like Chrysler built that mother."

With one eye on the road signs, Melvin twits the nervous driver who has already missed one exit, with an ominous *Dragnet* "dum-da dum-dum.

"Basso profundo," he rumbles. "I belong to a very rare breed. A very special minority."

He likes to say he was born "twelve pounds of bass and brown." His crying was so hoarse it drove people from the house. "Let me tell you, as a child I used to be called Froggy, and people would tease me and make me feel very self-conscious about it. And it turned into the ugly duckling type of story. Turned out to be my very best asset."

Since good bass singers are rarer than they were when he started out in the fifties, Melvin is never at a loss for session work, even when the

Tempts aren't recording. He has worked with everyone from the Captain and Tennille to Rick James, and he has a deep pride in being a skilled practitioner of a vanishing but venerable craft.

"I think I'm a composite of Sherman Garnes [bass singer with the Teenagers] and Ellis Johnson [of the Harmonizing Four], William Bobo [of the Dixie Hummingbirds], and myself. Ellis would let me spend time with him every year. And I think that we've never made a record that I couldn't go right down and show you something specifically that I thought Sherman Garnes would have done. My voice is lower than his, but the *way* he did it, his style and his knack, I think, personified the quartet bass singer."

Quartet singing is nothing if not emotional, and Melvin is up front about the way his singing and his emotional nature have shaped his life.

"Listen, I sing bass for a *group*," he explains. "My place takes care of me and my children. And *everything*. It is my way of life."

It is one of the few things he can call a constant in his life, and after years of personnel changes and the unpredictable eddies of the business, he frets about it constantly. During the negotiations for this reunion tour he says it was his big voice that wasn't too proud to beg.

"It worries me. That they may not want to stick; they may not want to stay. But they always do. Every time the man says, 'LADIES AND GENTLEMEN, THE TEMPTATIONS!' I know they're all here."

And every time Melvin Franklin allows himself a heartfelt profundo sigh of relief. Sure, he says, it's a long road, but you live for certain moments. He remembers one in the concert last night. It was a moment that brought the most emotional response from the audience as well.

It could have been corny, their near a cappella rendition of "Old Man River," an ebony chestnut first made popular by Paul Robeson and by the Ravens in 1947. Instead, it was a confirmation, an affirmation. Minus the horns and the lacy strings, stripped of all but a light rhythm section, the voices revealed themselves. Tenor, baritone, that big round bass all split and soloed in turn. More than the natty suits, beyond the pinpoint choreography, this short, still moment offered a resounding answer to the question of the night.

"Y'all still *got* it," a woman screamed, and the rest of the crowd clapped and hollered their agreement as Melvin's voice reached down, down to tote that barge and lift that bale. And if the audience felt it, this perfect resonance of mind and tissue and timbre, some of the singers were nearly overcome.

"When we got into 'Old Man River' and the audience stood up, tears were in my eyes," Melvin says. "I was trembling. They, the other guys, had to hold me 'cause I was trembling and it was beautiful. From the first moment I opened my mouth, I felt as if I was in my place in the universe."

He smiles, then jerks around to look out the window as we pull into the Philadelphia traffic.

"Mr. Bus Driver, yo. Left on Chestnut. Listen to me now, and we'll take this sucker home."

15
Roadrunners, Trouble Men, and Thrillers

Didn't worry much when it came time to go, no.
Motown helped me gold-plate my horn. But Motown
never did teach me how to blow it.

—JR. WALKER

SAXMAN JR. WALKER (formerly Autry DeWalt) was Motown's only real instrumental act, traveling with his three All Stars, ripping the rug of decorum from under people with party tunes like "Shotgun," "Road Runner," "Home Cookin'," and the like. He started doing vocals only by accident, he says, when Fred Paton, the singer assigned to help him, didn't make a session. Of all the ex-Motown acts I have encountered, Jr. is by far the most pacific. He smiles often and travels easy. Anytime, anywhere.

"I *am* a roadrunner," he says. "Ever since Berry Gordy told me to scare up a truck and git—he had some dates lined up for me—I got the truck and lit out. Same now. I travel. I blow some. People dance. And I like it."

Over the last couple of years I'd seen him in some very different venues, playing in Ukrainian community halls turned punk palaces, opening for

James Brown on a riverboat cruising the Mississippi, alternately blowing from a stand, a crouch, or lying flat on his back. Jr. is a consummate tease, getting folks wild with a snippet of "Shotgun," stopping, walking off, surprising them into screams and gyrations when he falls to his knees and starts blowing again. He isn't Coltrane; he's the guy who can guarantee a party. He says he hasn't changed, but maybe his audience has.

"I play colleges, schools, clubs. I have a ball. Big halls, Europe. Just did a picnic in Virginia where I had some little tots jumpin' on the grass. These kids, you know, they was raised on disco. And when they started listenin' to where disco *come* from, *wheeeeeooooo*. It was *sharp*."

He is laughing, turning to hunch over a rusty dressing-room sink to rinse out a few reeds for his horn. He is wearing a T-shirt instead of his regulation tux or three-piece suit, revealing a tattooed eagle stretched the length of his bicep. It spreads its wings farther with his exertions. Absently he lays one of the reeds on his tongue, then slips it back under the warm water, massaging it gently.

"Too funky," he mutters.

He is trying to remember exactly when he acquired this taste. He figures it started when he was a kid in South Bend, Indiana.

"I used to go to the house of a guy named George Mason. He blew a horn, tenor sax. He had an alto, and he had a tenor. I used to go to his house every Sunday. They used to jam every Sunday, and the police would bother us every now and again. I'd just go and watch and listen. I went over one day, and the band wasn't there. George was. So there was this alto sittin' there, and I picked it up and said to George, 'Well, show me.' "

Jr. turns off the faucet and begins drying the reeds on his shirt. His son, Autry DeWalt, Jr., the current drummer of the All Stars, dashes in for the car keys.

"I told George, 'Man, I like the crooked horn.' That's what I called it. So he showed me a few things on it, and I started blowing. Kept foolin' with it. He'd blow some notes, and I'd just go along with him. One day I guess I got too good, and he got uptight. He just looked at me, and he took the horn away. So I left."

Jr. was about fifteen, and he found other things to occupy himself; but he says he still kept his ear out for that sound. He was eighteen, married, and working in construction when one day his uncle came to visit from Chicago.

"I heard you was tryin' to blow a horn," he said to his nephew.

"Yeah. I'm gonna be *bad*."

"I got a horn at home. I ain't gonna blow no more. I'm gonna give the thing to you. Now I couldn't get into really big time. So I want you to *blow* it."

The next time the retired horn player saw his nephew, Jr. was blowing with a little band in South Bend. He had traded in his uncle's horn at Rosenbaum's pawnshop for a better one, but as he heated up, the dented old honker couldn't keep pace.

"My mother said, 'I'm gonna help you get your horn.' 'Cause she was workin', and I was tryin' still to work construction. She took me down to Elkhart, where they make horns, and she said, 'Just pick you out one of them *good* horns.' It cost about five hundred dollars but back then that was supposed to be cheap. She put it on layaway, and she was payin' on it every week."

That Selmer Mark 6 is the horn that made all the Motown hits, including his biggest, "Shotgun." He says that one was a bit of an accident. One night in 1965 he was playing a club when he noticed that a lot of the dancers on the floor were doing a two-handed sawing kind of step. It looked as though they were cradling a pump-action double-barreled shotgun. And that's what they called the dance. The Motown engineers grafted a gunshot sound effect onto the front, and it tore holes in both the soul and pop charts.

"I took that horn and gold-plated it," Jr. says. "Put it up on my wall at home. It *still* sounds the best, better than this one here, which I got in 1966 or '67. Sometimes I have to walk over and take it down. Oh, when I get to blowin' that horn, it's pretty."

He has chosen a reed and fits it into the mouthpiece, tightening the screws. He lays his tongue against it and sets the instrument down gently on an eviscerated sofa.

"I am just into makin' a joyful noise," he says. "No, I never did take to playin' no real sad songs. I leave that to the other men been talkin' through this kind of horn."

For the Coltranes, for the Dexter Gordons he has great respect. And with the good-time men, like the hornmen down at Stax and the late King Curtis, he feels a kinship.

"We make a wind blow them blues clean to Monday. It's Saturday night now, ain't it? And if you'll excuse me, I got a job to do."

Of all Motown's sixties soul men, Jr. Walker was the best equipped to keep moving on the road even after the hits had stopped. Classic party music is not a function of chart life, and having a self-contained band eliminates the pickup-musician nightmares suffered by Mary Wells, Martha Reeves, and a host of male singers who relied on Motown's house band and production teams to keep their careers going. Barrett Strong, Jimmy Ruffin, Marv Johnson, Edwin Starr, and Tyrone Davis were left adrift without Gordy's support system. On the other hand, some of his greatest discoveries chafed under the system and did their best material by finding the means to work outside it.

With the notable exception of Diana Ross, who enjoyed the special attentions of Berry Gordy, no female artist from Motown's golden decade would hang on to her success. (Gladys Knight had found her own sound before she signed with Motown and continued to have hits once she left.) With the exception of Smokey Robinson, who was so much a part of the corporate structure from the beginning, no male vocalist from those early days has retained—or gained—status as a major singer/songwriter unless he eluded Gordy's artistic confines.

Marvin Gaye, Stevie Wonder, and Michael Jackson did their best and most satisfying work only after either leaving the label or winning the right to produce their work themselves. Set loose in a studio with their own compositions, all three proved to be master synthesists who owed their success to flexibility Motown's formulas would not permit. In fact, all were able to out-Gordy their former boss, grafting urban sophistications onto the basic syncopations drummed into them in Studio A. All three were child prodigies, deeply involved with religious and mystical concerns inseparable from their work. At times each has been portrayed as moody, wary, reclusive—qualities that did not play well at Hitsville, U.S.A. As this book went to press, Marvin Gaye was shot to death, allegedly by his father, on April 1, 1984. On April 2nd, he would have been forty-five. Stevie Wonder is thirty-four; Michael Jackson, twenty-six. Their progressions are journeys through and past the sound of Gordy's Young America. They left behind a sound, in order to create some songs.

Michael Jackson left Motown with his brothers, the Jackson Five, and went to Epic in 1977. His debut solo album, *Off the Wall*, was far more appealing and sophisticated than the bubble-gum soul of "ABC" and "I Want You Back" that Berry Gordy preferred. *Off the Wall* became the best-selling LP of 1980, pop, rock, or soul, selling more than 7 million worldwide and spinning off four hit singles—a feat no other solo artist had ever achieved. *Thriller,* its 1982 sequel, had six hit singles and dominated both soul and pop charts for an entire year in 1983, selling a record twenty million copies and sweeping the Grammy and National Music awards. He accomplished this at twenty-five, having been in the business for twenty years.

When Stevie Wonder turned twenty-one in 1971, he demanded an accounting of his royalties. Finding them in order, he took a quarter of the $1 million that had been held in trust for him as a minor and set himself up in a New York studio with the freedom of a forty-track system and no producer but himself. He refused to renew his Motown contract and planned to put out his first self-produced album, *Music of My Mind,* on his own until Motown came back to him with an astounding offer. If he would allow it to distribute his records, songwriting royalties would be split 50/50 between artist and record company, instead of under the previous arrangement, which gave all money to Motown. In addition to acting as his own producer, Stevie Wonder could form his own publishing and production companies. In all respects, under a 120-page contract agreement, he retained full artistic control.

Marvin Gaye had to wait until he was twice that age—forty-three—before he secured that type of freedom for himself. It took him two decades to break from Motown contractually and sign with Columbia Records in 1982. He believed that his struggle and Stevie Wonder's victory were definitely related.

"When I was fighting for the right of the Motown artist to express himself, Stevie knew I was also fighting for him," Gaye told David Ritz, in *Essence* magazine. "He gained from that fight, and the world gains from his genius."

Marvin Gaye's genius revealed itself in cycles that he tended to describe in abstract, almost mystical terms. He spoke often of his dark and light sides, warned frequently of the movements of evil and an impending Armageddon. He did not seem to find it odd or insupportable that his own life had been governed by tempests. In interviews his tone ricocheted between rage and acceptance. Often this made for elliptical conversation.

"If one understands life," he once explained, "one must know that every positive period must have a negative period and every negative period must have a positive period. So the idea is to ride through one's negativity with disregard for it and total acceptance."

The movements of fate can make chart position look puny. And fate was a crucial concept to Marvin Gaye, who believed that his greatest successes were foretold before he had opened an eye to the world.

Well in advance of his birth, Marvin Gaye's grandfather had told his mother that her child's fortune would lie "under the grapevine." When Marvin's recording of "I Heard It Through the Grapevine" sold more than 4 million copies in 1968 and 1969, he sang the song on *Hollywood Palace, Joey Bishop,* and the *Tonight Show,* landing him in the cushy lap of prime time and pop. In the wake of that hit, *Billboard*'s polls found Marvin Gaye to be one of the nation's leading male vocalists, along with Glen Campbell and Elvis Presley.

The success of "Grapevine" planted a strange notion within Gaye. "That first decade was something," he told Ritz. "I screamed my head off about artistic control. And for most of the time I had the feeling I was screaming alone. Finally, in 1969, when 'Heard It Through the Grapevine' went through the roof . . . I thought to myself: Why? Why go on being led? I knew there was more inside me. And that was something no record executive or producer could see. But I saw it. I knew it had to get out there."

He succeeded in loosing it when he got the chance to produce his own album in 1971. Motown did not want to release the resulting LP, finding it too weird and different. Somehow Gaye prevailed, and *What's Going On?* yielded three singles that crossed over and hit the Top Ten. Released at the height of the Vietnam War, it was a moody, often bleak vista, despite the pleasing melodic backdrops. Front-page tensions ran through songs like "Mercy Mercy Me (the Ecology)," the antinuke "Save the Children," and "Inner City Blues (Make Me Wanna Holler)."

And then, the positive. Seer gave way to seducer two years later, with *Let's Get It On.* Erotic urgency has rarely been so well expressed. "Let's Get It On" is without question a top contender for Motown's most libidinous record. Certainly, ripped in just the right places with moans and screams, it is one of the most soulful. The singer is in a languorous rhythmic garden, and there is no evil in it. Chastity doesn't stand a chance there, but still, it is a holy place. Serpent-soft, Gaye's voice wonders in a whisper whether the lady knows the meaning of being sanctified.

Reconciling such ideal beauty with the evils of the real world is not easy within one record, and Marvin Gaye said he never tried. Instead, he repeated his hell-to-heaven cycle, following the ominous *In Our Lifetime* with the balm of *Midnight Love* and its hit single, "Sexual Healing," in 1982. But between those twin cycles, from 1971 to 1978, there was trouble under the grapevine and, with it, Marvin Gaye's strangest piece of work.

Shortly after the success of "Let's Get It On," the man PR releases had called the Prince of Motown found there was a tithe to pay for those heady first successes cut during his marriage to Berry Gordy's sister Anna, who was seventeen years his senior. In a divorce case bizarre by any standards, a court ordered that Marvin Gaye complete a financial settlement by recording two LPs and surrendering all resulting money to Anna Gordy Gaye. The artist obliged with a double album unparalleled in ironies and contradictions. He called it *Here, My Dear*.

It was, Gaye has admitted, an odd thing for a black man to be singing the blues about a multimillion-dollar divorce. But then, he was forced to make the album to satisfy the dictates of the American judicial system. It was stranger, still, that by releasing the record that would compensate his sister financially for her domestic pain, Berry Gordy was forced to contribute to her public humiliation. *Here, My Dear* is hardly coy in celebrating and condemning the couple's more intimate moments. Finally, in delivering such a personal "concept" album, Marvin Gaye was risking his own credentials as an up-tempo million-record seller. Divorce isn't altogether danceable.

The period that followed its release in 1978 was marked by a series of exiles. Some were self-imposed; others were flights from creditors, the IRS, and a federal bankruptcy court. Gaye was, in his own words, "snorting and smoking" extensively. At one point he lived out of a van on Hawaii. Reports from a bleak sojourn in London found him climbing out the window of an airport men's room to escape an unscrupulous promoter. He blamed the "unseen powers of darkness" that had been behind his divorce.

He was just coming out of that darkness, just beginning work on the record that would repay his debts and reestablish him on the charts, when Mary Wilson visited him in London. She says she was struck by something as he talked of rediscovery and redemption. "If they ever made a movie of Sam Cooke's life," she said, "I could think of no one better to play him than Marvin Gaye. In terms of his life and his music."

Beyond the fact that promoters billed Marvin Gaye as the heir apparent to Cooke's soul prince crown, the two shared the agony of getting caught between the wonderful and the terrible. Gaye's death, allegedly at the hands of his father, seems all too close to the tragedy of errors that killed Sam Cooke. And if Marvin Gaye did not possess the beauty and virtuosity of Sam Cooke's voice, he had a greater inventiveness as a composer and arranger. What his vocal expression lacks in pure quality and range, it makes up for in its idiosyncratic expression. Gaye's is a haunted voice, flickering through his own landscapes of love and loss, gliding on sexual thrill one moment, howling from despair's black hole the next.

Self-containment was the key to Marvin Gaye's musical growth from the time he began producing his own work. He'd sit down in a studio full of instruments and play nearly all of them himself. He recorded them, layer by layer, with the improvisations of a vocalist and the solid, canny basics of a natural percussionist. After all, he played drums at Motown before he sang there. To hear him singing, just over drums, as he does in "Midnight Lady," is to appreciate his counterpoint of finesse and funk. More than Stevie Wonder, more than Michael Jackson, Marvin Gaye was a willful soul alchemist.

It showed in his own musical preferences. He said that he thought James Brown had the greatest mind for syncopated rhythms and that Barbra Streisand had "superior soul." He liked and admired Peggy Lee and Aretha Franklin, Eydie Gormé and Sam Cooke. His ear was equally tickled in a supper club and a revival tent. He was known as a soul singer, but as he told David Ritz, that was never his intent. "I never wanted to sing the hot stuff," he insisted. "With a great deal of bucking I did it because . . . well, I wanted the money and the glory. So I worked with all the producers. But I wanted to be a pop singer—like Nat Cole or Sinatra or Tony Bennett. I wanted to be a pop singer like Sam Cooke, proving that our kind of music and our kind of feeling could work in the context of pop ballads."

The fact is, Marvin Gaye was one of those artists who forced themselves to live with and appreciate the tension of opposites. Instead of merging the fire and ice and coming up with harmless vapor, he had the effrontery to run hot and cold.

The music was no less schizophrenic than his life within it. Born the son of a preacher in a small, stern Pentecostal sect, he sang one day, at the age of five, at a religious meeting in Kentucky. The reaction was so intense that Marvin Gaye, Sr., hauled his small son with him from then on, letting the child hand him towels onstage, then setting him in the center of the congregation to sing. Even as a small boy Marvin was aware of his effect on the female faithful.

"It made me feel good," he explained in the liner notes to his *Anthology* triple album. "Mother kept me singing. She would say, 'Get up and sing "Journey to the Sky." ' " The ladies in the church, they would hug me and bring me to them. Psychologically, sensually, I liked this.''

When he was seventeen, he decided he wanted to fly and enlisted in the Air Force, in the hope he could pilot one of the graceful Skyhawks he saw in the recruiting posters. What he did not realize was that he had to march double time before he could fly. His discharge was honorable, but its message was clear: "Marvin Gaye cannot adjust to regimentation and authority" was the conclusion.

This was the same man who said he believed in the Lord Jesus but not the constraints of organized religion; who said that he loved women but hated womankind; who, in the same interview, referred to himself as an artist *and* a factory, as promiscuous but selective. Owing millions to taxes and creditors, he wore a quarter-inch-wide rubber band around his wrist to remind him that material things are not important. As "Sexual Healing" was about to be released, he installed himself in Ostend, Brussels, in the crosswinds of pig farms and the astringent breeze of the gloomy North Sea. Though his two failed marriages pained him, sex is sacrament, not sin in his songs. Sex was the soul of his musical success. And somehow, in this patchwork of contradictions, it seems fitting that he insisted the woman he duetted with so seamlessly was never his lover.

Tammi Terrell collapsed in his arms onstage at Hampden-Sydney College in Virginia, where they were doing a string of one-nighters in the summer of 1967. She was twenty-two, beautiful, and blessed with a voice that could embrace Gaye's phrasings perfectly. He had duetted with Mary Wells and Kim Weston, but when Tammi called out, "Talk to me," theirs was the most gorgeous of conversations. To millions of smitten couples, in 1967 and 1968, "our song" was likely to be Marvin and Tammi singing "Ain't No Mountain High Enough" or "Ain't Nothing Like the Real Thing."

Tammi fell unconscious just as they finished "Your Precious Love" and, when she was revived, admitted to needing "a pound of aspirins a day" to keep her going on the tour. Blinding headaches, which she said often came on after arguments with her boyfriend, had begun to debilitate her. The boyfriend, a member of one of Motown's most successful groups, had announced their engagement from the stage one night. Shortly after, she learned that he was already married. The headaches grew worse. Following her collapse there was brain surgery. She tried to resume recording, but weakness brought on by a forty-pound weight loss, a partial loss of muscle coordination, and difficulty remembering lyrics made it impossible.

After eight operations she died, in 1970, of complications related to a brain tumor. Marvin Gaye, who could not perform live for nearly four years following the loss of his partner, maintained his silence, saying only that there was a great deal behind Tammi Terrell's death that the public did not know.

Whether the skeletons in the Motown closets are real or imagined may never be known. What seems certain is that there was a dark side to the big, bouncy sound of Young America. But it was a relative darkness. Even Marvin Gaye admitted he was very lucky to be there.

"What you weigh it all against, all the good times and the bad, is the little bit of nothing you would have been handed if Motown never came along," Martha Reeves explains. She says that even if Berry Gordy was not a good shepherd all the way through, at least his initial instincts vouchsafed a lot of vulnerable young lives. "Stevie Wonder was a ten-year-old child who was black *and* blind," Martha says. "And I wouldn't want to guess what might have happened to him if Ron White of the Miracles hadn't heard him and pestered Berry to give him a listen."

Gordy agreed to listen to the child but had no great expectations. Half of adult Detroit was at his door with tiny geniuses in crinolines and sailor suits. Mary Wilson remembers the day in 1960 she, Diana, and Florence were about to leave the studio for the day when Berry Gordy stopped them.

"Stick around," he said. "I have this little blind kid coming up, and I've gotta listen to him."

"So Stevie came up," Mary remembers. "I think his mother was with him, and a couple of brothers. He's just a typical ten-year-old, comes running in, so Berry says, 'Can you play this instrument?' So he played the piano. He played the organ. He played the drums, the congas. He played everything there. And Berry said, 'You are signed.' Now when I see Stevie, I can hardly say Little Stevie because he's a man. And he always hates that because he doesn't want anyone to remember when he was a little kid. But he would run up behind all the girls and pinch them on the behind. He'd pretend that he could see by doing little things. He'd tell you what color jacket you were wearing and stuff like that. How he did it, I don't know. But the most amazing part was how he'd find us to pinch all of us. And we let him."

Like Michael Jackson, Stevie Wonder started out mimicking sexy adult stylings in a self-conscious falsetto until his voice and his testosterone level caught up with the lyrics. I remember seeing Stevie on a Murray the K TV special in the early sixties. They set him in the middle of a baseball stadium with his harmonica, and he stood there, wobbly-headed and ungainly until his ear picked up the cue and he put the harmonica to his mouth and lit into "Fingertips, Pt. 2," his first number one hit. The awkward, herky-jerky little figure took on an amazing grace, despite the boxy suit and the miniature Ray-Ban sunglasses.

As A & R secretary, Martha Reeves spent a lot of time with Stevie in the office and in the studio.

"I do want to get one thing straight," Martha says. "I was *not* Little Stevie Wonder's baby-sitter, though I have read that. Stevie's man Friday was Clarence Paul. If you'll look at Stevie's song credits, you'll see his name quite frequently in the beginning. He wrote a lot of Stevie's early stuff, and he was just in charge of him. Stevie came in every day after school, and at first we were told by some of the administration to stay away from him because we might be a bad influence. But it was okay to be his friend around the office. I remember sitting with him, day after day, with this little old tape recorder he liked to play with."

"M-I-C-K-E-Y." The kid picked out the Disney anthem on a keyboard, recorded it, then segued into a schmaltzy soap opera organ riff and talked into the machine:

"Today Mrs. Jones finds out that her entire family on her mama's side is in a coma and broke."

Brooooom, broooop broooom (more organ).

"An' she missed by one on the day's number . . ."

Brrrrooooop.

"The coal truck done run over her doggie . . ."

Brrrt-da-drooop.

"Aw, it was fun, Stevie at this Hammond organ, he'd play those silly chords, and we'd talk over them, make up dumb stories. We did lots of soap operas. I enjoyed Stevie Wonder as a child. Not being a baby-sitter or a nanny, but being his friend. He was truly a child genius. Seemed sometimes to be a spirit that's lived and is just here again."

Asked why she thinks Stevie had the strength and the wisdom to avoid the contractual and artistic disputes that plagued so many Motown artists, Martha is silent for a moment.

"Maybe it's because he wasn't fooled by the smiles. Didn't have to see them. There's a certain con to the business. But he wasn't taken in by those smiles, the looks on those faces."

She says that most of the adults saw him as a "natural child," an image he worked hard to shed later, along with the "Little" preceding his name.

But at the outset the image fitted. "Fingertips" was just a childhood doodle to Stevie Wonder, as was much of his early Motown work. He noodled along in a safe up-tempo way with hits like "Uptight (Everything's Alright)," "I Was Made to Love Her," and "My Cherie Amour." They sold, but he did not have another number one record until almost a decade after "Fingertips." In 1972 he cut "Superstition." It went to the top of the charts on the strength of his decision to accept the Rolling Stones' offer to tour with them as their opening act. By tour's end, when Stevie was joining Mick Jagger for a joint assault on "Satisfaction," he had established himself as an adult artist with a sound of his own. Onstage at Madison Square Garden, Stevie took a pratfall on a piece of Mick Jagger's giant birthday cake and came up smiling, licking icing. He was on his way, on his own. His three successive self-produced albums—*Music of My Mind, Talking Book* (both 1972), and *Innervisions* (1973)—sold in the millions and engaged the imaginations of critics who finally stopped thinking of him as Little Stevie, Motown marionette. He survived a near-fatal car crash and coma in 1973, won ten Grammy awards over the next two years, and in 1975 wrested from Motown what was then the richest contract in the history of the record industry. Besides artistic control, it awarded him $13 million over seven years.

Given his head, introspection continued to be Stevie Wonder's dominant muse, with titles like "Higher Ground" and *Fulfillingness First Finale.* Critics have carped about his pollyanna aspects, about the melodic pleas for human harmony, and the almost lunatic idealism in his notions of universal brotherhood. But it is not inconsistent with his early childhood as a junior deacon in church or as a teenager piping about the lofty ideals of romantic love in songs like "I Was Made to Love Her." Critical redemption came when Stevie revealed he could sing "both sides," when harrowing sound murals like "Living for the City" with its "git in that cell, nigger" sound effects showed that he was not blind to despair. Stevie Wonder's emotional range is not as extreme and intense as Marvin Gaye's, nor are his solutions as idiosyncratic. It depends, in the end, on just where you look for salvation. While Marvin Gaye is groping beneath the sheets, Stevie Wonder wanders off toward human be-ins. Never was the plea for racial harmony more simple and, some would argue, less compelling than in his 1982 single with Paul McCartney, "Ebony and Ivory." It was pabulum compared to the bite of "What's Going On?" And in the noncommittal eighties, it sold like crazy.

Later in 1982 McCartney recorded another two-tone duet with that other Motown prodigy Michael Jackson. Romantic rivalry was the theme. Again it had all the spice of tapioca; again it hit number one. Interviewing Michael for *Rolling Stone,* I was with him when the test pressing of "The Girl Is Mine" arrived by messenger at his temporary residence, a rented condo in Encino. Explaining that he had to check it for release, he ducked into the darkened den and put the disc on the turntable.

As he dropped the needle onto the vinyl, light from a giant screen—a video hearth that burns even when Michael is away from home—silhouetted him. He is painfully thin, ribs and shoulder blades protruding from a polo shirt. As he listened, his head was bobbing to the rhythm track, bony knees drawn up, feet moving slightly so that the undone tips of his shoelaces tapped against the floor. He had traipsed around all day like that, tripping over the laces, explaining that he was breaking the shoes in. They were new, picked out by a secretary, since he cannot and will not suffer the mob scenes in stores and cares little for any clothes except his stage costumes.

"He has no interest in things like that," his mother, Katherine Jackson, had told me. "Just like he has no interest in food. He says that if he didn't have to eat to stay alive, he wouldn't."

She says his precocity frightened her when he was five and six because she had no idea where the talent was coming from. His fierce concentration was always daunting.

"Don't like that degree of bass." Frowning at the turntable, he talked to himself as he listened to the test pressing. Directly beside him, a cartoon myna was spanking a naughty monkey, but the fracas failed to break his gaze. Before the tone arm had lifted off the record, Michael was on the phone, punching buttons, making calls to managers, production technicians, accountants. Between calls he smiled at the cartoons. He is the first to admit that there are two Michaels—the fearless, flat-out stage and recording artist and the shy, wispy-voiced young man who sat me at his living room table and explained, most convincingly, that sheer terror had kept him from doing interviews for more than two years.

"I was raised onstage," he explained. "And I am more comfortable out there than I am right now. When it comes time to go off, I don't want to. I feel like there are angels on all corners, protecting me. I could sleep onstage.''

Motown gave him a great musical education, he says. But he could have used a bit more instruction on getting on in the world at large. He says he conducts his private life ''just like a hemophiliac who can't afford to be scratched in any way.''

Though Young America has danced to his voice since he was a child, his constituency is largely unknown to the artist himself. Unlike Marvin Gaye and Stevie Wonder, who made all those bus and truck odysseys through big cities and bayou towns, Michael hit Motown when it had up-graded to jets and limousines. He did not learn street smarts along with harmony. Within him, he says, the tension between the performing and the private self can be so unbearable he must fast and dance every Sunday, sometimes until he falls down, to maintain his emotional balance. He is lonely, and he says he cries a lot. The funny thing is, he finds that some-times it makes his music better.

His most successful songs, like ''Don't Stop Til You Get Enough,'' ''Off the Wall,'' ''Beat It,'' and ''Billie Jean,'' are for the most part tense, tough dance cuts that flirt with paranoia, skittering between restraint and abandon, layering pop and soul idioms in a nervous, shifting counterpoint. His lyrics bite at themes of abuse and parasitism, loneliness and terror. But they're all very danceable. His arrangements—high, gusting strings and vocals over thudding, in-the-pocket rhythms tracks—are the logical progression of what Berry Gordy set out to do in the sixties. By virtue of his soulful past and pop aspirations, Michael Jackson became the perfect product for the eighties. The fanzine set is not scared off by raunchy lyrics and chest hair. But the R-rated uptown dance crowd can bump and slide right along the greasy tracks. It is now being called pop/soul by those into marketing categories. Michael says he doesn't care what anybody wants to call it. As a Jehovah Witness he believes his talent comes straight from God. His success, on the other hand, was a deliberate triumph of the will.

''I always knew I'd have to leave,'' he says of Motown. He was grateful for Berry Gordy's patronage but convinced that his star system would be limiting. From an early age he fell in love with performers who worked without restraint. He says his life was changed by watching wild, untamed creatures like James Brown.

''He gets so *out* of himself,'' Michael said. Getting out of oneself and into a performance is a ritual so essential, so much a part of Michael's life that like any serious acolyte, he completely devoted himself to learning the ways of the mystical elders. When other boys were collecting baseball cards, he was cataloguing James Brown's bag of dance tricks.

"I just love him. I do. I'd be in the wings," he said, "when I was like six and seven. I'd sit there and watch him for hours and forget where I was."

Michael's kindergarten was Soul Kitchen Number One, the basement of the Apollo Theater. He was too shy to approach the performers the Jackson Five opened for, everyone from Jackie Wilson to Gladys Knight, the Temptations, and Etta James. He says he had to know everything, how James Brown could do a slide, a spin, and a split and still make it back before the mike hit the floor. How the mike itself disappeared through the Apollo stage floor. He crept downstairs, along passageways and walls so funky they could grow hair. He hid there, peering from behind the dusty flanks of old vaudeville sets while musicians tuned, smoked, played cards, and divvied barbecue. After climbing back to the wings, he stood in the protective folds of the musty curtain, watching his favorite acts, committing every double dip, every bump/snap/whip-it-back mike toss to his inventory of night moves. Even now he can describe a set of red suits worn by Sam and Dave the way some kids would lovingly remember a set of electric trains: "Vented sides . . . pegged pants . . . matching patent leather boots."

In the Motown studio he was just as attentive to detail and determined to learn all he could. When the Jackson Five were working in Studio A, he fixed his wide brown eyes on the engineers and producers. He says he rarely asked questions. He just listened and watched.

"I was like a hawk preying in the night," he said. "I'd watch everything. They couldn't get away with nothing without me seeing. I really wanted to get into it."

He knew what happened to those who left the house of Gordy still dependent on production teams. When he left home, he vowed he would leave prepared. When the Jacksons switched to Epic, he was ready. At the outset Epic entrusted the brothers to Gamble and Huff, master crafters of Philly soul. But in response to the brothers' lobbying, it was agreed that the artists themselves could write two cuts on their first album for the label.

"I knew we were good," Michael said, "when we wrote this song 'Different Kind of Lady.' People went bananas for that song. And Gamble and Huff went back and wrote another song, in competition with ours.

They went back to the drawing board. They stayed in that room a *long* time. In fact, they left the producing up to us. And we said, 'Wow, look at this.' 'Cause to us, Gamble and Huff were like the ultimate songwriters. From that point on, we rocketed to doing our own album, *Destiny*. That was a big step, you know. That went platinum. Then after that came my album.''

And after the success of *Off the Wall,* there was *Thriller*. With the records, his show-stopping segment in the Motown TV special, and three exceptional video pieces, Michael Jackson *was* the music news of '83. But while both the movie and the record industries are busy investing in his future as a pop superstar, Michael is still curiously persistent in researching his musical past. He talks for hours with his producer, Quincy Jones, who says he found in Michael a precocity and professionalism he has seen only in the likes of Aretha Franklin and Lena Horne. Finding a person—friend, performer, interviewer—who lived through the sixties with a solid-state transistor and a full set of adult hormones, Michael is a tireless interviewer. He has heard, for instance, that there is a piece of film that caught James Brown's most astonishing bit of dancing. He had been searching for this get-down grail for some time.

"Have you seen it?" he asked as we drove through Encino in his gold Camaro. "Do you know what it is?"

It was *The T.A.M.I. Show,* I explained, a 1965 teen extravaganza filmed for TV with the Supremes, the Rolling Stones, the Miracles, and a host of other Motown and British invaders. Elvis Presley used to rent out a Memphis movie theater after hours and show the film over and over, just to watch James Brown. James says it was the fastest he ever danced in his life. He says if you look closely, you can see him collapse for a few seconds onto a stage monitor. For a moment he didn't know where he was.

"Because he was so *out* of himself, right?"

Michael was stopped at a light, daydreaming until traffic began to honk behind us.

"Will you help me find it? There are things I have to know. Things I very much need to see to understand what *I* do. . . .''

He figures that he was so young much of the influence must have been subliminal. When he studies film clips of himself dancing, he wonders how it all came together.

When you watch Michael Jackson dance, it's clear that he is the best, the brightest practitioner of Pentecostal dance boogie since James Brown.

There is nothing tentative about his solo turns. He can tuck his long, thin frame into a figure skater's spin without benefit of ice or skates. Aided by the burn and flash of silvery body suits, he seems to change molecular structure at will, all robot angles one second and rippling curves the next. So sure is the body that his eyes are often closed, his face turned upward to some unseen muse. The bony chest heaves. He pants, bumps, and squeals. He has been known to leap offstage and climb up into the rigging.

Despite such onstage coordination, he admitted his parents had to force him to learn to drive a car. The driving teacher told him that he did a wonderful job with the mechanics of it all. He was just a touch concerned about Michael's tendency to daydream. As he explained this, Michael drove us through Encino slowly and carefully, slowing to point out Clark Gable's old home, shoulders tense, his eyes serious beneath the sunglasses until a sound from the radio forced a smile. It was the Righteous Brothers and that masterwork of blue-eyed soul.

" 'You've lost that lovvvvin' feelin,' whoo-oh, that lovvvin' feelin . . .' Oooh, I *love* this, don't you?'' Michael was singing along with Bill Medley's big, aching voice. "It's one of my favorites. Those sixties were too much. The music from that time should never be lost to man. Never. They had the best songs and the best talent. Simon and Garfunkel, the Beatles, Motown stuff, the Supremes. Hey, was the sixties when they did 'Scarborough Fair'?''

Righto. Circa 1967. Same year "Sergeant Pepper" ruled the airwaves. Same year Aretha Franklin blew all asunder with "I Never Loved a Man," and Stevie Wonder was chafing under the "Little" that had so long preceded his given name. Marvin and Tammi had three hits; Martha Reeves was pining for "Jimmy Mack." Michael was nine.

"What's that song, 'Slow Down, You Move Too Fast'? Was that during the sixties?'' Michael looked over the top of his sunglasses, searching for the title. "I hope you don't mind all these questions," he said apologetically. "I do it to Paul [McCartney] all the time.''

Michael was only five when the Beatles crossed over to America; now he and McCartney were wrangling over the same girl in their duet. When they are together, he and Paul indulge in a mutual passion. They rent and watch cartoons like *Dumbo* and *Bambi*. And they gossip about the sixties. Michael asks fan questions ("What was your favorite Beatle song?''). Paul answers ("Yesterday"). And he asks about Motown.

"Paul loves Motown. He also loves gut music," Michael said. "Early, early American black music. And he goes to African hotels and Jamaica, bringing back different sounds, sticks, and some drums. He's recording things like that. But if you want to see him smile, just start talking to him about sixties Motown. He says he was a fan like anyone else. And since those years were real important to his career, his memories are very sharp, very sensitive about that time. I know he wants to hold on to it, so I tell him everything that I know, from being around the artists and the company.''

Sometimes this takes a little research. Michael was born the year Smokey Robinson and his Miracles cut ''Got a Job.'' By 1969, when the Jackson Five's first hit, ''I Want You Back,'' nudged ''Raindrops Keep Falling on My Head'' out of the number one spot, the Supremes were already broken up, the Temptations were into their ''psychedelic'' phase, and Smokey Robinson was already contemplating retiring from the road. The Jackson Five spent little more than a year working out of Detroit before Motown moved West. What Michael remembers most about it is the smallness and the cold.

''I guess I was just a little older than the company when they moved to California,'' he said, honking the horn for his sister Janet to open the garage door. ''The sixties at Motown still sounds like magic to me when I hear people talk about it. I mean, it must have been a charmed time. Don't you think?''

▮16
Aretha Franklin: A Woman's Only Human

▮ *Soul to me is a feeling, a lot of depth and being able to bring to the surface that which is happening inside, to make the picture clear. The song doesn't matter. . . . It's just the emotion, the way it affects other people.*

—ARETHA FRANKLIN

GROWING UP IN DETROIT, Temptation Otis Williams says, he heard wonderful things about the Reverend C. L. Franklin's young daughter Aretha. People said that the girl was special, that she was touched somehow, that she had a voice that could upend a stack of Bibles, a voice you'd never believe came out of the shy teenager who hung around the Arcadia Roller Rink and sang Sundays in her father's church.

"I got friendly with her sister," Otis recalled, "and I used to walk her home from school. I remember one day doing that and finally getting to meet Aretha. There she was, real quiet and shy—the same little girl who was layin' folks out in church. I guess I was surprised, she was *so* quiet. But then what *can* you say about Aretha? I don't know a person who can fit what she is into just the right words."

It had looked manageable enough on a newspaper assignment sheet. Aretha Franklin, appearing at Lincoln Center; interview and concert coverage. Never mind that more than a decade before, the first time I heard her voice over the radio, I ran my mother's wheezy Chevy through its first red light. The fan in me was thrilled. But the journalist was anxious. "Access" was a well-known problem with Aretha, and it had taken long and delicate negotiations to get her to talk. Apart from the obligatory three-minute phoners to promote records or concert tours, she had not done a substantive interview since 1968, when a *Time* magazine cover story spun Lady Soul into a fearful and deep-seated horror of the press. The cover pictured her as the radiant figurehead for the new soul music. But the text read like the Billie Holiday story, bulldozing into marital and family problems the way TV news teams cover Harlem murders and suicides. The descriptions of C. L. Franklin and Aretha's first husband, Ted White, were almost caricatures. Beneath a photograph of Aretha and White was the caption "Sometimes she prefers fishing."

"You can't tell me they would have taken the same approach with a Doris Day," said a member of Atlantic's publicity staff involved at the time. "What's more ironic is that despite a tough life, Aretha is far more sensitive to that kind of exposure. It was her first big break, and it traumatized her. I don't expect she'll ever fully get over it."

"Tread gently," then, was the advice. We agreed I'd start off at a respectable distance. I could watch a rehearsal. No questions, just stay loose.

I remember the strong smell of tar. A trail of oily footprints led from the newly paved street to the door of a low-rent West Side rehearsal studio in the shadow of the Port Authority bus terminal in New York City. There was no appreciable ripple among the musicians when Aretha walked in. She waved hello with a half-eaten cheeseburger, finished it off, and walked to a music stand in the center of the room. She was wearing a red velour slacks outfit beneath a loose gray coat. A half dozen packs of Kools filled a roomy black leather satchel. Aretha lit a cigarette, nodded to the stout, dashikied concertmaster, squared her shoulders, and took a long, deep drag of smoke.

Ten feet from the epicenter, I felt the first note square in the solar plexus. It hummed through every membrane in the room, saturated the gouged acoustic baffling, rising higher, louder, in a blue cloud of Kool smoke, echoing up the sooty airshaft, a Pentecostal crack in the dense city night.

"Jesus God," the studio watchman whispered. "Almighty Jesus God."

Another nod at the rhythm section, and Aretha worked herself into the melody, a do-right version of the pop chestnut "Still," the voice jousting, oh so gently, with the keyboard player, trading stratospheric "oooh yeahs" with his low, churchy fills. I remember holding onto the metal chair leg. It vibrated like a tuning fork. Aretha pushed the tempo, and the conga player began to sweat. Suddenly it was hot, and the room seemed far too small. The voice had become a physical entity, much too big even for the ample body that loosed it.

And the spirit became flesh and dwelt among them.

It felt like a holy moment. But suddenly Aretha ripped a note in half and ended the trance. The band froze.

"Let's try it again," she was saying. "That was just no good."

The conga player dashed off to hold his hands under cold water. Someone else was passing out paper towels. Aretha came over and lit another cigarette.

"I'm just fooling around with some loose edges here," she said. "You sure you want to hang around for this?"

I was startled at the change in the voice and in the woman. Aretha's speaking tone is so soft as to be inaudible past a couple of yards. Even her carriage is different. The shoulders hunch forward, almost as if to shelter the deflated, now vulnerable lungs.

That voice, I remember thinking, has a life of its own.

"It does get me out of myself," Aretha told me. "I guess you could say I do a lot of traveling with my voice."

"Miss Ree will see you now."

The voice is soft and almost playful as Aretha opens the door to her hotel suite. She is in a well-cut, white, take-care-of-business suit; behind her, the early-afternoon sun hits the henna-tinted hair. The glow is refracted through cigarette smoke.

"Relax," she commands, and, noting my startled look, smiles and explains, "Oh, not you. Just talking to myself."

Settling into the sofa, she points to my tape recorder. "Maybe you should move it closer. People have told me my speaking voice doesn't carry that well."

It's still surprising for a woman who has spent more than thirty of her forty-two years raising her voice in churches, clubs, studios, and concert halls. She says she was never a noisy kid—"just opened my eyes wide and watched"—along the gospel caravans when the Reverend C. L. Franklin moved his family from Memphis, where Aretha was born in 1942, north to Buffalo, then to Detroit and pastorship of the New Bethel Baptist Church.

"I guess I was about nine when I decided I wanted to sing," Aretha says. "The best, the greatest gospel singers passed through our house in Detroit. Sometimes they stayed with us. James Cleveland lived with us for a time, and it was James who taught me to play the piano by ear. But the ladies. How I loved my gospel ladies."

It is said that Aretha's mother, Barbara Siggers, was a fine, strong singer. But she deserted the family—there were five children—when Aretha was six and died four years later. Aretha says she always looked forward to visits from Mahalia Jackson and from Clara Ward, a longtime friend of her father's. Clara took a lot of time with C.L.'s girls, as did two of her singers, Frances Steadman and Marion Williams.

"They told me things girls should know," Aretha says. Much of the talk took place in the kitchen. Hands were busy, and strong voices talked above the roll of bubbling pots.

"Mahalia would come in, and she'd head right for the kitchen," Aretha says. "She'd put up a pot of greens. We'd sit around and talk. I was shy, but I guess I did have a lot of questions. Then maybe we'd sing. They were so strong, those ladies. And always there for me. Mahalia lived in Chicago, which was just a hop, skip, and a jump away from Detroit. And she'd sing in my father's church, and I would be thrilled, listening to her. And feeling so lucky she would come home, to our house."

She says that these wise, kind women seemed to understand her need to sing. "You can't explain it yourself," Aretha says. "But you can sense it in other people, I guess. Clara knew. She knew I *had* to sing."

Aretha says she has been secure in that knowledge for most of her life. She remembers that her first church solo must have been when she was eight or nine. She was trembling beforehand, but once she had taken her place in the big, rustling hall of her father's church, the terror left her. "Next thing I know, I'm just *out* there," she says. "Out there singing. But right then I knew that that was for me."

When church people began saying it as well, when she began to draw shouts and screams, when her idol Dinah Washington pointed at her and told people like Quincy Jones, "That one—C.L.'s girl—*that's* the one to watch," Aretha went about exploring the range of her gift.

"I suppose I might have been sort of a bully," she says. "As a kid I sang all day, every day. With my sisters [Carolyn and Erma] and with my friends. We had a little group. I wanted to go on through the night. And they'd be tired. And I would *yell* at them, 'Sing, sing, I want you to sing.' We sang all kinds of things, but mostly what we heard on the radio.

The Teenagers, the Drifters, LaVern Baker, and Ruth Brown. Ooh, I just loved Ruth Brown.''

Secular music was never forbidden in the Franklin household, nor were commercial aspirations discouraged. In the mid-fifties C. L. Franklin was enough of an attraction on the gospel circuit to command top scale of $2,000 to $4,000 for an appearance. His sermons made him a Chess recording star in the gospel market. Singing both sides was clearly possible for his daughter, who was young and versatile and always glued to the radio. When Aretha's favorite gospel singer ''made the change,'' as she puts it, the die was cast for her as well.

Sam Cooke went pop in 1956, when Aretha was fourteen. Many churchgoers grieved when Sam Cooke left off spending Sundays at New Bethel. But Saturday nights, when he headlined at the Flame Show Bar, young black Detroit pined anxiously at the door.

''Oh, I'd have *died* to get into the Flame,'' Aretha says, hands clasped over her heart. ''But I was too young. It drove me crazy. I guess I figured if Sam could do it, I could, too.''

There was, in her singing, a wisdom far greater than her years. (''I might be just 26,'' she told *Time*, ''but I'm an old woman in disguise, 26 goin' on 65.'') Despite her tender age—she was seventeen when she started making the secular demo records her father paid for—she says C. L. was always encouraging about her new direction: ''He never stopped me from doing the pop stuff, because he knew I'd never *really* leave the church.''

Her new career did take Aretha away from New Bethel and from Detroit. She lived for a time in New York City, went back to Detroit, then out to California, where she lives today. She says that it is a comfort that her old friend and mentor the Reverend James Cleveland lives in L.A. He has a church and a soul food restaurant there, and from time to time they get together for an at-home gospel rave-up. On hot afternoons in the San Fernando Valley she says she's apt to lie indoors listening to a record collection she calls ''extensive—everything from Sergio Mendes to Gloria Gaynor and Leontyne Price.'' And when she feels the need to ''free up some,'' she will motor at night to a golf driving range near her home in Encino and order up a jumbo bucket of balls. She plants her feet on the rubber mat, tees up, and sends dozens of tiny white balls rocketing into the dark.

''I'm a very private, shy person,'' she says. ''But I have my way of working things out.''

She has vivid memories of seeing other people let go and ''get happy''

under the roof of her father's church. They were flashes of complete and
enviable freedom, when self-consciousness blew away, when even crip-
pling shyness fled in the presence of the spirit. Sundays, people jerked
and fainted under the terrible roar of Aretha's father's voice. C. L. Franklin
was, in fact, "the Man with the Million-Dollar Voice," a master of the
rolling-thunder, bust-a-phrase-and-repeat-it cadence. Aretha sat in the
midst of working people as they were lifted by prayer, then carried off
by strong-armed nurses. But she was most taken herself with the passions
of the featured soloists. She remembers especially the time that Clara
Ward got happy at a relative's funeral, crouched like a discus thrower,
and hurled her hat toward the coffin.

"That *did* it," she says.

Of course, you couldn't plan on anybody's rebirth and redemption. But
you could stack the deck a bit with a great gospel bill. Aretha would anticipate the fireworks when she saw her father make up a Sunday program.

"I would hear Sam Cooke was coming," she says, "and I would be
beside myself. I truly loved that man. He would come to the house, so
polite and gentle. And so handsome. Wow! As much as anybody, Sam
made me want to sing. I thought to myself: If I can only do that. Sam
was very encouraging. He would just say, 'Sing, girl.' And believe me,
that was enough."

Sing it.

Aretha heard familiar voices shout at her as she watched the men from
Chess Records adjust their recording equipment. It was hardly a strange
sight; Chess had recorded more than seventy of her father's sermons. But
on that day in 1956 she was the featured soloist. Like Sam Cooke's first
outing with the Soul Stirrers, Aretha's first performance on record is hardly
tenuous. She chose a favorite made popular by Clara Ward, "The Day
Is Past and Gone." There is a beautiful solo rendition of that song leading
off Savoy's *Clara Ward Memorial Album,* recorded when Ward was in
her early twenties. You could almost lay fourteen-year-old Aretha's version over it and come up with a matched duet. Aretha's voice is wilder,
and it breaks every now and then; but her phrasings trace the signature
slides of her idol, right down to the sanctified ad-libs.

"Can I moan a little here?" Aretha asks the congregation.

"Go ahead," a man yells. "Let me hear you."

And when she does, the motherless child sounds like mother to all.
Aretha sang the song again seventeen years later at Clara Ward's funeral
in Philadelphia, and it was with what she describes as "a terrible hurt."

She had sent off Mahalia Jackson just a year earlier with "Precious Lord," at one of two funerals held for that great lady.

"Seems like I'm always missin' someone," Aretha says, and ticks off a list of lost friends. "Mahalia, Clara, Dinah Washington, Sam, King Curtis . . ."

Dinah Washington, who was a great family friend, died in 1963 of a sleeping pill overdose. King Curtis was Curtis Ousley, a New York bandleader, recording artist, and session man whose tenor saxophone pumped out some of the finest soul instrumentals and background work. He worked with Aretha from the beginning on Atlantic, toured with her, shored her up with the sassy horn and relentless good humor. Aretha says his horn spoke directly to her.

On the road he backed her as no one could. Aretha says she sang and felt her best when King Curtis stood to the side with Bernard "Pretty" Purdie on drums, Cornell Dupree on guitar, Richard Tee on keyboards. It was the same in the studio. "Going Down Slow," in particular, on her *Aretha Arrives* album is a beautifully choreographed chase between Curtis's horn and her voice.

"King Curtis could make me laugh *so* hard," she says. King Curtis was only thirty-seven when he was stabbed to death by a passing junkie, on the last hot night of August in 1971, outside the house he owned on Eighty-sixth Street in Manhattan.

"King Curtis was a soul superhero," Aretha says. "And I miss him still."

Aretha counts her father among those she misses. She says she will stop off in Detroit to see him before she goes home to California, but in all likelihood he will not know she is there. He has been in a hospital since he was shot by robbers in June 1979. (Shortly after our interview he was to lapse into a coma; since then Aretha has made countless visits, and done benefits, to see to his care.)

Aretha falls silent after speaking of these missing persons. A photographer arrives, and shyly she asks him to wait a bit, please. She lights another cigarette.

"I'll smile and say cheese," she says. "Just hold on."

Aretha's life has been full of tragic freeze-frames—the lost friends, a messy divorce, hospitalizations for "exhaustion," unexplained disappearances. She had three children by the time she was twenty-one; she grew up in a nice house, with a lawn, but gospel tours ensured a lasting acquaintance with the deprivations of segregation.

"We never went hungry," she notes, "except on the road."

It's easy, then, to do a "Sad-Eyed Lady" refrain on Aretha. She says she likes to do the talk shows, she knows it's good for her visibility and all, but the talk part is no picnic. They all have those blasted index cards with network-researched bios. Seated on the nubby divans of gabmeisters like Johnny and Merv, she tenses at the standard lead-in ("Well, Aretha, I guess we know things haven't been easy for you. . . ."). Always she stares straight ahead, polite but unyielding.

"Well," she tells them, "let's just say I'm experienced and leave it at that."

"A woman's only human . . . you should understand . . ."

She sings it. And though she lets go when she sings, she has learned to be very careful when she talks. Image, the celebrity's rugged cross, seems to have confounded her since the beginning of her years in the limelight. In 1968 a twenty-six-year-old Aretha innocently explained the dilemma to a reporter from *Downbeat:*

> If I started doing my exercises and singing from my stomach, I wouldn't have so many problems. But I forget. I'll do it at the piano, to get that big push. But sitting out there you sound all right but you don't look like a Marilyn Monroe profile-wise. And that's how I get into trouble, because unless I'm sitting at the piano, you know, relaxed, I'll sing from up here [her throat] all the time.

That kind of self-consciousness was not something she could have picked up in church, where no corset was strong enough to contain the Good News. Even when the Clara Ward Singers went showbiz, with Vegas dates, lamé robes, and impossibly tall wigs with curls and waves piled, cornucopia-style, like glossy black fruits, they hopped and jumped in ways that would have horrified the Supremes. Substantial women, arranged in a row, they popped up and down like runaway pistons, rising straight up, both feet off the ground, oblivious to the jounce of flesh or sagging nylons.

Every now and again Aretha will get that happy on a concert stage. She grins, and she takes off her shoes, grabs up a fistful of skirt and she *moves*. Her backup singers hop down off their pert lacquered stools; even rented, tuxed string sections start to smile and sway while Aretha's own horn players slip-slide into soul-step loop-the-loops.

Sometimes, after such a display, she'll come back for a bow with a mink draped over her shoulders like a prizefighter's robe, knowing she's done more than go the distance, and people scream.

Doctor Ree. Sister Ree. 'Retha. Girl. Mama. Oh, Mama. Baby. Baybee.

At moments like this she is all things, everything, anything they want. These are moments of utter possession, and long after the screaming has stopped and the lights have come up, even after the last sobbing balcony sitter has been led gently downstairs, the good Doctor is left limp and panting.

"Messy," she says. "Greasy and messy."

And oddly, it's only when Lady Soul gets prim and sophisticated, when she does not loose her little rhinestone bow ties or kick off her shoes or lay off with the feather boas, that her fans start grumbling about how she should clean up her act. Because they want mess from the lady. All this has backed Aretha Franklin into one sticky corner. The gift, the voice, is undeniable. The discomfort comes in deciding how to package it.

"My weight drives me crazy," she says, admitting that it was the ungentle gaze of cameras and spotlights that introduced her to the hard science of calorie counting.

"The trouble is," she says, "I love to feed people. I love to cook . . . I live in a houseful of men now. Between [husband] Glynn's children and mine, six boys. Lotta young men. Yeah, there's not enough women in that house."

As mistress of that house Aretha says she feels compelled to cook. Men are always wanting food. "Peach cobbler, fried ribs, spaghetti, pork chops—all those fattening things. Now I don't need a recipe to tell me how to cook something, just like I don't need anybody to tell me how to sing."

Jerry Wexler says it used to drive the studio engineers crazy when Lady Soul would clutter up the soundboard with saucepans and plates of ribs. She would cook for the musicians, hunting up provisions on her way from the hotel. Soul food was easy to come by in Muscle Shoals, Alabama, when they recorded at the Fame Studios. But when Jerry installed her in Miami for a session, in the suite usually occupied by Frank Sinatra at the Fontainebleau Hotel, she found the food service was heavy on bagels and herring. Under the ample wing of a local deejay named Fat Daddy, Aretha motored to the soulful side of town and came back with a brown bag full of pig's feet. Just as she was crossing the ornate marbled lobby, the bag broke, and several pounds of beknuckled *trafe* skidded across the floor.

Aretha took a powder as horrified employees poked at the desecration with mops.

"Lotsa talk, woman. But when you gonna cook for *me* again?"

Aretha's husband, actor Glynn Turman, a slim, handsome man who wears designer clothes and confidence extremely well, walks in from the bedroom. No man could ask for a greater sign of welcome. Aretha is on her feet, and the smile breaking across her face is enormous. In fact, she nods a go-ahead as the photographer tentatively unpacks his lights.

"Here," she says, "is my own Dr. Feelgood."

"Takes care of those pains and those ills . . ." Glynn sings, settling himself at the table and attacking a fruit salad. Aretha is very glad to have him here. She is far more relaxed, almost coquettish as she explains how it all came about. They were married in her father's church in 1978. Reverend Franklin performed the services, and the Four Tops sang Stevie Wonder's "Isn't She Lovely" as the bride walked down the aisle.

The couple met at a benefit Rosie Grier gave at the Dorothy Chandler Pavilion in L.A. Aretha's son was the go-between.

"You're my mother's favorite actor," he told Glynn.

"So who's your mother?"

The boy took him to his mother's dressing room.

"I told him that I was interested in drama, in acting, and he said he was an instructor at the inner-city cultural center. And I said, 'Oh, *really?*' I took the information down and told him I'd come to some of his classes. And I did go. I stayed the whole season."

Glynn looks up from his lunch and says yes, she was a good student, but he never graded her. "I married her. And if she's been acting all this time, she's *damn* good."

Aretha laughs and sprawls on the sofa, Theda Bara style, pantomiming just how exhausting she found acting. For her small segment in *The Blues Brothers* movie, she was on the set for hours. The result was an electric five or six minutes—clearly the best segment in the film. Aretha is cast as the proprietress of a Chicago soul food joint. When the Blues Brothers (John Belushi and Dan Aykroyd) try to recruit her musician lover (played by Matt "Guitar" Murphy, a real-life session man) to set down his spatula and rejoin their band, Aretha and her "girls"—cast as customers—face them down with a ferocious version of her 1968 hit "Think."

"When she sings 'Think,' " Pauline Kael wrote in *The New Yorker,* ". . . she smashes the movie to smithereens. Her presence is so strong, she seems to be looking at us while we're looking at her. She's completely there, and so funny . . . that you can't come down enough to respond to what follows.''

It is a segment worth putting on an endless loop. Strutting across the gritty tile floor in white scuffies, finger wagging, apron flapping, arms waving over her head, Aretha is a menacing warhead of female outrage and hurt, sheathed in institutional pink nylon.

"Think! Think about whatcha try'n' to do to me, yeah, THINK!"

"Guitar" is up against the counter; the Brothers are cowed.

"Freedom," she bellows, *"aw, freedom."*

A breathless moment or two later, the man gets it. Freedom, that is. With the Brothers, he strides past Aretha and out the door. The lady is left with a refrigerator full of bony-rumped chickens and an eternity of sticky Formica.

"Aw, *shit,"* she says, with the same look that Stella threw at Stanley Kowalski's receding back.

Aretha says that she would like to act more—TV, movies, video, anything. There has been talk of her starring in a film or a stage play based on the life of blues great Bessie Smith, and Aretha thinks she could do it. Having the Queen of Soul play the Empress of Blues is a reasonable leap. As Aretha points out, they both were signed to Columbia Records by the same man. John Hammond had found Bessie Smith working as a hostess in a Philadelphia speakeasy when he persuaded her to record for him in the thirties; he also "discovered" Billie Holiday. For the sixties he came up with Bob Dylan; and for the seventies, Bruce Springsteen. It was 1960 when he accidentally stumbled on the future Queen of Soul.

As he recalls in his autobiography, *John Hammond on Record,* Hammond found himself distracted by the voice on a badly made demo that a black songwriter named Curtis Lewis was playing for him in his office. Lewis was trying to sell his song "Today I Sing the Blues." But it was the performer, a gospel-trained teenager from Detroit, who excited Hammond's imagination. He made his interest known, and when Jo King, a woman who owned a Broadway recording studio, called one day to say that Aretha was rehearsing there, Hammond lost no time. He dropped in for a listen and signed her to Columbia.

Aretha's recollection of the six years she spent on that label are not pleasant. The record company kept her laced into restrictive pop songs, stylized jazz, or petrified show tunes. Atlantic was already sanctioning the gospel lunges of male singers like Wilson Pickett and Solomon Burke. Otis Redding was cutting heavy soul for Stax/Volt in Memphis. Columbia was hip enough to the trend to call one of Aretha's eight albums *Soul Sister,* but sticking her with tunes like "Swanee" hardly lived up to the LP's billing. For a time Aretha was actually under the direction of Columbia A & R head Mitch Miller, that goateed guru of prime-time middle-brow singalong. Miller swept her away from her gospel piano and set her, uncomfortably, in front of huge orchestras and gaudy arrangements. The company's indecisiveness is documented by John Hammond, who writes that while Columbia had faith in his ability to discover new talent, it would not let him produce his protégé's work for the hit singles market. Thus, he worked with Aretha only on albums. Other producers—Clyde Otis, Robert Mersey, and Belford Hendricks—tried 45-oriented pop material on Aretha, but nothing quite fit.

Live performances during the Columbia years were muted by ill-fitting material and by Aretha's blue mood. She worked small jazz clubs and big Caribbean resorts. She says she sang to the floor a lot during those days. She knew the chemistry was wrong, but she had to finish out her contract.

"I did what I had to," she says. But after more than half a decade as Columbia's supposed soul comet, she despaired over her lost momentum. She remembers a particular low point: "It was toward the end of my time with Columbia. They had a convention down in Puerto Rico. There was another young artist they'd signed. The guy had all these way-out lyrics, you know, like 'A hard rain's gonna fall' and all of that. We both *had* to be there. Anyhow, I was feeling pretty scared and down. And I remember looking out my hotel window at midnight. And there was this other artist out on the beach, just walking up and down, up and down alone. It was Bob Dylan. And I thought, My, he must be havin' a ball, and here I am miserable."

She laughs, waving away a cloud of cigarette smoke, and says that more than likely she and Dylan were so wigged out by the proceedings they could barely speak to each other, let alone chat up the merry conventioneers. In the few words they did have she sensed that the raggedy Jewish folkie from Hibbing, Minnesota, was as disoriented as she was.

"Believe me," she says, "neither of us knew where we were headed then. 'Cause neither of us was what you call—ah—mainstream."

Shortly after Aretha's contract with Columbia was up, she headed home to Detroit, "way, way down," she says, not about to quit, but not sure of her next move. Her husband and manager, Ted White, liked the deal Atlantic was offering. White heard that Jerry Wexler had been saying great things about Aretha, and the other black artists on Atlantic were doing well under Wexler's direction. The deal was cut, and on January 27, 1967, Jerry Wexler was waiting for Aretha in the Fame Studios at Muscle Shoals, Alabama. Ted White was somewhat puzzled. The plane had banked over the Tennessee River to the small, steamy Muscle Shoals airport that serves the town of Florence. Inside the unimpressive studio building Jerry had assembled his soulful A team: King Curtis and Charlie Chalmes on tenor sax, Spooner Oldham on electric piano, Chips Moman on lead guitar, Jimmy Johnson, also on guitar, Tom "Rooster" Cogbill on bass, and Roger Hawkins on drums. The band was half white.

"There was some initial weirdness," Jerry remembers, "but the trepidation was largely White's." Aretha settled at the piano. She listened to the funky rumble of Cogbill's bass; King Curtis joked and honked on his big friendly tenor. And they started working on a new song by Ronnie Shannon.

Atlantic loosed the thing on February 10, 1967. The Beach Boys were still going on about "Good Vibrations," the Beatles had just recorded "Strawberry Fields," and a made-for-TV group called the Monkees was selling dorky 45's between Saturday morning cartoons. The AM deejay shrieked above it all. And then, over the idle of a V-8 engine, over the straining defroster, vaulting out of the tinny speakers, the Voice: *"Yo' a no good heartbreakah . . . yo' a liar, and yo' a thief . . ."*

Suddenly real barbecue amid the bubble gum.

"That's a young lady named Aretha Franklin," aaaaooohed Cousin Brucie. " 'I Never Loved a Man (the Way That I Loved You)' is the record. Gonna be *big,* cousins, biggg, *waooooh, yeeeeeah!"*

More than a quarter of a million copies sold within the first two weeks of its release; shortly after, it went gold, selling a million. But none of those numbers were in when Jerry Wexler took Aretha into the studio in New York, again with King Curtis and most of the Muscle Shoals crew. On Valentine's Day of 1967, just four days after the release of her first Atlantic single, Aretha cut a bouquet of love songs and laments for her first album, *I Never Loved a Man.* They included that soulful declaration of independence written and first sung by Otis Redding, "Respect." "Drown in My Own Tears," "Baby, Baby, Baby," and "A Change Is Gonna Come" were in the can at day's end; by the end of the week they had knocked off "Soul Serenade" and "Dr. Feelgood."

Aretha hadn't hung up her first gold record yet—it was still being cast—

when "Respect," her second single, strutted to number one trailing the sassy Muscle Shoals horns. She had hits and, better still, an instant public ID. Lady Soul. *Aretha Arrives* trumpeted the title of her second LP.

Euphoria and adrenaline drove the Atlantic promotion department. Bob Rolontz, who then headed the team, huddled with Ertegun and Wexler. Fifteen years after mining the genius of Ray Charles, Atlantic had another phenomenon on its hands. And this time, given the more hospitable cross-over climate, the possibilities were dizzying. Before it was over at Atlantic, Aretha would win the Grammy Award for best R & B performance by a female artist eight years in a row. It became known, simply, as the Aretha Award.

"She started from zero, from zip, no hits, no one knew who she was," says Rolontz. "So believe me, and with all due respect to our efforts, it was that voice. It just grabbed people by the collar. That first record, 'I Never Loved a Man,' in three months was a national treasure. She just exploded. Now this was a black woman, a hefty black woman, certainly handsome and charismatic, but so damned *unlikely*."

Since Solomon Burke, Atlantic had been aggressively marketing soul. But never before, says Rolontz, could all the brilliant PR minds come up with such an effective one-word definition.

" 'Soul' was Aretha. What she did was something no record company could do, nobody could plan. Soul became as much of a trend as it did *because* of Aretha Franklin. Aretha came, and Aretha conquered and made that soul trend happen because it sort of united all the rest of the artists behind her. She hauled them along in a mighty wake."

She united pop and R & B audiences as well. In black neighborhoods and white universities, in the clubs and on the charts, her hits came like cannonballs, blowing holes in the stylized bouffant and chiffon Motown sound, a strong new voice with a range that hit the heavens and a center of gravity very close to the earth. Here was a voice with a sexual payload that made the doowop era, the girl groups, and the Motown years seem like a pimply adolescence.

It was a new kind of sexual lament that had the pain and knowing of the blues, without the resignation. Lady Soul was a fighter, but she was no quitter, perhaps owing to that gospel habit of holding out for hope. Aretha's sound had strength, with the determination to overcome. In the war of the sexes Lady Soul was a healer. The balm was homeopathic and applied directly. R-E-S-P-E-C-T. Just a little bit.

In 1967 the delivery and those lyrics went a long way. At a time when so many things were tearing the country apart, they were calling her Doctor Ree, tireless healer to those struggling to keep the faith. Some blacks called a few hot months of 1967 the summer of "Retha, Rap, and Revolt."

Nearly a year to the day after her first hit release, her hometown proclaimed the last Friday in February "Aretha Franklin Day." Martin Luther King, Jr., walked onstage in Detroit's Cobo Hall to present her with the Southern Christian Leadership Award. Less than two months later he was assassinated. While riot-ignited fires still smoldered in American cities, Aretha returned to the studio in New York on April 15, and with her trusted backup personnel, she cut "Think."

Working, driving toward the bridge of the song, Aretha reached down and hollered, sang, screamed the word "freedom" eight times in a row. Behind her, high and fierce, "the girls" hectored.

"Think about it . . . think about it."

They were just records—albeit hit records—but for some, they took on an anthem quality. "Respect" boomed through the warrens of inner city black culture and activist centers. "Chain of Fools" chugged across the airwaves as General William Westmoreland sent more lumbering troop carriers to the dusky mouth of another delta—the Mekong.

"We had been fucked over, and we knew it, right off," a Vietnam vet named Hobie told me at one Aretha concert more than a decade after the Paris truce. "This woman, Miss Ree, saved some of us, I swear. My CO had Aretha on his tape cassette. And after one of those suicide missions— you know, defusing booby traps with your own ass—after we fitted as many pieces as we could find into the body bags, we put on that tape. 'Chain of Fools,' I remember. And this may seem weird, but we danced. Like the fuckin' *fools* we were. We danced until we puked our guts out and laughed and cried. And I tell you, if we hadn't have done it, I might have lost my mind. I might have gone and died."

"I've had a lot of servicemen—Vietnam vets—come up to me and tell me how much my music meant to them over there," Aretha says. "I'm sure all those guys were in a lot of pain, something you or I can't ever imagine. But if they found pain *in* my music, it has to be their personal interpretation. What I feel singing it, and where it comes from, is something I keep to myself. Music, especially the kind I make, is a very emotional thing. And as an artist you're happy when people get *involved,* you know? But what they hear and what I feel when I sing it can be very, very different. Sometimes I wish I could make them understand that."

She does not quarrel with critics' contentions that she "lives when she sings," that music is her own highest freedom. But Aretha's deliverance has also been her burden. The greatness of her first Atlantic recordings set an almost unmatchable standard. And more than simply compete now with her early successes, Aretha's eighties recordings must contend with the sticky residue of her fans' emotional memory. She's that kind of singer.

Aretha says she doesn't try to tussle with the freight of those expectations. But there is a bit of Lady Soul mythology she would just as soon see cleared up. Yes, she was a child prodigy. Yes, she has always sung beyond her years, a *natural* singer. "But when it comes to the ABC's of music, I am no dummy," she says. "I always worked on my sound, my arrangements, *before* I went into the studio with a producer."

There is no better evidence than Aretha's own notes from those fabled sessions. They are written in a girlish, slanted hand on yellow legal pads. They actually look like homework, as Aretha claims they were. Her notes for the completion of her 1970 *Spirit in the Dark* album are punctuated with "Wow" and "(Smile)," commenting on cuts made with personnel that included Cissy Houston, Arif Mardin, and Jerry Wexler and musicians culled from the Dixie Flyers and the Muscle Shoals rhythm section. In between the ball-point curlicues are the savvy, decisive strokes of a fine technician.

For the title cut, she suggests, "Up the bass in spots, some turnarounds, tambourines on fast part and conceal or lower guitars on same part." On "Oh, No, Not My Baby," Miss Ree would like "just a touch more of the girls and Arif's strings and a groove would be to start them on a low F to a high F like Ah Ah. Like Sissy's [sic] approach to 'Ain't No Way,' the first notes."

The two pages of suggestions are capped with a small note to Jerry Wexler: "If the records flunk on my suggestions combined with yours, I had nothing to do with it. Ha Ha Ha."

"Nobody bothered us in the control room," Jerry says of their collaboration. "In general, the sessions went like cream. She'd take the song—she found most of them—or she'd write it. And she would work out a layout, working at home with her little electric piano and the girls. So you had three major ingredients: First of all, you had the arrangement implicit in the piano bars, you had her lead vocal, and you had the vocal background leads. She brings all this into the session. She'd sit at the piano and start to line it out, and the girls might or might not be there. So she might sing their parts, too. Then all we did was start to shade in drums, bass, guitar. We might make small changes, but it would always be by agreement with her. You know, change a bass line here and there. But those records were so damned good because she took care of business at home.''

Jerry says that the arrangements that always fitted best were those that flowed from Aretha's left hand as she worked things out on the piano. Whatever those fingers did became the bottom—the bass pattern—to support and float her melodies.

Even the most blasé session men would stick around the studio to listen to Aretha's playbacks. During those sessions, in Muscle Shoals, New York, and Miami, Wexler put together some of the most motley but inspired combinations on record. Atlantic's master session list shows a typical entry for Aretha's December 16 and 17, 1967, sessions in New York: King Curtis on tenor and, on guitar, the unlikely pairing of English blues hound Eric Clapton and soul man Bobby Womack. Duane Allman, the late guitarist from Macon, Georgia, also worked as a session man for Aretha. With the help of chief engineer Tom Dowd, Wexler and Mardin continued to work winning combinations in the studio, enough so that the "Aretha Award" was still hers in 1970, '71, and '72. Four singles in a row—"Bridge over Troubled Water," "Spanish Harlem," "Rock Steady," and "Daydreaming"—were certified gold. In 1971 she conquered an established rock venue with her concert album *Live at the Fillmore West*, which included a duet with Ray Charles.

Shortly after, Aretha and the Atlantic team went into the New Temple Missionary Baptist Church on South Broadway in Los Angeles in 1972 to record a gospel double album. Years before, Aretha had confessed to Mahalia Jackson that she wanted to record more gospel to "tell Jesus I cannot bear these burdens alone."

During the two nights of live recording in the church, she had plenty of help. Aretha was backed by the Reverend James Cleveland's thirty-four-member Southern California Community Choir, and Cleveland himself stayed at the piano until he broke down in tears during the title song, "Amazing Grace," and had to leave the church.

Sixteen years after she had first recorded the song as a fourteen-year-old on Chess Records, Aretha sailed into "Never Grow Old."

"I know a place where we'll never grow old."

This time the voice was far more controlled, the modulation of cries and whispers was sophisticated and deft. But the song crests in one of Aretha's wild, otherworldly ad-libs.

"Ain't never gonna grow old.

"Never NEVER NE-VAH!"

Clara Ward and her aged mother, Gertrude, were there to holler and sway behind C.L.'s girl, three generations of great gospel ladies standing and singing in the one place where truly they never would grow old.

Life is far from eternal on the record charts, and it wasn't long after "Amazing Grace," which went gold, that soul began to grow old to record buyers, overtaken by the new, smoother disco sounds and by loud arena rock groups like Led Zeppelin and Pink Floyd.

Throughout the remainder of the seventies, until she left Atlantic in 1979, by mutual consent, Aretha tried on new songs and new producers—everyone from Quincy Jones to Curtis Mayfield and Chuck Jackson—but nothing seemed to fit. Her last well-received album on that label was *You*, released in 1975. Her work with Curtis Mayfield on the sound track album for the movie *Sparkle* drew enough attention for the film to be briefly re-released after poor reviews had closed it. An early-day *Dreamgirls, Sparkle* was about three daughters of a black domestic who become pop stars à la the Supremes.

Like other fine soul singers—notably Smokey Robinson and Marvin Gaye—Aretha found herself in a peculiar limbo. Artists like the Supremes or the Marvelettes, who had styles and sounds created for them, could at least explain their decline as a shift in style. But for the great voices of sixties soul, downshifting to oldies' venues simply wouldn't do. Nor did their straightforward emotional singing fit the heavily arranged new styles of disco and macho/techno funk.

On record, then, nothing quite seemed to find the right groove. The confusion was even more apparent in Aretha's live performances. Her concerts were still packed with true believers, but they tested the heart and soul of many a fan and critic, even those helplessly in love with her voice, owing to her choice of material and stage productions. Once at the Apollo, bewildered fans watched dancers dressed in what looked like long johns shimmy around her; another time two male dancers tossed Lady Soul between them like a duckpin. At Radio City she popped onstage in a circus clown suit and red rubber nose, singing "That's Entertainment."

ARETHA, PLEASE COME HOME was the headline on a review of one weeklong stand at the Apollo that featured several changes of gowns and furs and only a half hour's worth of music. Another night it took two costume changes—one to rhinestone-studded black denim, then to a floor-length white mink—before Aretha finished that treacly credo "I Gotta Be Me."

The stage schizophrenia, coupled with sagging record sales, began to produce some mighty depressing reviews. Fans and critics have been vocal in saying who they think Aretha Franklin *should* be. They think that Aretha Franklin should sit, in comfortable clothes, at the piano and haul off with her best, her classic soul and gospel rave-ups like "Dr. Feelgood" and "Do Right Woman." They wish, loudly, that her soul be unadorned with showbiz trappings; they would like to have time stand still around the image of the 1968 twenty-six-year-old Queen of Soul. They want her to be the "natural woman" she sings so convincingly about. "Be your bad self," they holler at her.

"Of course I'm being myself," she says, a bit testily. "If I weren't being myself, I wouldn't be doing it. They might not particularly like what I'm doing. But I'm definitely being myself. Maybe the public just doesn't know me."

She agrees that some of the confusion may have to do with the fact that no one really knows Aretha's private self, that despite her emotional style of singing, the singer's true feelings remain a mystery. Since as a celebrity entertainer Aretha can't vanish into the congregation the way she did in her gospel days, she acknowledges the need to present a public self. And *that* Aretha has gone through plenty of changes—from gospel genius child to Lady Soul to Vegas headliner to solemn soloist on the Oral Roberts telethon. The public Aretha has been many different dress sizes, has appeared on the *Tonight Show* in an explosion of orange ostrich feathers, on *Saturday Night Live* in a cowgirl outfit and a mink, and in *People* magazine as a California wife and mother.

"I am most comfortable being myself in my own home with my own family," she says. "Just like when I'm singing, I'm me, and nobody else."

Abruptly she asks if I know anything about women's tennis and the players, and I tell her yes, I used to write about them.

"Aha. All right. Now I love to watch tennis, especially women's tennis. I get very involved because when they really get into it—just like singing—they are really *out* there. You are seeing the true Martina or Billie Jean. I love to watch Goolagong. That style, just beautiful and natural, those backhands. And they called her a genius, right? From the backwoods of Australia? And sometimes, on the court, she loses it a little. What is it they call it?"

"Walkabout," I tell her. That's the way Evonne Goolagong used to explain tossing away a crucial match. Somewhere in the middle her concentration went walkabout. She got distracted.

"Uh-huh," Aretha says. "And people would be yelling, 'Come on, Evonne, get with it, get back in the game.' "

They did. And the more tennis writers made of walkabout, the more it seemed to hit her.

"I rest my case," Aretha says, smiling.

"Oh, you should see her watch those matches on TV." Having finished his lunch, Glynn sits beside Aretha on the couch and fixes her with a wicked grin. "Sits there, practically inside the tube. Talkin' to those women. Especially if her favorite is down a set or so. Woman sits there, talkin' to the set. Says, 'Come on, girl, I *know* you can make it back.' "

"Technically, vocally, Aretha is as good now as she's ever been," says Jerry Wexler. "She's probably even better. At times she has been guilty of what I call oversouling—too much screaming and melisma. And I would question the choice in material. A lot of it just hasn't been up to her gifts. Now, as ever, it's a question of getting the right people around her, the right songs, a good band."

In addition to a wallful of Aretha's gold records, Jerry's home office contains other treasures, among them a cassette containing a baker's dozen of unreleased Aretha, cut before 1975.

The voice on the tape is strong and clear, the imprint unmistakable: Aretha as produced by Wexler, all full tilt, multioctave vocals neatly punctuated by answers from the horns and "the girls." Some are unfinished, just the voice and rhythm tracks. And ambling easily through it all is a joyful gospel piano: Aretha herself. She sashays into "Happy Blues," whoops and hollers through an old Willie John number, "Mr. Big Man You."

"Kind of like keeping a drop sheet over a Picasso, huh?" Jerry says. "There's a couple of albums' worth of stuff laying around, I'm sure. This is just the tip of the iceberg."

And, he explains, all this material—some of her best work—is imprisoned in the freeze-out between Aretha and her former label, which still owns the masters.

"Look," he says, "I'd love to produce Aretha again. One of us has to pick up the phone. I still have songs kicking around that have her name written all over them. I'd love to see her tear it up again. I would love to hear her sing in church again. On the album we cut in church [*Amazing Grace*] she is truly stupefying. If she really wants to, Aretha can use that voice to move any man, woman, or child. But she has to want it."

Aretha told me, during our interview, that she did want it, that after the release of *The Blues Brothers* movie, it was her intention to go back to what people clamored for most.

"Heavy soul. Rock-bottom soul," she said. "I am going back to the very best of soul with my new album. It's what I do best. And I think it's what the people want to hear."

As it happened, she didn't get down to it until her third album for Arista. She had just signed with that label when we spoke. *Aretha,* her first Arista album, was produced by Chuck Jackson and Arif Mardin and was dismissed as overarranged and uninspired. *Love All the Hurt Away,* co-produced by Aretha and Mardin, yielded two hit singles, the title cut, a duet with George Benson, and her remake of Sam and Dave's "Hold On, I'm Comin'." But it wasn't until her third Arista album, *Jump to It,* that Aretha made a good showing on the charts and drew reviews trumpeting "Aretha's Back." It made perfect sense that Aretha's *Jump to It* album, hailed as a "comeback" of sorts to a more soulful style, was produced by the man who fell in love with her voice in the late sixties. Luther Vandross got his start composing and singing ad jingles, yet, as he tells his concert audiences, his inspiration always hinged on three black divas: Aretha, Dionne Warwick, and Diana Ross. As a chubby teenager in Harlem he locked himself in with their records and emerged with a good working knowledge of the elements of style and soul. On *Jump to It,* he had the good sense to showcase the voice again, coaxing Aretha through some lighthearted scat singing, through hot mama asides ("tell 'em to come see Sugar Ray Aretha"), a bit of soulful rapping, and some mercifully unadorned ballads. Better still, Aretha went back to her old neighborhood in Detroit for a duet with Levi Stubbs on "I Wanna Make It Up to You," a song she wrote. It's a soulful reunion of two big, unafraid voices. And she floats through a composition by her old neighbor Smokey Robinson ("Just My Daydream")—with Cissy Houston behind her. Old fans were pleased with the last two cuts; the title song, laid over a very eighties rhythm track, played well even with the subteen set on Sugar Hill. Uptown, black junior high girls danced in and out of clacking double-dutch ropes while "Jump to It" blared from the boxy silver radio strapped to the rope turner's back.

Jump to It was still in production the last time I saw Aretha offstage. It was during another rehearsal, a sound check for a Radio City Music Hall concert with the Four Tops. The room was a sight bigger than at our first meeting. There was a full orchestra, musicians in jeans and T-shirts, tuning on the mammoth stage, and just a few of us scattered in the front rows, waiting.

Aretha, wearing a red suede Eisenhower jacket and slacks, sat with her feet up. Again she was finishing off a cheeseburger. She washed the last bites down with a Sprite and somewhat wearily climbed up to the mike at center stage. There was a small disturbance as a group of black schoolchildren, on some sort of field trip, settled in about twenty rows back to watch the rehearsal. They whispered and giggled among themselves, passing milk cartons and *Star Wars* trading cards. Doubtless they weren't born when their parents shook it to "Chain of Fools."

"Oooooooweeeedat-n-dah, dah, aieeeeeeeaaahhhh. Test-test-test."

Aretha's scat sound check startled the children. They sat still, eyes front, as the band worked past the introduction to her single at the time, "Hold On, I'm Coming." It would win her a Grammy—the first in seven years—and at that moment, it was winning her a flock of ten-year-olds.

"Dontchu evah feel sad, just lean on me when times get bad . . ."

Out in the aisle a little girl started to dance, oblivious to the teacher shushing at her like a steam radiator. Plastic beads bounced on the ends of her braids; she danced faster, banging a lunchbox against her jeans in perfect time.

"Hold on, I'm comin'—ho-wo-old on."

Two more girls were out of their seats, but Miss Ree didn't see them. She was smiling, looking up at the big gold ceiling, gone to wherever it is that voice takes her, the three heavenly ladies whooping behind her, the trumpets flashing. Her fists were clenched at her sides, and 5,000 velveteen seat cushions were not enough to absorb that sound. Eyes closed, Aretha held a finger behind her at the drummer, and the band shut down on a pinpoint, leaving the ladies to finish it alone, in one mighty shout.

"Hold ON!"

17
They Also Sang

> *It would have been nice to be on Motown in the sixties,*
> *with all that support. But to do that, I would have had*
> *to become a Motown artist, with a Motown sound*
> *instead of my own. That isn't something I wanted to*
> *do, then or now.*

—JERRY BUTLER

EVEN BEFORE MARTIN LUTHER KING, JR., honored Aretha Franklin's spiritual contributions in Detroit, another city soul sermonist named Curtis Mayfield had worked up an impressive R & B doxology:

> *Keep on Pushing.*
> *People Get Ready.*
> *Amen.*

It was in Chicago, the city where delta blues had found their northern stronghold. Chicago was also a gospel fortress. Professor Thomas A. Dorsey wrote most of his gospel classics there and sold the sheet music from his home on the South Side. Sallie Martin and Mahalia Jackson settled there between revival tours. And as one of the next transitional generation,

Sam Cooke grew up there a church singer and was eulogized there a pop star.

Curtis Mayfield's grandmother was pastor of the Traveling Soul Spiritualistic Church in Chicago. Once he left the choir and turned to R & B, soul music found its most unabashed moralist. Mayfield wrote message lyrics and, singing them with the Impressions, made them danceable, national hits.

Working with his friend Jerry Butler, with the Impressions, and later by himself, as a songwriter, guitar player, and singer, he was responsible for the sixties' most direct soul homilies like "It's All Right," "Choice of Colors," and "Mighty Mighty Spade and Whitey." In 1968 "We're a Winner" was banned by some stations, presumably for its uppity advice to "keep on pushin', like your leaders tell you to." Some of those leaders, like Martin Luther King, Jr., and Jesse Jackson, did adopt "Keep On Pushing" as an on-the-march fight song.

Later, in the early seventies, when soul and the civil rights movement moved on to tougher, less visible struggles, Curtis Mayfield left the Impressions for a solo career and kept on pushing himself. There were a few somewhat flaccid message songs, among them "(Don't Worry) If There's a Hell Below We're All Going to Go." But wrapped in slicker, more contemporary studio sounds, Curtis spun some deadly nursery rhymes like "Superfly." As the title song of that granddaddy blaxploitation flick, it seemed to deify a ghetto drug czar, and as such, it was a wild commercial success. But a close listen offered a more circumspect, Chicago-style understanding of the soul man gone bad. On screen, Superfly's fur-lined macho cool was his own perverse vindication. To Curtis Mayfield, Superfly's MO was a horror of damning, poor, urban sameness.

"Can't be like the rest is the most he'll confess . . ."

In the person of Superfly, morality has lost out in a razor fight with survival. Over it all, beyond the verses that act as an uneasy apologia for the dope dealing, the violence, the trouble "with his woman and things," the root motivation is explained in that old gospel lyric, sung in Mayfield's deceptively gentle falsetto: *"Tryin' to get over . . . jes tryin' to get over . . ."*

"Freddy's Dead," off the same sound track, was a tougher, mordant epitaph to a junkie. Mayfield's sinister guitar lurks beneath the breezy, light flute and strings. Again the sweetness of the voice belies the message. But when it comes, it's a neat stiletto to the overblown H-wood black dude mystique pandered to by the likes of *Superfly, Shaft,* and the wave of conk-and-karate screen thrillers to follow. It comes as a question: *"Why can't we brothers protect one another?"*

By 1972 some black listeners were already finding such questions hopelessly naïve. Still, in "Freddy's Dead," the milk chocolate voice won't let it rest. Soft and melodic, it lilts: *"If you don't try . . . you're gonna die."*

Curtis Mayfield's voice was loudest in the mid- to late sixties, composing for and singing with the Impressions. The group began as a fledgling doo-wop outfit and grew into its preacherly name by singing tight-harmonied, trumpet-laced gospel soul. It went through various incarnations, split, re-formed, and split again. Its last major chart entry was "(Baby) Turn on Me" in 1970.

In 1983, a year jammed with soul reunions and anniversaries (Motown's twenty-fifth was among them), the Impressions organized their own thirty-city silver anniversary tour. Unlike the Tempts' Motown reunion tour, there was no record company behind it, though Curtis Mayfield was recording on the tiny Boardwalk label at the time. Budweiser came forward with sponsorship, and by early spring original Impressions Jerry Butler, Mayfield, Fred Cash, and Sam Gooden, plus "newcomers" Nate Evans and Vandy Hampton, had put together an evening that offered a sampling of the best of Chicago soul.

As with most of these shows, their appearance at Manhattan's Beacon Theater drew a set of over-thirty baby boomers, ex-preppies and hippies, post-teenage blacks, and veterans of sixties peace/equality campaigns of both colors. In the beginning segment, when all seven men forged through some of the sixties hits, people hollered and clapped and sang along. But the mood quickly downshifted when Curtis Mayfield took the stage.

The lights dimmed to just a single blue spot; even the band left. He intended to accompany himself with just the lean, moody guitar lines that made all those lyrics track so well. Mayfield, Jerry Butler has noted, "was as important to R & B guitar as Wes Montgomery is to jazz guitar." To hear him play alone was a rare treat. Without the band, he toyed a bit with phrasing and rhythm. Seconds after he had begun, it was unusually quiet in the house.

Curtis stood alone, his guitar slung over a forty-plus stomach, gray-haired, balding, peering over the trademark wire-rim specs with the air of a disappointed patriarch. The silence grew deeper when he worked slowly into a slow, half-spoken parable. Things had changed, the song acknowledged. Black and ofay, doin' same jobs for same pay. But still not talking.

"Ain't nobody sayin' nothin' . . ."

The pretty falsetto hung in the air like a rebuke. There were a few limp amens and "right on's," and bodies fidgeted, caught in some uneasy reminiscence. Standing in a spot now burning red, hardly looking up, Curtis had dared take it past the safe perimeter of Top Forty nostalgia.

"Ain't nobody sayin' nothin' at all . . ."

"He's shamin' us," the guy behind me said. "The man is shamin' us, and the man is right."

It was a strange, brave performance, one that flitted between grief and sarcasm and sheer technical virtuosity. Some people applauded heartily; others squirmed. In singing "those songs," he had turned the high beams on his own youthful delusions and pinned them there.

"At last that blessed day has come . . ."

Curtis had heralded the hoped-for new dawn with that line in 1964, in "Keep On Pushing," and it had played well alongside "I have been to the mountain." Of all the men post-sixties history has turned into martyrs or failed prophets, Mayfield gave voice to the jauntiest, most up-tempo optimism. In 1968, *Billboard* called it "black hope" music, a phrase that a few artists have since found to be a nasty contradiction in terms.

Curtis finished his set without fanfare that night, and it was with great enthusiasm that the crowd welcomed Jerry Butler and a retreat to the less rocky memory lane of love songs. Some of the best were composed by Curtis Mayfield, who could write about romance as well as revolution. At first, as Butler has pointed out, they were wildly abstract flights of fancy like the Impressions' "Gypsy Woman" and "Minstrel and Queen." But for Jerry Butler, he cowrote simpler, more realistic tunes like "He Will Break Your Heart" and "I'm a-Telling You." That Chicago soul was as warm and romantic as the song that had launched the Impressions— "For Your Precious Love"—a mood carried on by the Impressions' "I'm So Proud," and the Dells' "Oh, What a Night" and "Stay in My Corner."

In addition to Butler and Mayfield, Chicago turned out a crop of fine strong singers who remained largely in the soul backwaters, save for an occasional brief appearance on the national charts. In this way, longtime soul men and women of prodigious talent turn into "one-hit artists" in the industry's harsh appraisal. Among them were Fontella Bass, with "Rescue Me" in 1965, Major Lance and his 1964 "Um, Um, Um, Um, Um, Um," Gene Chandler and his goofy, doowoppy "Duke of Earl"

(1962), and Tyrone Davis's great spasm of regret "Can I Change My Mind?" (1969).

The most durable Chicago acts have been the Dells, the Impressions, and, in their various incarnations, Butler and Mayfield. Their Chicago soul used a pleasing combination of emotion and technique. It was a polished, distinctly city sound. The Dells, who were actually from Harvey, Illinois, just outside Chicago, learned their harmony courtesy of those doowop Jedi, the Moonglows. Before the Moonglows' smooth, urban tutelage, the Dells practiced what baritone Chuck Barksdale calls fish harmony ("Fish go everywhere, and that's how our voices went when we sang"). Class was in session for three years, until 1954, when the El Rays, as the Dells were first known, released "Darling I Know." Thirty years later, in the dark of clubs and big hotel ballrooms where the Dells are assured of healthy bookings, they still work in pluperfect harmony. And no matter the venue, there is nothing like the moment when Barksdale leans into the spot and asks, with the voice that did all those dusky bedroom monologues, "Do you recall that *night? That very special, that oh so very special night? Do you remember the girl? That very special girl? Well, to the old and to the new, we dedicate this song to you. . . . "

A beat; then the ecstatic wail of Marvin Junior: *"Oh, what a night!"*

They first cut it in 1956, and it was suave, pleasant, and durable enough for the Dells to get another hit with their own remake in 1969.

The Impressions were never as mannered and smooth as the Dells. But as a strong, tight gospel-based R & B outfit, they were a jump ahead of the Temptations, who were working on a similar sound just across the peninsula in Detroit. The Impressions had "Gypsy Woman" in 1961; the hipper "It's All Right" hit in October 1963, six months before the Tempts scored their first triumph with "The Way You Do the Things You Do."

The Impressions first recorded on Vee Jay, a Chicago company formed in 1953 by Vivien Carter Bracken, her husband, James Bracken, and Vivien's brother, Calvin Carter. It was black-owned, with a shoestring budget and a vast catalogue that included gospel and R & B. Ironically, Vee Jay was the first American firm to sign the Beatles, but its good fortune and its future were lost when its parent company, Capitol, appropriated the Fab Four for itself. Vee Jay began bankruptcy proceedings in 1964, just as Motown was hitting its stride. And during its last year, until 1965, Vee Jay was kept alive mainly on the sales from a white group, the Four Seasons.

Though both Chess and Vee Jay were out of business by 1968, their differences reflect a crucial shift in the recording and marketing of black music. Chess scouted and canned undiluted blues originals to service a mainly black market; Vee Jay looked ahead to crossover pop markets. And while the Brackens may have shared Berry Gordy's goals, Vee Jay was unable to match Motown's marketing genius.

Chicago soul was born of the same gospel and blues migrations that made things happen in Detroit. As the strongest of the postwar, black-oriented labels, Chess, with its subsidiaries, Checker and Cadet, ended up with the deepest catalogue of blues and gospel soul antecedents. Keeping to its policy of not tampering with the product, they were able to record the classic works of bluesmen like Muddy Waters, Sonny Boy Williamson, Howlin' Wolf, Little Walter, Willie Mabon, Willie Dixon, and Otis Rush, plus groups like the Flamingos and the Moonglows and R & B pioneers Bo Diddley and Chuck Berry.

Perhaps because of their company's blues-oriented and hands-off production policies, Phil and Leonard Chess didn't aggressively seek out the young wave of Chicago soul artists, save for a few efforts on Checker with Fontella Bass and on Chess with Billy Stewart. When soul took off nationally, it was too late; the company was sold shortly after Leonard Chess's death in 1968.

Chess did continue recording bluesmen through the sixties. But recording the majestic Muddy Waters was just a matter of turning on the tape and letting him go. The younger, city-raised singers required more; they were partial to a slicker, more produced sound; even their orientation was different. They seemed to borrow more from the church than from the barroom. And so Chess passed on Jerry Butler, on Tyrone Davis, and dealt only briefly with Curtis Mayfield as songwriter/producer on one record. This being the case, most Chicago soul singers had to cast their lots with small, shaky outfits like Vee Jay or Bandera or go outside the city. Jerry Butler would cut his biggest hits in Philadelphia for Mercury, the Impressions recorded in New York for a time on ABC, and much of Curtis Mayfield's seminal work as composer/producer was done for Okeh, the R & B subsidiary of Columbia. Both Major Lance and Curtis Mayfield were signed to Okeh at the urging of a Chicago A & R man named Carl Davis. Were it not for Davis's lobbying with Okeh's New York management, Chicago soul would probably have traveled an even harder road.

Unlike the bluesmen who recorded on Chess labels, Chicago soul artists could be considered first-generation city kids. If they were born down South, most had come up very young and barely remembered any other home. Jerry Butler was of that generation. He moved North from Mississippi when he was just three. Butler's mother taught him hymns, and he sang in church. But blues rolled out of the tavern directly across the street from his home on the Near North Side—just two blocks south of where Old Town now stands. He remembers it as "poor and ugly" but full of beautiful noise. He loved a new sound he heard in the early fifties. It came out of the radio, and he also heard it outside taverns prosperous enough to have live bands.

He wasn't able to give it a name until he saw it printed on an Old Town jukebox: rhythm and blues. These were newer jukeboxes and different from those on the Chicago Gold Coast, where the teenage Butler delivered newspapers. There black music was still called jazz, and the records were by more sophisticated acts like Billy Eckstine, Sarah Vaughan, Nat "King" Cole, and Ella Fitzgerald. But on the R & B box, Butler punched up the latest from the Drifters, the Clovers, and B. B. King. These were affordable music lessons, three plays for a dime.

The voice basics were already in place. Butler developed his husky baritone in a quartet called the Northern Jubilee Gospel Singers. In Chicago, as in New York and Detroit, the best quartets traveled between churches in a harmonic Little League, trying hard to please their coaches, straining at Sunday collars stiff and shiny with Argo starch, working to sing rival quartets into late-inning submission.

One day, when Curtis Mayfield was singing at his grandmother's Traveling Soul Spiritualistic Church, he met a visiting quartet member named Jerry Butler. Butler was about seventeen, Mayfield fourteen. They have been friends ever since. When gospel turned inevitably to doowop, Butler left his group, the Quails, and talked his friend into leaving another go-nowhere outfit called the Alphatones. Butler and Mayfield joined Sam Gooden and brothers Richard and Arthur Brooks and became first the Roosters, then the Impressions. They fought it out with dozens of other hopefuls for school and rec center gigs until they landed a job as the entertainment for a ritzy Chicago fashion show. They worked hard, and they played well enough to accessorize all that style and runway glide. A scout from Vee Jay subsidiary Falcon was persuaded by the good offices of one Mrs. Vi Muzinski, who saw them at the show, to give them an audition.

Neither their name nor their performance drew a rise from Vee Jay exec Calvin Carter until they lit into a song that Jerry Butler had originally written for his high school English class. Butler stepped forward and took the lead; behind him was Curtis Mayfield's weird, evolving high tenor.

Soon after, "For Your Precious Love" was cut on Falcon, and in 1958 it sold more than 150,000 copies in two weeks. It was also the end of the original Impressions.

The trouble arose when Vivien Carter Bracken had labels printed that read "Jerry Butler and the Impressions." What disturbed the group even more, according to Butler, were the theater marquees that had his name in huge letters and "the Impressions" in tiny type. Everyone was upset, and, Butler says, there was too much weird fallout to put things back together, musically or otherwise. He left the group in 1958 but stayed with Vee Jay. The Impressions split up. Later they would re-form, with Mayfield, the Brookses, Gooden, and, as new lead, Fred Cash; a third incarnation would see the Impressions as a trio when the Brooks brothers dropped out.

All of them were still struggling, Butler with a languishing solo career, the Impressions with unsuitable and tired Coaster and Isley Brother sound-alikes, when Butler asked his old friend to help him out on guitar. Curtis obliged, and when they sat down together and began to toy with the idle but appealing riffs that came from Curtis's guitar, they found themselves writing again. With those songs—"He Will Break Your Heart" and "I'm a-Telling You"—Jerry Butler was back on the charts, and Curtis Mayfield began building his credentials as a writer and producer. Convinced of their future as writers and of the need for black artists to retain control of their compositions, they formed the Curtom Publishing Company in 1961. Though Thomas A. Dorsey had formed a company to publish his gospel songs, in R & B only Sam Cooke had moved to protect his compositions with his own company.

Even with their publishing rights battened down, Butler remembers the early sixties as a rough go for Chicago R & B. Hoping for a more mainstream audience, he recorded "Moon River" in 1962, though he has since referred to it as a "prostitution." The facts were plain: He had to eat. He kept up with lessons in cooking, restaurant management, and ice sculpture, so he could turn out restaurant entrées and centerpieces if the music thing didn't work out.

It wasn't until after "Moon River"—and after Mayfield had banished the fairy tales from his early love songs—that Butler felt their work had the right balance of soul and substance. He traced the change back to the day he and Mayfield were driving from Philadelphia to Atlantic City, and part of a melody popped into Butler's head. The two of them noodled it out in the car. The appeal of "He Will Break Your Heart" wasn't mystical

or even overly romantic. It was soulful because it was basic, as Butler
explained to writer Vince Aletti:

> "He Will Break Your Heart" was something that I'd lived: you
> go into a town; you're only gonna be there for one night; you
> want some company; you find a girl; you blow her mind. Now
> you know this girl hasn't been sittin' in that town waitin' for you
> to come in. She probably has another fellow and the other fellow's
> probably in love with her; they're probably planning to go through
> a whole thing, right? But you never take that into consideration
> on that particular night. You're lonesome, you want company;
> she's available or she's *there* and—you know. But looking at it
> from the standpoint of the guy that's in town all the time and
> that's been lovin' this girl for years and years—that was basically
> the reason for that lyric. The lyric was an experience rather than
> a revelation.

Butler is fond of calling R & B "people music" for this reason, contending it has survived its many incarnations because of its durable, stay-
pressed themes. "It's not the music that gets revived," he says. "The
music survives. It's the artist that gets revived."

This he learned firsthand by leaving Chicago in 1967 for the Sigma Sound
Studio in Philadelphia and the cool, vibraphone alchemy of the songwriting
and production team of Kenny Gamble and Leon Huff. They revived Butler's sagging career with a softer, smoother sound, less churchy than the
Mayfield-inspired material, slicker and more highly produced, and emi-
nently salable.

Philadelphia sounds were never as raw, never as greasy and toothsome
as those of other cities, with the leaping exception of gospel acts like the
Clara Ward Singers. In pop, in the long view, Philadelphia music has
tended to flourish when little else was going on. Between the wildness of
fifties rock and before the advent of Motown and gutbucket southern soul,
Philly scored with the adenoidal outpourings of Italian geldings like Frankie
Avalon and Fabian. Bobby Rydell, Freddy Cannon, the Dovells, and the
Orlons rode the same bland wave. It was, after all, the original home of
American Bandstand, purveyor of Clearasil, Dentyne, and Dr Pepper. It
wasn't until Motown had taken firm hold, until Dick Clark was larding
his road shows with Berry Gordy's acts in the mid-sixties, that the at-

mosphere was right for Gamble and Huff and producer Thom Bell to turn Philly into a latter-day soul center.

Gamble and Huff began their collaboration in the mid-sixties and got their first national hit with the Soul Survivors' "Expressway to Your Heart" in 1967. It was crammed with car horns and freeway sound effects and a thudding dance rhythm track the worst dance klutz could shuffle his desert boots to. A firm, dominant rhythm section had given some backbone to G & H's early hits with the Intruders as well, lending danceability to silly novelty songs like "Cowboys to Girls" and "(Love Is Like a) Baseball Game." Soon, having formed their own label, PIR (Philadelphia International Records), Gamble and Huff oversaw a prospering stable of talented black artists, writers, producers, and arrangers. Dynamism was hardly their signature. Like Motown, PIR's formula was the key to its chart success.

Stylized, updated doowop with more emphasis on arrangement than on voice assured reasonable airplay for the Delfonics, the Intruders, and the Stylistics. Gamble and Huff also masterminded the Three Degrees, the O'Jays, Bunny Sigler and Harold Melvin and the Blue Notes (who spun out "Teddy Bear" Pendergrass and his "rub me down with warm oil" macho ooze).

For young, new groups, G & H, sometimes in collaboration with Thom Bell, custom-tailored sounds and images finished with a veneer of studio sweetening—strings, vibraphone, harpsichord, woodwinds, French horns. The ultimate in such saccharine soul was the Thom Bell–written ballad "La-La Means I Love You" by the Delfonics.

Some had begun calling it pop/soul, and for established black acts, Gamble and Huff did have a genius for adjusting backgrounds and beats to bring R & B up to contemporary, crossover viability. Working as independent producers for other companies, they tore down and rebuilt sounds. Epic sent the Jacksons to Gamble and Huff when they left Motown. According to Michael Jackson, they ultimately found the Philly sound as confining as Motown formulas. He points out that the Jacksons' first platinum album, *Destiny,* was the first they were allowed to produce themselves. But until they had earned that freedom, Michael says, he watched G & H "like a sponge with eyes" to soak up studio technique. At Atlantic's suggestion, Wilson Pickett put himself in Gamble and Huff's care and came up with "Engine Number 9" in 1970 and "Don't Let the Green Grass Fool You" the following year. G & H worked with a neglected

Spring Records soul man named Joe Simon, and in 1971 and 1972 he had three hits, including the beautiful "Drowning in a Sea of Love." But of all these resurrections, Jerry Butler's was the most successful, with a new and bigger set of hits and a retooled soul man persona.

Knowing about Butler's study of ice sculpture as he was casting about for an appropriate sobriquet of urban cool, Philadelphia deejay George Woods dubbed him the Ice Man. And while his partner Curtis Mayfield was heating things up on the ramparts with "We're a Winner" in 1968, Jerry Butler posed sunk to the waist in a huge block of ice for his *The Ice Man Cometh* LP. That album and *Ice on Ice* yielded hits: "Western Union Man," "Only the Strong Survive," "Never Give You Up," and "What's the Use of Breaking Up?"

Despite his commuter success, Butler remained very much a Chicago loyalist and continued to live and work there. By the late sixties, city soul was blowing hot and cold. Curtis Mayfield's messages were superheated but delivered from the lofty upper registers of his gospel-schooled, otherworldly falsetto. The Ice Man delivered torchy ballads; groups like the Dells—and a bit later the Chi-Lites—used a workable counterpoint of unchecked emotion and controlled harmony. At Motown and later in Philadelphia, formula and a big beat were their own seductions.

Down South, in Memphis, New Orleans, and Muscle Shoals, Alabama, things had been heating up as well. And once the skids had been greased by the smoother sounds of city soul, deep, muscular country sounds would gain a toehold in the national market.

It's likely that southern soul would have had to spend a bit more time on the chitlin circuit, had it not been for the audacious breakthrough soul of James Brown. It was a requisite of the times that he had to go North, to a city, to be heard. Besides New York, Chicago, Detroit, and Philadelphia, city soul had many small but entrenched pockets, out West with Art Rupe's Specialty label in L.A., and in Cincinnati, with King Records and its subsidiary, Federal.

Syd Nathan's King Records sent scouts from Detroit to Mobile to bring 'em back black, talented, and bankable. By the time James Brown arrived King had already recorded a progression of black blues and R & B artists, from Ivory Joe Hunter to Wynonie Harris on up through Billy Ward and the Dominoes and Little Willie John. And from 1956 to 1971 King served as a pipeline for the loudest, the rawest, the most fundamental in-your-face soul ever pumped up from the green hills of Georgia.

Though he had a huge urban constituency, though he moved for a time to New York and cut his most successful LP at the Apollo Theater, James Brown was and is deeply, loyally southern. And long before the blazing years at Stax in Memphis and the dominance of southern soul, James Brown turned something awesome loose in Nathan's little Cincinnati studio. He was as far from city doowop or "sweet" soul as a man could get. He was, as Albert Goldman wrote, "the scream at the end of the dial."

To Syd Nathan, he was an unfathomable curiosity and the most valuable property he could ever have signed. James Brown has never had a number one hit on the pop charts—he is *that* black—but he is behind only Elvis and the Beatles in terms of total records charted.

Even Syd Nathan, who knew the crossover limits of his black artists, threw out the customary gauge when it came to James Brown. He spoke about his hopes one day early in their association as he addressed his A & R troops at King on the bald facts of the record business. Now the music business was no freak thing, he contended. Wasn't like getting hit in the head with a pin and dying from it. It was a business, like the coffin business or any other damn thing. You bet only on a sure thing. And sure as James Brown was black, he was going to be a huge money-maker for King.

"From one minute to another, you can't tell how this guy James Brown is going to act," Nathan observed in his feisty lecturese. "But we all love him, and we consider and respect the fact that he has made it. Now we are hoping that he not only has made it but stays there for many, many years. The same as Bing Crosby and Sinatra and Como have made it."

Part 3
Southern
Soul

I lived in a chicken house for two years. I used to get twelve bucks for two nights in a club. And I used to ask the lady for a little old slice of potato pie. Didn't have a car, and I didn't want nobody to know where I lived. So I sat around the club till everybody went home, and I'd walk the fifteen miles. Over the fence, into the chicken coop, off to bed. Sang in there, too. Yeah, them chickens had soul. Although the rooster didn't like me none.

—JOE SIMON

18

Superbull, Superbad

RAIN IS GLANCING IN through the corner of the limo skylight. Reflexively James Brown tucks his own overcoat across his father's knees and scrunches down to puzzle out the back seat tape deck.

Spiritual adviser and aide-de-camp the Reverend Al Sharpton is shuffling through papers in the front seat. A heavy transaction has just gone down. Striding into the Island Records office in the *Newsweek* building on Madison Avenue, James had waved the master for what *he* believed should

265

be his first Island single. He had just signed with them, and he wanted his new employers to give it a listen.

"There was no argument," he says, unable to contain the grin that's been tugging at his mouth all morning. "Nobody can tell James Brown how to be James Brown."

"OW!"

The tape is rolling and the sound is definitely *James*, singing aloud in the back seat and bawling through the speakers. His boot raps along a guitar riff; the voice fills in around the bass with a couple of live "good God's." James is moving to his music, head bobbing, right hand tracing the precise geometry of a spring-tight JB horn pattern. It is a good record, one of the best he has cut in years.

"Feels so gooooood," he yells, oblivious to the stalled traffic, the rain, the bleating horns. He is JAMES BROWN, riding downtown in a white stretch Lincoln that is coal black on the inside and full of funk, armrest speakers vibrating with the promise of hit.

"Sound good, Junior." Joe Brown, who has just turned seventy, is sitting, rather stiffly in his pinstriped city suit, up from Augusta mainly because his son wanted him along for the two-day trip. Unless James watches him carefully, Joe is apt to sidle off and commence working—in the yard, on the cars, mending a pump. Work is a habit he acquired at the age of eleven, when he struggled to control a four-mule team grading Carolina backroads. Not too long ago the elder Brown sneaked off and found himself a job operating heavy equipment—tractors and earthmovers—on a construction site in Florida.

"Six months and twenty-eight days befo' they found me," he says, chuckling. "Ain't had so much of a good time befo' or since."

"Aw, Pop, you like to killed yourself that time." The Hardest-Working Man in Show Business was not amused at his father's truancy. Says he came back limping.

"I wanna show you something," James says to me, and he hikes the belled bottoms of his suit pants to reveal his knees. They are an appalling sight, scarred, furrowed, and discolored like those of any longtime professional athlete with a high tolerance for pain and orthopedists. Bloody knees, wardrobe mistress Gertrude Sanders told me, are a persistent James Brown laundry problem. Though it is more than a quarter century since he first punished cartilage and bone by dropping down during "Please, Please, Please," James Brown says he still cannot get up off his knees.

"They made my daddy crawl. Crawl under cars, behind mules. Crawl

all kinds of ways. Four years ago they made me go down on my knees—
my comeback they called it—to prove I could still do it. That at his age
James Brown can still get *down*."

James admits to "fifty plus," and his knees hurt like hell some nights.
When it is pointed out that perhaps his work habits are as irresponsible
as his father's, he smiles, turns up the tape volume, and ducks back into
the music.

"*So tahred of standin' still . . . I gotta move.*"

"I think it's what people want," he is saying. "After all these years I
feel it. I *got* to move. Keep movin'."

"Sound like a hit, Junior," says Joe Brown.

"Aw, we running, sure. Gonna do it this time, Daddy."

As the limo finds a hole in the midtown traffic and shoots through,
James turns up the volume loud enough for pedestrians to stop and peer
inside. Recognizing him, some grin and wave. A black teenager with a
box radio does a Jamesian pirouette and raises a fist.

Twenty-six years after his first hit record, after an eight-year hiatus in
which he rarely toured, James says he is working more and thinking back
to the days when he used to give out hundreds of sets of souvenir cuff
links in the space of one week. Some promoter has approached him with
a design for pennants to be sold in club and concert hall lobbies. It will
have a silk-screened picture of the Godfather. And this message: "I'm
Back!"

The banners were printed and sold. But the single we heard in the car
never made it to the market on Island. A lapse in a distribution agreement
with Warner Brothers made it impossible for Island to release James's
single; the deal fell apart, and James took back his master. He called,
early one morning, to tell me the news. It was one of the rare times I
have actually heard him sound tired and a bit depressed. I asked him if
he wasn't angry, if it wasn't incredibly frustrating after all this time to
have the thing sit in the can, and there were two beats of silence on the
line.

"I do not ever *stay* angry, no. Because I believe in God's justice. I
believe there will be justice, or I could not go on. Could not keep runnin'
the way I do. I will tell you that I'm a bit tired just now. But God is fair
and true. And if some record company, if some deejay don't want to know
me, don't want to recognize me in all that stuff you hear in the Top Ten
today, well, all right. Because God knows James Brown good as I do. In

the year 3000, people say, 'Who was James Brown?' Now I bet *you* got an idea who James Brown is. But it ain't the same answer as His and mine.''

There are flash card answers to the question, of course, many of them invented by James himself or his longtime announcer, Danny Ray. The Godfather of Soul. Soul Brother Number One. Mr. Dynamite. Mr. Sex Machine. Mr. Please, Please, Please. The Hardest-Working Man in Show Business. James "Butane" Brown. Or by the mid-sixties, simply and magisterially, *James*.

James! he was then shooting out of the wings like a pinball off the spring with a "pleeeeeease" that could pop a hairpin at fifty feet. *James,* skittering sideways on one leg that drove and twisted in quadruple time, while the other kept a backbeat in the air. *James*, leading the guitar player with his shoulder, the horn section with his knees, the drummer with a nod. *James,* so hot he sweated through his shoe soles; so salable that papa's traveling bag bulged with up to a quarter million dollars in small bills from a single date—one of 350 he played a year. *James,* who got down in front of 3 million concertgoers in 1967 alone, selling more than 50 million records that incendiary year. *James,* who racked up seventeen hits in a row in two years, a flaming sixty six weeks on the charts with his landmark *Live at the Apollo, Vol. 1. James,* who had himself crowned onstage and draped in superbad raiment: 500 suits, 300 pairs of shoes, the personal jet, the diamonds, the cars, the funky castle in Queens, New York, with the black Santas on the lawn at Christmas. *James,* summoned to the fore in Boston and Washington, D.C., during the 1968 race riots for a march and live TV spots to cool the constituency. *James,* funky lyricist turned sloganeer: *Don't terrorize, organize! Don't burn, learn! "James!"* they bellowed that same year when he choppered through Vietnam for the GIs who craved more swing than Bob Hope's golf stance could deliver.

And then, he says, "I took some mess."

By the early seventies there was, to James's thinking, a backlash mess. After songs like "Say It Loud, I'm Black and I'm Proud" whites were afraid to come to his shows, and once the movement had cooled, blacks danced off to more commercial beats. There was a financial mess as well, one he couldn't shimmy his way out of. The tax division of the Treasury Department claimed he owed $4.5 million in taxes for the years 1969 and 1970. Brown's three black radio stations (in Augusta, Baltimore, and Knoxville) failed, as did plans for a catfish and collards fast-food chain and his TV venture, a *Soul Train* clone called *Future Shock*.

There was an image mess as well. Within the James Brown band there were mutinies triggered by excessive work, low pay, and even less musical credit. Talented musicians like Bootsy Collins, Fred Wesley, and saxman Maceo Parker left. And politically many blacks found it disconcerting to see Soul Brother Number One dallying at the Nixon White House. In 1976 things got uglier still when Charles Bobbit, formerly James's manager, testified in the U.S. district court in Newark that he had paid New York deejay Frankie Crocker nearly $7,000 to get Brown's records played. (James denied the charge under oath, and Bobbit's testimony was later ruled inadmissible on a technicality.)

There was no respite at home. James grieved for his eldest son, killed in a car crash. His second marriage was foundering. To please his wife, Deirdre, he had moved from New York to a sixty-two-acre spread in South Carolina, just across the Savannah River from his native Augusta. He stayed home, he says, and "tried to be a father" to his three surviving sons from his first marriage and his two daughters by Deirdre. Bookings tapered off; those that remained were no longer lucrative enough to warrant keeping the most prized symbol of his success: a black and green D-125 Sidley Hawker jet with his name painted on the side and operating costs of $550 an hour. After its last $52,000 tuneup the jet was sold. Shortly afterward Deirdre swung open the custom-made gate that says "Jaydee Ranch" in wrought iron and drove away with the girls.

Ask James Brown where he's been, and he will sum it up as "down."

In his mind the turning point was a 100-degree day in 1977. He walked through his empty house and out into the glaring afternoon sun. On the lawn, his father knelt, knuckling chickweed and tearing it out in clumps.

"Daddy, what you doin' there?"

"I'm diggin' this grass up," he replied, " 'cause we ain't able to hire nobody."

James dropped to his knees alongside his father and slid his fingers into the matted turf. He worked until the sweat came, and he felt the tension ease. He says it was handling the dirt that made him feel clean—baptized. After all, the land was his, in a neighborhood where most blacks pulling weeds by a swimming pool were still yardmen. Yardmen and their families grew up on the land, his father pointed out, "but didn't have no address."

"My daddy is a very independent man," says James. "He got his son back together."

"Young lady, what is it they call them kind of eatin' places now? Got some word for it. I know I heard of it. . . ."

Driving his son's flashy black van down an Augusta four-lane, Joe Brown points out the windshield at the squat plastic fast-food huts that squawk poundage and billions sold from two-story signs.

"Franchises?"

"Fran-chise. Yeah, I know I heard it. Now when I come up, you didn't have you no franchises. At least no black man had one. No, you ride this road. Or probably, you walk it. And you don't see but red and green. Now I know real well the color of Georgia clay when it wet. And when it so dry it choke a mule. Got a different color then. But, young lady, I tell you. This black man didn't think he'd live so long as to lay his eyes on colors like that to bloom in Georgia."

He chuckles, and of course, he is right. Nothing in the Lord's paint box could approach Burger King orange.

"You know Junior my only child? My onliest son. If you got a mind, I'll carry you around to where he come up. Some people, they think James Brown, they think of the Apollo. And big cities and them clubs, them football places. Now I lived up North myself. Philadelphia, fourteen, maybe fifteen years. Sure. But I never did think to stay. I tell you this, I could buy me a fancy house on that Long Island, you know, outside New York. And every day I'm gonna lay my head on my pilla, scared thinkin' some white man been nice to me at the gas pump gonna blow me sky-high. That's right. Northern white man sneaky. Southern white man, least he let you know where you stand. He tell you to go 'round to the *back* door to get your sandwich, you gonna find a sandwich. Period."

If James Brown ended up with a genetic mother lode of soul, it would be the legacy of his daddy, whom he loves and depends upon above all others. Joe Brown was just twenty when his wife, Susan, gave birth to James, in a shack out in the country, "so little a place the windas never seen a glass." When he was certain all was well, he walked several miles into Barnwell, South Carolina, to register the birth.

"He look like my boy, don't he?"

Joe Brown is wiry and thinner than his son, but he has the same deep-set eyes above high, wide cheekbones. He wears black-rimmed glasses and a straw workingman's version of his son's trademark cowboy hat. There are grass stains on his blue cotton pants, and there's dried mud on his work boots.

"All my family been singin' since before I was born," he says.

Baby James came to music shortly after he could walk. "He was always a little bit different. People called him a godsend chil'. He could make a song and sing it when he was fo' years old. He would sit there and *stare* at you.''

Out in the yard he watched James buck dance, sing, and play the mouth organ.

"He would do alla that when he was six, just as good as now. Splits? Aw, yeah."

It was just the two of them by that time. "We come apart" is all Joe Brown will say of his marriage, which ended when James was four. He was away a lot, working among the many turpentine camps that dotted the vast pine forests. He says he walks across a supermarket parking lot every now and again, watches his boot go into the sun-melted tar, and remembers "them big white steam clouds. Full of rozzum, pine spirits, you know?''

Pine resin stuck in your throat unless you loosed it with some blues and maybe something wet.

"Young lady, I could howl in them woods. Be so dark, you looking up the trunk of an eighty-foot pine, you can't tell where it ends and them black heavens commence. Yeah, I was out there a bunch of years or out country farmin'. Grow them vegetables, pick 'em, haul 'em on in, then do it ag'in."

It was hard to keep a child in the country, so he carried his son into Augusta to live with James's aunt, a woman named Handsome Stevenson, better known as Honey. After a time Joe got a town job in Eubank's furniture store, where he was able to cadge a three-legged pump organ no one would buy. He thought his son might like it.

"I come and leave the organ at the house lunchtime," he says. "Prop it up with a cheese crate. And I come back that night, and I see a crowd of people standin' on the porch. And he was there, playin' the organ, and he never seen one before. Those kinds of things you watch in a chil', you know?''

Traffic honks behind us. Unlike his son, who can make an engine do the Popcorn at eighty miles per hour, Joe pilots the big Dodge van slowly. He says he is very careful with it because of all his forty-odd cars and trucks, the van is James's favorite. He is always adding to it: more chrome, new side mirrors, bigger mud flaps to keep the Georgia clay off its Simonized black flanks. Cushioned swivel seats rise out of thick char-coal-colored shag; the gray velveteen ceiling is tucked and padded like the inside of a coffin. There is a bar and sink, a Formica table, and a brace of what James Brown calls disco lights, some of which are

trained on a sign bearing a female nude and the florid red lettering "MAS-
SAGE PARLOR."

"Oh, he love this truck," his father says. "He love it to death. Now
look there. See that doorway?"

We drive slowly past a constellation of stoops, storefronts, banks, and
boarded movie theaters, spots where Joe Brown could pass thirty-five
years ago and be satisfied to see his son at work shining shoes, sweeping
up, racking pool balls, delivering groceries, and, for a time, working
alongside his father in a gas station.

"Taught him to wash them cars, greaz them cars. . . ."

We continue past the railroad tracks where the long World War II troop
trains would idle long enough for James and his friend Willie Glenn to
make Honey's rent money, $5 a month. James danced; Willie, Honey's
grandson, was the pickup boy. Supplements to their board came from the
dice games beneath a canal bridge by King Street.

"That's the place," says Joe Brown, "where all them kids got into
trouble." Here James Brown turned JD, pinching bikes, stealing car bat-
teries, but often with honorable intent. His seventh-grade teacher, Miss
Garvin, called him a Robin Hood, stealing for other kids—pants, sneakers,
and shoes. "All the kids had to do is complain they got no shoes or jacket
or something," says his friend Henry Stallings, "and he'd try to get it.
Like if they didn't have no pants, or they was holey and whatnot."

Shoplifting was one thing, but teenage devilment could turn deadly in
the alley behind King Street. And if you were caught, forties Georgia law
was not known for tempering its vengeance. And so it was that a night's
lighthearted escapade of breaking into four cars landed most of the boys
in prison, each sentenced to nearly as many years as he had lived.

"I knowed they couldn't keep a young boy like that," Joe Brown says.
"In my heart I knowed he would be home befo' too many years. Still,
wasn't right. Couldn't do nothin' to help him. Used to walk on by that
jail they first had him in, over to Fo'th Street. Just stand there. Tear at
you, you got someone inside."

WE SIGN BONDS ON AUTOMOBILE WRECKS. Peeling, but still prominent,
the ad for Bob Rayburn's twenty-four-hour bail bond service stands on
a corner lot just adjacent to the Richmond County Jail on Augusta's Fourth
Street. James himself has driven us here, having decided to show me the
place his father spoke of. Seconds after he has lighted from the van, the
clamor rises from inside the jail.

"Jaaaaaaames!"

"Yo, God-fathah. Get me out."

James hooks a gold-ringed finger into the chain-link fence and peers up at the yawning darkness beyond the brick façade. No faces are visible, just rows of fingers, most of them black, curled around the thick iron grillwork.

"I been in there," he yells back. "The Man had me, an' I know what it's like, bruh."

When he was arrested on the break-in charges, James arrived here, in shackles, to await trial. The court records reveal that it all went down without benefit of bail or counsel. "James Brown waives copy of indictments, list of witnesses, fill panel, formal arraignment and pleads Guilty" is what the docket book says.

"Oh, yeah,"says James Brown. "I waved my fool arms off, lookin' for help. Wasn't nobody lookin'."

He was in this jail for a few months, before he was transferred to a larger facility out in the country. He says this jail was old and crowded even then, in 1949. He found himself back here—on the outside—in May 1970. A sixteen-year-old black had been beaten to death inside, triggering the worst racial riots in Augusta's history. Then-governor Lester "Pickax" Maddox—the man who proudly sold plastic souvenir ax handles commemorating his lunch-counter resistance to desegregation—found himself telephoning Augusta's most celebrated black citizen for help. James was doing a date in Michigan when the call came through.

He flew home and got on his radio station to try to talk them down, but before it was over, 6 more blacks had died; 50 businesses and homes had been destroyed or damaged. More than 1,000 national guardsmen and 50 state troopers were called in, the papers reported, to guard the city's "130-block Negro area," a sprawling aggregate of rickety frame houses also known as Niggertown. The jail was filled, and the bondsmen were busy. Outside, the air was leaden with smoke and tear gas.

"First thing that gets you in there is the noise," James says. "Then the smell. Like a zoo."

There is a faint whiff of institutional ammonia in the muggy courtyard on Fourth Street. As more inmates spot the stocky figure in the silver bomber jacket and cowboy hat, the din grows, punctuated by shrieks, laughter, and radios.

"Jaaaaaames. Where you *been*, James Brown?"

Now inmates from the women's cellblock have seen him, adding squeals and screams to the din. Bars are rattling now. Loud thumps and shouts bring a fat, uniformed guard to the door. He stares through mirrored shades and calls down from the steps, "Now what y'all doin' rilin' these boys up?"

The commotion has drawn children from a nearby playground, and a second guard has appeared.

"Get in the van. Right now." James is tense and frowning.

He says he hadn't expected this, forgot how hot it was inside. The racket peaks as he pulls away, rolling up the window against a few angry curses.

"You hearin' rage and frustration," he says over the hum of the air conditioner. "And those are things I left behind. Where I been is not where I am, no, thank you."

"Top Notch," the secretary says into the phone, "a James Brown affiliate."

She is sorting through a pile of mail in the small reception area of James's Augusta headquarters, a five-room suite he rents in an "executive park" populated by chiropractors and small businesses. Past the reception area the small corridor is lined with warping 45's, spray painted gold. The only genuine article is a framed, certified gold LP from *The Blues Brothers'* sound track. I find James in his office, sitting beneath a zodiac plaque showing his star sign (Taurus) and proclaiming him the "new minister of funk." On the opposite wall there is a framed color photograph of Hubert Humphrey's grave.

"These are real men," James is saying, gesturing to his staff, comptroller Fred Daviss, manager Al Garner, and boyhood friend and factotum Willie Glenn. "I call 'em the first family of soul," he says, laughing and slapping five with the two white men, Garner and Daviss. Garner left the firm shortly after my visit, after nearly twenty years, because of family and health problems. Daviss is a wiry, talkative southerner who says he passed up an airline career to work for James Brown. Though he was a licensed jet pilot, Daviss was working in an Atlanta airport bank when he first met the boss. It was James's custom to stop there on his way in or out of Augusta. No teller liked to see James Brown stride in with his bulging satchel. Papa's bag was a pain in the ass.

"The tellers would go hide when they'd see him comin' 'cause they knew they'd be there till eight at night counting that money," Daviss says. "It was gate receipts. You could get a few hundred thousand in ones, fives, and tens. And top people at the bank would shake their heads at all that money and say, 'Hey, the nigger's just goin' through a fad.' "

Now Daviss's business as James's moneyman often takes him through that same office.

"Fifteen years later I see that same guy," he says, grinning. "And I say, 'Hey, the nigger's *still* goin' through the fad.' "

"These country boys," James says. "*Us.* They ain't gonna beat us. Whatever comes up in my life, they'll be a part of it."

This is not to say that working for James Brown is a day at the beach. "Mister" is the preferred form of address; on the hottest Georgia afternoon, the staff scurries to straighten ties when the boss walks in wearing sleeveless denim. The legend of Brown's system of fines and rules for his musicians—having to do with lateness, grooming, and performance—is based on truth, Henry Stallings says. James Brown's relationships with his musicians have been stormy over the years. At times they've quit en masse; some have been fired and rehired a dozen times.

"Maybe I been fired a few times, I don't exactly recollect," veteran saxman Sinclair "Pink" Pinkney told me. "Most people say he's a hard man to work for, and I'm sure he'd say that, too. He loves precision, he's an absolute perfectionist, and the man is absolutely unbelievable as far as foresight is concerned. He makes predictions, and they happen. Time and time again. You say, 'Hey, the man's crazy. Where's he comin' from? Gotta be out of his mind.' And before long, whatever he predicted—musically, whatever—becomes a reality."

Even more mystifying is the boss's stone memory. He remembers fans from ten and twenty years ago, and his mind stores a full Rolodex of phone numbers. Though his are "head" arrangements in the studio—built off a simple bass pattern or just presented to the band full blown—James is insistent that anything onstage be played, note for note, the way it was that first time on record. James says the *fans* remember them that way— off the records. Pinkney knows this is true. For years James's main linchpin in the band was the incomparable Maceo Parker on tenor sax, and the fans remember his ground-breaking riffs. James himself considered Maceo "magic—anything I threw at him he came through on." Though Maceo walked out somewhere around 1970, Sinclair Pinkney still hears it onstage.

" 'Maceo, hey, Maceo, blow it, Maceo.' They say, 'Hey, I've been watchin' you for a *long* time, Maceo.' And I say, 'Thanks, bruh, but I'm not Maceo.' They flip out. But it does tell you exactly who they're lookin' at up there. It *ain't* the band."

Sometimes, James admits, he has even gone after less sterling musicians on purpose, to get his sound the way he wants it. Virtuosos like Maceo Parker are simply too inventive to take orders for so many years. This can lead to what James himself calls a battle of "beats, grooves, and egos." It's a matter he is not shy to discuss.

"I had a lot of problems with my musicians, you know. A lot of times they thought they were doin' it themselves. So what I did, in order to teach Maceo and them somethin', I took Bootsy out front. And when Bootsy thought *he* had something goin', I took musicians that couldn't hardly play at all and cut bigger records with them. Cut 'Hot Pants.' I wanted them to know it wasn't them doin' it."

Of those who departed, he contends, "They never did make it."

In fact, bassist William "Bootsy" Collins has had considerable success as a funkmaster with Bootsy's Rubber Band. Collins, Maceo Parker, and Fred Wesley (trombone and keyboards) have all recorded, under names like Maceo and All the Kings Men, and Fred and the New JB's, but with the exception of Bootsy's puckish funk and Parker's and Wesley's alliance with George Clinton in his Parliament/Funkadelic camps, few other JB alumni have found comparable employment, despite their considerable individual talents. The JBs always worked best as a churning stage-show engine. What might have made life as backup men just too debilitating to their pride were the lengths to which the boss would go to prove them dispensable.

Henry Stallings remembers that one night at the Apollo James dispatched a Lear jet to Georgia two or three times, at astronomical cost to himself, to pick up all the members of a replacement band when he fired most of the JBs a few hours before showtime. Things were hardly different in the recording studio.

"One time," James says, "I was doin' a record, and the drummer said he had to go to the rest room. And at that time I *felt* somethin'. I said, 'Go,' and when he come back, I had cut a million seller playin' the drums myself. 'Night Train.' "

On the road the band knows its place—generally in less expensive lodgings. "We stay in different hotels because you know, with him, he has to be the prestige," says his wardrobe mistress, Gertrude Sanders. "He don't be stayin' with the *band*."

She remembers one night at Caesar's Palace in Vegas when James Brown arrived for a soul extravaganza a trifle early for a reservation—at

2:00 A.M.—and had a sleeping couple rousted from the presidential suite he had reserved.

Reverend Sharpton confirms the story: "He's got the suite, with three bedrooms, just for him. The next day everybody's downstairs—Aretha, Barry White—down gambling. He says, 'This is how you be a star. Ain't nobody gonna see me till showtime. They see them all day, they gonna be used to 'em; it don't mean nothing.' Sure enough, that night, everybody got polite applause. But when they introduced James, the place went crazy. And here he was, sittin' there sufferin', watchin' that stupid stuff on television all day while everybody else was havin' a ball."

Occasionally, says Sharpton, Soul Brother Number One will engage in a little playful market research, checking out the recognition factor in the streets of New York. "He and [Muhammad] Ali, they like to stop traffic in New York, you know, see who stops it the most blocks."

Sharpton has enlisted the aid of dozens of black entertainers, from B. B. King to Teddy Pendergrass, for his various black youth crusades, but James Brown remains his personal hero. It's an image of manhood, he explains. "My mother and father broke up when I was ten, and my only memories of my father were that he used to take me to the Apollo to see James Brown. One of the impacts of black entertainers that a lot of whites don't understand is that they become substitute fathers. We know how to dress from watchin' a star; we learn how to walk. We look at James Brown, and we say, 'Hey, *that's* how I'm gonna be a man.' "

Just who James Brown is beneath the zippered and coiffed manhood of style, few people, if any, really know.

"I ain't never seen him crack," says Henry Stallings, "and I'm with him all the time." It's a mental toughness Henry says he can trace back to their days together at Floyd Elementary School. "I remember him comin' to school barefooted in the winter. He would never grumble or complain, 'bout the same as he is now. I always refer to him as a sergeant or somethin', a man who can't show weakness to a lot of people who work under him. I know he feels things, but he never shows it. Maybe he goes behind closed doors and breaks down, but I never seen it."

Despite the tax troubles, the divorces, the slipping record sales, there was only one incident that Henry remembers as having visibly shaken his friend. When nineteen-year-old Teddy Brown drove his car into a tree in upstate New York, James flew up in his jet to identify the body and bring his son home. The funeral was jammed. Teddy was James's first child, born in Toccoa, when James was struggling to feed him by singing gospel in country churches. By all accounts, he was the spitting image of his father. He had started college, and he was James Brown's greatest pride, even though James admits he was tough on the boy. Henry Stallings was so upset himself he watched the service from the back of the church.

"They had Mr. Brown up there, talking and whatnot, with the preacher. But suddenly he rushed outside. I left myself and went the other way 'cause I can't have him and me both breakin' down. But I tell you what: the next day—right back on the job.''

There was one other time, Fred Daviss remembers, when the Godfather nearly lost his cool, and that was over the open casket of his friend of twenty years, Elvis Presley. The night after Elvis died, James chartered a jet and flew to Memphis, where a special unmarked police car sped him through the hysterical crush to Graceland, Presley's mansion. Eyes filled, he stood staring down at the bloated face, stroking the King's arm.

"Elvis," Daviss heard him say, "how you let this happen? How you let it go?''

Having seen his own fortunes rise and fall, JB says he has dug in, out in the country, where he feels comfortable and safe.

"I have the one thing which means somethin' in this world, which God gives to no man. Yet man sells it. I have land. For my kids. They need a place where they can pick up dirt and let it go through their fingers and say, 'It's mine.' As far as man's law, that dirt belongs to them, and I feel good about it.''

He says it was his daddy, and the country in him, that convinced him of the worth of land. He admits that before he got into acreage, he made a lot of investments—the radio stations, the fast-food franchise—and could not keep them. He lost fortunes—$50 million by his reckoning. One night, over a dinner in the company of a dozen or so friends and acquaintances, all of them black, he explained his hard-won perspective on the American economy in a way that had everyone nodding and laughing and thumping the table. He started in a low, somber tone.

"I know that racism in this country is a part of the economy. It is economically *fruitful* to keep blacks in a certain position. Once they were valuable to use for work. As slaves, yeah.''   ·

"Got no jobs now," someone put in. "For slave wages or otherwise.''

"Right *on,*" James said. "Now blacks are valuable to *buy.*''

"Negro persons do *spend,* don't they, Professor?'' A wag at the end of the table was getting into the lecture, and James rose to it, grinning, his voice getting louder.

"Blacks are important to the, ah, economic base, sir, of this country, because . . ."

Pause.

"They *spend* twenty-five percent more than they make."

Applause, table thumping.

"And when you take the money from them, you take the cash flow, do you not?"

"Right outa the K Mart register, ooh, yeah."

James was half out of his seat, roaring.

"We are so *depressed* that if we make a hundred dollars a week, we spend a hundred and fifty dollars. They give us a credit card, and what happens?"

"We are slaves once more."

James Brown is very serious about protecting the riches he still has left. He will tell you how many hundred acres he owns, but he will not tell you exactly where ("south of the Mason-Dixon Line, that's it"). He will drive a visitor to the very gate of his private retreat, up in the Carolina hills. But at that gate he stood guard over an accompanying photographer, while his father drove me down the long, winding dirt drive to the family compound.

The house itself is a handsome but modest ranch of deep tan brick. The two-car garage holds a silver Mercedes and a gold Excalibur. There is a fenced-in pool and poolhouse, though James himself never swims. A pair of floppy Afghan hounds loped up to the van. They let me past them to the huge hewn oak door. James had told me I could make a phone call there; but I found the door locked, and oddly, Joe Brown could not find his key.

Back at the gate James chided him gently and winked. After all, he said he had planned on the visit, had already evacuated his mother, Susan, who spends a lot of time there. "I keep her hostage," James explained, "and away from the press." Such protection was not necessary for his father, he said, because "my daddy can handle much more than I can. My daddy watches me like a hawk watches chickens."

Wheeling the van back onto the dirt road, James hit the accelerator hard and whirled us through a billowing mess of red dust, up a hill to a combination poolroom/gas station/general store. A clutch of old black men sat atop piles of blown-out tires, talking and smoking. Younger men, shirtless under overalls, shot pool in a dark back room. No one seemed startled by James, only by the strangers.

Asking me for a dime, James handed it to the man behind the counter and motioned me to the phone.

"Don't wander none," he said. "I can guarantee you ain't never been *this* far country."

While I made my call, James ducked behind a counter and wolfed down a package of Twinkies in an eyeblink, hiding the wrapper in his back pocket like a little kid. Outside in the sun, men talked cars and crops. James decided it would be nice to have a photo with the poolroom regulars, and as photographer Michael Halsband complied, a few of the old men came over to check out the commotion. They looked blank when James said, *"Rolling Stone."* He tried again. "National magazine. Full-length feature article."

"Aw, fellahs, lookahere. They gonna make this country boy famous. *Again.*"

James himself had been skeptical about the ability of another article to raise his visibility. But his pessimism lifted with an interlude at the Atlanta airport. We were sitting in a Delta gate area, waiting for the connection to Augusta, when a plump, pink-cheeked lady from East Georgia walked over with an open travel diary. She adjusted her mink stole and tugged apprehensively at the chain holding a pair of harlequin-shaped reading glasses. She asked if she might read aloud her most recent entry, and James, who had spoken to her earlier, said he would be delighted. The entry, she noted, would probably be reprinted in the mimeographed newsletter of the Sixty-Plus Travel Bugs.

"I have just met Mr. James Brown, the singer. He's traveling first class, and I'm not. He was a shoeshine boy on his way up the ladder which is wonderful. I was first to recognize him and he signed my boarding pass and wished me good luck and told me I was a stunning lady. Now ain't that somethin'?"

He was tickled. The legend had reached white, over-sixty Dixie. But on the drive back in from the airport he conceded that after all these years a little more detail wouldn't hurt. The following day he would deliver an old and trusted friend.

"Here now," he said, "I got someone waiting for you in my office.

Leon Austin make the best piña colada in Augusta, G-A, 'cause he stir it with his finger. Play the best piano you want to hear. I know 'cause he taught me. And if that ain't enough, Leon fix your hair. Leon, my man, tell the lady about James Brown. I got to see my dentist.''

Leon bowed, and smiled, and took off his homburg. He was on a break from overseeing his club, a friendly downtown boîte called Leon's DeSoto Lounge.

"I been knowin' him most of my life. Yeah, we done some piano playin' together way back. I was a spiritual player, you know. Church style. Did whole-hand chords. He played with three fingers, and I showed him how to play with four or five, so he could make the note larger. And showed him minor chords and things like that. I had the edge 'cause I had the piano. He'd come by, and we'd play together, we'd sing. We were just true friends.''

Their friendship, which has included several volatile business arrangements, has had its ups and downs.

"We get warm with each other" is how Leon puts it. But somehow, it always cools down and things are copacetic until the next time. He says that all that stuff—about fining and firing band members, threatening promoters, even jiving reporters—is true, and then some.

"He's selfish, and he can't help it," Leon says of the celebrated Brown ego. "If you try to overpower him, then he'll show you how much he *don't* need you. And then, when you do somethin' for him, he'll come back and fall on his knees and thank you.''

Leon figures that ego is a necessary lubricant for the James Brown machine.

"Daily it's all James Brown. And he's not afraid. Maybe I get afraid to just keep tellin' you about Leon. I'm afraid you gonna get tired of hearing Leon. But he don't care whether you get tired; he's gonna keep tellin' you *James Brown, James Brown.* It's been good for him because if nobody else love him, *he* love him. And things keep workin'.''

Leon says his friend's well-developed sense of self probably hauled him through a particularly tough time, shortly after the jet had been sold, when folks began to snipe about how James did go and Tom himself at the Nixon White House. But long before that, in 1968, the constituency was split on Soul Brother Number One. Imamu Baraka, then LeRoi Jones, speaking at a black power conference, called him "our number one black poet," while H. Rap Brown backhanded him as "the Roy Wilkins of the music world." Of the Nixon visit, Leon says: "Oh, it hurt him, it really hurt. Blacks didn't understand. See, poor people—not just blacks—just can't find places to love leaders because *they're* not leaders. Deep down in 'em, they don't mean to envy you, but they do. With Nixon bein' a leader and takin' a fall like he did, James Brown took a fall, too. He is a black leader. A lot of kids love him. And it is an amazing thing to witness. You should see him in Africa. Somebody says, 'James Brown.' Even *whisper*, 'James Brown.' Every corner you pass, it's like an echo, even out in the bush. And by the time you get to the corner you see them in thousands. Like bees. Come out of mud shacks with James Brown albums, don't never play them, no electricity, for sure no Victrola. But they know who is *James Brown*. I was in Zaire with him the time Muhammad [Ali] was goin' to fight [George] Foreman [1974]. That was the first time I got a little afraid. Cats got spears, them drums, boom, boom, boom, Muhammad and James, they walkin' along in the middle of this swarm, and I am bodyguardin'. I was sure thinkin' about another line of work.''

Their most serious falling-out came when Leon stayed behind in Africa to do some work (''hair and whatnot'') for James's friend President Omar Bongo of Gabon. But when Leon came home, it didn't take long for them to get back together.

''Look, I have a lot of pleasure in life with him,'' says Leon. ''We can talk, and we can free down. I'm one of the ones that don't forget who he is. And what he thinkin'. I don't have no animosity. And he have his way about things, you know. People say he's crazy sometimes, but no. He's got a *good* heart. He know how it is. To be down. Because he witness and seen it so many times. Trouble was, when he faced it, he was the only one there. He was alone, and that was the worst cross to bear. Because when he made the song 'Black and Proud,' he wasn't makin' it because he was a militant. Nothin' like that. He was makin' a song that the blacks could feel proud of themselves. It was a song that was *good* thought of. It made lots of people feel good. But it broke him. The white people still loved him but were afraid to go *there* with them NEGROES, cussin' and chantin' about proud, proud, proud. Then there were the blacks who betrayed him. He made them proud of not bein' proud of him. Like I say, black leader get whipsawed every which way. Some people name you militant; some people name you Tom. So what you gonna do?''

The way Leon sees it, James Brown did what his daddy always taught him: shut up and work. Work so hard and so well that you shut them all up.

''When you pay your money, you gonna enjoy him 'cause he gonna be workin' hard, hard, hard. He's not gonna come out there and be cool, and he ain't gonna have on this pretty suit that ain't gonna get dusty. He gonna *wallow*. He's gonna just be splittin', dancin', fallin'; he'd jump outa a air-o-plane, I swear. Mess up his knees so he can't work the next job. Or he may scream so hard he can't sing the next night. But he ain't gonna worry about that."

Onstage James Brown doesn't worry. And that's where it all shakes down. Like the gospel ladies that give themselves so freely to possession, at his peak, James gave it up one, two, three times a night, and from *out there*, from the audience, it truly looked as though he'd "do it to death." Body fluids oozed and spattered and vaporized in the red and blue lights; the hair collapsed like wet licorice; dust and blood mingled and spread across the knees.

"Can your heart stand it?" he would scream, and they screamed back, honestly fearing for his.

"Jaaaames!" They called him back from wherever it was he'd up and flown to, but every time he lit for just a moment, stood stock-still, and looked straight ahead, until the body jerked and took yet another dance form.

"Popcorn!
"New breed boog-a-Loo!
"Mashed po-tayyyyyy-to!"

Successive dance steps transformed the short, tight-torsoed body, twisted it, shimmied it, wound it up, and drove it the length of the stage on one skinny, stovepipe leg.

"Jaaaaames!"

He did not hear them.

"Jaaaaaames, please!"

Screaming hard himself, he could not hear them. Nothing seemed to reach him, he was not there, gone, sunk to the floor, the drums still crashing over his limp form. Then, miraculously, he responded to a hand on his shoulder. Gently the first cape fell over his shoulders; tenderly he was lifted and drawn, wobble-kneed, toward the wings. And savagely he threw it all off—the cape, the arms.

"Ohmygod, Jaaaaaames! No!"

They were hysterical with terror, with awe and gratitude and envy. Who else had such strength, such freedom? To shun the second cape, and the third . . . Who else? Live, onstage, James Brown came up with his own four-dimensional conjugation of the verb "to be." He lived until he seemed nearly dead. And then he'd snap back, miraculously, in full, grinning possession of himself.

"Ah'm tahred," he always said. "But Ah'm *clean!*"

It was no surprise in the sixties that a lot of white kids wanted to be as free as James Brown, at least in their fantasies. It was something that went past the free speech, university-strike, "student-as-nigger" conceit, past that basic adolescent white longing to be black and be anointed by said automatic mantle of spade cool. It was the longing to be specifically and only JAMES BROWN. To do it to death as only *he* could. To rise out of the numbing comforts and constraints of tract developments and Bay Ridge row houses, of SAT scores, of orthodontia, of aspiring to all the right (white) things and eating Mrs. Paul's fish sticks every blessed Friday night, and be . . . *different.*

"I wanna be James Brown." White rocker G. E. Smith went so far as to sing and record that secret wish in a song called "James Brown." Even Mick Jagger wanted to be James Brown—probably wished to hell he were the night he had to follow the Godfather on *The T.A.M.I. Show.* Members of James's staff remember pulling Jagger in out of the hallway at the Apollo and lecturing him about his own safety, all those nights he showed up there, nearly twenty years ago. They say he always sat quietly, in a corner of the dressing room. Miss Sanders used to keep an eye out for "that skinny, polite little Jagger boy" who didn't seem to have enough sense to stay off 125th Street on a Saturday night in high August.

"I dream of being James Brown." In a tiny apartment in a Connecticut rooming house in 1983, a working-class Italian kid confessed this desire, no secret to his friends. They call him James in the freight company where he works as a clerk, though his given name is Paul. A cassette blared ten seconds of every song James Brown has ever recorded—including such rare treasures as "Santa Claus, Go Straight to the Ghetto"—lovingly spliced together from the stacks of James Brown singles and albums that line the walls beneath posters of the Godfather. Paul keeps scrapbooks—clippings, photos. Anything that merely mentions the name gets sealed in clear Mystik tape.

Anytime James plays within fifty or seventy-five miles, Paul is there, right in front, no matter what it costs, anticipating every rim shot, mouthing the words, screaming right along on the horn break: *"Take me to the bridge an' drop me!"*

Down he goes, if there's enough room, just like James. Except that

Paul is wearing roller disco kneepads, the better to get down with. He says he lives for these moments. Once James bought him a club sandwich when Paul dogged him to a Manhattan deli.

"James remembers," Paul says, and it is true, he does.

Leon Austin has seen all these crazy white kids when he's out on the road with James, and he says he can dig where they're coming from. But for blacks it was something else.

"Being black in this country is what you'd call *different,* ain't no doubtin' that. Sometime you get a place, look around, feel like a ant caught trackin' up a white-frosted weddin' cake. James show the ant how to *dance* hisself off. Without gettin' squashed."

Out there, even on the *Ed Sullivan Show*, even after the producers had threatened to cut him off at the waist as they did Elvis "The Pelvis" Presley, James Brown had the courage to lose it anyhow, to get out of himself, as his fan Michael Jackson puts it, and celebrate a kind of blackness impenetrable to whites. James Brown cut loose with a swaggering pride few men of color dared express in mixed company. Even among blacks, it ruptured the stratification of "high complexion" versus low.

"A darker person would probably be named as ugly," Leon explains. And James Brown is dark.

"So," says Leon, "he made the ugly man *somebody.*"

He did it by getting pretty, in ruffled shirts and rollers. "I used to wear my hair *real* high," James explained. "And people would ask, 'Why you wear your hair so high?' And I tell 'em, 'So people don't say *where* he is?' but '*There* he is.' "

Such notoriety has its price. Leon Austin estimates that James spends $500 to $700 per week on stylists and supplies. Two dryers and two suitcases filled with rollers, creams and shampoos, and relaxers are part of the road equipment. Depending on how many shows there are to do, James may have his hair done three or four times a day. He says it doesn't bother him; he goes on about his business.

It's a standard assumption that hairdressers are privy to the most intimate secrets, and Henry Stallings is no exception. He has had the closest vantage point to the rise and maintenance of the James Brown legend. In fact, he says that you can chart James Brown's career by studying the changes in his hairstyle.

In the beginning, when he needed to be noticed above all else, it was jacked up past the bounds of Little Richard's outrages. The hits and

James's growing confidence rolled the sides back smooth as Caddy fenders; the top foamed into a dizzying cataract of waves and curls. The late sixties were tough. "Processed" hair was not cool, but for James, a true Afro was just *too* kinky. Henry Stallings bridged the gap with a processed Afro. It was the hardest to maintain. And for James, it was a psychic torture.

"It was like givin' up somethin' for Lent," James explained. "I wanted people to know that one of the most prized things I let go of was my hair. It was a real attraction to my business, but I would cut it off for the movement."

"Like I say, he did it for the ugly man," Leon says. "For the darkest of dark."

For all the outrages perpetrated against it, the hair has never betrayed him. Its health and luster cause lots of people to think it's fake.

"Feel it," he insisted one day, wishing to dispel any wig rumors. It has the strength and texture of industrial-grade nylon. You could knit a trampoline with it.

To maintain the image from the neck down, James counts on the able assistance of Miss Gertrude Sanders, his wardrobe mistress. For over two decades she has been trainer, confidante, seamstress, and dressing-room bouncer. The lady says she "brooks no jive" on the road; her frown can scorch like a steam iron. Visit James backstage, almost anywhere, and you will see Miss Sanders unzipping garment bags, pressing velvet capes, blowing the steam off a container of chicken broth, and worrying lawdamighty aloud about the shortcomings of the new synthetics. Polyester. Phewy.

"Whipcord," she told me. "That's the toughest. That stretch knit is pretty good 'cause he does a lot of splits. And he falls on his knees, and that can tear a pair of pants first time out."

She has been wardrobe mistress since 1959, after brief gigs with the Isley Brothers, Odetta, Etta James, and the Shirelles. In the beginning she stitched, pressed, packed, *and* drove.

"I got to keep after him 'bout his health, his weight and all," Miss Sanders says. Yes, she confirms, Gatorade has replaced the glucose and B_{12} intravenous solution that a personal physician would administer after shows that robbed James Brown's body of seven to ten pounds of fluid. On the road she urges bland soups and egg salad; at home housekeeper Ella Overton is sparing with slices of his favorite corn and potato pie. Southern poor boys can rise up to sirloin, James says, but some can't outlive a craving for starch. Growing up, he knew some poor kids who chewed laundry starch, and he mentions that Elvis was into starchy junk food, too. James confesses that visits home are murder on his waistline. Good country food and middle age find him working closely with simpatico tailors for what he calls slimmin' suits.

Slimmingest of them all is what Miss Sanders calls "the gorilla suit," a forty-pound extravaganza exploding with studs, rhinestones, and beads that James wears for his finales. It was made by Alamo Clothes, the same firm that created Elvis's high-collared, studded-belt Vegas excesses. Two people must help the Godfather into the gorilla; as Henry Stallings peels off the first soaked suit, Miss Sanders flies in with towels and talc and the gorilla, all with astonishing speed. When he comes offstage in the gorilla, after perhaps only two more numbers, it can be a pound or two heavier.

"He come off that stage," says Miss Sanders, "and he say now he know how Elvis felt."

Again, and forever, Elvis. It was Elvis James spoke of one afternoon as we drove through the black neighborhoods in downtown Augusta. Every few blocks, when he saw someone he knew hosing down a car or sitting on a porch, James stopped the van to chat. Always the conversation was easy and friendly, cars and cousins and the like.

"Elvis couldn't do this. Couldn't walk around where he came up."

Elvis was an honorary G-man, though. He was very proud of the legal prescriptive he got from Richard Nixon that proclaimed him a federal narcotics agent. Elvis was a proud American.

"Here," James said one day, "I want you to have this." And from his wallet he produced a photocopy of his visitor's pass to the Vice President's Gallery in the Senate chamber, signed by Hubert Humphrey. "James Brown," someone has handprinted beneath the official lettering, "The World's Greatest Singer." And proud American.

"Elvis loved this country like I do. Loved cars. Loved his daddy and his mama. Elvis was basic. And look how they done him."

A few times James has expressed his belief that someone who's worked for him will write a tell-all book the way Elvis's bodyguards did. He figures it might sting him some, but he will not admit to any great worry—about his career or his future.

"Mortality ain't no big deal," James told me, "except where it concerns my parents and my children."

He says that he is strict with his sons because in order to grow up right, they must learn the meaning of work, the same way his own father taught him. They are in their twenties, all polite, respectful young men. And they all work, mainly for their father's business concerns. They mow the lawn and wash the many cars. And they are mindful when their father dispenses one of his many Lessons in Life.

Larry Brown was with us one day in Augusta when James pulled the van up to an abandoned warehouse. He motioned Larry and me to a rusted oil drum beside the warehouse, where he says he rooted for dented cans as a child.

"Puffed-up cans of vegetables," he said. "I guess they was spoilt."

Larry looked a trifle uncomfortable. "Daddy, you ate garbage?"

"Never did get sick."

Driving away from the place, James allowed that he's probably a bit overprotective with his parents. He guards them closely now, aware of their vulnerability to age. Only they dare confront him with the harsher truths, to tell him when he's acting foolishly, even to scold him.

"My daddy won't let me gamble," he said, seeming to enjoy his obedience.

"He likes to keep them around," says Henry Stallings, who spends a lot of time at the house. "I think he just wants to sit around where they can baby him. He wants to lay back and holler 'Mom' or 'Dad.' He'll ask for something, and his mom will tell him, 'Well, you don't need it.' He likes that, you can see it. He wants to be a baby again, sit back, and say, 'Mama, why is this?' "

"Unless you do puzzles," James said, twitting me, "you cannot hope to understand James Brown."

Unless you appreciate the tension of opposites, he's right: proud of the country that first brutalized him, then mythologized him; a grown godfather who plays out the childhood he missed; funky revolutionary confronted with the fear of becoming a has-been. It's a tug-of-war that echoes through his lyrics as far back as 1960's "I'll Go Crazy." He screams, *"If you leave me I'll go crazy,"* and then, punched out with strident horns, that jarring non sequitur: *"You gotta live—for yourself, for yourself and nobody else!"*

From the stage he bellowed it again in "Superbad" (recut as "Superbull, Superbad"): *"I don't need nobody else . . ."*

Not always, anyhow.

"Sometimes," he yelled, *"I feel so good I wanna jump back an' KISS myself."*

He throws off dependence as though it were just another stifling cape. Then the strutting Sex Machine can spin around, drop to his knees, and plead, "Try Me," without losing a bit of manhood. As a lyric, it's danceable; as a life-style, the footing can be tricky.

"Well now," he says, "I got to believe my own song, 'It's a Man's World.' It is a man's world, yes. But it wouldn't be nothin' without a woman or a girl. I just ain't found the *right* one yet."

If it's lonely in the gorilla suit, beyond the footlights it's a party whenever James Brown plays. His music is a very social thing, in the spirit of the polyrhythmic, call-and-response involvement of African forms.

"Get up offa that thing," it screams, dance music above all else. This is not the kind of soul pinned on the intimacy of a Smokey Robinson or the aching, hoarse humanity of Otis Redding. It's not the kind of music you need lyric sheets to understand; James Brown's funk works its best mojo from the neck down. You love it or hate it; it's magic or just screams. At its best, it won't let you rest; at its worst, it keeps the motor running.

Criticism of some of James's later albums on Polydor/Polygram points out, rightly, that many of the cuts are simply remakes of old hits, like (after 1969's "Popcorn") "Mother Popcorn, Part I," "Popcorn 80's," and "It's a New Day So Let a Man Come in and Do the Popcorn." When I asked James about it, he shrugged and said it's beyond his control.

"When I solo on the organ, it's like somebody's guidin' my hands. I don't have to look for it. Writin', too. It's like the tablets were written for Moses. Yes, ma'am. And everything I do hasn't been finished yet. So I can go back and keep *tryin'* to finish it. All those songs I put together are about ten percent of what the songs *should* be."

Sometimes, he points out, the public just isn't ready yet. Even now, he says, with a straight face, that he is working up something called "nuclear soul—just too powerful to be unleashed yet." After all, "Please, Please, Please" was a major aberration in 1956. Twelve years after that, he told *Downbeat* of the market's persistent limitations.

"I tried the heavy approach two or three times, and every time I tried, I'd get stopped. Just have to keep coming back and simplifying it. It's a funny thing. You make a little three-finger chord on the guitar and they'll sell a million copies, and the minute the cat spreads his hand out across the neck, you can't give the record away."

Long before multitrack systems synthesizers and heavy overdubbing got the public used to complex, layered rhythms and far-out, funky instrumental asides, James Brown was fussing with Syd Nathan of King

Records to let him stay on the keyboards and lead his band through these uncharted areas. Martin Machat, who was his lawyer at the time, says that the dispute reached the nation's highest court. The issue also involved James's intended move to Mercury from King. Nathan claimed his contract had not run out; James claimed it had and he could sign with Mercury.

"We won in the Supreme Court," Machat says. "And it was taken up on appeal. The appellate division, in their wisdom, divided James Brown into two parts. They said as a vocalist he was still bound to King, but as a musician he was not. So in the sixties James Brown actually had two recording careers, one as an instrumental orchestra, which he pursued with Mercury, and the other, vocal, with King. Some years later Polygram bought out Mercury; it had previously bought King, so all the pieces came together."

Since then the James Brown sound has been studied, amplified, busted into components—diffused in any number of ways into current forms of black music. George Clinton took the funk and flew to another planet, though he is mindful to thank the Godfather on his album jackets; Sly Stone cozied up the self-contained stage band and made it a less autocratic, more electric "Family Stone." Rick James performs the soulful repetitions, but with the uninspired boredom of a Nautilus workout. You can even hear James Brown in the efforts of Grandmaster Flash and the Furious Five, who lay spoken raps over shifting rhythmic grooves. After all, the first rap record was James Brown's "America Is My Home." Lyrically it's the polar opposite of Grandmaster's "The Message" ("It's a jungle out there"). But it was a groundbreaker nonetheless.

Henry Stone, who has scouted, signed, and produced black acts since 1945, says he was the one who convinced James to cut "Rap Payback (Where Is Moses?)" for his *Soul Syndrome* album in 1980.

"I really believe James Brown's the father of all this music you hear, of all these grooves and beats," Stone says. "And he really needs the recognition. We're talking about a pioneer of music that's really world-wide."

Lack of recognition is one of the few things JB gets "warm" about. "They keep gettin' people out of my camp to give recognition to," he says, "but they're afraid to give it to me. They don't want a man to have that kind of power."

He says he's never had that problem anywhere else but in his own country. Martin Machat, who has overseen James's interests for many years, agrees. "In France he's still a superstar; in England he's a legend;

in countries like Italy and Spain he's enormous; in Japan, Africa, he can fill arenas. In the U.S., the customer is the most fickle.''

Like the bluesmen who were "rediscovered" after the English invasion, James was being courted again by reverential foreign acts. In 1980 the Clash invited him to tour with them, but he declined, not having ever heard of them. Mick Jagger asked him to open for the Rolling Stones in Madison Square Garden—the very show Screamin' Jay Hawkins opened—but last-minute management snarls KO'd that dream double bill. Recording deals continued to fall apart, until, in 1983, James produced an LP, *Bring It On,* on his own Augusta Sounds label. Since getting airplay was an uphill fight, with or without record-company promo machinery, James figured he was better off keeping it all in the Augusta family.

"I am not a fighter," he said. "But James Brown don't take no sucker punch, no, ma'am.''

Besides his parallels to Elvis, boxing is a frequent theme in James Brown's conversations. Like Screamin' Jay Hawkins, Jackie Wilson, even Berry Gordy, James Brown had a brief career as a prizefighter. Along with his friend Henry Stallings, he got the taste for it in Augusta as a kid. James says he trained there with the fabled Beau Jack.

"You boys got to *know* about Mr. Beau Jack." James was in a lecturing mood the night we ran into prizefighters Leon and Michael Spinks in the Stage delicatessen in Manhattan. Ex-Olympic champion Leon was every bit the sweet but ill-fated sad sack in the headlines for drug busts and car wrecks and unregistered pistols. Leon ordered "a Muhammad Ali sandwich"—lots of bloody roast beef—and took out his front teeth to get down to business. Michael leaned over and questioned James about Beau Jack.

"Beau Jack come up in them battle royals," James said, and the brothers nodded. This was a quaint sporting ritual held by Augusta National, a white country club. Members rounded up as many as six black boys at once, blindfolded them, and shoved them into a makeshift boxing ring. The last one left standing would collect a dollar or two. A shoeshine boy named Beau Jack was left standing so often a few club sports sponsored him on a campaign up North, as a professional. In 1944, admission to one of his fights raised more than $35 million in war bonds; in 1982, Beau Jack was washing dishes and shining shoes again.

"Beau Jack have the heart of a lion," James insisted. He went on about dignity and money, strength and street smarts. The white men who floated around the Spinkses rolled bread pellets and sucked on cigarettes. James got loud as a preacher.

"And I tell you, you got to *keep* what you get punched in the head for. . . ."

"Yes, sir," Michael said. "I know, sir."

"Mmmmpf," Leon said, through a mouthful of rye.

"For all them boys, who count you heroes . . ." James pointed over his shoulder. Outside the glassed-in restaurant front, a bunch of young black boys hopped and slapped on one another's palms, waving at James and the fighters, raising clenched fists, feinting boxing moves and dance steps. James leaped up suddenly, having forgotten that Vice President George Bush was talking to the United Negro College Fund folks at their splashy dinner in a hotel across the street. He headed over for a quick howdy, and Leon and Michael fell to their meals.

"I love that man James Brown," Michael said, adding that when Leon was snagged in all his troubles, James took pains to talk with him, even yelled at him to straighten up. As he swept back in from his veep visit, James stood over Leon with a hand on his shoulder and promised to bottle him up some of the magic spring water that gives him so much energy.

"Yes, sir," Leon said. "Thank you. Need water."

At the brothers' request the management packed up some takeout cold cuts. After many long good-byes we watched them leave, each holding a foil-lined doggie bag. Out on the sidewalk, they sparred with each other like frisky twin mastodons, swinging the bags, hugging and cuffing, until each became aware of the toy handler tugging at his sleeve. Two limos idled in the Seventh Avenue traffic. Reluctantly they allowed themselves to be separated and led off. There was on James's face the closest thing to sorrow I have ever seen him show.

"Them boys love each other," he said. "And if the vultures get their way, if they make weight class and stay clean and fit, they're gonna be tearin' at each other in Caesar's Palace. Yeah. An eighties battle royal. Those boys could hurt each other bad."

He says he is not one to condemn another black man for the self-inflicted pains that are the price of making it. He has merely to look at his own knees. Only now is he beginning to make concessions to age and abused cartilage. He dances less, and on one occasion I saw him turn the dance spotlight over to a younger man in a flashy white suit. He says that he is a survivor above all else, and very proud. He would rather go out as the uncontested soul heavyweight. It would be unthinkable to sink into a split he could not rise up from.

James had explained all this, another night, as we sat in the dark in a

TV network dressing room. The lights had been turned off at the request of another heavyweight. Slumped in a chair, Muhammad Ali admitted that his own retirement from the ring was so wearying—the sports commentary, the endorsements ("Hotel, Co-sell, Ho-tel")—that his eyes simply couldn't take the light. His speech was slurred; frequently he seemed to doze off. The two men were about to make a TV appearance for another one of the Reverend Sharpton's campaigns. This time the subject was to be the need for black heroes to inspire black youth. James was keyed up, shadowboxing in the dark, urging Ali to try the Gatorade and ginseng concoctions he feeds the drummers who try to keep up with him. Ali drowsed, then snapped awake at the sound of the Rev preaching out in the hall about moral direction and the burden of black heroes. The prizefighter wondered aloud why his seventy-year-old father had more energy than he did. James stopped dancing and walked over to face him.

"He only got to be your daddy," he said. "Just like my father only got to be that."

19

Soulsville, U.S.A.

*Now what we were doing was called the Stax sound or
the Memphis sound. It wasn't Chicago, and it wasn't
New York, and it sure wasn't Detroit. It was a
southern sound, a below-the-Bible-Belt sound. It was
righteous and nasty. Which to our way of thinking was
pretty close to life itself.*

—STEVE CROPPER

IN 1962, WHEN JAMES BROWN asked Syd Nathan for the money to record
his show live at the Apollo, Nathan refused, insisting that no one would
want to hear live versions of hits he'd recorded already. But then Syd
Nathan didn't get out of Cincinnati all that much. James knew full well
his effect on a crowd, and he was sure that a live record would bear little
resemblance to the things that went on in the relatively sterile confines
of Mr. Nathan's modest studio.

"I was determined," James told me. "So I decided to do it myself. Do
you know how much it cost me? Oh, you won't believe it. *Live at the
Apollo*—the biggest album smash I ever had—cost me five thousand dollars
to make. Naw, I didn't worry about my investment. *Live* is what soul is
all about now, ain't it? *Live* made me. Made soul."

Live sold. *Live at the Apollo, Vol. 1* was on the *Billboard* album charts
for sixty-six weeks, beginning in 1963. It hit number two on the pop LP

charts, something no R & B record had ever done. Mr. Brown's competitors took careful note.

One Saturday night in November 1963, Atlantic Records sent a crew to the Apollo Theater to record, live, what promised to be a very interesting show. The resulting LP, *Saturday Night at the Apollo,* on Atco, captures a turning point: a flux of urban and country soul that previewed the late sixties dominance of southern soul and what became known as the Memphis Sound.

At the insistence of Jerry Wexler, Atlantic Records was already on the case, having made a distribution deal with a new tiny Memphis label called first Satellite, then Stax. The first joint release, a duet by father and daughter Rufus and Carla Thomas called "Cause I Love You," dropped to the murky bottom of the R & B charts. But soon Stax would eclipse Sam Phillips's Sun Records as the main Memphis label. The Atlantic/Stax venture was nearly three years old the night Atco (an Atlantic subsidiary) set up its recording equipment to capture the State of Soul at the midnight show.

The urban half of the roster included the Coasters, James Brown protégée Doris Troy, and the headliner, Ben E. "Mr. Soul" King. The show was opened by the Falcons, a Detroit group featuring Wilson Pickett on lead. They were recording on Lu Pine at the time, but within a year Pickett and fellow Falcon Eddie Floyd would be working in Memphis, on Atlantic and Stax.

Despite his own city orientation, *Saturday Night*'s headliner remembers finding the country half of the bill very intriguing. "You had the shape of things to come that night," says Ben E. King. "There was the fifties R and B thing, with the Coasters, which was still in the limelight. And I was doing those soul ballads, 'Stand By Me' and all, and I guess I was at my peak in terms of billing and sales and whatnot. And then you had the guys from down South who were really coming on."

The show had just begun, he recalls. It was a bit past midnight, and the opening act moved like Saturday night but sounded like Sunday morning. The Falcons sailed into "I Found a Love" behind the preachy invocation of the not-yet-Wicked: *"Unnnhhhh . . . said can I get a LOVE this mornin'?"*

They worked a classic gospel format, tight harmony on the background, Pickett ad-libbing about the midnight hour, about needing love—late in the evening, early in the morning, yeah, yeah.

"Baptist," Benny said to himself, *"Walkin'* Baptist, even in those pointy shoes."

With nearly two hours to kill until his show closer, Benny wandered into the wings, where he happened on a big, bearlike man who was sweating and trembling, worrying aloud about his suit, his voice, the house band. It was Otis Redding's first appearance at the Apollo.

"Now just about everybody had heard about this real soulful singer from down South who was recording on Stax out of Memphis," says Benny. "Otis told me he was up from home—he lived in Macon—and he was *terrified*. I mean, already Otis had to know he could kill an audience, any audience. And he had that great ballad cut, 'These Arms of Mine.' It was the record that got him the spot on the show. No big money, no band, no nothing. Otis kept saying he was worried 'cause he was country. Well, he sure was. But by then people were willing to listen to that, to southern soul. They were ready for the rougher stuff. Otis, he was a great, great showman. But rough. Otis whipped up on a song. Had a voice could mug you on the first note."

"He can *sing* baby, he can *sing*" is how the emcee introduced him.

"Sing it pretty," a woman yells on the record, and despite a scrappy sound system, the crowd noise, the nerves, that voice flies out like an arrow.

"Pain in my heart . . . treatin' me cold . . ."

The horns tagged along unobtrusively; the rest of King Curtis's house band lay back while Otis worked his changeups, stuttering "n-n-na-NOW," fracturing phrases and repeating them in halves and quarters.

"Lil pain in my heart . . . someone STOP this pain . . . someone . . ."

This was the real thing, so direct, so loose that even after the big hits had come, the tours, the awards, the private planes, TV lip-syncing would always be impossible for Otis Redding.

"We used to laugh about that," Benny says. "Tell Otis he had too much soul for Dick Clark. Man could sing a hit song a hundred times, but he'd sing it a hundred different ways depending on how he felt."

The only effect that first Apollo appearance seemed to have on Otis Redding's free-form soul is a bit of weird, stylized pronunciation on "These Arms of Mine," but even that drops away when he lets the band fall back and pleads, *"Be my lover!"*

"I could tell by the crowd's reaction that a lot of kids had heard that record," Benny says. "Dimly I recall that the people at Atlantic were perking up their ears then, leaning South. Now Motown was giant by then, and the Beatles and all. And the city acts were cruisin' pretty well—myself, the Drifters, and the Coasters, all those guys. Of course, guys down South had been working for years. They weren't slick, you know. They kept it simple, and for the most part they kept it to themselves. That's southern. You make your music for yourself and your friends, and if some guy walks in off the street and taps his foot to it, fine. If he doesn't, what the hell. *You* still got something going.

"Otis said to me, 'You really think they're gonna go for what I do, what *we* do down home?' But as long as I knew him, Otis never did get over that little bit of stage fright. He looked over at Rufus that night. You know Rufus Thomas was on the bill after him. And Rufus was so cool, very relaxed. 'Cause Rufus *knew*. Rufus always had a huge ear. He was what—in his late forties then? At least twenty years older than Otis. And all of a sudden Rufus had soul hits that were selling to kids."

Rufus Thomas was hardly the ingenue that night. Then forty-seven, he was a wily trouper who had begun as a comic in black vaudeville with the Rabbit Foot Minstrels in the mid-thirties. In the early forties he recorded jump blues and began spinning discs for WDIA in Memphis. He ran talent shows, package shows, and R & B extravaganzas there in the fifties. In 1953 he had a modest hit with "Bearcat" (an answer to Big Mama Thornton's "Hound Dog") recorded on Sun. When he made the first Stax/Satellite record with his daughter in 1959, it was on time borrowed from his radio work and a job overseeing eight huge boilers at a textile bleaching plant. Once he got rolling again at Stax, it was largely on the appeal of novelty dance hits, beginning with "The Dog" in 1962.

All this, after twenty-five years, had made him a protean entertainer. He had a deejay's feel for dance beats, a comic's sense of timing, and the wry, self-mocking black humor that had made Louis Jordan so popular in the forties. Rufus Thomas aimed at the cartoon generation with his funky chickens, dogs, and the like. He wore capes, hot pants, feathers, sequins, even zipped himself into a Funky Penguin suit. And while he was a good-natured trickster, Rufus Thomas was, literally, the Daddy of Memphis soul. Carla Thomas's "Gee Whiz (Look at His Eyes)," released on Atlantic in 1961, was Stax's first major hit, reaching number ten on the pop charts. Before Aretha Franklin could lay permanent claim to the title, post 1967, Carla Thomas was the Queen of Soul, duetting with Stax king Otis Redding months before his death.

"Rufus and Carla got the whole thing started, in terms of engaging our interest in Memphis soul," Jerry Wexler says. "When he's eighty, Rufus will still have a very spry ear."

It was no understatement, then, when Rufus looked out at his young

Apollo audience that night and began his set: *"When I get to rockin' I don't need a rockin' chair . . ."*

"Rufus was real Memphis," Ben E. King says. "And no matter what the rest of the country was doing, Memphis *rocked*. Look, when I was coming up, my music was tied to the neighborhood. You know, sometimes the world ceased to exist below the Hundred-tenth Street subway stop. Down in Memphis, I guess it didn't have to go much past the river."

Memphis, Tennessee, sits midway between New Orleans and Detroit, on a wide loop of the Mississippi where three states meet. Much of black America migrated North through Memphis. And there have been as many waves in Memphis sound as ripples in its western state border—courtesy of a fickle river and the American habit of seizing on a local fad and running all to blazes with it.

Piggly Wiggly, one of the nation's first supermarket chains, began in Memphis. The first Holiday Inn was built there. American legends were nurtured and murdered there: Elvis Presley and Martin Luther King, Jr. Memphis was named for the famous city of ancient Egypt, burial ground of the great pharaohs; surely Presley's mansion, Graceland, carries on that grand tradition of sepulchral excess.

Memphis's musical dynasties have been anything but mournful. For a century and a half the city has turned out a variety pack of black and white musicians who mixed blues and Baptist and hillbilly idioms. In the fifties they fused in a spectacular way in the persons of Jerry Lee Lewis, Carl Perkins, and Elvis Aaron Presley, all cutting for Sam Phillips on Sun. And in the sixties those country and blues mongrels came up with Memphis soul. Hi Records would deliver Ann Peebles and the lambent gospel soul of Al Green; Chips Moman's American Studios gave Bobby Womack a start as a studio technician and session man; some of Atlantic's King Curtis and Dusty Springfield sessions were cut there. But for the most part Memphis soul was Stax, and its subsidiary, Volt, a white-owned label using black and white musicians. All of them operated in what one Stax veteran calls "a very funky, very isolated little world." In the beginning, at least, that world ended at the Memphis city limits.

"Aw, maybe it got as far as the other side of the river to the cruddy clubs where we went and hung out with black guys, playin' music, feelin' young and tough and hotter'n shit," says a white Stax session man. "So if you wanna get technical, we extended our horizon to the honkytonks in West Memphis, which is hanging like a fat old tick on the corner of East Arkansas. But that was the world as we knew it. That was *it.*'' The very isolation that let Memphis musicians make such great, unself-conscious music would eventually limit them once rockabilly, then soul slid off the charts. But then that was Memphis.

The city itself went through some drastic changes. As a river commerce center it was particularly vulnerable to the ebb and flow of American economics. As a result of its prime location, it boomed as a commercial center in the mid-nineteenth century and all but disappeared following a yellow fever epidemic in 1878 and 1879, losing so much of its population that its city charter was revoked. But Memphis rose again. And the music, like the river, never stopped churning through it.

Despite that continuity, it always took some startling aberration—be it the genius of W. C. Handy, the two-tone pink-and-black rockabilly of Elvis, or the gutbucket soul of Otis Redding—to make the rest of the country even listen to the music it would eventually snatch up and carry off in a thousand variants. And to its native sons, Memphis music was atmosphere, languid and changeable as the weather rolling in from the West.

"Wasn't something you studied up on," says Isaac Hayes. "You breathed it, is all."

The most technical term you can find for it is "head arrangements."

"That's not at all pejorative," says Jerry Wexler. "It was different down there—a total departure from anything we'd known in New York, since it veered away from formal, written arrangements and back to head arrangements. By that I mean it put the creative burden back on the rhythm section, to a symbiosis between the producer and the rhythm section. It's instinctual. You don't know why you're doing it—maybe some of it comes from subconscious memory. But it's southern, very southern. Which is to say extremely ad-lib."

The extraordinary history of Memphis music is resolutely ad-lib, beginning with the work of its most venerated progenitor. W. C. Handy just happened to be sitting in a Mississippi train station when he heard a black man playing the guitar and singing something called the blues. Handy brought his black dance band to Memphis in 1909 and, shortly after, began to put some of what he'd heard in that train station into his own compositions. Handy was the rare black musician who wrote and published then. And when his pen bolted off from the G clef, zigzagging through ragtime piano figures, through stately dance rhythms, and back into the bush again, the blues were heard nationwide in his sheet music. Minor chords and blue notes came out of the backwoods and into the parlor.

A white man named Sam Phillips oversaw the next series of happy accidents. At a small studio he called the Memphis Recording Service, Phillips cut sides on the black musicians he liked to hear like B. B. (Blues Boy) King, then a WDIA deejay, Little Junior Parker, and other itinerant bluesmen. Phillips had a guitar and keyboard player he also used as a talent scout, named Ike Turner. Turner brought Howlin' Wolf (Chester Burnett) and Little Milton to Phillips's Sun label, which he formed in 1952. Turner also recorded with his own band, the Kings of Rhythm.

Turner had a girl friend, known first as Annie Mae Bullock, then as Bonnie Turner, now as Tina. Thirty years down some very bumpy roads, after a bitter divorce from Ike, Tina Turner would find her greatest recognition not as a soul act but as a rock goddess, opening for the Rolling Stones, starring as the Acid Queen in the Who's rock opera film *Tommy*, singeing the eyelashes of live audiences from Vegas to lower Manhattan with her Ikettes, her leather Sheena suits, and a pair of thighs that could crush a car chassis. The Hardest-Working Woman in Show Business, just showered and sipping herb tea, wasn't keen on talking about the old Memphis days when we met one night after an evening of Tina-in-the-round at a Long Island dinner theater hall. She allowed that in the late seventies, Ike had laid down his guitar and picked up some mighty nasty habits. He got busted for cocaine. He shot a newspaper deliveryman in the leg. Put closed-circuit cameras in their bedroom, the way George Burns used to spy on Gracie. But it wasn't funny. When things were working for them, they used to do this little thing in the middle of Otis Redding's "I've Been Loving You Too Long." As Tina moaned through the bit about "can't stop now," Ike leaned into the mike and growled, " 'Cause you ain't ready to die." Once life at home threatened to imitate art, Tina split.

"The only thing that remains of Ike from back in Memphis is the music," Tina said. "He is the best. When I met him, I was in awe. I gave myself up."

Her surrender is audible on her earliest records. There is nothing to connect the mike-swallowing Acid Queen with the timorous child singing "Old Brother Jack" and "Way Down in the Congo," recorded on Sun in 1953. The voice has all the confidence of a starving child singing for its supper. "Death" is Tina's description of the later years with Ike. "Hard schoolin' " is how she describes those Sun years. She says she is grateful for all she learned, that Ike taught her everything, that he is a standout rock original. Still, some memories come to her when she stands up in front of adoring audiences that include famous actors and artists and rock stars and lights into her 1971 hit "Proud Mary." That record was the high-water mark of her years with Ike, making it to number four on the pop charts. But, she says, the lyrics touched a few of the lows as well.

"Cleaned a lot of plates in Memphis . . . "

Tina left the church at seventeen, heading from a Tennessee eyeblink for the city named after the repository of the Egyptian dead. Though she is now a member of a Buddhist sect, Tina believes that most of her karma comes from Egypt. Voluntarily she will take you through some of her past lives, as a convict in an English prison and a French dance hall girl. She says her current success must be the payoff for a mother lode of bad karma. There's no other reason the first half of this life would have been so bad. No, she does not believe in accidents. Ike was no accident, although their marriage might have seemed like a slow-motion wreck on the highway. And Memphis has its own weird destiny. Still, she acknowledges, people tend to think of Memphis music in terms of things "just happening." Tina believes that rock and roll was indeed born in Memphis. Ike himself is credited by many to have made the first rock and roll record. Ask her if she believes "Rocket 88" to be just another karmic glitch, and Tina Turner just smiles and closes her eyes.

It was, by all accounts, a typical Memphis accident. "Rocket 88" was recorded for Sam Phillips and released through Chess in 1951, when it hit number one on the R & B charts. The sole artist listed is Jackie Brenston, who was actually the Kings' sax player and vocalist. It's a high-energy vamp, heavy on girl/car lyricism, with an odd, appealing fuzzball electric guitar played by Ike Turner. The "new" guitar sound was born of improvisation and impatience.

The story goes that Ike's amp came loose from its lashings atop his car and took a few hard bounces along the highway on the road into Memphis. Sam Phillips wanted to get on with the scheduled session, so he stuffed some paper into the busted amp, and the guitar sounded as if it was being played through the Sunday supplement of the Memphis *Commercial Appeal*.

After "Rocket 88" hit, Phillips kept experimenting in that vein with black and white artists until that fateful 1954 break for coffee and Cokes when he overheard some bit of foolishness in the studio. Jamming with

Sun sidemen, a young, white Memphian named Elvis Presley sang Arthur "Big Boy" Crudup's "That's All Right." Having long toyed with the notion of recording white vocals of black blues, Phillips recorded it and had his hunch rewarded with a legend.

It was similar, racially mixed tomfoolery that made Stax records and began its soul dynasty. The record that truly put the company in business was an instrumental, "Green Onions," cut as a casual afterthought by a black and white studio band calling itself Booker T. and the MGs. It reached number three on the pop charts in 1962 and breathed new confidence into a shaky family venture.

Stax was white-owned but black-oriented. Estelle Axton and her brother Jim Stewart bought the Capitol Cinema on East McLemore Street, in a black neighborhood of Memphis. In 1959 they founded Satellite Records, which was renamed Stax (for Stewart and Axton) a year later. As a sound and as a corporation it had a comparatively short life-span, from 1959 to 1975, when it went bankrupt. The peak years, from 1961 to 1971, coincided (until 1968) with Stax's association with Atlantic Records.

"There were three phases for us," Jerry Wexler has said of those years. "There was Carla Thomas, then there was Booker T. and the MGs, and then there was Otis Redding. And when there was Otis Redding, the ball game was over. That was it."

It's an oversimplification, of course, since many of the artists worked throughout the sixties and a second crop of black singers and musicians produced fine, if less commercial, work in the final years. Still, as Wexler says, Stax is best remembered for the earlier stuff. Besides those first hits by Rufus and Carla, William Bell hit in 1962 with "You Don't Miss Your Water." By then the strong studio band had coalesced into Booker T. and the MGs; in 1962 they were the label's top LP-selling act. That same year an unknown chauffeur named Otis Redding got his first hit with "These Arms of Mine." In terms of output, sales, visibility, and stage presence, he dominated the label until his death in 1967.

By the mid-sixties, once soul and Stax were well established, the roster swelled. The Mar-Keys and the Bar-Kays were also session bands that moved on to recording and live gigs. Eddie Floyd, late of the Detroit Falcons, became a Stax writer, producer, and recording artist; Sam Cooke's gospel protégé Johnnie Taylor, Little Willie John's sister Mabel John, Sam and Dave, and Little Johnny Taylor did their finest work on Stax. Isaac Hayes, who had worked in tandem with David Porter as a songwriter/producer and session man, turned to recording himself and pulled Stax into the seventies on the strength of his dance and production innovations, beginning with his 1970 LP *Hot Buttered Soul*. Post 1972, the only Stax sound to hit the pop charts was the up-tempo gospel soul of the Staple Singers. By staying black in the seventies, Stax was willingly recommitting itself to the R & B charts.

Wattstax, a highly successful seven-hour concert in an L.A. football stadium, seemed to prove that the company still had a decent future in 1973. Despite the death of Otis Redding and the departure of Sam and Dave, there were still viable acts such as Isaac Hayes, the Soul Children, the Emotions, the Dramatics, Little Milton, Albert King, the Staple Singers, Margie Joseph, and Mel and Tim, as well as that stubborn soul man Johnnie Taylor. On the heels of Otis and Carla's "Tramp" in 1967, Taylor's "Who's Makin' Love" was a funky manifesto of black sexual politics. He recorded it in 1968, followed with a string of between-us numbers like "I am Somebody, Part II," "Cheaper to Keep Her," "Steal Away," and "Jody's Got Your Girl and Gone."

"While Johnnie Taylor stayed at Stax, he stayed funky, which is to say, black as could be," says ex-MG and Stax guitarist Steve Cropper. "Which meant he made real good records that did well on the R and B charts and just nibbled at the pop."

With the exception of "Who's Makin' Love," which hit number five pop in the soul boom year of '68, this was true. Johnnie Taylor got his only number one pop hit in 1976, two years after he had left Stax for Columbia. The song was "Disco Lady," and its title pretty much tells the story. Even if there were some artists remaining at Stax who kept the faith, nobody, save a small, loyal black audience, was listening anymore.

Changing styles on the national charts aside, there were internal problems in Stax's two-tone family. Without the help of the departed Al Bell, a hard-working black A & R man, Stewart seemed unable to guide and market his black talent. Worse, he diluted it, branching, unsuccessfully, into rock, jazz, and country. By 1975 even Isaac Hayes and the Staples had departed, and the company was consigned to liquidation proceedings.

"Running a record company strikes me as being like playing Russian roulette—with five bullets in the chamber," commented a judge who oversaw the dissolution proceedings.

As it was, Stax's most successful era—from 1961 to 1971—was, in the best Memphis tradition, characterized by serendipity and a series of spectacular detonations: first the Thomases, then Otis Redding, Sam and Dave, and Isaac Hayes. It was tough and southern and uncompromising and very black. As such, Stax succeeded in spite of its dark self. In its entire history it had just four records make number one on the pop charts. At Motown the Supremes alone had a dozen. But Stax always charted well with R & B.

The difference in outlook between Stax and Motown was written boldly on their studio buildings. Motown declared itself "Hitsville U.S.A." in fat blue script. Stax, housed in an old movie theater, put its slogan on the marquee in worn black clamp-on lettering: "Soulsville U.S.A."

Soulsville was where Stax fans lived, and at least for its first decade, it was where the company was determined to stay. Once, in a momentary spirit of do-goodism, Stax replaced the slogan on the marquee with "Stay in School." The neighborhood kids stoned it.

Soulsville was just the place for wild, wild young men of both colors. One of them was Steve Cropper, a pale, skinny Vitalis-head from Messick High. Cropper and his buddies Donald "Duck" Dunn, Don Nix, Charlie Freeman, and Packy Axton had themselves a little band. They had big ears and quick hands and a sense of adolescent adventure that drew them into black neighborhoods, into clubs where blood, beer, and music washed over them night after night. They made some money by lightening the music they heard a little and playing it at white high school and college dances.

"We were getting fairly popular," Cropper remembers. "Everybody wanted us for their proms and all. We played R and B basically, a soul band. We played Ray Charles and Hank Ballard and James Brown. And a little Jimmy Reed and Chuck Berry and so forth."

Twenty years had passed since his rambunctious high school days when I hunted Steve Cropper up in California. He says he left Memphis once things started going bad at Stax and has since been recording, producing, and doing session work—some for Motown and other California-based labels. He and Duck Dunn enjoyed a brief reunion playing and touring behind Belushi and Aykroyd in the Blues Brothers Band; they appeared in the movie, on the sound track, in concerts, and on the Blues Brothers' subsequent LP.

When we spoke in Los Angeles, he said he was "laying back some," looking for a good act to produce, and working on some tunes himself. There was little to suggest the pale, bony studio rat of the early sixties. He is tall, fit, and bearded. The tan is Californian, but the voice still says Memphis.

The portraits in this section were made by Fredrich Cantor, in New York City, 1981-82.

Twenty years after his biggest solo hit, "Stand By Me," Ben E. King reminisces: "Remember, it started as a *neighborhood* thing. And your buddies, the guys who [sang] with you, they were your *heart*. You could get so in tune it seemed you all had but one heart between you. Those street years were the best of my life. Listen, it's real hard to describe the feeling a quartet gave you. You never felt alone, is all."

Martha Reeves: "When people say, 'Where are the Vandellas?' I say *men* broke up my group. Men. I've loved each one [of the Vandellas]. And now I'm godmommy to their babies."

Shake me, wake me! When an airline lost their luggage, the Four Tops, lords of cummerbund cool, played Radio City Music Hall in sweat suits.

Jr. Walker's new set of All Stars includes his drummer son. "I *am* a road-runner," he says. "Ever since Berry Gordy told me to scare up a truck and git—he had some dates lined up—I lit out. Same now. I travel. I blow some. People dance. We make a wind blow them blues clean to Monday. It's Saturday night now, ain't it? And if you'll excuse me, I got a job to do."

Mary Wells, with her friend Curtis Womack. "When I listen back to those records, I can hear the difference in my voice, from when I was seventeen. I'm a divorced mother struggling with family and career. I don't have the peace of mind I did on those early tours. We were just a bunch of kids growin' up together. It's something like what I've heard people describe about their college years. Those were *our* years of higher education."

Aretha Franklin: "What I feel singing, and where it comes from, is something I keep to myself. Music, especially the kind I make, is a very emotional thing. As an artist you're happy when people get *involved,* you know? But what they hear and what I feel when I sing it can be very, very different. Sometimes I wish I could make them understand that."

The Hardest-Working Man in Show
Business, Mr. Please, Please, Please, the
Godfather of Soul, James "Butane"
Brown: "If some record company, if some
deejay don't want to know me, don't want
to recognize me in that stuff you hear in
the Top Ten today, well, all right. Because
God knows James Brown. In the year
3000, people say, 'Who was James
Brown?' Now I bet *you* got an idea who
James Brown is. But it ain't the same
answer as His and mine."

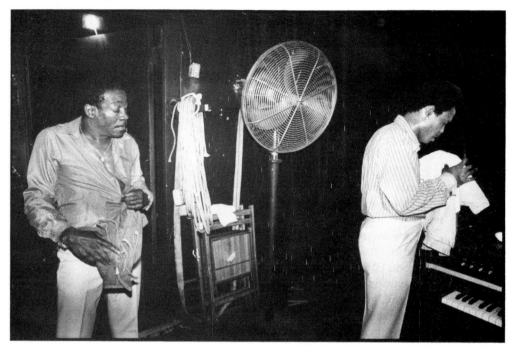

Dave Prater (left) and Sam Moore made beautiful harmony onstage from the early sixties to their breakup in 1981. Offstage, Messrs. Double Dynamite had not been on speaking terms since 1969.

The Soul Clan rides again, at a one-night reunion in the summer of 1981. Left to right: Ben E. King, the late Joe Tex, Don Covay, Wilson Pickett, and Solomon Burke.

Stompin' at the Savoy: The Soul Clan closes out its Manhattan one-nighter with a tribute to fallen member Otis Redding. Left to right: Joe Tex, Wilson Pickett, Don Covay.

Pickett, the Midnight Mover: "I AM THE WICKED. Dig? I am NAMED the Wicked, I got to BE the Wicked. Don't you be *writing* nothin' nice 'cause you'd be jivin' people. Now git!"

Cropper says he was not born in Memphis, he came from the Ozarks in Missouri. But he grew up in Memphis, in a safe, suburban upbringing, made bearable, he says, "by consorting with what some folks called wild Nee-groes." His suburban buddies weren't from the "most likely to" set. Those white boys were just the wrong kind of upwardly mobile. They actually had a dread of turning out like the regiments of madras-clad Kappa Sigs their band played for.

"Could be we just grew up hearin' different," Cropper says, and smiles. "You suppose it could be, ah, organic?"

The sound they heard and liked was racially mixed. They couldn't *be* black, but they tried to sound it, graduates of the hey-I-can-do-that school of honkytonk hard knocks. Cropper acknowledges that when he was a teenager, the ultimate cool was to hang with the black and the hip. He's a bit embarrassed, though, when asked the name of that first group he played in. It was the Royal Spades.

"We changed it to the Mar-Keys, so let's call it that," he says. "Now one day in school this kid came up named Charles 'Packy' Axton, and he wanted to join. Said he played saxophone. I said, 'How long you been playin'?' and he says, 'Well, I've had three or four lessons.' So I was kind of heehawin' around a bit, you know. Then he says, 'You know, my mom owns a recording studio.' And I said, 'Okay, show up at the next rehearsal.' "

Packy Axton's mom, Estelle, was favorably disposed toward recording a band her son played in. After all, the boy was about to graduate and he needed a trade.

"It was during the summer we graduated from high school," Cropper remembers. "We came up with a little tune. It was called Last Night,' and on the *Billboard* charts, I think it got up to number three. We wound up doing a little tour, going to Philly to do *Dick Clark* and all."

Released in the summer of 1961, the record was the first hit for Stax (then Satellite), hanging on the pop charts for three months. It was a bigger R & B hit, putting the band of white boys in the odd circumstance of playing the chitlin circuit.

"Somehow we pulled it off," Cropper says. But soon he decided he wasn't crazy about life on the road, and he left the Mar-Keys to join the Stax rhythm section as a guitar player. The house band leaned heavily on the talents of two blacks—keyboard wizard Booker T. Jones and drummer Al Jackson, Jr.—and two whites—Cropper and Dunn. Soon they became Booker T. and the MGs (for Memphis Group).

Like Motown and Atlantic, Stax began as a casual all-under-one-roof operation. Jim Stewart hung the acoustical curtains and nailed up the tiling himself. And before the studio began to pay in any serious way, employees worked double shifts.

"They had a record shop out front," Cropper says. "It belonged to the studio. So I'd work in the record shop during the daytime, and then at night I would help in the back—call musicians, set up sessions. 'Cause Jim Stewart, who was the president of the company, was still working in a bank."

In off hours Stewart was recording Billy Lee Riley, a southern rockabilly original responsible for songs like "Flyin' Saucers Rock 'n' Roll." Cropper was part of the slapdash rhythm section put together for his sessions. It was, as he remembers it, one of the first instances of Stax's weird synchrony that put the company solidly into the black.

"We had just finished with Billy," he says. "And we were just kind of jamming around, playing some blues. Jim heard us playing and he pressed the record button. We didn't know he was taping it. After five minutes of jamming he called us in and said, 'Hey, you guys better listen to this back.' It sounded pretty good. Booker and I had been working on this for a couple of weeks—he had a riff and I had a riff, and we switched them around. Anyhow, I guess we made two tapes on it. And that was 'Green Onions.' "

It was an instrumental, and Cropper doesn't think it hurt that there were no identifiably black voices to consign it immediately to the R & B charts. Still, it was hardly a pop sound. Drummer Al Jackson held a steady, uncomplicated beat beneath Booker T.'s low, almost ominous organ. Duck Dunn's bass rumbled out a danceable funk, and over it all, cutting across the top like a sugarcane machete, was Cropper's sharp, mean guitar. In August 1962 it sold more than a million copies. Its success, along with Carla Thomas's "Gee Whiz (Look at His Eyes)" and William Bell's "You Don't Miss Your Water," was the beginning of Stax's soulful decade.

"From about 1959 to 1967 or '68, Stax was exactly what we had intended it to be," Cropper says. "What it ultimately wound up to be was not what we intended. But in the beginning it was a form of community music that just spoke for the black person. And it was a step above what people call the blues. It was slicker, but it wasn't *too* slick. It wasn't Motown. You know, to me, Motown was white music. R and B music, black music, to me was James Brown and Hank Ballard and Little Willie John. We fit in Carla and Rufus Thomas and Little Johnny Taylor and people like that.

Once Eddie Floyd had hit records, and Sam and Dave and Otis had hit records, Stax was a real record company."

And by the mid-sixties the tide had turned, giving new opportunities to southern singers, hauling artists like Wilson Pickett and Aretha Franklin back down South to record as well. The English invasion had begun to loosen its stranglehold on the charts, and soul was at last getting its due.

"The emergence of the Memphis Sound, a much darker mixture than Motown or Atlantic of Mississippi mud and country blues, suggested that white record buyers were ready for the real thing—not white kids singing or playing black, but black vocalists singing and playing black," Arnold Shaw theorized in a special issue of *Billboard* dedicated to soul. Shaw saw it as an R & B revival, but record company ads in the same issue claimed it was something black and shiny and new. Whatever the root, soul artists were cashing in, even on the Vegas Strip. In 1969 black artists filled casino marquees: Aretha Franklin, Ray Charles, blue-eyed soul man Bill Medley (of the Righteous Brothers), Gladys Knight and the Pips, and Little Richard. Johnny Carson began using Flip Wilson and Bill Cosby as guest hosts for the *Tonight Show*, and they brought in acts like Jimi Hendrix, Joe Tex, and Wilson Pickett. Dick Cavett featured Smokey Robinson, Edwin Starr, Dionne and Dee Dee Warwick, and B. B. King.

Network soul wasn't especially funky. James Brown was told he couldn't sing "Don't Be a Dropout" on the *Ed Sullivan Show*. And as Jerry Butler told writer David Hinckley, talk show appearances weren't exactly that:

> Sure, during the period when soul was big in the sixties we could get on TV, because guys like Johnny Carson figured that to be hip, they needed black artists. But we weren't really guests, even then; if you noticed, we'd mostly sing our songs and leave. The thing was, Johnny never felt comfortable with us. He didn't understand us; we weren't the kind of people he played golf with, which meant he couldn't tell his golf jokes, and since a talk show host has to be glib, that makes him look bad. He can't afford to be uncomfortable. So we were never really in the mainstream, even then. It was just another glimpse of the promised land.

Even the musical segments on those shows could be problematic for a soul artist, owing to the low funk factor of TV studio bands and the impossibilities of lip-syncing the more untamed soul cuts. As the funkiest of them all, Stax artists didn't get quite as much TV exposure; Sam and Dave did *Where the Action Is* once or twice, and a few live spots were available for self-contained bands like the MGs.

Up until the mid-sixties, commercial image hadn't been a pressing concern at Stax. But once the Memphis soul men began to realize their appeal beyond the city limits, they became acutely conscious of the need to manage it.

"We'd have meetings," Cropper says. "We sort of all gauged records and judged them. You know, this is an A side, this is a B side. But we really got smart on the road. Booker T. and Al Jackson and myself, we'd play all these places, we'd do weekends. This was in the days where a joint could afford only one band. So if we were on an hour, and thirty minutes off, then during that half hour, they'd play records. We'd watch the kids dancing in Detroit and different places. They'd do different dances than they were doing on *American Bandstand*. And different than they were doing in Memphis. And we'd get with these kids and say, 'What are you all doing?' One of them happened to be the swim, so we'd go back and write instrumentals that had that swim beat. Another was the jerk."

It was the jerk, that spine-snapping, bent-elbow spasm, that dominated rhythm tracks in 1965. There is a story that Wilson Pickett's "In the Midnight Hour" was restructured to fit the dance, as demonstrated by Jerry Wexler in the studio at Stax.

"That's a true story," Cropper says. "I couldn't believe it. But right during the cook [the instrumental bridge], he came running out of the booth, doing this thing. It wasn't the jerk as you know it. It was so funny. I take it he remembers it."

Months later, when I asked about it, Jerry Wexler stood up in his Manhattan office and laughed. And jerked. "White kids danced like this, all shoulders," he said, freezing into a stiff-spined, Frankenstein herky jerk. Then he shook it off and switched to some Blaze Starr hip action. "*This* is what it was all about, right? *Below* the waistbands of all those legions of Levi's. How else was I gonna make them understand? Draw a diagram? By hopping around the studio, we set it on the right groove that was funky and marketable."

By then the traffic in the Stax studio was heavy. Jim Stewart hauled his acts off the road and cut on them whenever he could. And when New York called, under the distribution arrangement with Atlantic, he worked to make time for Jerry Wexler's soulful commuters. According to Cropper, a lot of the fever to record at Stax was tied to the initial success of Pickett's

Memphis sessions. It all started with "In the Midnight Hour," a composition credited to Pickett and Cropper (though the Wicked insists it should have been his alone). By 1982 Cropper estimated that they had been paid for more than 150 cover versions of the song, "which means," he added, "that about five hundred have been done."

As it happened, such a rock and soul classic was hatched in a moment's desperation. One day Jim Stewart called Cropper aside and told him that Wexler was sending down a new act. Though Wilson Pickett had a modest northern following for his work with the Falcons, none of the Stax session men knew who he was. Cropper walked into the record shop out front and began rooting through the bins.

"I pulled out some of the old spiritual records. And everything that he sang lead on, he wound up doing this ad lib in the end. Sounded like 'the midnight hour' on the end of every record. I said, 'This is this guy's favorite statement.' That day Wilson flew in, and we started writing in the afternoon. I think we wrote 'In the Midnight Hour' in about an hour. I thought Jerry had made a good decision in bringing him down because I think we were his kind of people. And he was generous. Wilson was the first guy that called Jerry or Jim and said, 'Get these guys an extra session, do something for them for helping me out.' He was one of the first people ever that acknowledged what the guys were doing in the studio."

Not every session went as smoothly. The next time Pickett was scheduled to descend from New York, Cropper tried to work out some songs ahead of time with Pickett's old partner Eddie Floyd. They made an odd but effective writing team.

"Yeah, a white country boy and a black city dude. Eddie had been living up in Detroit, you know; then he moved to Washington. He'd been on the stage, and he knew what was going on. He was real helpful to me. Eddie knew the pulse in the street; he knew the pulse of the ghettos in Detroit and Chicago, and I didn't know jack shit about that. I knew what was going on in Memphis, Tennessee, and that's as far as it went."

It was in December 1965, before Pickett's second session, that the two of them wrote for a solid week, "looking for another 'Midnight Hour,' " Cropper says, and they came up with something called "634-5789." When they picked the Wicked up at the Memphis airport on December 19, they started jabbering at him like excited kids.

"I said, 'You *gotta* go by the studio and hear this tune we did for you.' He said okay. We went straight to the studio. We got the tape and put it up and handed Wilson a set of lyrics."

Pickett leaned against the control board and listened while the other two searched his face for the onset of rapture.

"This is it? This is my hit tune? This is a piece of shit!"

Pickett rolled up the lyric sheet and tossed it at the trash can, and before it hit bottom, Eddie Floyd had leaped across the room straight for him. They went down like scrapping bearcats, flailing at each other until Cropper managed to get them apart.

"These guys are big, you know. I thought Eddie was gonna kill Wilson. But they'd been doing this sort of thing all their lives. Anyhow, I got them apart, and I took Wilson to the hotel and got him checked in. I called him later, and I said, 'Well, you feel like writing?' He said, 'Yeah, you and Eddie want to come down?' And so I called Eddie, and I guess he had calmed down, too. On the way down to the studio, about two blocks away, there's this big Coca-Cola sign. And they had a brand-new slogan out, called 'Ninety-nine and a half won't do.' "

Coca-Cola had, in fact, borrowed the phrase from an old gospel lyric. You had to love your Lord *all* the way.

"Well now," says Cropper, "we figure you gotta have all her love, instead of your co-cola. The three of us sat there and within an hour or two did 'Ninety Nine and a Half.' The next day we went in and cut it. Then we mentioned looking at '634-5789' again. It was like that fight never happened. Wilson listened, and this time he said, 'Sure, that's pretty good.' Just like that. That's the way Wilson is, he can turn it on and turn it off. He doesn't hold grudges. He's not an evil person. He can just be real belligerent if he wants to. A real soul man and a half, you know."

■20

Soul Men

■ *I'm a workin' man. Been gettin'* down *so long, I don't be thinkin' about will I make it up again. Now what's a music man like me gonna do? What's he do, 'less he entertains till he dies?*

■ —DAVE PRATER of Sam and Dave

"GIVE IT UP, I say. Yeah, mama—you. Give it UP. Huh. Ungh. Owwwwww."

Long past the midnight hour, the Wicked's gold leather pants are welded to his thighs with sweat; salt water rolls down his chest and drips off the gold-plated Rolls-Royce key he wears around his neck. He is holding the mike with some difficulty. The fingers of his right hand are swollen, and dried blood rims the nails beneath a makeshift gauze bandage.

A leggy blonde in a vinyl miniskirt has climbed onstage, and Pickett is facing her down, mugging, rolling his eyes, rocking his hipbones, the fingers of his free hand fluttering over his heart. They dance toward each other from opposite ends of the stage. They are just about touching when Pickett lowers his center of gravity, leaning into the woman to wrap her, neatly, around the curve of his thigh. She nearly swoons in his arms as he growls into the mike: *"Awl you wanna do is ride, Sally, ride . . ."*

Another night, another Mustang Sally. Since that song hit in 1966 there have been thousands of them, throwing off inhibitions like so many fussy prom gowns, leaping onstage or making a scene in the aisles—nice girls, all of them, caught in thrall with the nasty. Even grandmamas are not immune. There is one, a graying black lady in a knit suit, bumping with the bass player. Even Pickett seems amazed as she moves her rock-solid self toward him.

"Stac-ko-lee!" the Wicked screams. "Where you *at,* man? I need some help."

When the song finally ends on an explosive rim shot, Pickett looks as if he could be posing for a statue atop the Tomb of the Unknown Soul Man. He is panting and grinning, the blonde hanging from his waist like a dead quail, the black woman leaning against his shoulder, fluttering feebly with a white hankie.

"I learned how to love before I could eat."

Sam and Dave sang the anthem "Soul Man," composed by Isaac Hayes and David Porter. In that song, and in many others, the soul man appears as a mellowed descendant of the mythical Staggerlee. He's a ferocious lover. But he's capable, even willing to be an "only boyfriend" as well. There was a soul man for all persuasions and a great roster of macho marquee titles: the Wicked, the Midnight Mover, the Man and a Half, the Godfather, the Sex Machine, the Ice Man, the Big O, Love Man. The hype was good-natured. And the goods were genuine.

"During that time we all had our own style," Ben E. "Mr. Soul" King explains. "No one really copies anyone. Coming out of gospel, which most of them did, they had their own way of stepping and jumping and moving and standing. Wilson still performs the way he did when I first saw him. Still has that very Baptist way of presenting himself. Which makes for a totally honest performance. What you see is what he is."

Opposite a Pickett there was the sweet, mournful country soul of Percy Sledge, at his best when he sang with an icepick in his heart. Joe Tex was a wry, fatback philosopher who sang and rapped parables like "Hold What You've Got," "Skinny Legs and All," and "Ain't Gonna Bump No More (with No Big Fat Woman)." Sam and Dave kept up a melodic counterpoint of brass and butter, high-stepping through dance songs like "Soul Man," then melting into a ballad like "When Something Is Wrong with My Baby." Big, blind Clarence Carter edged his genial soul vocals with a stinging blues guitar. And later, at the outset of the seventies, came the wild, holy

fire of Al Green, the last of that era's great soul men and currently
a preacher once again. In 1973 Al Green had three Top Ten hits; the
following year his career came to a momentary halt in a bizarre caricature of the soul man persona. While he was in the bathtub, the woman he refused to marry scalded him with a pot of hot grits, then killed
herself.

The majority of sixties soul men were deeply, vocally southern. Working
in Memphis, Muscle Shoals, Miami, Nashville, and New Orleans, they
included Johnnie Taylor, Eddie Floyd, Arthur Conley, James Carr, William
Bell, Z. Z. Hill, Arthur Alexander, Aaron Neville, Jesse Hill, Ernie K-
Doe, and Bobby Womack. James Brown and Otis Redding held the elevated titles of "The Godfather of Soul" and "The King of 'Em All (Y'all)"
respectively. Still, for sheer ferocity and conscious management of the
soul man mystique, nobody looked, walked, and talked the part like Wilson
Pickett.

"Oooh, you are *wicked*," an Atlantic Records secretary named Lurleen
told Wilson one day after he'd delivered one of his poetic comments on
the length of her skirt. "When that chick bent over, you could see clear
to San Francisco," he says in his defense. But that day Jerry Wexler was
out of his office like a shot, hollering, "That's it, you're the *Wicked!*"
For the newly Wicked Pickett, there was no problem working out a life-
style to fit the image.

The local police weren't as understanding as Mr. Pickett's record company the night they hauled him into an upstate New York jail for shooting
at the door of the Isley Brothers' motel room. He wasn't after them, he
insisted. They all were on a hunting trip together. It was late, and he
wanted somebody to play with. Just figured he'd wake them up with this
bitty two-shot derringer. The night I first interviewed him—the evening
of the bashed and bandaged fingers—he was using phrases like "a dis-
agreement of the personal sort" to explain his latest sports injury.

"So. I fucked up again. Someday they gonna ride me outa this town
on a rail. Yeah."

Despite having had to miss the first night of his weekend gig, Wilson
is actually cheerful, greeting friends in his Times Square dressing room
in Bond International Casino, a converted clothing store transformed into
a cavernous but short-lived disco.

"Awwwwweeeeeoooooh. SHIT."

For a moment he has forgotten himself and tried to shake hands. The
pain ebbs, he smiles, but seconds later he plunges the injured hand into

a cardboard container of french fries, and the acidic sting of ketchup makes
him holler again.

"Wil-son, Wil-son," a friend is saying. "Ain't you never gonna slow
it? Lookit you now. Don't you know? Handsome man ain't supposed to
bleed over silk."

"Dirty, filthy Broadway, don't I like ya, Brrrrroadway . . ."

Pickett is singing now, sidestepping the fries, pulling on a Heineken,
yelling, dancing, rolling his eyes like a preacher shaking down the thunder.
But the message ain't sanctified.

"Well, I be shit," he bellows. "Revival? You askin' about a soul revival?
That mean I been dead?"

Calming some, he sits down and says of course he lived through a bad
time, through the lean years following his departure from Atlantic, through
a bad scene with RCA, from a run of solid, certified gold to nothing—
zippo in five head-spinning years, something he now calls his "career
breakdown."

This was when Wilson crashed head-on with what he calls "the Big
Lie." He says he had thought that America had accepted soul men as
permanent, respectable citizens, when really it was only a fad.

"I should have known," he says. "Even a motherfuckin' *monkey* make
it to the Johnny Carson show."

Such perspective escaped him at the time. He says he was amazed but
pleased at how willing America suddenly seemed to celebrate the strength
and talent—the soul—of the black male. Merv and Johnny made room in
their lineup, if not on their sofas. More and more soul artists were entrusted
with the national anthem at ball games. Even *The New York Times Magazine* paid attention, offering translations of the soul man's special argot.
Its glossary of terms included "fox," "dap," and "gig." Chitlins, it noted,
were also known as "ruffle steaks" or "wrinkles." And for the soul man
himself, a concise definition: "Main man: A woman's boyfriend; a man's
closest friend. Feminine form: main squeeze."

What began as a feeling and solidified as a sound was then given a peck
on the cheek from high fashion. Ray Charles was celebrated in *Vogue*.
White folks slipped into militant uptown chic, a penchant Tom Wolfe flash-
froze in his *Radical Chic & Mau-Mauing the Flak Catchers*. Black Panthers contemplated fondue forks at white cocktail parties. And uptown,
enterprising blacks hopped on the soul train for a brief but profitable trip.
In 1968 *Newsweek* found Harlem merchants "Selling Soul Style." One

Jason Benning explained that his New Breed clothing shop specialized in "fashions with a philosophy." The word "dashiki" described the loose, printed, African-style cotton tunics enjoying a vogue and also, Mr. Benning noted, "means freedom" in an unspecified African tongue.

Soul had become "music with a philosophy," as *Billboard* described it, an up-tempo "black nationalism in pop." It seemed to have reached its peak in 1968, when *Billboard* reported, R & B DISKS SWING TO "BLACK HOPE." Within a year it would declare, BACKLASH CUTS SOUL ON TOP 40. But while the mood lasted, artists were winning "payoff sales" with message songs like the Impressions' "We're a Winner" and Hank Ballard's "How You Gonna Get Respect (When You Haven't Cut Your Process Yet?)"

Later, sociologists produced statistical and lingual evidence to link such songs to changes in the black's social position. In *Right On: From Blues to Soul in Black America,* published in 1975, Michael Haralambos made a careful study of the radio airplay given to different types of black music in the sixties and a concomitant change in black lyrics. Among his observations: The "back door man" of the blues had been replaced by the soul man, a lover possessed of both guilt and morality. The "I" of the bluesman had become "we" in soul music. And having borrowed so much from gospel, soul music was bullish on hope. Activism, while still suicidal in some quarters, had gotten a booster shot of faith with the Civil Rights Act of 1964. "I Have a Dream," from Martin Luther King, Jr.'s 1963 speech, became the official slogan of radio station WCHB in Detroit. Even WDIA in Memphis adjusted its pitch to "50,000 watts of Soul Power."

The stunner, says Wilson Pickett, is that despite all this, the charts, the record companies, and, in the end, the country treated soul like just another pop culture curiosity.

"Stuck us in a closet in mothballs like some raggedy-ass Nehru suit."

Wilson is up again, stalking around his dressing room, tugging on his car-key pendant so hard it's leaving furrows in his neck.

"I ain't just blamin' whites. Plenty of black people didn't want to listen. Wanted somethin' new and not so messy and dangerous. But I been tired of sittin' on my ass. I don't like this bullshit about our music is gonna happen again 'cause our music never went *nowhere.* Shit, you can't play no songs without using some chords from the twelve-bar blues. R and B is the twelve-bar blues. Rock, punk, new wave, you call it whatever you want. . . ."

This is not to say that the Wicked begrudges the white boys their success with R & B covers. Rolling Stone Bill Wyman is Wilson's "good partner." So are Ringo Starr and Peter Wolf, then lead singer for the J. Geils Band.

"But listen, those boys are on Lear jets. And I'm still here runnin' my ass off. If I ain't sittin' on it, waiting for some sorry gig to turn up. Now you get tired of runnin', but you get more tired sittin' on your ass thinkin' about it all. I tried some experiments a few years back. Cut two albums myself on the Wicked label, released one. Went back to Muscle Shoals and recorded my album *Funky Situation* with Rick Hall. But Rick is more stubborn than I am about change. We stuck to pretty much the old groove, and the record didn't do shit."

As a longtime sultan of style Wilson says he is not naïve about the necessity of altering things a bit, just to keep up. He talks, a bit abstractly, about a "more tailored, more sophisticated R and B" that he believes would reach old and new audiences. What he could not and would not stand was disco, where the arrangement, not the singer, was the star, and the premium was on a producer instead of on a voice. He says he sang about it on *Funky Situation*. The cut, called "Time to Let the Sun Shine on Me," was about the rise of disco and his attempt to deal with it. He cowrote the song in 1978 with his old Falcon buddy Mack Rice, and it opened with a little bit about some brother walking in and telling Wilson to listen, pull up a chair, 'cause Pickett gotta go disco. The Wicked sang back: *"I changed my clothes, but I didn't change my soul."*

"Yeah, well, like I sing in that song, I'm ready to express myself. I'm near to bustin'. I still got a lotta soul left. I sung that in the song, too, but wasn't nobody listening."

His friend Don Covay keeps telling him, reassuring him that disco is dead, that with all that overload it finally committed suicide.

"I hear," said Covay, "disco jumped off the Brill Building."

Pickett says he wants to see the corpse and stick a mirror under its coke-blasted nose. He is leaping around the room again, preaching some more, bellowing, stopping for just a second to express horror at his reflection in a mirror.

"Will you lookit this nigger's *hair?*" He fluffs it over a small scar on his skull, wheels, and catches a frantic signal from his manager of the month ("they don't last long").

"Aw, shit, I clean forgot my new project. I guess it ain't so new. Like in the sixties, with all that marchin', you realize maybe you can't do a whole lot alone. So me and the rest of the soul men are gettin' together.

You remember the Soul Clan? It was me and Covay, Otis Redding, Ben E. King, Solomon Burke, Joe Tex, Arthur Conley. We put it together years ago on Atlantic. Had plans for some sessions together, a tour. What we're gonna do now is bring it back. We got to show a little unity and strength."

Ushering me out, Wilson promises an invite to the upcoming Soul Clan show. He taps at the tape recorder, smiles, and asks, "You got enough? Too much? Well, just remember this now: If it don't fit, don't force it."

Cackling as only the Wicked can, he closes the door.

For all his yawping, Pickett is still privy to a lot of the good-times touches that songwriting royalties, Vegas dates, and semi-regular gigs have assured: the custom-made leathers and lamés, the lizard boots, the manager, the hairdresser, and, at shows around Manhattan, a club owner's excited intelligence that stars—a Mick Jagger or a David Bowie—have been seen in the audience. Wilson owns a Rolls-Royce and a Stutz Bearcat, sends his children to private schools, fishes off Fire Island and Puerto Rico, bought a house for himself in New Jersey and one for his mother in Kentucky. No, he concedes, he isn't exactly poor. But he is needy. "Otis Redding sung it—gave the word to it. To what we all want—which is respect."

When I caught up with soul man Sam Moore, he was singing the same tune. "Call it a blues," he said, "but it's just statin' a fact."

At the time he and Dave Prater were still Sam and Dave—they have since split for the umpteenth and last time—and they were enjoying a resurgence just after the Blues Brothers covered "Soul Man" on *Saturday Night Live*. Sam and Dave were invited to appear on the show, and they did, but John Belushi would not sing *with* Messrs. Double Dynamite.

"I asked him, and he went pale and said, 'Aw, no, man.' Cat wanted us to come out, do two bars of our song 'Soul Man,' then turn it over to the Blues Brothers and leave the stage. The four of us, okay. But not that way, not Sam and Dave as emcees. No, I don't need that. I am grateful for the chance again, don't get me wrong. But I won't do nothin' that is disrespectful to myself."

"Where's Dave?" The staff at Manhattan's Lone Star Café was nervous. Ten minutes to showtime, and still, only Sam had shown up. For years Sam and Dave were given to arriving separately, often from vastly distant places. I'd spoken to them several times, but they never sat for an interview together; it was impossible even to photograph them together unless it was onstage. As far back as 1969 I'd gone to a show of theirs that ended up being the Sam Revue. The weirdness persisted for nearly thirteen years. That night, at the Lone Star, would turn out to be one of their final appearances together. Still, Sam stonewalled on the subject of offstage relations. "Let's just say I need the work. *Have* to work. And leave it at that."

"Who gets the pitcher?"

A busboy had come in with a beer pitcher filled with water and a dishtowel. Sam reached for them, shaking his head.

"Twenty-six years on the road and still shaving out of a beer pitcher. Shee-it." He laughed, and set about unpacking what he called the soul man's one-nighter kit. It was a worn small Leatherette bag with a shoulder strap, packed with an engineer's precision. He extracted clean socks, toilet articles, and a straight razor rolled in a clean pair of Jockey shorts. A pearl-gray three-piece suit hung in a garment bag from a nail.

Though he regrets, bitterly, the excesses of his life within show business—booze, drugs, fortunes lost—Sam insisted he was still sure he had made the right choice when J. J. Farley, manager of the Soul Stirrers, approached him one night in 1956 in his hometown of Miami. Farley had heard him in a club, knew Sam was the gospel-trained deacon's son, grandson of a Baptist preacher. Farley offered him a chance to go out with the Soul Stirrers to see if he could replace Sam Cooke, who had left to sing pop. Sam was ready to leave Miami that Monday morning, but over the weekend Jackie Wilson came to town.

"I went to see him, and his show that night changed the course of my life," Sam said. "I saw what he could do with his voice in the broad range of songs he could do, and I was hooked. I went back and told Farley I couldn't go with them. I loved gospel, but I wanted to do like Jackie."

He stayed in Miami, working small clubs. He was onstage one night at the King of Hearts Club, trying to emcee an amateur show over the bar clamor, when he was joined onstage by a guy in baker's whites. Dave Prater was a laborer's son from Ocilla, Georgia. He had lit out for the city, hoping to sing for pay. He was working as a short-order cook and baker's assistant when he hopped onstage during one of his breaks. A little fumphering around, and Sam and Dave found in each other a pleasing counterpoint. Dave had a gritty, hoarse bottom to his voice; Sam could wail at the top of the register, and together, their harmonies were sweet and jelly-smooth. Dave was so nervous, he dropped the mike; Sam caught it in mid-air and the crowd went berserk.

They talked and realized they could be part of a very specialized partner tradition. There had been Don and Dewey and Sam Cooke's protégés the Simms Twins. The duet tradition was furthered, in the sixties, by Don and Juan, by the blue-eyed soul of the white Righteous Brothers, and by James and Bobby Purify. The latter got their first hit, "I'm Your Puppet," in 1965, the year Sam and Dave left Roulette Records for Atlantic. Veteran R & B producer Henry Glover had them recording in New York for Roulette. But it wasn't until Jerry Wexler sent them down South, to Stax, that anything solid came together for Sam and Dave. He had signed them in Florida, where he found them, then made a handshake deal with Jim Stewart to record Sam and Dave with the Stax studio band and production team.

"Those guys were like Siamese twins when they came to us," Steve Cropper remembers. "They were incredibly tight."

So was their production team. When they arrived, they found a sheaf of songs composed by Isaac Hayes and David Porter, who established themselves at Stax largely on the strength of their work with Sam and Dave.

During the years when nearly every session yielded a hit, from 1966 to 1968, a big silver bus ferried the thirty-five-member Sam and Dave troupe to clubs, colleges, arenas, and dance halls. THE SAM AND DAVE REVUE, the destination sign read, in white lights. They carried red suits, white suits, three-piece lime green suits, all with matching patent boots and co-ordinated silk hankies woefully inadequate to absorb a soul man's nightly outpourings. Both Sam and Dave talk a lot about sweat. To Dave, it's proof that he's worked for his pay. For Sam, it's essential, almost mystical. He says he can't work without it.

"Unless my body reaches a certain temperature, starts to liquefy, I just don't feel right."

Outside the dressing room someone hollered, "Five minutes," and I left Sam to shave in his pitcher.

"Where's Dave?" The booking agent was sweating. Downstairs, on the tiny stage, the eight-piece band was setting up. A trombone slide narrowly missed a waitress. Sugar Bear, a mammoth keyboard player in flaming orange polyester, settled gingerly on a tiny stool. The drummer's elbows knocked the back wall. He nodded, then drew screams as he counted the band into the familiar rumble that signals the start of a brassy soul revue: *thunka-thunka* from the drums and bass; advance heat lightning off a poised tenor sax. A trumpet kicked into the opening strut of "Hold On, I'm Coming,'' and the announcer bawled showbiz soulspeak over it all: "The one, the only, the HEATERS of 'Hold On, I'm Coming,' the sultans of SWEAT, DOUBLE DYNAMITE, Sam and . . .''

At last, Dave. He was looking older, tiny corkscrews of gray in his hair, but once he had grabbed the mike, ten years fell off his face and landed somewhere in the front row. It was a good, happy crowd, pressing up against the stage, faces upturned to the almost instant mist of sweat. In unison, the gray jackets flew off, then the vests. After ten minutes the white shirts clung like sandwich wrap, nearly transparent. Fifty wet minutes later they were climbing the curved stairway to the second-floor dressing rooms, running a gauntlet of upturned palms, slapping five, ten, twenty before they made it past the bar and into the stairwell. Dave had stepped into his dressing room to towel off when Sugar Bear filled the doorway, looking puzzled.

"Where's Sam?''

Seconds later someone spotted him, a flash of gray silk heading out the downstairs exit, to a waiting car and the airport.

"Yo," Sugar yelled. "Soul man Sam, what you know about that Buffalo gig?''

The only answer was the sweep of traffic noise in the stairwell.

Six months after his last appearance with Dave Prater on New Year's Eve of 1981, Sam Moore was free of heroin for the first time since 1968. Over the years he had overdosed twice; the second time nearly killed him. At one point his weight dropped to 120 pounds. He says he was always depressed and bloody, full of holes, reduced to stealing methadone at times, working, as he'd said he had to, just for the next fix, which, he claims, show business "friends" were only too happy to provide.

"Word got out," Sam says, "Sam and Dave are bad news. We were reduced to playing toilets. I'd lie, I'd miss shows, I'd find guys in my dressing room who'd heard about my habit. And they were always there with more. You become scum, you deal with scum. I had a phone book with every dealer from Harlem to Kalamazoo. Got to a point they'd charge me more because of who I was. That night we talked at the Lone Star, why you think I left so fast? I'd shot enough to do the show, but I came off that stage *hurtin'*.''

He admits he hadn't the strength to stop it himself. Having seen a TV program on experimental treatment with an opiate blocker called naltrexone, Sam's new manager, Joyce McCrae, got him into a program.

Slowly, hellishly, he kicked. His weight went back up to a healthy 200; he was working out in a gym, counseling addicts on a hot line, and singing. Beautifully and alone. He talked, too, about addiction and shame and depression and, finally, about the longtime freeze-out with his former partner. In 1968, Dave Prater shot his own wife in the face during a domestic scuffle. She lived, but Sam's respect for Dave was dead.

"I told him I'd work and travel with him, but that I would never speak or look at him."

When he explained all this, Sam and Dave were speaking to each other only through attorneys. Having found another "Sam," Dave was billing his act as "The Sam and Dave Revue." Sam was getting solo bookings, but it was problematic.

"You get club owners questioning why they should pay Sam Moore twenty-five hundred dollars a night when they can pay 'Sam and Dave' eight hundred dollars a night with a band. Who cares about the original when a club owner has to pay eight hundred dollars for two shows?"

By January of 1984, Sam Moore was back in a recording studio. Alone. His voice was strong enough, he said. Strong enough to bust a beer pitcher.

Ask any latter-day soul man for a full listing of his gigs, and inevitably, despite the media attention given to the "revivals" and "anniversary" shows in concert halls and white rock clubs, the bulk of his work will be down South or in the black neighborhoods of northern cities. There they find faithful, appreciative audiences. They love stars like Solomon Burke and Percy Sledge. Big names are nice, but for a two-buck cover, big voices will do, those of forty- and fifty-year-old soul men with more modest nicknames like the Tan Canary.

Johnny Adams—the Tan Canary—has been making a living in Louisiana and Mississippi clubs for more than thirty years. An Elks' lodge in McComb, Mississippi. Prout's Club Alhambra. The Busy Bee. John J's Lounge. The Tan Canary has flown from countless Greyhounds to his own Buick. Had a few records, still hoping for a hit. Picks up fifty, sixty bucks a night serving as the tall, trim swizzle stick that stirs the passions of countless small-town Saturday nights.

Black audiences still give such soul men a respectable, if tenuous, living. And for the next level—the guys a notch above the itinerant cougars and canaries—there are still small black record companies and a stalwart audience to keep buying good soul records. At the outset of the eighties, black charts have supported hits by Bobby Womack, Tyrone Davis, and

Johnnie Taylor. Z. Z. Hill kept making his raspy, adults-only epics on tiny Malaco Records out of Jackson, Mississippi. Otis Smith's Beverly Glen Records, out of California, cut Bobby Womack's album *The Poet,* and it sold, making it to pop album charts as well, on the strength of beautifully sung and produced cuts like "Just My Imagination" and "If You Think You're Lonely Now." Womack is still Wilson Pickett's favorite songwriter and running partner. Pickett, Womack, and Don Covay show up at one another's shows when the feeling hits them, no matter what the venue. They yell and dance and hug each other and tear up with their own stuff, an Otis Redding song, a Sam Cooke song, maybe even one of Covay's new ones.

"I still write songs all the time, still keep in it," Covay says. "I wrote 'See Saw' for Aretha in five minutes. And I still get royalties. I got something for her in the vault right now. Ain't no one else can do it. I'll just hold on to it till the time is right. A song a day keeps the rent man away."

Copyrights, he notes, last longer than record labels. One night, over dinner, he and Pickett played a game, shooting out the names of dozens of small labels that popped up to service sixties soul men: Dial, Date, Lu Pine, Shout, Soul, Soul Power, Charade, Jewel, Dynamo, One-Derful, SSS, Minaret, One-Shot, Solid State, Ric Tic, Minit, Money, Ronn, Dionn, Groovesville, Verve, Capitol, Fame, Mercury, Smash, Kent, Uni, Tangerine, and Wilson's own short-lived Wicked label.

Now many soul men find their work reappearing on French, English, and Japanese labels. Like so many tons of surplus wheat, after its late-sixties bumper crop, soul became most valuable as an export. It is still easier, in most places, to find a copy of *This Is Clarence Carter* or Otis Redding's *Dictionary of Soul* as a Japanese import. Some black artists, like Arthur Conley and Marvin Gaye, moved permanently to Europe. Even Ben E. King confessed he's toyed with the idea of moving to England. The soul circuit overseas is still lively.

Booking agents, like Otis Redding's brother Rogers Redding, are aware of this disparity and wisely divide their clients' dates between black venues in the South and longer, more lucrative European tours. Redding, who is still based in Macon, works with a roster of soul men that includes Clarence Carter, Percy Sledge, and Rufus Thomas. He had booked Clarence and Percy, along with Carla Thomas, for a "Night of the Living Legends" at the Ritz, a large rock club in lower Manhattan. Clarence, Redding advised, was the ultimate soul man, one of the very few who never left the road, even when what Clarence calls "that disco bidnis" turned the jet planes and fancy buses of the Atlantic boom years into six-cylinder pumpkins.

When Clarence pulled into Manhattan for the Ritz date, the grille of his band's station wagon was still clotted with red mud. They had just motored in from Savannah. Clarence hadn't even unpacked when I met him in his darkened hotel room. Mr. "Too Weak to Fight" was busy on the phone when he let me in, "just shoppin' this record around some," calling deejays in Newark and Long Island to scare up some airplay for his latest LP, recorded and produced himself for tiny Venture Records.

"You boys gonna give it a shot now? Air, yeah, baby, Clarence is just gaspin' for air. . . ."

Patiently Clarence answers the jock's standard "So where you *been,* baby?" with a simple "Out there." Lately he's been spicing up his string of VFW dates and outback BYOB socials with featured bookings in Manhattan, Washington, and Philadelphia, billed with other soul steadies like the Spinners. Copies of his 1968 *This Is Clarence Carter* are going for $25 in oldies' marts. His new album, *Let's Burn,* is more of a bargain, but just as tough to find. When he's on the road, sometimes Clarence sells them out of the back of his car. While looking for the light switch, I fall over a pile of them, and Clarence is apologetic. "I forget you sighted folks got the handicap of needin' lights."

Light from the unshaded overhead bulb reveals a clutter of tapes and guitar picks on the worn chenille bedspread. A flame red suit with sequined lapels glows beneath its plastic sheath. On the night table Clarence's mink cuff links huddle like field mice.

"This soul man stuck it out," he is saying. "And man, it was rough out there. Now I'm doin' all these rock clubs, and I don't mind it none. I got to go out there and fish a little bit. See what turns 'em on. Most of these white clubs like to hear the old hits best. 'Patches,' 'Slip Away,' 'Too Weak to Fight.' I just start 'em off and jiggle the bait. And lately I been catchin' pretty good.

"Don't know what all I'll give 'em tonight. Worse comes to worse, I just stand up there and laugh."

He busts into his trademark laugh, a big, wicked *hyuh-huh-huh,* the one that larded cuts like "Thread the Needle" and "Looking for a Fox."

"Ain't nothin' changed for me. Do me one favor, though. Set it straight. They've written me up as a gospel singer for years, that I started in church and all, 'cause that's the standard R and B artist bio, you know. But no. I didn't do it that way. I am a *blues*man.

"I learned how to play guitar from those old blues records. John Lee Hooker, Lightnin' Hopkins, Jimmy Reed, I used to imitate them. John Lee used to come down to Montgomery, where I come up, and every

time the club owner that was booking him would get the same thing. John
would say, 'What the hell you got to back me up? If you ain't got those
blind boys down there, I ain't comin'.''

Clarence started singing with a partner, Calvin Scott. They called their
act Clarence and Calvin.

"It all started with Calvin at Fame Studios in Muscle Shoals. I called
up Rick Hall and booked me some studio time. Cost me eighty-five dollars
to do two sides, 'Step by Step' and 'Rooster Knees and Rice.' Zenas
Sears—he was a big deejay in Atlanta, managed Chuck Willis and all—
he called Jerry Wexler and got him to do a favor and put the record out.
But by the time Jerry was ready to sign both of us, Calvin had gotten
married and the woman figured he should *solo*. So he put me down.''

Wexler signed Clarence as a solo and assigned Rick Hall to produce
the records for Atlantic. Working with Hall, Clarence stayed at Atlantic
from 1968 until 1974, then tarried briefly at ABC. But as disco and funk
outmuscled soul, Clarence took to the chitlin circuit again. He still writes;
but recording is sporadic, and sometimes, he says, it isn't even planned.
Take the song "Love Building," which he chose as the single from *Let's
Burn*. Clarence says that song came to him "outa all that smoke and
screamin' and carryin' on, on Sat'dy night. I was working the chitlin circuit, yeah, yeah, and I toted along a tape recorder one night in . . . lemme
see . . . Aiken. Aiken, South Carolina. Got into this little bit of a thing
with the people there.''

Like the night Ray Charles first tried out "I Got a Woman" in a Pittsburgh nightclub, it started late, very late, when the artist had exhausted
his repertoire, but the crowd hadn't quite worn down the clock or the
Seagram's. It started with a soul stutter.

*"Ah-ah-ah-ah-'ll tell ya'll about it. When I be makin' luhv, I don't be
foolin' around . . ."*

Clarence cocked an ear and heard some amens. Worked with it, talking
more about luhhhv, about working on the ol' love building. Got to *build*
it, right, girls? The band was trawling nice and quiet behind him, watching
his big old Dacron back, the way he had taught them, for the moment the
shoulders hunched and the people got a taste of the blues guitar John Lee
Hooker was so partial to. A loose-jointed organ punctuated the chat.

"I bet some of you girls got some men so JEALOUS . . ."

Clarence tossed it all in, suspicion, jealousy, steppin' out, makin' luhhhv,
on mundy-toozdy—makin' luhv EVERY NIGHT—pulling laughs,
screams, and amens into a sound track so live you can feel the beer seeping

into your shoe soles. He would play the same song in the rock clubs; he planned to try it out later at the Ritz, the evening that I interviewed him. But he wasn't expecting anything more than polite applause.

"Like I told you, darlin'," Clarence says, "ain't nothin' changed."

"Ain't much room for what you call happy accidents no more."

As Clarence prepares for his set, Percy Sledge is recalling how he came to compose his biggest hit, "When a Man Loves a Woman," a compact bundle of sexual truisms guaranteed to drop any sixties nostalgic, weeping, to his or her knees. Percy was just twenty-five when the record was released in 1966, but when he sang it, his voice sliced through the stone, bronze, and petrochemical ages of human love. He says he composed it in a vale of tears, and even now he has to be careful not to get too involved with the "thing" onstage or he'll lose it and set to drizzling all over his starched-up tux front.

He was moonlighting from his job as a hospital orderly, singing with a local band at a club in Sheffield, Alabama, and he was so low with woman troubles he couldn't even make it through the Smokey Robinson and Beatles songs he had been doing at dances and clubs. He turned to bass player Cameron Lewis and organ player Andrew Wright and just asked them to give him a key, any damned key. He half sang, half bawled along in his mammoth, achy baritone, just a bunch of stray thoughts on the blindness and paralysis of love: *"If she's bad, he can't see it . . ."*

"Wasn't no heavy thought to it," he says. "I was just so damned *sad.*"

Sometime later, when he had calmed down and refined the thing into a slow, anguished ballad, he gave Lewis and Wright songwriters' credit. By then Percy had won an Atlantic recording contract by auditioning in a record shop in Sheffield for a local producer named Quinn Ivy. The song was cut there, in Ivy's South Camp Studios, with some personnel borrowed from Rick Hall's Fame Studios in nearby Muscle Shoals. Percy grew up in Leighton, not ten miles from the Fame operation. So he says it all felt right—the musicians, the place, and the song. "When a Man Loves a Woman" was Percy's debut on Atlantic, and it sold more than 1 million copies in the spring of 1966 and stayed at number one on the pop charts for two weeks.

For the next three years he cut mainly lush ballads, working with Quinn Ivy and at Muscle Shoals. He did Elvis's "Love Me Tender," plus "Warm and Tender Love," "Take Time to Know Her," "Dark End of the Street," and the sublimely wrenching "Sudden Stop." Percy says it felt like family from the start at Muscle Shoals. His cousin Jimmy Hughes had already worked on the Fame label in the early sixties; so had Arthur Alexander, who had a broad country sound he so admired. Like Stax, Muscle Shoals had a mix of black and white studio personnel. The sound was part church and part hills, with Spooner Oldham and Barry Becket on keyboards, bassist David Hood, Jimmy Johnson on guitar, and the drumming of Roger Hawkins. At times some of the Memphis musicians worked there, too. Wilson Pickett's 1966 "Land of 1,000 Dances" session there included horn players Wayne Jackson and Floyd Newman, bassist Tommy Cogbill, and producer Chips Moman.

From 1966 to 1969 the tiny Florence, Alabama, airport saw the best of soul deplane, blinking, onto its hot scrap of tarmac. Candi Staton, whom Clarence Carter discovered and later married, cut her best records there. Southern expatriates like Ben E. King, Pickett, Aretha Franklin, and Don Covay cut there for Atlantic, as did the Sweet Inspirations. Etta James and Irma Thomas recorded there for Chess, James and Bobby Purify and Solomon Burke for Bell, Joe Tex for Dial, Joe Simon for Spring, and Bobby Womack for United Artists.

Percy acknowledges that it was the musicians and the producers who drew artists to Muscle Shoals, but he insists there was a deeper, more basic appeal to the place, especially if you were interested in cutting deep, deep soul.

"What drew everybody to Muscle Shoals . . . well, it sits right at the bottom of the mountains. Mountains all the way around us, and we have the best bass sound in the *world*. When you got mountains standing that high up over you, all the way around for, like, fifty, sixty miles, *then* you've got a bass track."

Having been reared nearby, Percy says he was comfortable with the Muscle Shoals frame of mind as well. As a boy he had learned the wisdom of country patience—had lain out on a trail all night long, stalking one deer. And to his mind, Muscle Shoals musicians were just as knowing and patient when it came to nailing down a tune.

Allowing that he was often referred to, on the southern college circuit, as "the big, gap-toothed nigger" with the audacious lungs, Percy tells stories late into the night about playing wild frat parties at Ole Miss and up on Stone Mountain outside Atlanta.

It's crept up to 2:00 A.M. by the time Percy is called upon to close this "Night of the Living Legends," and the house is peopled with no more than fifty dead-on-their-feet loyalists. The pieced-together pickup band is fumbling disastrously, and after just one song Percy loses patience and walks off the stage. As he undoes the mink cuff links in his dressing room, Clarence Carter instructs a band member to gas up the car for the morning.

"Yeah, slippin' away just after dawn, I expect. Got to make it to Sumter, South Carolina."

"We all been *out* there. Out there, alone."
Once again, Pickett is preaching.
"All these years, Lord help us. Well, now we're together. Check it *out*. Take a good look. We're all alive, dammit. And we ain't quit yet."

On a sticky July afternoon in 1981 the music press was summoned to a "soul meeting" in the Savoy Theater just off Broadway in Manhattan. The Soul Clan reunion that Wilson had prophesied was set for the following night in the form of a concert, with plans for a national tour. Things looked good; the show was sold out. Five soul men faced the press from behind a table: Solomon Burke, Joe Tex, and Don Covay wore cowboy hats; Ben E. King wore a suit. And Wilson Pickett wore black leather pants and a bright yellow silk shirt. The concert they had gathered to promote would dissolve in near chaos as busted sound systems, dead mikes, band miscues, and "unauthorized backstage personnel" scuttled hopes for the tour.

As he had back in 1967, Don Covay masterminded the get-together. Originally, a joint LP, including Otis Redding, had been planned. Otis had been waiting for his throat to heal from surgery; that was why they hadn't started earlier. After his death, one session, including Otis's protégé Arthur Conley, Solomon Burke, Ben E. King, and Joe Tex, was actually cut in Nashville in February 1968, yielding two unreleased sides, "Soul Meeting" and "That's How It Feels."

"Some funny stuff went down at Atlantic," Covay was telling the assembled reporters. "And of course, Otis's plane went down. And okay, over ten years have passed, but here we are to say the Clan lives."

After some applause the five men sat fielding questions. Solomon Burke beatified; Don Covay mediated; Ben E. King was reserved, contemplative; Joe Tex grinned and rasped. And midway through the proceedings, after he had tongue-lashed record execs, disco, deejays, radio format, the system, the tax structure, several reporters, and the show's own promoters, the Wicked offered an aside.

"I think you all realize we all have our own personalities and our way of expressing ourselves. Me? I'm mad as shit!"

"I ain't mad," Joe Tex offered, once the conference had broken up and the assembled were tearing into a fried chicken and Kool-Aid "Soul Clan buffet." "There *is* such a thing as a satisfied soul man. Yeah. Ain't got to prowl and holler all the time. No reason to run, run, run. Depend where your mind lay."

Joe said his own was in a piece of bottomland in Navasota, Texas, not far from Texas A&M, the Aggies, and his beloved Houston Oilers. He said he was a fifth-generation farmer and, as such, a patient man. He had been with the same record producer, Buddy Killen, for twenty years on Dial Records out of Nashville. He ended up on Atlantic when Dial let it take over its distribution in 1964. He found his groove in Muscle Shoals in late 1964 with "Hold What You've Got." He flew to New York a few weeks later, in December 1964, and cut a couple of novelty tunes, "You Can Stay (but That Noise Has Got to Go)" and "One Monkey Don't Stop No Show." After that he went back South and cut hits like "Skinny Legs and All" and "S.Y.S.L.J.F.M. (The Letter Song)," making the pop charts with some regularity between 1964 and 1969.

"You want to know my secret for gettin' a crossover hit? I used the same formula every time—half soul musicians, half country musicians. Still do."

He said he purposely recorded with a hoarse voice; once the Soul Clan show was over, his voice would probably be beat-up just right for an upcoming recording session in Nashville. He was planning to finish a new LP called *Joe Tex Rides Again*.

"Got a picture of me on my horse for the cover. Got the single all picked out."

This was a ditty called "Do the Earl Campbell," a tribute-*cum*-fight song dedicated to his dear friend Earl Campbell, the Houston Oilers' running back. Joe had rigged an act to go with it, complete with block-and-tackle choreography. He had already taught the steps and a rap/cheer to the Houston Oilerettes cheerleaders.

Joe was on his feet, slapping out a martial rhythm on the tabletop, flinging out a sample:

Uhnnnh . . . now whenyagetcha Gatorade, gimme a swalla
  All for Earl Campbell, stand up and holler . . .

He guessed that a lot of Sunday dates would have to be canceled since he had promised to be on the sidelines with Earl in the fall. He had been limiting his gigs to weekends, anyhow, and tried never to be away from home for longer than a week. He usually made it home by Sunday evening, Monday at the latest.

"Mondays I rest, play with my son. Tuesday I get up at seven-thirty, put on my overalls, chop in my garden, see if anything's ready for pickin', feed my chickens. Just watch them planes fly over—without me in 'em."

We fell to our meal for a moment, until Joe looked up at the sound of another commotion. It was Wilson, a yellow flash of agitation amid a knot of reporters. He had one arm in the air, another flung around the bony shoulders of singer Peter Wolf, a lupine white soul fan and friend in black beret and shades. Beyond them Solomon Burke was organizing rides to a radio station promo across town at WBLS with deejay Frankie Crocker, the dandy don of NYC black airplay.

"I'm tellin' you right now, it ain't gonna work."

Joe was shaking his head. "I hate to say it, but it ain't. We are five very different men. Most of us are loners, if you get what I mean. We love each other, we do. But we been having to make it on our own so long it's hard to get in step. A soul man is that. Singular. Soul Clan is more a beautiful idea to me. I would have given it a chance if Otis had lived. Man's head was on straight. Didn't *nobody* fight with Otis Redding. I always looked to Otis sort of as . . . oh, hell, I don't know. An ambassador for us all. Talk to white, talk to black, don't piss nobody off, but don't Tom neither. So far as I am concerned—and if this tour takes off, I'll love it, don't get me wrong—but so far as I see, the future of the Soul Clan died with Otis Redding. Now here I go, though, rappin' outa my head. But that's me. That's my motor mouth."

As one of the original rap bards, Joe had been obliged to field a lot of press conference questions asking his opinion of the wave of current rap music, by artists like Grandmaster Flash and his Furious Five, Kurtis Blow, and deejay Afrika Bambaataa's Soulsonic Force. Most of them were still too far uptown or out in New York's boroughs—in Brooklyn and the Bronx—for Joe to have heard of them out in Texas. But he said he knew enough to say that theirs seemed to be a very city thing, whereas he'd cut his syncopated parables as country wisdom. Couldn't see a kid from Bushwick coming up with "Ain't Gonna Bump No More (with No Big Fat Woman)."

"I love what these kids are doin' now," he told me. "But you know there are some things in what I said that are still true."

He was up again, slapping out another flat-palmed stutter rhythm, going on in his sandpaper singsong. A few lines into it, I realized he was playing around with his 1970 song "You're Right, Ray Charles":

"Tellya now a song don't have to say much now—nuh I tell yuh givem beat—beat BEAT . . . eighties kids don't wanna hear no words . . . they wanna move they big ol' feet . . . *eeee-eyah.*"

His voice dropped to a whisper after the effort. "That's it now, ain't it? Some of the lyrics I've heard on these city rap records are real clever. I like 'em a lot. Some are real angry, much more open about stuff than any of us could be. And that's good. But wouldn't nobody listen—in Harlem, in Watts, nowhere—if it didn't have that BOOM BOOM BOOM, that crashin' almighty beat."

Joe sat back and poured some more Kool-Aid down his throat. Don Covay was rounding folks up for the trip to the radio station. Joe tipped his cowboy hat and rose to leave.

"The Clan is callin' this black man, and he is pleased to go. Now ain't *that* a kick in the head?"

Following the next night's disastrous concert, the next time the Soul Clan met was at the funeral for Joe Tex in Navasota. He was home on his farm when he was stricken with a heart attack and died, on August 13, 1982. Just before football season.

21

Respect When I Come Home

Fa fa fa fa fa fa fa fa fa.

—OTIS REDDING

TWO WEEKS BEFORE CHRISTMAS of 1967 Solomon Burke arrived in Macon for Otis Redding's funeral, carrying a new fishing knife in his pocket. He had bought it months before, anticipating his next visit to the Big O Ranch. Otis's boys were just babies; so was his daughter. But Solomon had bought it, figuring their daddy could break it in for them on some shiny fat trout. Otis was the soul of patience at the end of a fishing line.

"Otis ran a stone soul picnic there," says Solomon. "It was family. Kids, dogs, horses, fishing, and just about any soul star you could name at the time. We all went to visit like summer camp."

Lots of singers have stories about sojourns at Otis's ranch, about terrified city soul men on runaway horses and huge barbecues and kids rolling in the high grass. The ranch, Solomon says, was like the man himself, "big, sprawling, and generous."

As a farmer's son Otis knew a good deal about the dirt he bought and

331

how to get the most from it. Solomon Burke says Otis told him his ancestors had been slaves on that very land, so he knew it had been well tended. Before his career took off, Otis said he trucked a lot with dirt. He earned $1.25 an hour drilling through layers of shale and clay and loam for well water. In 1965, just a year after the Apollo Theater had offered a mere $400 for the "newcomer" from Macon, Georgia, he had earned enough to buy nearly 400 acres and stock it with horses, cattle, and hogs and build houses for himself and his parents.

"Otis liked to fly over his land, you know, liked to look at it from away up there," says Solomon. "He'd bank, dip the wings for the babies when he went over the house. That meant Daddy was coming home."

Otis Redding died on December 10, 1967, when the small plane carrying him and the Bar-Kays fell into icy Lake Monona, an inconsequential little puddle just two minutes from the airport at Madison, Wisconsin. *Sepia* magazine later ran a photograph of his body strapped in its seat, with an eyewitness account by the only survivor, Bar-Kay Ben Cauley. Otis's longtime friend Joe Simon says his hands and feet went stone cold when he heard the news of the crash.

"I was always scared of those bitty planes. Now, Otis and I both worked for [manager] Phil Walden. And Phil's father and Otis were always trying to get me on this little plane to Muscle Shoals. Anyhow, this time I made up my mind to go ahead and get on it. Otis was always trying to help me, see? And he was gonna help me break pop; we were gonna open at the Fillmore West. So we were trying to get some things together. Something came up at the last minute, but I was supposed to be on that plane with him when he was killed. Ain't that a gas?"

Instead, along with Joe Tex and Johnnie Taylor, Joe Simon was a pallbearer. Otis's widow, Zelma, asked him to sing "Jesus Keep Me Near the Cross" at the services in the Macon City Auditorium. Booker T. Jones played the organ while Johnnie Taylor sang "I'll Be Standing By." There was no shortage of beautiful voices, for the mourners included Aretha Franklin, Stevie Wonder, Percy Sledge, James Brown, Fats Domino, Don Covay, and Little Richard. A eulogy was delivered by Jerry Wexler, who noted the fact that Otis's fellow performers constantly asked him why he still lived in Macon when he was rich enough to live nearly anywhere. Otis maintained that he was happy there and that he believed southern blacks who had made it should stay there to help others find a toehold. With this in mind, he'd taken twenty-year-old Arthur Conley down to Muscle Shoals and set him up in the studio with his band and his own composition, "Sweet Soul Music," a hit in April 1967. Like his idol Sam Cooke, Otis Redding had formed his own publishing company and a management firm. All of it was run out of Macon, where his previous business experience was limited to parking cars and mopping floors.

"Otis's composition 'Respect' has become an anthem for peoples around the world," Wexler's eulogy concluded. "Respect is something Otis achieved for himself in a way few people do. Otis sang, 'Respect when I come home.' And Otis has come home."

After the services Otis was buried in his land. At the request of Atlantic Records, Steve Cropper went back into the Stax studio to finish the song that Otis had intended for his next single.

"It seemed impossible," Cropper says. "It was hard just to go into the studio. Otis *was* Stax, and we were in pieces. But we did it. Sent the first version to New York, and Jerry sent it back, saying you couldn't hear Otis's voice enough. I still disagree with him. But I respect him, so I changed it a little bit."

In 1968 "(Sittin' on) the Dock of the Bay" became Otis Redding's only gold single, selling 1.4 million copies. It was also his only single to reach number one on the pop charts. The tempo was more languid than usual, the voice just a bit rougher owing to his recovery from throat surgery. And the sound was a touch more complex and plush than the standard Stax issue of the time, spiffed up with rolling surf and sea gull cries. The lyrics were partially composed as Otis sat on a rented yacht in California, but the voice was that of a broke, homesick southern black man. Like the man in Gladys Knight's "Midnight Train to Georgia," he was 2,000 miles from home, no prospects, nothing to live for.

"Look like nothin' gonna change . . ."

Unlike the hapless, becalmed man in "Dock of the Bay," Otis had plenty of wind in his sails, was at the peak of his career at just twenty-six, happy, genial, and in no particular hurry. The last we heard of his voice it trailed off the end of "Dock" in a lazy, ambling whistle.

"Everybody thinks that was on purpose," Cropper says. "The whistling was a one-shot deal. Otis couldn't think of anything to say to fade out, so he started whistling."

Cropper says it bruised his ego and disrespected his late friend when a few people in the company suggested that it was Otis's death rather than the quality of the record that made it such a big seller. But he and Otis worked closely together, cowriting and producing. And "Dock of the Bay" had been part of a plan they had to widen Otis's market a tad.

"There was a little more pop in it than anything Otis had ever done. But my theory was, and Otis's, too, was that if we're really going to break it, we're going to have to have a little pop. You can't just keep doing R and B songs like 'Mr. Pitiful' and all, because it's only going to cater to a certain amount of people. I think a lot of Otis's pop recognition came from things like 'Satisfaction,' stuff that people were familiar with, from the Stones, and 'Loving You Too Long,' which is a real *slick* R and B song. It's not blues; it's real crafted stuff. And I think *that's* what got Otis happening."

Though he had been recording three years—pillow drenchers like "Pain in My Heart" and "That's How Strong My Love Is"— it wasn't until 1965 that Otis had a huge hit on the soul charts with his own composition "Respect."

"What Otis was to be came together in that record," Cropper says. Lyrically it was undiluted Otis, simple but insistent. R-E-S-P-E-C-T. *Got* to have it. Musically it was Otis by way of Stax, hammering busted phrases directly over Al Jackson's rolling snare, running straight up a verse with that wide, loud voice, trailing the horns behind him like so much spent rocket fuel. If there is a single word to describe Otis Redding's career and his vocal style, it's *ascent*.

Onstage he built his delivery from a crouch, unfurling the big, tall body, rising with the horns and the tempo, arms high, face lifted, singing *straight up*. Live and on record, Otis Redding could levitate. And if it looked natural and easy, it was, as Cropper says, crafted, like a thundering but thought-out sermon. From the start, once he gave up trying to imitate Little Richard, a boyhood idol, Otis was possessed of complete control— of the arrangements and the histrionics. He wrote lyrics, but refused to be confined by them. He let his voice go where it wanted, but he made sure the horn and guitar lines fitted snugly around it. It was plain, deliberate music. And it all came together at just the right time.

Unlike so many soul men before him, Otis Redding did not have to make his way in an overwhelmingly hostile landscape. People were ready to listen, as Ben E. King suggested, to deeper southern soul. In 1965 James Brown had breached the pop charts with his first Top Ten hit, "Papa's Got a Brand New Bag"; Pickett scored with "In the Midnight Hour." And the English groups topping the charts were doing so with a lot of unabashed soul covers. The year of "Respect," 1965, the Rolling Stones' *Out of Our Heads* album was nothing less than an homage to

American soul, with covers of Don Covay's "Mercy, Mercy," Solomon Burke's "Cry to Me," Marvin Gaye's "Hitch Hike," and Otis's own "That's How Strong My Love Is."

Black and white artists were giving one another the high five across the Atlantic. *Ebony* magazine followed the Animals' Eric Burdon on a pilgrimage to the Apollo, accompanied on the subway by neophyte photographer Linda Eastman (now married to Paul McCartney). And in 1966 Otis Redding paid the Rolling Stones the highest compliment by cutting their "Satisfaction" as a solid soul song. *"Got-ta, got-ta,"* Otis's trademark soul stutter hauls the song to the instrumental bridge and dangles it there. "Keep onna groove," he hollers at the Stax musicians, and they do, horns answering the guitar, rhythm set by the cheerful tyranny of Al Jackson, a drummer so forceful he often used the butt end of his sticks. When at last Otis crashes through the final verses and trails off, yelling that he wants it early in the evenin', in the midnight hour . . . "Satisfaction" ends not as an I-can't-get-no complaint but as a triumph.

Respect and satisfaction were appropriate titles for that pivotal year, 1965–66. By the time Otis Redding was twenty-four and really selling records, he had achieved a fusion of old blues and new rock, of rough country music and sophisticated commercial hooks. His soul could play Vegas, given the current soul tide, but the roots were stubbornly, proudly Macon by way of Memphis.

By 1967 that tide was strong enough worldwide to propel Otis Redding to the number one spot in England's *Melody Maker* poll for best male artist, knocking out that other Memphis hybrid who had owned the title for nine years running, Elvis Presley. In that year Otis Redding sold more records than Dean Martin and Frank Sinatra combined. Janis Joplin was a fan; Bob Dylan went to see him four nights in a row. Though his triumphant appearance at the Monterey International Pop Festival in June 1967 has been ballyhooed as Otis's crossover high point, he had done it long before, in the studio.

It was not your standard string and show tune–sweetened crossover. Except for that slight mellowing on "Dock of the Bay," Otis Redding did not change his music. It can be argued that he couldn't have if he'd tried—would probably have roughed up "Yankee Doodle Dandy" with a crossfire of fa-fa-fa-fas. Instead, Otis Redding made pop audiences cross over to meet him. His acceptance at Monterey was just a media-exposed replay of what had already happened when he toured overseas and played before white southern and college audiences in America. By 1967 Otis "Love Man" Redding, the Big O, had elbowed the soul man into a more hospitable place.

In his own mind he was simply carrying on what others had begun. It was his sole intention, he told an interviewer, to "fill the silent void caused by Sam Cooke's death." And what he may have lacked in comparison with Cooke's awesome vocal beauty, he made up for in warm, big-boned grace.

"No weirdness, no scandal," says Cropper. "There was something totally different about Otis, but at the same time it was real common. He didn't have the personal hang-ups most artists of his caliber have. And I don't think he had an ounce of prejudice anywhere in his system. If he did, he sure as hell hid it. Otis took crap like any other black man. He had his down times. But Otis knew how to turn it around. I would say he had a real big capacity for joy. Hell, he could wallow in a blues. But I fell most in love with Otis when he just tore it up to celebrate."

The first music that Otis said he remembered was the happy *ad hoc* stuff that floated from parties and picnics his parents took him to as a child. Otis Redding, Sr., was a farmer and a preacher. He had moved his wife and six children to Macon from Dawson, Georgia, where Otis was born in 1941. Picnicking out at Sawyer's Lake in Macon, Otis heard everything from blues to calypso. A childhood favorite was the Caribbean-infused tale of a black fugitive called "Run Joe," a song redone recently, New Orleans style, by the Neville Brothers. Otis said he loved anything Hank Williams did, and he dug Eddie Arnold. He heard gospel as well. Otis, Sr., led the congregation at the Mount Ivy Baptist Church, and all his children sang there. Otis was eight when he joined the choir and an impressionable thirteen when he heard the bizarre carryings-on of a local R & B singer who had changed his name to Little Richard. He was enthralled by the lunatic, eye-rolling delivery. By his mid-teens, Otis "Rockhouse" Redding was creating his own tenuous ruckus, scaring up local gigs with various bands and blowing rival contestants off talent-show stages with his lung-shredding versions of Elvis Presley songs. Fifteen Sunday nights running he walked off with the top prize at one show. On the sixteenth they wouldn't let him go on.

One of the groups that came in a consistent second to Otis was a black band called the Heartbreakers, managed by a white teenager named Phil Walden. By the time he hit his thirties, Walden would be a rock and soul impresario, guiding the careers of Otis Redding and the Allman Brothers and soul men like Sam and Dave, Eddie Floyd, Percy Sledge, Johnnie Taylor, Clarence Carter, Al Green, Joe Simon, and Arthur Conley. Besides the Walden talent agency, he would later start Capricorn Records, a southern rock label he masterminded with Jerry Wexler. The whole empire grew from just another teen infatuation.

Though he grew up in the city where Little Richard and James Brown did their chitlin apprenticeship, Walden was a stranger to black music until his older brother, Allen, came home from the Midwest with some R & B records and set off pinwheels behind his kid brother's eyes. Soon Phil Walden was wild for the Coasters and Hank Ballard. He was also partial to an up-and-coming local weirdo who actually got a record on the national charts. Though he had reinvented himself as Little Richard, Richard Penniman was still a dishwasher in Macon when his "Tutti Frutti" hit in 1956. Walden was sixteen and already booking bands for local dances when he made friends with Little Richard after spotting him on the street and hollering "Tutti frutti" at him. Richard shot back an "all rutti," and Walden fell deeper in thrall.

There were obstacles to his obsessions. Walden still couldn't get into the clubs he booked his black bands in. But he was outdoors, at Macon's Lakeside Park, in the middle of a white teenage crowd when he finally got the opportunity to meet the singer who had been consistently burying his acts at the talent show. Their encounter began a business partnership and a close friendship that lasted throughout Otis Redding's life.

Walden started booking Otis as a vocalist for a local band called Little Willie and the Mighty Panthers. Still, day jobs were a necessity. Otis had married Zelma in 1958, after a courtship that began when a band he worked with, the Pinetoppers, took to rehearsing next door to her father's house. Their son Dexter was born a year and a half after their marriage, and singing wasn't quite enough to make ends meet.

He couldn't give it up, though, and twice the habit cost him dearly. He got fired as a lot attendant for singing in parked cars and lost a second job as a hospital orderly for vocalizing in the halls. And so it went, until the much-vaunted "break." It happened at Stax, in Memphis, during a recording session Walden had arranged for Johnny Jenkins and the Pinetoppers. As driver and factotum, Otis went along. It was October 1962.

"I don't know how many stories you've heard, but there really is only one. I was right there," says Steve Cropper. "Now I'd come in contact with Otis, but I didn't pay any attention to him. I was dealing with Johnny [Jenkins] all day long. But according to Al [Jackson], he'd talked to Otis on a couple of breaks. And Otis told him, 'You know, I drive for Johnny, and I set up the stage and all that, but during the shows, I always go up and do some numbers.' Otis always came off sincere 'cause he was. So Al was real inquisitive. I don't know if he asked [manager] Joe Galkin or Johnny if Otis was legit. All I know was that when we got through cutting Johnny, Al says, 'Wait a minute, before you go.'

"The musicians were tired. A few had already left. Al says, 'Let's just see what this guy's got.' And so Jim [Stewart] says, 'That's fine, get him over here.' And he starts out with this tune 'These Arms of Mine.' We didn't have a piano player 'cause Booker was out for a bit. But Johnny still had his guitar plugged in, and he knew the song, and he played. I sat at the piano and just started playing the triplets. And Otis opened his mouth, and everybody went, 'Waaaaaaaaaa. Oh, my *God,* this guy is oozing with it, get the tape rolling.' We scrambled and pieced together a band."

The session log lists Johnny Jenkins on guitar, Booker T. Jones on keyboards, Lewis Steinberg on bass, Cropper on guitar, and Jackson on drums. Besides "These Arms," they cut a B side, "Hey Hey Baby."

"We cut that thing in about three or four takes," Cropper says. "And after that one, Otis had seventeen in a row. Never a flop. Ever. They all didn't sell a million pieces, but he never had what we call a stiff."

In Memphis in 1963 and 1964, Otis cut a mess of covers, like "Louie, Louie," "The Dog," and "Lucille." He had been writing for himself as well, songs like "Security" and "Mr. Pitiful." By 1964 he had recorded enough to release his first album, *Pain in My Heart.*

The title cut was a more passionate, masculine version of a ballad recorded by the first lady of New Orleans soul, Irma Thomas. Originally titled "Ruler of My Heart," it was written by R & B artist Aaron Neville, who produced Irma's records, and it was published under the name of his mother, Naomi. Recording that song the way he did was the start of a grand tradition for Otis Redding, who, in addition to writing his own stuff, could recut an old tune in ways the composer never dreamed of. On "Pain," Otis, who was never terrific at remembering lyrics anyhow, ad-libbed his words, addressing his vocal not to a tyrannical lover but to pain itself, making it a living, willful, attacking thing, his own voice taking a sledgehammer to Neville's melody, breaking it up with his own repetitions and asides ("someone stop this pain!").

As his records shot up the soul charts, Otis played more and bigger live dates, mainly in black club venues or white colleges. Though he was not overly fond of the road, things went well—except for one day, when he pulled into Houston with his band and discovered, to his horror, that James Brown was headlining across town the same night. When the two ran into each other that afternoon, Otis was almost inconsolable. He didn't think anyone would show up to see him since James had already sold out the Coliseum. Brown's then-manager Al Garner recalled that his boss just nodded and told Otis not to worry.

That night, at the Godfather's instructions, Garner had a car waiting outside the Coliseum. From the wings he heard James wind up his show by inviting everyone to join him at the Continental Showcase to see Mr. Otis Redding, his very good home friend from Macon, Georgia. So if they'd excuse him, he was heading on over. . . .

James's car was at the head of a mad soul road rally through the streets of Houston.

"We packed the place," James recalled when I asked him about it. "Me and Otis, we had a great time. His band knew all my numbers. We did 'Cold Sweat' together and a few other things."

The crowd, by Garner's account, was delirious over the dream double bill. A James Brown show was often memorable to Garner in terms of what it did to his wardrobe. That night he suffered the customary shredded suit. But never before had he lost his shoes.

Otis counted both wild men and sophisticates among his musical heroes. And though he got over his Little Richard imitations quickly enough, he made no secret of his devotion to Sam Cooke. Only one of the albums he put together himself did not contain a Sam Cooke song. It was with Cooke's "Shake" that Otis went all to blazes onstage, especially at Monterey. His album *Otis Blue,* cut just after Cooke's death, is clearly a tribute, with three of Sam's songs.

"Sam Cooke was Otis's complete idol," Cropper says. "He talked about him a lot, how Sam worked for a white company but was a black man to the end, that he was in total control of himself with his publishing and starting to manage young singers like Johnnie Taylor and all."

It does seem that Otis demanded the same commitments of himself. Besides forming his own publishing and management companies, he was an honest, eager-to-please performer who had no Sinatra-esque aspirations.

"I am not a blues singer or an R and B singer," he insisted. "I'm a soul singer. We go into the studio without anything prepared, just record what comes out. That's soul—the way you feel."

His description of the process is consistent with what Steve Cropper remembers of their sessions at Stax. By 1965 Otis Redding and Steve Cropper had become close friends and collaborators. Cropper played guitar for him and produced for him at times, and they wrote together often, from "Mr. Pitiful" right on up through "(Sittin' on) the Dock of the Bay."

"He'd have a few ideas, and I'd have a few ideas," Cropper says. "I guess he was heavier than me on melody because a lot of his lyrics were ad-libbed. There were instances where he would literally forget lyrics that he had written the night before and he'd just make up something on the fly. And that's what went out, if that's what was cut. You still cut your monos in those days. No way to take his voice off and redo it. You got what you got."

It followed that Otis was just as ad-lib with other people's lyrics. At one point the myth took root that Otis Redding, not Jagger and Richards, had written "Satisfaction." Cropper found it necessary to debunk the story by explaining that he had written out what he believed to be the correct lyrics by listening to the Rolling Stones' record. Cropper handed them to Otis, but halfway through the session they were on the floor. Once Otis had figured the proper trajectory for a song, the correct words were beside the point.

Often one night's live blooper could ripen into a habit. One evening, momentarily forgetting the words to "Respect," Otis frantically cued the band through a few extra choruses until it came to him. He picked up the missing verse, then took it all home in a mile-high finish. It became a favorite tactic, especially onstage. It wasn't as broadly theatrical as James Brown's cape routine, but it could lay them out just as flat.

In the studio, spontaneity was often a function of tight schedules. "So much of it was on the fly," Cropper says. "We'd grab him off the road and cut whatever we could find."

All those hurried sessions within the two years following *Pain in My Heart* resulted in two more albums, *Soul Ballads* and *Otis Blue*. But soul as practiced by Otis Redding was never more clearly defined than in his 1966 LP *Dictionary of Soul*. Contrary to what the title may imply, it was not cut as a "concept" album. Stax, as Cropper points out, was still a black record company. And black buyers were still buying more singles than albums since singles were all they could afford. Until the mid-sixties black LPs were cut only as sure things—bargain packages of already proved singles.

"In those days, once you got enough hit singles, you put out an album,"

Cropper says. "At the time Otis cut *Dictionary of Soul,* we were just getting out of that, thinking about doing albums on him. And we didn't have much product."

Dictionary of Soul, then, was business as usual, a random mix of covers, a standard or two, and, in this case, seven Redding compositions or collaborations. Still, it's a distinctive collection for its display of just how much that frayed, untidy voice could do.

"Try a Little Tenderness" is the shining light on the record and one of Otis's best-loved soul ballads. It's built on that zero to sixty vertical structure that worked so well for him, quiet and thoughtful at first, then louder and more deliberate, up to a flat-out fit at the end, all big horns, reaching that wild, hiccuping summit of gotta-gotta's. "Fa Fa Fa Fa Fa (Sad Song)" was something Otis came up with while trying to line out a horn pattern for Jerry Wexler. The collection includes two outright wallows, "I'm Sick Y'All" and "Hawg for You," a blues that has the singer root-root-rootin'—and it's not for truffles.

He kept making gutsy, sweaty records right up until his death, and according to his songwriting partner, he intended to do more of the same. He was an instinctual, episodic writer who claimed no divine inspiration. He said he got the horn introduction to Arthur Conley's "Sweet Soul Music" from the bloop-bloop of percolating coffee on the Maxwell House commercials. "Mr. Pitiful" came to him one night after an especially dispiriting gig.

"Some polite folks name it basic," Cropper says. "Hell, it was *black.* Otis worked in simple, basic black. Now that limited him on the charts, and it also made him great. The man would make Gershwin sound greasy. Whatever changes we might have made if he'd lived, you can bet they wouldn't have been drastic. Just look at what he was doing right up till the day he died."

The duet album he made in early 1967 with Carla Thomas, *The King and the Queen,* gave the best indication of Redding's resolute sense of himself. "Tramp," a remake of the old Lowell Fulsom song, has been called "one of the blackest sounds ever to come out of the south." Otis and Carla are at each other like wolverines, back and forth in a raucous, funky domestic disturbance.

There is little film footage of Otis Redding save the well-known segment from the film *Monterey Pop.* But I do remember seeing a riveting TV clip, circa '67 and probably long since lost, of Otis and Carla doing "Tramp." They stood on one of those stiff, creepy cardboard sets, but once they got to it, the action was nothing like that you'd ever see on *Shindig* or *Hullabaloo*. Packed into a short, tight skirt, Carla advanced her tiny self, mouth flapping, finger wagging. Otis bent backward under the assault, then came to himself, leaned over her, and bellowed back. It was *The Honeymooners,* sepia style, a complete crackup and oddly hip for sixties TV.

The rest of the *King and Queen* LP was also a return to blues and R & B roots, with Aaron Neville's "Tell It Like It Is" and Otis's own "Ooh Wee Baby." They cut the whole thing, eleven songs, in three days in February 1967. Then the entire Stax road show flew off to Europe where *Otis Redding Live in Europe* and *The Stax/Volt Revue Live in Paris* were recorded.

The Stax/Volt European tour in March 1967 stunned the Memphis crew. They knew they were selling well at home, but nothing had prepared them for the outpouring of adoration on the other side of the ocean.

"From day one," Cropper says, "we got off the plane, and there's like a hundred reporters, hundreds of fans. We were expecting to sort of sneak into the country. It was Otis, Sam and Dave, Arthur Conley, the Mar-Keys, Booker T. and the MGs, Carla Thomas. We literally had to stop the show, I think it was in Liverpool. Sam and Dave were on, and the people in the balcony were rocking so much the security men thought it was gonna fall. Once word got out about our shows, we were told beforehand by security that Sam and Dave or Otis could not go into the audience, couldn't shake hands and all that stuff 'cause it could be riotous."

Perhaps it's the intensity of that reaction captured on record that makes those *Live in Europe* sides more vibrant than Otis's half of the Redding/Hendrix LP recorded live at the Monterey Pop Festival. Though the Monterey appearances have been likened to the discovery of the Dead Sea scrolls for the "emergence" or "crossover" of Redding and Hendrix, they were completely unrelated to their distinction and maturity as artists. For both of them, all the elements had already been in place.

Both Otis and Jimi faced the 50,000-plus crowd as "new artists" despite the fact that between them they had more rock basics than the rest of the acts combined. Hendrix had knocked around some of the same clubs in Macon as Otis, having done time in the R & B backwaters playing with Little Richard and with the Isley Brothers. Sam and Dave fired him from their band for his weird innovations, but before he bent and fractured those root guitar lines and blasted off for Electric Ladyland, Hendrix and his Fender Stratocaster had been part of the heaviest soul band in Harlem under the direction of King Curtis. As part of the session band Hendrix had cut "Soul Serenade" with Curtis for Atlantic.

Tucked into a bill with the likes of the Association and The Mamas and the Papas, both of them blasted the sandals off the tie-dyed celebrants at Monterey, and both were doubtless elated. Still, though the Hendrix/Redding liner notes burble on about "the strength and joy of a new culture" promised for the Love Generation, neither man would make it to thirty. Stax and soul were peaking, too, headed, unwittingly, for the end of their good, good thing.

Beyond the live performances recorded in 1967 and the duet album with Carla Thomas, Otis had not cut much else, partly owing to throat surgery for the removal of strain-induced polyps. In December, when he felt his voice was strong enough, he went back into the studio. His last session was on December 7, three days before he died.

"That week we did 'Dock of the Bay,' we did a bunch of stuff," Cropper remembers. "We had just gone to a four-track system. So we had a lot of things in the can with Otis's vocal on a single track, and he was singing so good. We would stay after the sessions, which were in the daytime. We would stay overnight, just [Bar-Kay] Ronnie [Caldwell] and Otis and I. The three of us made two or three records with us playing all the instruments. But we also went in and redid his vocal on about ten or eleven songs. So when Otis died, we had like fourteen good tracks left in the can, all good, clean vocal tracks."

For nearly a year following Otis's death Steve Cropper spent a lot of time in the studio working with his friend's voice. Beyond the "Dock of the Bay" single, he worked with Duck Dunn and Booker T. to remix some tracks for a double album, *History of Otis Redding*. The posthumous *Dock of the Bay* album was most noteworthy for the title cut, but *The Immortal Otis Redding,* also released in 1968, contains a lot of those final session songs; ten of them were recorded during the last six months of 1967. Despite other collections released since, including *Otis Redding Recorded Live* (previously unreleased live material recorded at the Whiskey A Go Go and rediscovered in the Fantasy Records catalogue), the Stax studio cuts on *The Immortal* are far superior. One song, a lovely ballad called "I've Got Dreams to Remember," was cowritten by Otis and Zelma Redding. "Think About It" was a funky collaboration with Don Covay. Like the duet album with Carla Thomas, it was bedrock soul. And if Otis Redding intended to make any changes in his style, indications are that he might only have deepened that intensity and just slicked things up a bit.

"Ten days before his plane went down, Otis asked me to produce him," Jerry Wexler says. "Why? He had, like, a horizontal texture to a lot of Atlantic stuff. And Stax was vertical. Otis was great at taking a tune to the moon. But he wanted to change a bit. He said he wanted a denser sound."

This wasn't inconsistent with feelings Otis expressed in an interview with Jim Delehant a few months before his death. Delehant asked whether Otis felt R & B had changed a great deal. He said he thought it had, and it was a good thing:

> I'd like to say something to the R & B singers who were around ten years ago. They've got to get out of the old bag. Listen to the beat of today and use it on records. Don't say we're gonna go back ten years and use this old swing shuffle. That's not it. I know what the kids want today and I aim all my stuff at them. I'd like to see all those singers make it again. I'd like to take Fats Domino, Little Richard, Big Joe Turner, Clyde McPhatter and bring them into the bag of today. They'd have hits all over again. The blues changes from day to day. It all depends on what the kids will be dancing to, what they're moving to. I watch people when I sing. If they're stompin' their foot or snappin' their fingers, then I know I got something. But if they don't move, then you don't have anything. Five years from now, I know the kids are going to be tired of my singing. If I can keep a good mind, with the help of the good Lord, I'm gonna keep producing records.

Otis often said that he wanted to get more into the production end. Within a year, he told Cropper, he wanted to work with more new artists and take some time off the road to experiment a bit in the studio.

Said Cropper: "He was actually talking about quitting the road for a year or so, renting a house in Memphis. Said, 'We're gonna write for a solid year.' He talked like that up till the day he left Memphis. And he died three days later."

The end of Stax's glory years wasn't far off either. The year after Otis died, Stax's distribution agreement with Atlantic ended, and artists began to leave the label.

"Like someone blow on a dandelion. Poof. We scattered," said Sam

Moore. He and Dave Prater left in 1968. The same year Jim Stewart sold the company to Paramount Pictures, a soon-to-be-subsidiary of the giant Gulf & Western. He stayed on to run Stax and eventually bought it back four years later. But in 1969, talking to *Billboard*'s Paul Ackerman for a special issue devoted to the Memphis sound, Stewart was adamant about maintaining Stax's soulful integrity: "We keep abreast of the changing times, but at the same time we remain close to the roots. . . . The roots are basic, and that pure, virgin stream must remain uncontaminated."

On one level Stewart kept to his promise, recording black acts like Albert King, Little Milton, the Dramatics, and the Emotions. The Staple Singers rivaled Curtis Mayfield in soul sermonizing, securing two of Stax's rare number one pop hits with "Respect Yourself" in 1972 and "I'll Take You There" in 1973. Isaac Hayes spoke to blacks with rhythm rather than lyric, in seamless, highly arranged dance tracks that presaged the disco years.

"Some very funky stuff went down at Stax in the end," Hayes insists. He blames the company's "failure of management." Steve Cropper believes the fatal blow was dealt during Atlantic's merger with Warner Communications when, he feels, "nobody cared what happened to Stax." Others insist the decline was due to distribution and production problems Stax experienced once it was bought by Paramount.

Whatever the reasons, the decline was swift and irrevocable, and it had its effect on the entire Memphis music scene, much the way Motown's move to Los Angeles affected Detroit. In the last three years before Stax's bankruptcy in 1975, Stewart took to avoiding the press and the inevitable questions about trouble in his happy interracial house. His sister Estelle Axton hopped on the disco train long enough to record a novelty miscreant, "Disco Duck," part of the contamination Stewart had railed against. Booker T. and the MGs began to lose their hard groove edge, recording limp sides like "Mrs. Robinson." After 1972 they ceased working together in the studio, then split up.

By then Stax's original studio musicians had certainly earned their spots as company execs. But the next crop of studio recruits was not as well disposed toward the old, manual methods that had yielded all that dark, dense funk. They liked to sweeten things with orchestral touches in the vein of the ultraslick Philly soul that was charting well by the early seventies. The rest of the stuff on the charts was schizophrenic at best, strung somewhere between the caftaned excesses of black Romeo Barry White and arena rock acts like Led Zeppelin and Elton John. Disco and heavy metal made a lot of loud, homogenized noise, and across the country, regional sounds were becoming extinct. Chess had folded in Chicago in 1968; Motown had left Detroit in 1971.

And in Memphis the exodus continued. Native son Al Green enjoyed a brief, flaming few years as a primo soul man—he had virtually no competitors at that point. But shortly after the death of Al Jackson, whose drumming had provided the crucial rhythms for his soul hits, Green disappeared back into the sanctuary of the church. Both Booker T. Jones and Steve Cropper moved West to California. Producer Chips Moman, who had worked at his own American Studios and as an independent producer for Stax, moved to Nashville to work with country artists like Willie Nelson. Isaac Hayes resettled in Atlanta. Stax assets were first sold at auction in 1975, on the steps of the Shelby County Courthouse. Even its catalogue left Memphis; it was bought by California-based Fantasy Records, which has since marketed reissues and collections of old Stax hits. Not to be outdone by other rock mythmakers, Stax's decline ended on a sinister note, when MGs' drummer Al Jackson was murdered by an intruder in his Memphis home in 1975. All in all, Memphis remained true to its history, losing most of its homegrown goodies to the rest of the country.

Phil Walden, who has said on several occasions that southern rock, if not soul, shall rise again, did record a thirteen-year-old black singer in Macon on his Capricorn label in 1972. The song was called "Love Is Bigger Than Baseball," and it did very well in England. The flip side was called "God Bless." The artist was Otis Redding's son Dexter, and when I spoke to him in the offices of Epic Records, distributor of what he calls his "adult" music, he said he preferred to forget he had made it.

"Aw, it was a kiddie record. I didn't know what all I was doing."

Dexter and his younger brother, Otis, III, along with another Macon musician, Mark Lockett, formed their own group, the Reddings, a few years ago. They played the same kinds of talent shows in Macon that their father had, though the house band often included a few members of the Allman Brothers Band. Instead of Little Richard and Elvis covers, they sang Top Forty stuff by the Jackson Five.

Now that they have completed a third album, their own sound is more funk than R & B, thanks in large part to Dexter's precipitous bass and the fact that they moved to the city—Washington, D.C.—in order to record. They had a dance hit, "Remote Control," that made it to number three in the soul charts in 1981, and that wasn't a bad debut. Their mother, Zelma, has gone out with them on the road. All of them make decisions about the family record company. It's called Believe in a Dream.

Otis and Dexter say they do love their father's work, especially that first ballad "These Arms of Mine." And though they were just babies during the heyday of southern soul, they came of age smack in the middle of the wave of southern rockers like the Allmans, Marshall Tucker, and the Charlie Daniels Band. They listened to them all in Macon the way their father had listened to white country musicians, and played with some of the Allmans at those talent shows. But when the big break came—a fifteen-city national tour—it was as the opening act for Motown funk king Rick James.

"I guess you could call us hybrids or something," Dexter said. "We came up in Macon, and we grew up listening to soul and southern rock; but we were really into Top Forty and the Jacksons and such. Once we went to live in D.C., we started being hip to what city bands were doing."

"Even though we spend a lot of time in Washington, Macon is still home," Otis said. "It's still the place. You know, our father's legacy is a real nice thing. Everywhere we go, people stop us and go on and on about what he meant to them. He gave them a lot of memories. But for us, there's home. The land he bought, the ranch. The music was for everybody. But home—that was for us."

"There may not be anybody recording in Macon just now—in much of the South, for that matter," Dexter continued. "That doesn't mean there's no music there. If you came up there, you know where to find it."

22
And the South Shall Rise Again

Continue to work with the faith that honor and suffering is redemptive. Go back to Mississippi, go back to Alabama, go back to South Carolina, go back to Georgia. . . .

—Reverend Martin Luther King, Jr.

"SHERMAN BURNED IT, but the Sun Belt has turned it." The voice on the Atlanta radio station is going on, in Vegematic-ad pitch, about the miracle possibilities of the New South. Racial understanding . . . newfound industrial prosperity . . . Peachtree Street high rises sprung from the heart of this old southern city. The announcer's voice echoes off the bare walls of the apartment Isaac Hayes keeps for his musical and physical workouts. Though he has a home outside town, he comes here at least five days a week.

The six-room apartment is sparsely furnished but heavily wired. There are more phones than pieces of furniture, as well as video equipment and stacks of games like Crypto-Logic, Odyssey, and Alpine Skiing. Bodybuilding equipment rests on the floor, alongside canisters of protein supplements, piles of muscle magazines, and a weight training encyclopedia called *Bill Pearl's Keys to the Inner Universe*. A gray steel electric piano has a room to itself. Phones ring, and on a TV screen opposite the sofa, Richard Simmons is whining about why you shouldn't bad-mouth tofu. For an empty apartment, there's a lot of chatter.

The sound of shower water stops, and finally Isaac appears, looking like an eighties Othello in a black and white vertically striped caftan. Even in soft terry cloth, he is as imposing as the Isaac Hayes who used to appear onstage in a tuxedo jacket made of chains. Wincing at the sound, he switches off the TV and the radio and hits a button to still the four phone lines that have been blinking, ringing, and buzzing.

"My electronic smoke screen," he says, folding himself onto a sofa. He says that he realizes he's a tough man to catch up with. Since his well-publicized bankruptcy in 1976, he says, he has kept mainly to himself. He has been putting things back together, here in this capital of the New South. Though he grew up in Memphis and grew to love it, his last years at Stax were not pleasant.

The high points he remembers fondly—the heady years as writer/producer with his partner David Porter, when they barreled off hit after hit for Sam and Dave and Mabel John. And when that wave of Memphis soul began to fade, Isaac Hayes came up with *Hot Buttered Soul,* a solid but experimental LP that augured a brief, final boomlet at Stax. That was in 1970. A year later, when the pneumatic platform raised Isaac Hayes, his bare torso draped in chains, into the midst of the 1971 Oscar ceremonies to play his composition, the nominated track from the movie *Shaft,* millions of viewers worldwide watched, fascinated, or at the very least amused. It wasn't exactly *The Sound of Music.*

"There you had black Moses ascending," Isaac says. "Here was my weird black self elevated, so to speak, just beaming out over the whole world. If you had any doubts about yourself, a moment like that will make you believe."

"Shaft" won the Oscar and made it to number one on the pop charts, and by the end of 1971 Isaac Hayes had become the Stax franchise, responsible, he claims, for 69.5 percent of its gross revenue. He had a gold-plated limousine, a cavern full of designer furs, and a spit-shined bad and bald image. In the era of the Afro, a smooth, shiny bald skull put a reverse macho spin on black pride.

"I suppose bald was as black as you could get," he says. "And I don't know, maybe some people saw the beard as sort of menacing. But I never really thought about it. People still tell me that *Hot Buttered Soul* is one of those must-have records and how much they dig the cover with just that over-the-top shot of my head on it. I was just fooling around with the photographer. We did it as a joke, but everyone liked it 'cause it was different and it was out front.''

Stax album art was traditionally pretty lame, featuring photo heads on cartoon figures, or weirdly floating silhouettes, or, as in the case of Otis Redding's *Otis Blue,* a creamy, dreamy blond woman. Isaac was relieved that by the time he left producing for performing, he didn't have to mess with that kind of careful Sambo marketing. Following *Hot Buttered Soul,* his *Black Moses* cover featured Isaac cloaked and hooded like some desert prophet. Onstage he got "kinda outrageous" as he stood slamming at his keyboards in tights, tunics, and gold and silver suits of mail.

"I had a chain dinner jacket, chain shirts, even a chain tux with tails," he says. "That tux was *bad.* But I had to watch how I landed on the piano stool."

Looking so bad could be exhausting throughout a two-hour stage show. By 1972 the Isaac Hayes touring company was featuring no fewer than forty players, including backup singers and strings. All of it, plus thirty or forty pounds of two-inch metal links, was a lot to hold up seven nights a week, at Tahoe or on the concert hall trail.

"I was just thinking the other day that it might be time to go back to the chains," Isaac says. "People are always telling me they'd like to see the 'old Isaac Hayes,' whoever he was. I'd be in better shape for it now, that's for sure."

With discipline that sometimes surprises him, Isaac has been resculpting his body with diet supplements and punishing workouts. He says he started running during his bankruptcy mess, pounding up and down country roads, just listening to the blood in his head.

"Miles and miles and miles," he says. "Right now I'm heavily into karate. In fact, I hurt like hell today. I go three times a week, and to the body-building gym nearly every day. But I work on a different part of the body every time. I do it all—squats, clean and jerk. From a squat I can do three hundred and fifteen pounds, which isn't so bad."

He says he got into all of it to escape the bad memories, which are a lot harder to lift. He is only forty-two, but by his reckoning, he has had a few distinct lives. He has been poor and black, has gone from hard-core R & B to dance to soft-core sepia mood music, from rich and black to comfortable and black, and lest he forget any of those stages, they're all set down on vinyl and magnetic tapes.

"I am glad it exists in the mind," he says. "Glad that sound survives time. Because damn near everything else was sold at auction. I have been auctioned too damn many times."

It first happened in 1975, when Stax went under and the rights to some Otis Redding and Sam and Dave material went to the highest bidder, a bank. Soon after, in his personal bankruptcy, caused, he says, "by too many management types and not enough management," marshals and IRS agents disposed of Isaac's cars, home, clothes, linens, even his croquet set, to offset half a million dollars in IRS liens.

"At least I got out with my health and my sanity."

His mother lost both, shortly after Isaac was born in 1942, in Covington, Tennessee. His was a sharecropping family, and after generations of hard, hard times one or two in a family will just drop the bucket from sheer exhaustion.

"You can die of thirst," Isaac says, "two feet from the well."

His mother never quite returned to herself after his birth and died in a mental institution when he was a year and a half old. At seven he moved with relatives to Memphis. He sang gospel while he was a student at Manassas High School. He had a little R & B group, Sir Isaac and the Doodads, and always he had a big pair of ears.

"I was a radio kid. The first stuff I heard was country and western, Hank Williams and all that. Then I listened to everything—jazz, the Hit Parade. I was always in little bands; we played basically R and B stuff. I lived with a jazz musician for a time, and he taught me a lot. And of course, I grew up listening to Rufus Thomas on WDIA. He was pretty adventurous; he'd play stuff that wasn't well known; he'd break records locally. He had a show in the late afternoon, for an hour or two after school. Really my ears were open to everything. The first electric guitar I ever heard was from Sister Rosetta Tharpe, if you can believe that.

"I really liked Nat 'King' Cole. He was just about everybody's idol at the time. But I was also crazy—*crazy*—about Sam Cooke. He was in a car accident nearby, and he was hospitalized in Memphis. With some guys from the group I was in, I snuck into the hospital to see him. We found him, but he couldn't talk, had this thermometer in his mouth, and he smiled and mumbled, 'Can't talk, guys.' Then the nurse came in and threw us out. But it was good to see him in person, big as life against that pillow. We were just thrilled. He was such a beautiful man. And what was so important to us was that he was so sophisticated.

"That's what we wanted, you know. I was the same as any other black kid growing up in the fifties. I mean, in the white scheme of things, the blues weren't going to help you advance.

"I had to grow up about it. I listened hard to the blues and said, 'Yeah, that cat is talkin' about me.' It just took some time to free myself up and embrace it as part of myself."

That began to happen once he had signed on as a session musician for Stax, playing keyboards. Originally he filled in when Booker T. Jones was off at college. His first session was backing Otis Redding in July 1965, when he cut "Respect," "Satisfaction," and "I've Been Lovin' You Too Long."

"I worked as a session man for a good while. I already had a family to support. I teamed up with David [Porter] in 1963 or '64. I knew him. He went to a rival high school, and we were always competing against each other in talent shows. We teamed up, and it worked well."

It's fair to say that the Hayes/Porter partnership was responsible for the blazing success of Sam and Dave, thanks to songs like "Soul Man," "Hold On, I'm Coming," "I Thank You," "You Got Me Hummin'," and "Small Portion of Your Love."

"I took care of the instrumental end, the melody," Isaac says, "the horns, and the rhythm tracks, and David stood behind the baffling with the singers, teaching them the songs."

I ask Isaac about a few especially pretty horn and piano sections on some of those Sam and Dave songs, and for the first time he smiles.

"I had so much fun with those songs. I was a bit of a renegade. I messed with the horns quite a bit. Like the intro on 'Wrap It Up.' "

"Dah-dah-daa-dadadada-doodah dandn-dah dah dah . . ." He is singing the horn parts, poking the air with an index finger, the way he did when he was teaching a horn player during a session or trying something out on Jim Stewart beforehand.

"Now there were some disagreements in the happy house of Stax," he says. He is grinning and shaking his head. Asked to spell it out, he hesitates.

"Oh, well, okay. For some reason Jim Stewart just did not like minor keys. Yeah, yeah. The bread and butter of gospel and blues. He *hated* them, in fact, and would order something done over. Of course, you couldn't be at all funky and innovative if you didn't use some of those options. So we were always at work sneaking them in."

He closes his eyes and laughs, then segues into more dah-dahs, instantly identifiable as the opening riff to "Hold On, I'm Coming," a song that took root when David Porter was bellowing for Isaac to come on out of the studio bathroom.

"Dah-dah-dah dadn-dah . . . oh, I loved that. Those horns were a real stamp that said Stax."

Generally the horn section included Wayne Jackson on trumpet, Andrew Love and Floyd Newman on sax. They often worked with the MGs and became known as the Memphis Horns. They did other Memphis sessions for Chips Moman's American Studios, and for Stax, they filled out many a spare or oversimple tune. They could yank a listener into a song head-first, heralding the midnight hour or keeping a macho strut through "Soul Man."

With Otis Redding especially, the horns were exhorters, instrumental Raelettes, so to speak, spurring his vocals onward and upward. All those tight blasts pumped him to his vessel-popping "gotta-gottas." It's unsatisfying to hear any of those songs played in versions without the horns or, worse, to hear those horn parts souped up with slides and half note geegaws. The appeal of the Stax horn lines was their simplicity. They were neat, economical, and nearly always played with all instruments in unison.

"I loved the way those guys *heard,*" Isaac says. "They listened with one giant ear between them. Which, I guess, is the ultimate head arrangement."

I ask him about a lovely, ringing introduction to "Small Portion of Your Love," the kind of piano playing that made people call it *sweet* soul music.

"Yeah, that was me. I was in that studio *all* the time. Never went on the road, nothing at first. Just took care of business at home. Memphis was my universe—more specifically, that old movie house we worked in."

The leap from studio craftsman to recording artist came with the spectacular success of *Hot Buttered Soul.* It was Isaac's second album; he says he would rather forget his debut, *Presenting Isaac Hayes.* "It was done while I was, ah, under the influence of alcohol, and it was full of mistakes."

The second album was the result of another kind of intoxication—complete freedom. "That record was all me," he says. "I just went ahead and did what I wanted. I had all the studio time I needed, and there was no pressure on me. We were putting out twenty-six albums that year, so if twenty-five sold, it wouldn't matter if mine didn't."

The torrent of LPs was the result of an agreement Stax had made with its new owner, Paramount. During a lunatic two-week period nearly every artist on the label was hustled into the studio to produce material to satisfy contractual obligations. In the midst of such confusion Isaac found himself at liberty to experiment.

The resulting innovations—the extended soul rap on the eighteen-minute version of "By the Time I Get to Phoenix" and the layered, almost symphonic arrangement on "Walk On By"—have been credited with anticipating a new direction in black pop. Vocally Isaac veered away from the rawer Stax sound. Where Otis Redding sobbed and groaned, Isaac Hayes sang in a buttery croon that opened the door for the later excesses of bedroom bards like Teddy Pendergrass and Barry White.

Rhythmically Isaac's highly arranged, repetitive, insistent dance beats would broaden into disco; once it hit, he'd record an album called *Disco Connection,* in 1976. In 1971, he says, it was just an experiment.

"As a writer, I had always felt constrained by the two forty-five time limit. I wanted to try longer stuff because I felt I had to get deep, real deep into the listener's head with those repetitions, to keep at it until even if the head was stubborn, the body couldn't resist. I did that later on the *Shaft* album, too. When I have what I think is a good melody, I like to draw it out and play with it."

He says that it's okay if people want to call him the father of disco; he doesn't care, but he won't claim any special forethought. Stax always had such a straight, simple sound that it was like bingeing after a strict diet— so tempting to fill up a track with strings and wah-wah guitars, to heap on layers of sound.

"How much the long cuts, the repetitions, and all influenced dance music to come, I can't say. I didn't have any inkling that dance was going to become so big again. I mean, people have never stopped dancing. I just did what I felt like at the time, without any intentions other than what I felt within me."

By 1978 the record industry had turned the stuff of inspiration and rhythmic improvisation into an aural lobotomy kit, setting cartoon figures like the Village People out as costumed mouthpieces for the robotic repetitions in "Macho Man" and "Y.M.C.A." The dense curtain of sound that Isaac Hayes had experimented with became petrified in the hands of packagers, rather than producers. Most late seventies compositions were untroubled by the slightest breeze of melody or wit. But by the time white America was taking its first tentative steps to this sanitized-for-your-protection sound, blacks were already dancing to more sophisticated, idio-syncratic funk and rap beats.

"Well, you know it takes a good deal longer for white audiences to become hip to different forms of black music," Isaac says. "The stuff that's going on now, this funk, with all those sophisticated grooves, all that overlay, is beyond white audiences just now. Black audiences are tough. It's so much a part of the culture, the black experience, to be immersed in music that you better be *damn* good, or somebody will say, 'We can get ten kids off the street to do the same thing better.' White artists can get away with more mediocrity. Whites copped to disco so easily, I think, because the beat was so overwhelming."

It was the rigors of pleasing a tough black audience, Isaac says, that hatched his marathon soul rap on his cover of Glen Campbell's "By the Time I Get to Phoenix."

"I was doing a gig in a black club. People were just talking; they weren't paying attention. I figured I'd better do something. Now I knew they were going to think I was crazy to be doing a song by a white pop singer, so I figured I'd explain. And I started talking. Explaining why, as a black man, there were things I could draw on in the song, weaving in some personal stuff—I was going through a lot of heavy personal stuff at that time. And pretty soon they quieted down, and they were listening to me. So I sang the song, and at the end people went crazy. Some were crying. It was wild and very gratifying. I tried it again in a white club, and the response was the same."

Somewhere, he concedes, that kind of soulful spontaneity got blunted. Or buried. But for a couple of years, at that critical juncture in the early seventies, Isaac Hayes was the main pivot man. Gutbucket soul was being abandoned by threatened whites and restless blacks, and Isaac Hayes offered something to soothe both sets of aural jitters, with his tough chains and rhythms and his massaging love chatter. Two more albums, *To Be Continued* and *The Isaac Hayes Movement,* capitalized on the same for-mat. Then *Shaft* hit number one.

"Life got beautiful," Isaac says. "And then it got weird."

He wasn't the same guy who was grateful for an extra Otis Redding session. He lived unbelievably well, but sometimes things looked damned funny. The Stax office was still in the ghetto, so barbed-wire fences and armed guards had to stand vigil when Isaac's Rolls was in the parking lot. His lyrics were laced with more upwardly mobile reveries and less realism.

"I can see the difference in my perspective when I look at the songs I've written," he says. "I mean, in the beginning, I was writing funkier stuff, more for the masses. And for a certain kind of woman. Then, as I began a more affluent way of living, the feeling changed. And in the lyrics I was making love to a different type of woman."

Whoever she was, she stopped listening. Sales were down, and the public view of Isaac Hayes was becoming like the celluloid caricatures in the blaxploitation films he was acting in and scoring, films such as *Tough Guys* and *Truck Turner*. He wrote background sounds for ghetto smoothies, pimps, and shiny ladies, all jeweled and minked outcasts.

"My life was looking like a weird movie, I guess. It's wild to go back and listen to the early stuff. And I can relive every moment, precisely, on some of those songs. I remember what I was going through at the time, how I felt, whether I was up or in a depression. I do write the best stuff when I'm feeling bad, definitely. I did lay off writing for that rich dream woman. She was killing me. I think I'd like to go back and write more of that mass-oriented stuff again, which is more real to more people."

Working in this stripped-down apartment, noodling on the piano, heaving around slabs of steel, Isaac says he has had a lot of time to think about what pricked his pretty bubble. He left Stax for ABC Records in 1974. But not before things had started to go bad at Soulsville, U.S.A.

"I stayed just about until the end. I really had no choice. Like I said, some very funky stuff went down. Stuff I can't really talk about in detail now. Basically I think it was a failure of management. I mean, Otis, Sam and Dave, the MGs were gone, but they still had some good acts. They had the Dramatics, the Staples. But by then there were so many people trying to copy the Stax sound it just got diluted. The intensity, the feeling, the denseness of the sound—well, watered-down, it didn't work. But look, all three companies and their soul acts—Motown, Stax, Atlantic—experienced this boom period. Growth is inevitable, and when you get too big and too corporate, of course, the product gets diluted. And you can't give the artists the same attention they were used to. Yeah, at bottom, I'd have to say the problem was management and leave it at that."

His own finances didn't fare much better. He says it was somewhat of a relief to have himself declared a bankrupt, to lose all the things and step out of the gold Cadillac and the chains. Black Moses had expired on the charts of relatively natural causes, like changes in style. Isaac says he could deal with that, but what astonished him was the lack of respect people showed at his wake. The bankruptcy sale received national coverage. When I mention that I recall reading that they'd even sold gold records right off his walls, Isaac is silent for a moment.

"You know what? I think what hurt the most was not the process, but the stigma. People were saying, 'This guy is finished, it's horrible, he's ruined, it's all over.' But most people don't understand the function of declaring bankruptcy. It's to clear the decks, to make a new start—not to end it all. Some gold records did go, I guess. It was disgusting. It was a crazy scene, people grabbing my stuff. I mean, they were buying monogrammed bars of soap. I didn't really care about the stuff I lost. I mean, they'll make more of whatever, right? I was already in the studio, working again, when the auctions were held. What hurt the most were some paintings done by fans. I had one I loved, by a boy who later drowned, and I wanted to keep it forever. During it all I tried to stay as removed as I could. I helped myself by getting physically stronger. I jogged; I lifted weights; I worked out like crazy to keep myself occupied. I've been working at that for a long time."

For now, Isaac concedes, he is caught in a funny kind of place. People keep telling him they would like to see the "old Isaac Hayes" again, with the chains and the funky R & B. And though he would like to try acting what he calls sensitive roles, casting agents keep coming up with stuff like "The Duke," the snarling bogeyman he played in the futuristic gorefest thriller released as *Escape from New York*.

Since Hollywood "still hasn't got its shit together" about fitting black people into movies ("guess art imitates life on that score"), Isaac says he is content to stay in what he calls a rest and reconstruction phase. He likes Atlanta and notes that a lot of other soul artists have returned back South "now that they've quit runnin' all over the place and figured out who they are." Gladys Knight and the Pips are in Atlanta. Ex-Temptation Eddie Kendricks moved way back down to Birmingham, Alabama. James Brown has consolidated his holdings in Georgia.

"It feels right again," Isaac says. "I'm in no hurry." In a little while he's due at the gym for a few hours' work with the metal and the mats. He's begun to click on phones and collect a stack of tapes for his car stereo.

"Quiet is very nice, but once in a while it's spooky," he says. "Besides, like I told you, most of what I have kept from those years is sound. It's solid in its own way."

Again he says that he doesn't really miss the things. They got to be a pain in the ass to look after. He will always be amazed at how much maintenance wealth and leisure require.

"There's just one thing I'd like. There's this piano I really want. It's a big black concert grand we had at Stax. It's got everyone's name carved in the leg. I think I know who bought it, and I'm going to try and track it down. That piano was in my office; then it was in David's. It would mean a lot to have it. Where is it? Stax sold it. At an auction."

23

No More Runnin'

> *New Orleans music is like a fly trapped in amber.*
>
> —JERRY WEXLER
>
> *I'm not sure, but I'm almost positive, that all music came from New Orleans.*
>
> —ERNIE K-DOE

IT IS IN THE CITY with one of the most infamous auction blocks in American history, New Orleans, that more kinds of black music, soul among them, survive, intact and undisturbed by the vagaries of marketing and record charts. Two centuries ago a slave buyer could drive his wagon into the Place du Congo, the auction square, and choose bloodstock from more than a dozen distinct African tribes. The haggling was in French, English, Spanish, and Carib-infused dialect. And louder than the voices were the scores of shifting rhythms.

Though slave drumming had been outlawed in the rest of the nation as blasphemous and seditious, the beat never stopped in New Orleans. Every week, on the day Christians called their Sabbath, slave dances in the Place du Congo kept the sound of tribal drums alive.

It is still very much a city of tribes, parceled into eighteenth-century parishes, divisible, to its natives, by family, by sound, by style, even by

359

the physical distinctions in a piano man's flat fingers or the quick, rare talent for "slap-tonguing" a clarinet reed. Musical societies—funeral and marching bands, feathered and moccasined "Indian" tribes like the Wild Magnolias—rattle out rhythms that sound more like the West Indies or West Africa than anything east or west of the Mississippi.

The more formal bands use drums and horns and woodwinds; behind them, in any street procession, the "second line" of celebrants keeps the beat with anything available—trash can lids, chair legs, hubcaps, wash buckets, coat hangers, and car antennas. It can be argued that the entire city is a stubborn, lively second line. I saw a guy walk into a Crescent City Burger King, well lubed on Jax, the local brew, and holler that ages-old chant "Iko iko." A dozen or so patrons looked up from their Whoppers and ikoed right back. Behind the counter the fryman clacked out his own second line with an aluminum potato scoop. There's a noticeable lack of big boxy radios and Walkmans in New Orleans. It's a city where people never stopped dancing in the streets.

"Who wanna go buy it canned," one Wild Magnolia told me, "when you kin go and pick and chomp it fresh-fresh?"

New Orleans R & B, soul, jazz, calypso, the generational platoons of second-liners—all of that served to put the "roll" in rock and roll. For if Memphis and other points southeast came up with the soulful and hillbilly voices, New Orleans came up with the rhythms. New Orleans piano men, in the persons of Huey "Piano" Smith, Fats Domino, and Henry Roeland Byrd, known best as Professor Longhair, had an awesome reach that leaped into R & B nationwide yet curiously kept the originals in their hometown. Twenty-five years after Ahmet Ertegun and an accomplice went crashing through bayou swampland to find the genius they'd heard about, Longhair died, sick and broke, on January 30, 1980, the day his long-in-the-making album *Crawfish Fiesta* was released. He was a victim of neglect and his own bullheaded insistence on staying *home*. Having made music all his life, he considered it absurd to tour "behind" a record. Living the music made more sense to him than promoting it. Though many New Orleans piano men—from Fats Domino to the late James Booker— came up listening to him, as late as 1970 Longhair was sweeping out a record store for a living. In the end there could be no more fitting patron saint for New Orleans R & B. He stayed put, but his music racked up incredible mileage.

Longhair was the undisputed savant of New Orleans R & B. But behind him was no shortage of other homegrown originals. Jesse Hill, Ernie

K-Doe, Allen Toussaint, the Neville Brothers, Lee Dorsey, Betty Harris, Clarence "Frogman" Henry, Deacon John, Walter "Papoose" Nelson, Irma Thomas, the Meters, and the Dixie Cups all have made their careers living and working in New Orleans. Some would see sporadic national exposure—Ernie K-Doe with his novelty hit "Mother in Law," Aaron Neville with "Tell It Like It Is," Lee Dorsey with "Ya Ya." Some have trucked briefly with outside labels like Atlantic, Imperial, and Specialty. But most have done their best, or only, recording on small local labels like Bandy, Minit, Ric, Ron, Dover, Rip, Polka Dot, and Sansu.

"Some artists may be bitter that record companies from other cities once raided the talent or that they've been passed by," says Jerry Wexler. "Some of them have every right to be. Still, if they never got the big break, the contract, the heavy promotions, all of that, the city itself—that place—embraces them. And that's no small thing. Call it the marvelous arrogance of clan. Being counted and revered as family confers its own blessings. The past and the future have never been distinct things in New Orleans. Whenever I'm there, I hear voices."

There is, in fact, a ghostly work tape, recorded accidentally one night in 1969 when Jerry sat in a New Orleans studio with Dr. John (Mac Rebennack), the man who sang the line that could easily describe the position of New Orleans R & B: *"coulda been in the right place . . . coulda been the wrong time . . ."*

Jerry and Dr. John are at the studio piano, tired—it's late enough to be early—and they are free-associating with the aid of some particularly uplifting sensimillia. After a bit Dr. John's left hand takes off on its own, possessed, in turns, by piano figures that conjure a half dozen Crescent City piano men. They are identifiable by signatures—double-note cross-overs, stair-step chords, some big old perverse bass notes, very wrong notes dropped in just the right places. Then Dr. John's foot hits a *boom-wacka-wacka,* courtesy of Fess, as Longhair was also called. Fess used to kick the bejesus out of pianos—smashed them. Sometimes used a kick-board under there, abused it with his big fat left foot.

"Fess don't know nothin' on the jukebox. Don't know no Top One Hundred."

Dr. John laughs and lets his hand find the opening notes to Longhair's signature "Mardi Gras in New Orleans," a song that has so much in it— Latino rhythms, whistling, stomping, knuckle rolls—that it sounds like the orgy it's named for.

"Every time Fess hit this tune, I don't know *where* it come from. . . ."

"With yo' ticket in yo' hand, you wanna to go New Orleans . . ."

This was Jerry's advice, too, when he sat, listening and chuckling over the tape one night. Longhair is dead, and soul may be dead on the charts, and in too many places R & B may be embalmed or disfigured by synthesizers or just caught in some cryogenic format deep freeze. But any dirge is premature. And if you want to check the pulse of any black music, you just have to hop a Delta L-1011 and make it down to New Orleans in time for the annual Jazz and Heritage Festival.

Jazz, soul, calypso, salsa, R & B, blues, reggae, even the chant of the Wild Tchoupitoulas Mardi Gras Indian Tribe—they're all collected on riverboats, in band shells, concert halls, and open fields, a late-spring rite guaranteed to shake off the draggy effects of anything that ails you.

Early on the first weekend morning the rhythms are already shaking the springy wooden planks that lead the faithful over the track to the infield of the Fairground Racetrack. The hawkers line out a chant before the first drum is struck: "Hot-un-greazy, go down easy. Cajun pork una dirty, dirty rice now. Gator tail fry, get you high. Get gumbo. Get down. Get Jesus. Get saved."

There are no well-dressed A & R men here, no TV crews, no live recording permitted. Just, over ten days, about a quarter of a million people. Black babies and blond freckled teens, grandmas in flowered housedresses, oil rig workers in gym shorts. Tiny rumps in rubber pants wriggle along to the beat, but mama knows the words, stands up and grinds her Wedgies in the grass and dances and sings: *"Whip it on me, pretty baby . . ."*

Jesse Hill is singing that old hit with his Full Ooh Poo Pa Doo Revue at one bandstand. Fifty yards away local soul man John Wright has come down off Stage Two into the growing crowd, crouching, wailing, shaking sweat from his eyes during the chorus of Sam Cooke's "Bring It On Home to Me."

It smells like wet grass and talc in the gospel tent, a huge canvas womb where clear-eyed, handsome singers in groups like the Randolph Brothers plant knife-creased pants legs and shout, backed by respectful snares and a Fender tremolo laced with arpeggios and organ flutters. The tent spews out spent believers after each set. They lie on the spiky, parched turf, cardboard fans waving like mammoth butterflies on the sunny field.

The Wild Magnolias have attracted a battery of clicking cameras as they tie themselves into beaded and feathered headdresses and Indian costumes, a gaudy riot of fuchsia, turquoise, and orange plumes. Some sit on their instruments—plastic wash buckets—to contend with pesky legging ties. Off to the side, one of the Magnolias, an ancient, wrinkled black woman, tickles a two-year-old with her feathers, teaching him a chant. "Sing it fuh me, baby chil'. Singa heyyyyy pocky-way. Ah-hey, pocky-way."

The kid blows a raspberry, then explodes like a popcorn machine. "Pockapockapocka."

Back inside the gospel tent, another lesson. A woman stills her Scotch-taped Mahalia Jackson fan long enough to speak the truth to a wide-eyed grandchild: "Reason for any revival, honey, is to show you the spirit ain't dead."

Just maybe it ain't commercial for a time. So you box it out with playlists and formats; you find new trends. Cut off air time and leave it gasping. Haul the soul men off the road. Pile the bare bones of its timeless rhythms with enough electronic gimmickry to fool another generation. But damn if it doesn't come back, stubborn as crabgrass in a junkyard lot.

"They can't kill it, aw, no, ma'am." James Brown is shouting from beneath the drone of a hair dryer inside his pricey New Orleans hotel suite. They, they, they. They are the record companies, tax men, station managers, advertisers. The format people, perennial bogeymen. But even they have little relevance just prior to showtime.

"Right now," James says, "my biggest worry is that old boat. That river. Too humid."

Ah. The hair.

"Mr. Stallings!"

Painstakingly, Henry Stallings rolls a section of the hair and coats it with some protein-loaded spray. I leave Mr. Brown gulping black coffee and head for the river. In line for the midnight show on the SS *President,* a man who has seen James Brown twenty-nine times is trying to explain the experience to an unenlightened honeymoon couple from Tupelo: "All I kin say is, you gonna *enjoy* yourselves."

On board the ship Chief Jake and the White Eagle Nation have already worked folks into a frenzy with their jackhammer chant and percussion. They have no fancy costumes like the Wild Magnolias. They look like ten guys in T-shirts who all work in the same car wash, beating on upended buckets, whacking pairs of sticks, shaking tambourines crisscrossed with oily masking tape. There isn't a hint of melody in "Indian Maid," but the rhythm is enough to draw a few hundred souls into wet and wild second, third, and fourth lines, rapping with pens and cigarette lighters, beer cans and sunglasses.

The drum of so many feet vibrates louder than the big boat's engines. Plastic beer cups splinter and crunch on the metal deck. Moths sizzle against the spots trained on Jr. Walker, the evening's next act, who is down on his back, feet kicking, blowing some of his party songs. When he's done, frantic stagehands mop up treacherous pools of sweat before the JBs strut their shiny high tops onstage. Horns flare; the three winsome Sugar Bees put it in gear, and a nod gets the chorus: *"We are the funky men . . . been funky since the world began . . ."*

A tired-looking but game Godfather gets down and up and down again, doing it standing, kneeling, and sideways, until, just as the song says, it's *too* funky in here. No one is seated; the deck is slick with sweat and drink. Wilted prom queen coifs, undone shirts, lost shoes, and a silver anniversary black couple back in certain love. A couple thousand voices sing happy birthday to Mr. James Brown when announcer Danny Ray lets it slip, in well-miked sotto voce, that this Taurus, this Superbull, the Godfather is, well, a year younger tonight. By the time James encores in his gorilla suit, the gray catbirds are already twittering in the trees by the Canal Street pier, and the sky has begun to lighten.

"Soul, soul, soul . . ." JB's parting chant, amplified by those still able to yell, echoes past the refineries and out toward the Gulf. The *President*'s engines shudder down, and the people drift off, through the railyards and up Canal. The capes, the hair dryers, the sodden gorilla suit are heaped on a dolly and rolled down the gangplank. Within hours all the festival "guest" artists will be gone. And for the homegrown musicians, it's back to business as usual.

"What you see is what you get."

Wearing a housecoat and terry-cloth scuffies, Irma Thomas unbolts the screen door of her tidy peach-colored bungalow. The house is set on a small fenced-in lot in the shadow of the Mid-City Baptist Church on the outskirts of New Orleans. The living room is webbed with Irma's macramé work—planters, wall hangings, and curtains. On the wall is a handsome framed version of the poster available in countless French Quarter tourist shops and record stores. It is a silk-screened portrait of the artist, along with the lettering IRMA THOMAS, QUEEN OF NEW ORLEANS SOUL.

Irma is one of those southern soul women, singers like Betty Harris, Ann Peebles, Doris Duke, Betty Lavette, Barbara West, and Tommie Young, who sang big and charted small—female counterparts to the southern soul men, with just as many hard knocks and more often than not, a clutch of children as well. Mabel John had modest success at Stax. Two soul women with the good fortune to be discovered by bandleader Johnny Otis fared considerably better. In Chicago Etta James enjoyed a good, if stormy, tenure at Chess, and Esther Phillips made some great sides for Atlantic.

Irma Thomas, who recorded on New Orleans labels like Ron, Bandy, and Minit and on California's Imperial, often had her sides produced by Aaron Neville. She did most of her best-known work—songs like "For Goodness Sake," "I Done Got over It," and "Time Is on My Side"— in the early sixties, when Diana Ross was just graduating from high school and Aretha Franklin was struggling with pop confections at Columbia. Irma Thomas was a teenager, too, and the mother of three.

"I had no idea what I was doin'," she says. "That they were calling it soul, that anything was even a hit. I figured New Orleans mirrored the world's tastes when it came to music. Then I got out a bit. Played the Apollo with different headliners like Smokey Robinson and the Miracles, Mary Wells, Dionne Warwick, the Temptations. Toured some with James Brown. Even went to Europe once. But I guess I knew I would come back to New Orleans.

"I live here. I went away for a bit, but New Orleans had too much of my soul. I tried runnin' to those outside record companies, some tours. But I always run back. Yeah, like Longhair, I guess I don't feel quite right anyplace else. Pulls me like a tide I can't figure. I left here and went to California to live after the big storm, Camille. Camille was in August of 1969. I left in January of 1970. Under more clouds, 'bout like what you see now."

Irma stands at the screen door, pointing to a western sky that's as rippled and iridescent as the inside of an oystershell. A wet-smelling wind is coming in. It has been raining on and off for two days. Just the night before, in the middle of a torrential downpour, I'd dragged into a bar on St. Philippe and punched up Irma's "It's Raining" on the box. Though it was released in 1962, it's still on a lot of local jukeboxes, a pretty, lonesome dawdle with Irma's girlish voice framed by a teen queen chorus of female voices chanting "drip-drop, drip-drop." On the record, Irma's quite calm and melodic explaining the situation—It's pouring; her lover's nowhere near; this would be the best time to have him around—and then she ends with an ancient, sweet-voiced female shrug: *"I guess I'll just go crazy to-night . . ."*

The way Irma sings it, resignation and dementia aren't opposing concepts. She says that song was always something special to her. Just the other night, when she was doing a sound check on the riverboat, a reporter from *Billboard* asked her if she had heard the version on the album of Jerry Wexler's latest protégée, a white Texan named Lou Ann Barton.

"I told him I haven't. Don't know who-all she is. For a time I was on Atlantic, and I wanted to recut that song; but Jerry wouldn't let me. He must have picked that one out for this new girl, though."

Other artists have had successes covering tunes that Irma did. Otis Redding recut her "Ruler of My Heart" as "Pain in My Heart," and the Rolling Stones stayed on the charts for nearly three months with "Time Is on My Side."

"None of that is any matter to me," she says. "I didn't write the songs. I am glad that those people once listened to me, though. I guess that's nice."

A low thunder is rolling in. Irma walks back to the door, inhales, and says she gives the storm about an hour to hit.

"You know, I could never relate to the climate in California. California was kinda burnt around the edges. Besides which, I was mostly breathing plastic and air conditioning."

Her career was becalmed when she lit out West with four children to support. Hurricane Camille had literally wiped out some of the clubs she counted on for her living, and divorce washed away the second paycheck.

"I had relatives out there," she says, "so I felt that if all hell broke loose, at least my family would get a meal until I got myself on my feet. But I didn't have too much trouble 'cause I'm very ambitious when it comes to making a living."

Ambition had cost Irma her first job when she was a seventeen-year-old waitress with three children. In 1958 she was working in a club called the Pimlico on South Broad when Tommy Ridgley asked her to sit in and sing with his group. She did a couple of things with them for fun, but the owner fired her for neglecting the customers. Ridgley took her to a recording studio, and she auditioned for Joe Ruffino, who owned Ric and Ron records. That week she recorded her first song, "You Can Have My Husband (But Please Don't Mess with My Man)," and it was released the following week. Soon after, it was pulled off the radio in New Orleans for being too suggestive. She says she didn't understand all the fuss.

"I was just seventeen. Now I had kids, but half the time I wasn't sure how they *got* there. I was one of them folks that learned by trial and error, you know. It was a song, a record, a way of getting into show business. I was so naïve. Now I know better. I try to make things work for me. I don't wanna be hawkin' shock absorbers again.''

She sold auto parts in a California Montgomery Ward to support herself and her children. She never sold the wrong size fan belt, could prescribe effective treatment for high idle. But when the company sought to reward her expertise with a promotion to manager, Irma balked. The responsibility might interfere with her working club dates on weekends. The kids were a handful, and the job was tiring, but she couldn't let the music go. "You curse it, but you love it. And it's not like a divorce with some paper there to cut you loose.''

Besides, New Orleans wanted her back. Twice she returned for six- or ten-week engagements in the supper rooms of the big hotels. The third time she stayed. She met her second husband, Emile Jackson. Things worked out. The kids got older, and the gigs stayed steady. She would probably take more work, but Emile, who manages her, puts on the brakes from time to time.

"I'm working toward a point in my life when if he and I want to go on vacation, we can afford to do it without having to catch up on bills. And I'm getting near to where we can. It's close; it's real close.''

For now Irma relies on small escapes. She does her macramé, puts her feet up, and once in a while she tunes in to one of those morning TV shows where women get up and speak their minds.

"Who's that gray-haired fella? Donahue? It's a riot. It's funny to see these women saying, 'I can't get it together, I don't know what I'm gonna do, this don't work for me, for my relationship . . .' Lord. I'm not gonna say I did the best job of it, but in some way I managed to raise four kids, work on a daily job, do weekend work, and buy a house. I didn't go runnin' to a psychiatrist. I didn't have to take Valium. I didn't drink. So when I see this, well, girl, it's a joke. I mean, children are still children, work is still work, a dollar is still a dollar. Almost.''

Irma is still Irma, too. Some people consider it bullheaded to refuse to change with the times. But in New Orleans it isn't necessary. In fact, it can get you hissed off a stage. Irma says people want to hear what she does best, which is deep soul.

"And as you can see,'' she says, flicking the hem of her housecoat, "image was never a real big deal. I'm not gonna show half my rump. I'm not gonna dye my hair purple and wear a miniskirt. I didn't do it when I was younger. I would never go to any extreme to sell records. And that's what happened with me in the past, with the bigger companies. I'm not an artist who would do any damn thing to get a record."

She says her last session for Atlantic, the one she had high hopes for, was a complete disaster. She flew to Detroit to record an album and found a pair of producers who wanted to do a Motown Pygmalion number on her.

"They had me singing in keys I'd never sung in before, that didn't fit me. They gave me material that was more suitable to a pop singer. Then they told me that I couldn't sing. They told the company that I didn't have it anymore. All my kids were home at the time. I had to take time off from work and lose money to cut the record. I got back from Detroit, and two weeks later my release came in the mail. Lord, I don't even remember what was on that session."

I tell her I've heard it. I'd brought a tape of it along, intending to ask her about it.

"Good. 'Cause if we listen to it, you'll see what I mean."

A very different voice leaps out of the living room speakers.

"My sweet Lord." Irma is leaning forward on the couch, hugging her knees and wincing. The record is hardly cringe quality, but it's hardly Irma.

"Oh, God, this is where they wanted me to be Diana Ross. They actually said that."

The breathy voice is squeezed into a key that's too high and too tight for it. Irma grips her knees tighter and lets out a small moan. I start to apologize, tell her I feel as if I'm flashing photos of a car wreck or something, and Irma smiles and shakes her head.

"Hey, it's okay. This session was one of the most painful experiences of my career. But it taught me something. Which is that I am Irma. And I sing in a soulful way that is *all* Irma, and if it's not in fashion, if somebody else is makin' millions with whatever's hot, it has nothin' to do with me. I am a southern black woman raised up singing what goes down right in New Orleans, Louisiana. And if I ever get to wantin' something else, I'll just slip this tape on."

She winces again as the voice vamps uneasily.

"Swamp Dogg," she says, "where were you when I needed you?"

Swamp Dogg, also known as one Jerry Williams, Jr., is a singer and producer who calls himself the "world's most spectacular failure." Coaching Irma through an album called *In Between Tears*, using guitarist

Duane Allman, himself on piano, and an aggregate of strings and horns he calls the Little Swamp Dogg Symphony, the Dogg came up with a soul stew that includes lighthearted sexual upmanship ("You're the Dog [I Do the Barking Myself]"). The Dogg turned Irma loose for "Coming from Behind," an extended, ad-libbed rap. It's a *femme* State of the Union message shot with nuggets of romantic and carnal truth that far outshines anything Millie Jackson would later come up with in her own raunch raps. It starts out simple enough:

"You know, a man is a hell of a thing."

Irma struts (*"Anytime you men two-time, we women can THREE"*). She hurts, since she's in love but miserable. She ponders creation. Women are not meant to be angels, yet they're put on earth to bring forth angels. All children, even men, start out that way.

On the *In Between Tears* album, the rap breaks into a reprise of one of Irma's best cuts, "Wish Someone Would Care." It is the only song Irma has ever written, and like a lot of the best soul music, it came together in one perfectly awful flash of anger and hurt. Things weren't going well with her recording career, and her first husband was about to become her ex. She says she cried a lot. One day she sat down and sang about it into a tape recorder. It's all hers, but for all of them, for Betty Harris, Esther Phillips, for Fontella Bass, and even Florence Ballard, it could be the flip, distaff side to Sam and Dave's jaunty "Soul Man":

Sittin' home alone
Thinkin' bout my past
Wonderin' how I made it
And how long it's gonna last
Success has come to lots of them
And failure's always there
Time waits for no one
And I wish—how I wish someone would care.*

"When I wrote that song, it had a big meaning to it," Irma says. "At the time I was having difficulties with my marriage, and that's how I wrote the song. Out of anger. I haven't written anything since. I don't ever want to get that mad again."

---

*"Wish Someone Would Care," by Irma Thomas, © 1964 UNART MUSIC, a Catalogue of CBS SONGS, a Division of CBS, Inc. All Rights Reserved. International Copyright Secured. Used by Permission.

She says Emile does his best to keep that from happening. He is a big, genial man with musical, Creole-infused speech.

Emile knows where to go to find good New Orleans sidemen, and he has put together a tight, reliable backup group for his wife, the kind Irma's ex-producers, Aaron Neville and Swamp Dogg, would have found for her.

"Emile takes care of business," Irma says. "Without him I'd be a dish-rag. I'd be doin' all sorts of things that would wear me out. Emile can stop me with five little words: 'Baby, you don't need it.' " And sometimes, when she's being mule-headed: "What you runnin' off to? What?"

He asked her that when some promoter offered her an insulting $750—with no band or travel expenses—to play a club in New York. And when a so-so recording deal came up. And whenever one-nighters are too close together on the calendar and too far apart on the highway map. He has prescribed a few days of layabout after the weekend, but already Irma says she's a tiny bit restless. Offering to drive me back into town, she slips into a cotton dress and shoes and backs a new powder blue Mercedes out of the narrow driveway.

The storm is still threatening, flapping leaves on the banana trees and hurling heat lightning low on the horizon. On the way back Irma tells funny stories, about those sixties gigs at southern colleges, where well-meaning coeds picked up the star of "It's Raining" at the bus station, planning to put her up in the sorority house—until they got a look at her.

"Had you some blushing little Chi Omegas."

Once in the Quarter, people honk and wave at intersections. A cabdriver leans out and blows a kiss. "Irma, my lady. How is your boo-ful self?"

As we pull up in front of my guesthouse, the rain has begun. Irma cranes her neck out the car window, looking at the clouds.

"If this keeps up, I ain't makin' it to that gig in Bogalusa. I've done my share of crazy runnin'. Don't fancy drivin' up along that old Pearl River in this. Nope. No more runnin'."

Index